THE
LOST
SPY

THE
LOST
SPY

AN AMERICAN IN STALIN'S SECRET SERVICE

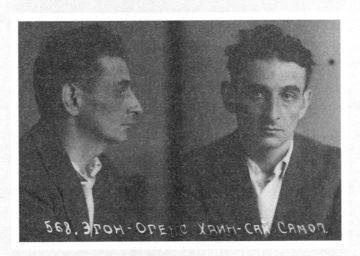

568. ЭТОН-ОГЕНС ХАИН-САК САМОЛ.

ANDREW MEIER

WEIDENFELD & NICOLSON

London

First published in Great Britain in 2009
by Weidenfeld & Nicolson

This edition published by arrangement with
W.W. Norton and Company, Inc.

1 3 5 7 9 10 8 6 4 2

A CIP catalogue record for this book
is available from the British Library.

ISBN: 978 0 297 85655 9

Book design by Barbara Bachman
Map on page 193 by Adrian Kitzinger
Typeset by W.W. Norton & Co, New York
Printed and bound in the UK by CPI Mackays, Chatham ME5 8TD

The Orion Publishing Group's policy is to use papers that
are natural, renewable and recyclable products and made
from wood grown in sustainable forests. The logging and
manufacturing processes are expected to conform to
environmental regulations of the country of origin.

Weidenfeld & Nicolson

Orion Publishing Group Ltd
Orion House, 5 Upper Saint Martin's Lane, London, WC2H 9EA

An Hachette UK Company

www.orionbooks.co.uk

for Oona

CONTENTS

■

THE
LOST
SPY

ARREST

■

HE OPENED THE DOOR, KNOWING WHO STOOD ON THE OTHER SIDE.
They had come, as they always did, at night. Three men in
dark blue raised their badges—a blur of Cyrillic letters in red
leather. They asked for his name, although they knew the
answer in advance. Then they seized his passport, although
they, or, more precisely, someone in the depths of their
organization, had created it. They gave him a moment to
gather his things.

Sixty-one years later, in the winter of 2000, the room
remained austere, a drab single with scant adornment. The
narrow bed sagged low, and a lone bulb lit the bathroom. A
wooden table stood nearby, only big enough for an old metal
lamp. The faded green-gray walls were bare save for a
mounted radio. In the old days, the *tochka* had piped the
voice of the Leader, day and night, into every room across
the empire.

The Moskva Hotel, a hulking cement tower in the heart
of the capital, was a centerpiece of Stalin's dream. It was
intended as a model of the new world—"bright," "happy," and
"invincible"—that Stalin promised to build. In 2000, the view
from the airless room on its top floor remained as spectacular
as it had been in 1939. A pair of tall windows opened onto Red
Square. When you turned the rusted latches and leaned out,
you saw the worn cobblestones stretching below. From this
vantage, the square, the unbridled bazaar of medieval times,
seemed almost without end, an endless flow of people streaming over the stones like black water.

The snow was falling that night in 1939 as the three men came through the hotel's double doors. It fell in unending swaths, muffling the trams that hurtled by and whitening the ZIS limousines idling in a row beside the hotel. At the Bolshoi, across the way, the new aristocrats were taking in a spectacle. High above Red Square, the klieg lights of the Kremlin, red and white and smoking in the cold, cast halos against the sky. As the square glowed and the air on the street turned sharp, the men inside passed beneath the bald head of stone, the unyielding hero of Great October. They walked on undeterred, stopping only at the bank of new elevators. On that night, the twentieth of February, 1939, they came to claim a man. They came for the American.

·

HE OPENED THE DOOR AND OFFERED HIS PASSPORT WILLINGLY. AFTER all, he had been waiting years for them to come. The portrait inside, stamped and signed, was his, although the small black-and-white photograph scarcely resembled him. The tortoiseshell spectacles, thick and round, darkened the brown eyes and lent an intellectual air; the silvery streak of gray amid the black curls added a sober confidence; the high-collared shirt was unbuttoned and the cravat loosely tied around the thin neck.

The passport, however, was false. It was a Czech one cobbled together—a "boot," as such things were known in the trade—solely for this trip, the last of his journeys, as things turned out, after more than a decade of traversing the globe. The name inside was an alias, too. But the secret policemen had long known this Czech mask, as they had the others. They had kept careful records, cataloging it with all his other inventions.

The American stood silently as they asked his true identity. Even now, on the cusp of middle age, he possessed the air of a young intellectual, a bon vivant at home in any café or university across the continent. He spoke fluent German and French and several other languages, not all of them well. Russian, however, he could scarcely make out. When the most senior of the three read aloud the warrant in his hands, the American could only nod.

Yes, he said, repeating the surname scrawled in dark cursive on the long white paper: the name written there was Oggins.

Cy Oggins, early portrait, date unknown.

CHAPTER I

"THE AMERICAN PROFESSOR"

■ ■ ■

THIS IS AN IMPROBABLE BUT TRUE TALE. IT IS ALSO AN ATTEMPT TO resurrect a man's life, one lived on the frontiers of the twentieth century's longest war.

Isaiah Oggins was one of the first Americans to spy for the Soviet Union. For more than a decade, beginning in 1928, he served in Joseph Stalin's espionage networks in Europe, Asia, and America. At each station along his odyssey, Oggins gained greater responsibility in the underground and greater respect in Moscow. At the time of his arrest in the Soviet capital during the endless winter of 1939, few Americans —if any—had served longer or climbed higher in Stalin's spy world.

This is also the story of a man who did everything possible to cover his tracks. Devout and methodical, even when the chaos of the times rose high above his head, Oggins traded identities and addresses with ease. No diaries or last-minute confession survived him—just one notebook, a handful of telegrams and handwritten notes, and a single letter.

For half a century, Oggins's life remained a mystery without an investigator. In exploring it, I discovered a man of astonishing faith and innocence, and a story of desire and dedication nearly impossible to imagine today. As I searched across three continents, the discoveries began to accrete. In time, curiosity bred a quest. After six years, the research filled a dozen large boxes; interviews, State Department dispatches and memos, declassified files from the KGB and the FBI, survivors' memoirs, and even postage stamps revealed a remarkable journey.

Both an Everyman and a singular exception, Oggins was born into the proverbial American Dream. He attained success early in life, only to abandon it. Oggins sought to climb higher, daring to believe that he could remake the world. He envisioned a utopia on earth, a realm of harmony and justice, not a world ruled, as he and his comrades saw it, by the lust for profit and violence. He imagined himself an American Robin Hood among the Bolsheviks, and he risked all for the good fight. In doing so, however, he crossed a line, and in the end fell prey to his own blind faith.

Isaiah Oggins belonged to the generation of intellectuals betrayed by "the God that failed." He forsook everything, only to find himself forsaken. In the light of history, some may forgive him. Others may not. Now, at least, his story, obscured for so long both by his own design and by the political forces that long outlived him, is no longer hidden.

•

I WAS STILL LIVING IN MOSCOW, WORKING AS A REPORTER, WHEN I began my search: I was looking for anyone with the surname Oggins.

Robin Oggins I found by pure luck. A half-dozen Web pages formed a rough résumé: Robin S. Oggins, professor of history at the State University of New York in Binghamton, author of a pair of pictorial histories (the cathedrals and castles of Europe) and an authority on the royal sport and business of medieval English falconry.

At once, from Moscow, I sent him an e-mail message. "Are you or do you know anyone who is related to Isaiah Oggins, also known as Cyrus?" I asked.

By nightfall I had my reply:

Dear Mr. Meier:
I am Cy (short for Ysai, never, to the best of my knowledge, Cyrus) Oggins'
only child—and son. I doubt if I can help you very much but am willing
to try.

It was the winter of 2001. Robin had just turned seventy, and after four decades of teaching was nearing a long-awaited retirement. He lived on a rural road, in a small house at the end of a long driveway. When I called him the following Sunday morning, he answered on the first ring. His voice was measured, quiet but firm.

"This is the call I've been waiting for my whole life," he said.

Upstate had been snowed in. Robin was working at home, down in the basement in a dark study ringed with leather-bound books and metal filing cabinets. He was revising the last of several hundred footnotes, references pertaining to young men holding falcons in the medieval illustrations of the ages of man.

To his joy, Robin had nearly completed his "life's work," *The Kings and Their Hawks*, a meticulous study of medieval English falconry. He had begun it back in Chicago as a graduate student in the 1950s. But so much had gotten in the way—first the jobs, then marriage, kids, teaching. He had always had to work, to provide. Now, for the first time in years, Robin had time on his hands. Time, he told me during that first telephone call, to listen to inconvenient questions, file requests for documents, and help me reassemble the broken pieces of his father's life.

FOR ME, THE JOURNEY had begun in Norilsk, that Pompeii of Stalinism in Russia's far north. Hundreds of miles above the Arctic Circle, Norilsk is a place of permafrost, precious metals, and, for ten months of the year, little but the frozen white desert of the tundra. For generations, ever since its founding in the 1930s as an island in Stalin's archipelago of labor camps, the city has loomed in the Russian imagination as one of the most remote and forbidding corners of the country.

In the summer of 2000, I traveled to Norilsk as a reporter to learn about the gulag from the survivors, a few dozen men and women, then in their eighties and nineties, who had stayed on, even decades after the camps had closed. At its height, the gulag had held prisoners from more than thirty countries. In Norilsk, there were Poles and Germans, Swedes and Koreans, even Afghans. Had the camps held any Americans? I asked in interview after interview, spurred solely by curiosity. Over and over, the old-timers shook their heads. But at last, on the afternoon before I left town, the large round eyes of a small birdlike woman lit up with a look of recognition.

"Yes, there was someone here," she said. " 'The American,' they called him. 'The American professor.' "

A FEW MONTHS LATER, I traveled to Paris to see a French survivor of Norilsk. Jacques Rossi, at ninety-one, was something of a celebrity among camp veterans. His *Gulag Handbook*, an encyclopedia of camp life, was a landmark in the canon of Soviet persecution. I went to see Jacques because I knew he had spent years in Norilsk. Yet when I knocked on his door, I had no idea that he knew the answer to the question that had seized me in the Arctic.

Jacques seemed to have shrunk inside his body. His bones jutted against his thin checked shirt, but he was still a force, animated and ardent. Only now, like so many once-zealous followers, he reserved his passion for his hatred of communism.

Jacques, too, had been a spy. From the late 1920s into the 1930s, he had lived and worked in the Soviet underground. He had served first as an agent of the Comintern, the Communist International, before being pulled deeper, into military intelligence, the espionage arm of the Red Army.

Jacques lived on his own, visited by the Polish nuns of a nearby convent. The apartment resembled a monastic cell, two rooms filled with little but books, on the rue de la Resistance in Montreuil, the suburb on Paris's eastern edge. The working-class district remained defiantly left-wing. Across the way, a park housed a museum dedicated to the French socialist and workers' movements. Jacques, however, had found a new calling in Paris. He was one of the favored witnesses of the French right wing, called upon regularly to testify to the evils of communism.

Like hundreds of fellow believers, Jacques had worked longest as a courier, crisscrossing Europe with clandestine messages. "Microfilms in heels," he said, tapping a shoe. "That's how we carried Moscow's secrets." Agents would travel nonstop. "Paris, Venice, Prague, Istanbul, Oslo" were routine destinations. Side trips to

Moscow, for training, debriefings, and shipments, were normal. In the spring of 1937, at twenty-eight, Jacques was sent to Franco's Spain. The civil war raged. The Nationalists were sweeping the north, but Guernica had not yet been bombed. "The Center," as agents called the headquarters of Soviet intelligence in Moscow, had lent him a party "wife" and a collapsible radio transmitter. At night Jacques blacked out the windows with cloth and tapped out the news gleaned from informants.

One night he took down a message that would break his life in two: *Rentrer au village,* "Return to the village." He wrote down the letters, knowing the village was Moscow. In 1937 he walked into the Comintern headquarters on Mokhovaya Street, the grand building across from the Kremlin, and was arrested. He would not leave the USSR until twenty-four years later, in the spring of 1961.

JACQUES ROSSI HAD known the American professor. But he seemed surprised by the question. It was as if no one had ever asked him. Jacques said he had served with the American in the Norilsk camps. He could not remember the precise years, though he was certain they had met "before the war"—before Hitler launched Barbarossa and set 3 million men against the Soviet Union in the third week of June 1941.

"His name was Oggins," he said. "Cyrus Oggins."

It was the first time I had heard the name—either the first name or the last.

Jacques knew few details of Oggins's life before the gulag. They had never spoken of it, but Jacques was certain that the American had also been a spy. "You never asked," he said. "You had to trust your senses. It was not unlike hunting. Like a fox, you had to smell the rabbit."

Years after Jacques finally left the USSR, he visited New York. He tried to track down his friend from the gulag. He found nothing—no home, no relatives, and no news. The absence haunted him. One memory, however, remained close. Oggins, Jacques said, was in fact a professor. "A professor of history, at the Columbia University in the city of New York," he said, drawing out each word, as if to summon a spirit. "At least, that is what he *said* he was."

■

IN THE FALL OF 2001, ON A CHILL OCTOBER FRIDAY WEEKS AFTER THE terror struck in New York City and Washington, D.C., I rented a car and drove to see Robin.

He and his wife, Ginny, lived in a modest wooden house perched on a steep hillside overlooking a pastoral stretch of the Susquehanna River in upstate New York. The house was warm, and the kitchen, lined with pine cabinets, dominated. Robin and Ginny had lived half a lifetime on the hill. They had raised their three children here, yet the house retained the feel of a cabin. The woods—white birches and red maples—filled the windows, and beyond them, down below, the river turned gently through the valley. Outside the kitchen, goldfinches, titmice, and nuthatches dipped into a pair of birdfeeders. Wild turkeys and deer were also known to come close, and in early spring and late fall even the occasional bear.

Robin had last seen his father when he was seven years old. It had been in Paris, in the anxious year of 1938. On the telephone, he had told me that somewhere in the back of his mind—"ever since I can remember"—he had hoped someone might appear on his doorstep. "It wasn't a fixed thing," he said. "Just a thought—that someone, someday, would pick this thing up and follow it."

When Robin and I met, I had already seen a photograph of Cy Oggins. Robin had sent it to me in the mail. Over the years that followed, I would gather other photographs of his father, but this was the first—and the earliest.

Cy is already a young man in the portrait. It was taken in a photographer's studio, it seemed, on the eve of his high school graduation. He wears a tight double-breasted suit with leather buttons that glisten, and a white shirt bound by a white tie. His face, caught in the flash, is pearly white, nearly porcelain. His hair is ink black, trimmed and pomaded for the occasion. His head is torqued, twisted a quarter-turn for the formal moment, leaving one ear visible, white and outsized. His nose is aquiline and straight, lips broad, and eyebrows dark and rounded. The flash, reflected in one eye, casts a shadow on the wall behind him. It is a dramatic portrait, an apt image of a young man on a precipice.

Robin seemed to have none of his father's taste for drama, and little of his passion. He was fond of flannel shirts and workman's trousers. He did, though, inherit his looks—the penetrating brown eyes, broad, flat cheekbones, and sharp jaw. Yet unlike his father, Robin was short. As a child he had suffered a string of accidents and illnesses, and a broken hip had left him with a limp. But he spoke with authority, and his presence filled a space. It was as if the secret history, the weight of his father's mystery, had lent him a hidden strength.

Father and son, whether by blood, chance, or fate, had stretched across the years and formed a bond. When we first met, Robin had a sense that he shared his father's first love and his first profession. He had heard that his father had also been a professor. But he had never known whether the stories were true.

"There's just so much I don't know," Robin said. "I was never told—or not told the truth." He had no control of his memories. "I can remember details of eighteenth-century London better than my own past," he said. He had heard so many stories, often contradictory, more often vague, that he now had trouble sorting fact from fiction. There were so many dark holes, he said. Things he did not know. Or did not trust. Or did not want to know. There was so much uncertainty in his mind about his father's life.

"Why did my parents go over to Europe?" he asked himself. "I don't really know. At one time I was told they were students. At another, that Dad worked for American Express. That he had a job and was working there. They both spoke a lot of languages, visited many countries. They loved travel."

Robin yearned, even now, to hold on to any excuse. It was hard, though, not to hear the doubt in his voice. He had a file of clippings, newspaper articles about his father's case that had appeared in the first years after the Soviet collapse. Boris Yeltsin, hero of the new Russian revolution, one of the articles said, had even handed over documents on the case. A memoir, too, had come out, a confessional by a Soviet spymaster, a favorite of Stalin's. Robin had not read it. But he knew of "a book in the local library" that his son had come across. It had said "something about Dad's case." Just what, he had never asked.

One thing Robin did know for certain. The gaps in the family history far outnumbered the moments of clarity or logic. Whenever Robin dove back in time, trying to retrieve the memories, he would stop short, falling silent in midsentence. Over time, in these silences I sensed another presence—the witness who had kept his father's secrets.

Nerma Oggins had died in 1995. Robin had never heard much about his father from his mother. "She didn't want to dredge the memories," he said. But without fail, in his telling of the past, Nerma would reappear, as if rearranging the fragments of her son's recollection, camouflaging his memories. At first I could imagine her only faintly. Later, as Robin traced his steps through an itinerant and bewildering childhood, Nerma emerged clearly, casting and recasting the past.

Robin was far keener to speak of his father. He wanted to learn the truth about the man he always just called "Dad," to have some answers to the questions that had haunted him since childhood.

He had, however, made one discovery. It was a terrible find, stumbled on by accident in the 1940s. Robin was still a teenager when one day he unearthed a stack of letters "squirreled away in an old steamer trunk." The details were sketchy, half hidden in the bureaucratic language of official government letters. It was a convoluted story, but to Robin the nightmare was clear. The truth seemed unavoidable: the U.S. government had helped kill his father.

ROBIN AND I TALKED often in the years that followed. We compared notes on the telephone, and when enough questions or answers accumulated, we met at the house upstate. In time I assembled boxes of documents culled from archives around the world. We would sit together at the kitchen table and try to sift the facts out of the paper trail. It was not easy to wade through decades of Soviet and post-Soviet falsification. Nor was it easy to rob a man of his illusions. It was not easy to tell Robin how his father had died and how his mother had deceived him.

Toward the end of my first visit, Robin invited me to see the woods beyond his house. We went for a walk. On the ground, wet leaves, copper and gold, spread out around us. He had one more thing he wanted to say. He wanted to thank me.

"It'll be a gift," he said, "to know the truth at last."

I did not know what to say. "You may not like where this leads," I told him.

Robin stopped and looked at me hard.

"I don't care where it goes," he said. "I'm a historian. Remember that. If it's out there, find it."

Willimantic, ca. 1909.

CHAPTER 2

THREAD CITY

■ ■ ■

THE OLD HEADSTONES NO LONGER STOOD STRAIGHT. IN ROW AFTER row, the granite seemed off-balance. Some of the markers leaned to a side; others were pitched forward or back. Many were so worn their chiseled letters spelled out clues, not names. The gates had no sign. Only the half-eroded Hebrew on the stones told the history of the graveyard, a burial ground for Jews in a forgotten corner of New England.

The cemetery was small, a quarter so intimate it was surprising that it remained. Across the street, beyond the iron fence, the eighteen-wheelers, and the pickup trucks, stood a drive-in movie theater, one of the last in the state. Next door was a doughnut shop, and across the way a liquor store. They had buried the Jews here in the nineteenth century, on the advice of Dr. Thomas Morton Hills. The doctor was the force behind the ban on burying "Hebrews" within the town limits. It was a matter, he argued, of the purity of the water table. So they had gone out West Main, just past the town line, and marked off a small square to leave for the Jews.

Someone, though, still came here. The grass was deep green and freshly cut. Many of the headstones bore the signs of visitors: pebbles piled atop the stones, in the Jewish tradition. Five rows in, six graves to the right, lay Simon M. Oggins, father of Isaiah. On top of his headstone, too, there was a pile of small rocks. No member of the Oggins family had lived here for nearly a century, but someone maintained the line of remembrance.

■

ISAIAH OGGINS'S EARLIEST MOTIVATIONS IN LIFE, HIS ZEAL, ANGER, AND ego, were rooted in "the Thread City," as Willimantic was called at the time. The town lies in the northeastern corner of Connecticut, tucked away off the interstate nearly halfway between New York and Boston. As I drove in one humid Sunday evening in the summer of 2005, I followed the old post road, a meandering byway from colonial times. Along Route 6, it was not hard to imagine how Connecticut was once largely trees and farmland, divided only by rivers and lakes. In the state's northeastern corner, the macadam rolls over hill after hill, offering a glimpse of the original topography. Route 6 passes no malls and no McDonald's, scarcely even a billboard. Only on occasion does a shingled A-frame or forlorn trailer appear in the blur of roadside green.

Oggins was born in Willimantic on July 22, 1898. A younger, far larger sibling of Windham, the Yankee village and county seat a few miles to the north, Willimantic was known across New England for its contribution to the growth of America's textile industry. It also ranked among the more popular destinations for the country's growing underclass of immigrant laborers. At the Willimantic mills, the backbone of the workforce—80 percent—was young girls. Uneducated, unskilled, and mercilessly underpaid, the girls kept the mills alive. They endured long hours in stifling conditions for a dollar a day. Few workers in America suffered greater exploitation, as their champions, the Wobblies (the Industrial Workers of the World), would cry.

Willimantic's history, from its accelerated growth to its sudden decline, mirrors the evolution of industrial America. Named by the Algonquin—Willimantic means "land of the swiftly running water"—the town rose quickly on the promise of its water power. In 1833 it was established as a county borough within Windham, which dates from 1692. By the mid-nineteenth century, as demand for cotton and silk grew, immigrants flooded in, lured by the prospects of employment. In 1860, Irish laborers began to dig stone from the river, giant slabs of granite to build the mills. When completed in

1880, Mill Number Four was one of the largest factory buildings in the world, and Willimantic became a destination for commerce across New England.

By then the town was divided along class and labor lines. The managers of the mills and the attendant industries lived in the Hill District, a leafy neighborhood of prim Victorians overlooking the farmland valley beyond. On top of a steep hill, two- and three-story gable-roofed homes testified to the new industrial wealth. Down below, hewing to the banks of the river, sprawled the tenement districts, home to the workers' families. Yet what united both halves was their envy of the world beyond. For the residents of Thread City, Boston and New York, the cities at the ends of the railway tracks, dominated the daily news and their imagination.

SIMON AND RENA OGGINS HAD COME TO AMERICA A DECADE BEFORE Isaiah's birth, among an early wave of Russian Jewish immigrants arriving in New York Harbor in 1888. They were both twenty-five years old when they abandoned the western edge of the czar's empire for the Lower East Side of New York City. Simon and Rena were both born near Kovno—today Kaunas, Lithuania—and raised in the same village, the shtetl of Abolnik. The eldest of three boys, Simon was the first to leave home. Somewhere along the journey, his surname, Melamdovich, serendipitously became Oggins. It was a name so rare, and with such a resounding Scotch-Irish ring, that its fabrication, as those who carried it for generations would discover, was obvious. The invented surname would also, in time, as ambition grew inside a young man, and a career took shape, become aptly symbolic.

One of the countless Russian immigrants in New York's rag trade, Simon worked as a peddler. He and Rena had made the crossing with their firstborn, a two-year-old named David. Like so many other Jewish immigrants, they lived in a sunless tenement—on East Broadway, three blocks south of Hester Street.

A daughter was born in 1892, four years after their arrival. In their eagerness to cast off their past, Simon and Rena did not give their first American-born child a Russian name, or even a Jewish one. Molly, they named the girl—a nod, if anything, to the Irish who lived on the edges of their neighborhood. Not long thereafter, in the spring of 1893, Simon appeared in Superior Court and swore to "renounce and abjure all allegiance and fidelity . . . to the Emperor of Russia." At the first chance, he became a naturalized American.

The following year Simon sailed back to Europe. Whether he went on a trading trip or went home to claim an inheritance, he returned in August 1894 with enough money to escape the slums. He did not just move out of the Lower East Side; he took his family out of the city altogether. After six years in New York, they moved to Willimantic.

TODAY WILLIMANTIC SUFFERS the blight of so many New England towns. Its mills long closed, much of it is a dead end for the working poor, a place of new immigrants and little employment. Main Street, however, still shows its history. It is lined with graceful buildings that date from its industrial ascent in the second half of the nineteenth century.

In 1854, the owners of the biggest mills in town united to form the Willimantic Linen Company. After the Crimean War, as the supply of flax from overseas was nearly cut off, linen became almost impossible to make, and cotton boomed. The Willimantic Linen Company made cotton thread. (The name was a ruse to throw off the British.) After the Civil War, as Indian cotton arrived on the East Coast, demand for the high-grade thread grew. By 1882, Willimantic produced the best six-cord cotton thread in America. At the Linen Company, spiraling profits brought more mills, great hulks of granite that towered over the river and stretched nearly a mile. At its peak, the company employed more than three thousand workers, nearly all foreign-born.

In 1898, the year of Isaiah Oggins's birth, a group of British industrialists struck back, buying up the thread factories of New England and forging a conglomerate, the American Thread Company. They intended the name as insurance against jingoist attacks. American

Thread, as it became known, also thrived. Willimantic now teemed with arrivals—first the Irish, Poles, and French Canadians, and then the Germans, Italians, and even Syrians. And in the decade that preceded Oggins's birth, from across Eastern Europe and the far-off lands of the czar, came the Jews.

SIMON, RENA, and their two children settled into 74 Elm Street, a tall house with pine walls and narrow windows. It was a markedly better home than any on the Lower East Side, but it was a tenement nonetheless. Like all the houses on the street, it was a triple-decker, home to three families stacked one on top of another.

In the 1980s, a fire leveled 74 Elm, along with the other houses that had lined the street a hundred years before. Where the tenements once stood is a vacant lot, a patch of brown dirt littered with abandoned cars. Still, the contours of the old neighborhood remain. Elm Street cuts near the river, along Willimantic's southern edge. It runs up a hill and backs up, as it ends, at the railroad tracks. When Simon Oggins settled here with his family, the noise was unbearable. All along the street, the thin walls shook with the passing of each train. In the 1890s, the tracks provided the main link between Boston and New York and the route of the New England Limited. The Ghost Train, as the locals called it, was painted white and glowed at night.

In time Simon found a footing. He had experience and savings. He opened a little shop, dealing, like most Jews, in dry goods. It was far from the center of town, at a good remove from the Hotel Plaza, the druggist, and the livery and feed stable, but it provided a modest income.

Simon moved his family as often as he could afford to—first, in 1896, across town to North Street, and then, in 1899, to Center Street, where they would live in various houses for nearly two decades. Willimantic, as the new century opened, had a small population of Jews. Nearby lived the Murphys and Olinses, Almonds and Viegards—Irish and French Canadians, nearly all spoolers and weavers at the mills. But on Center Street, the Jews dominated.

The street became the heart of the Jewish district, a ghetto without gates. Next door, at Number 22, the Newburgs, from Austria, had a brood of seven children. Abbie Golden, a mill worker, was at Number 5; Max Levine, the local rabbi, at Number 19; Joseph Astmann, the sausage maker, at Number 27; and across the street, at Number 20, Abraham Glouskin, a shoe salesman with a store on nearby Union Street. On the far side of the street from where the Oggins family lived, in a converted Spiritualist church, stood the Sons of Israel Temple.

Hyman Israel was the man who got the temple built. Israel, who had also fled from Russia, held the reputation of the first Jew to settle in Willimantic. In the years that Isaiah was a toddler, Israel ran the lunch wagon on Railroad Street. Each day before dawn he would hitch the wagon to his horses and take it to the rail crossing downtown to serve the passengers. Willimantic was a hub then, the nexus of three railway lines. With more than forty passenger trains crisscrossing the city each day, including the Ghost Train, which stopped only in Willimantic, Israel never lacked for customers. In town, he enjoyed the respect of Jew and non-Jew alike, as so many Jews of that era in small-town America did.

Simon and Rena were still on Center Street when Isaiah was born, in the summer of 1898 in St. Joseph's, the town hospital. That he was not born at home, as his sister seems to have been on the Lower East Side, was a sign of the family's progress. The following fall, a second daughter, Rebecca, arrived. By 1900, Simon and Rena had four children; David, Molly, Isaiah, and the newborn Rebecca. In the fall of 1903, Rena, at forty-one, gave birth to a third daughter, Ethel Dora. The infant died, though, of pneumonia on January 5, 1905, at seventeen months. When the baby died, Isaiah was not yet seven years old.

David, Isaiah's elder brother by twelve years, soon left home, and Molly moved out in the fall of 1911. At nineteen, she married a twenty-four-year-old Russian émigré in Rhode Island. By 1912, the thirteen-year-old Isaiah was living with his parents and twelve-year-old sister, Rebecca—the aunt Robin knew as Betty.

Following a typical American tradition, Isaiah went to grammar school across town at the old Natchaug School, a yellow clapboard building—the very image of a New England schoolhouse—built in 1874. Then it was on to Windham High, the elegant new school on the edge of the Hill District. It was a public school, but the sons and daughters of the men who ran the mills dominated. Walking across town from Center Street each morning, Isaiah passed their tall Victorians. It was a small school, with nearly two hundred students in four grades, but for the mill town, the pretension of elegance was hard to justify. Two campanile towers overlooked the pyramidal roof, and a row of Doric columns flanked the granite threshold. Isaiah had nearly completed his first year when, in the spring of 1913, the new school burned to the ground.

The townsmen rebuilt the school within a year, and in the spring of 1916, Isaiah graduated. He began the summer—America's last summer of peace before the Great War—with hope. For him, a chance had arrived. He could leave the city of giant mills and child workers

■

DESPITE WHAT MIGHT APPEAR TO SOME A HALCYON CHILDHOOD, ISAIAH grew up in a veritable battlefield. The tensions that shaped turn-of-the-century life in America's large cities pervaded Willimantic. Labor disputes arose and were put down with frequency and brutality in the years of his youth.

Isaiah was only thirteen years old when the mill workers in Lawrence, Massachusetts, a day's train ride north, went on strike. The 1912 Lawrence strike became a landmark in the history of American labor. More than 20,000 workers took to the streets, where they were greeted by policemen carrying bayonets. In the end, "Wild Bill" Haywood, the bearlike leader of the Wobblies, carried the day. For Haywood and the Wobblies, Lawrence was far more than a single victory. It was the harbinger, long awaited, of the great upheaval to come.

Within weeks the Wobblies descended on Willimantic. Isaiah was just a schoolboy, but the strike was sure to make a strong impression. For the first time in his life, the Willimantic mill workers forged a political force. It was not just the men. Everyone walked, even the young girls and gray-haired women. First they dared to take on the old union, the United Textile Workers, the domain of labor officials far more conservative and pliant than the Wobblies. But the ultimate goal was brazen: to force American Thread to its knees.

It began on a Friday, April 27, 1912, when more than half of the two thousand workers left their stations. Willimantic was paralyzed. Workers and their families flooded downtown, and all along Main Street, boys in breeches and caps climbed the trees to get a better view. Even young Isaiah, a freshman at Windham High already lost in his books, would have had a hard time forgetting the haggard faces and the jackbooted policemen, many on horseback, who tried their best to beat the strikers back to the mills.

On Sunday a mass meeting was held in the center of town. The workers stood together, vowing not to return to work. At last feeling their power, they issued a single demand: a 10 percent wage raise. Before long, Elizabeth Gurley Flynn, the flame-haired Irish labor agitator, arrived. "The Rebel Girl," as her fans called her, had quit school to join the Wobblies and given her first street-corner speech at sixteen. By 1912, at twenty-two, she was a celebrity—"an East Side Joan of Arc," in the words of Theodore Dreiser.

The strike did not last long. On Monday, American Thread caved, granting the raise. For the Willimantic mill workers, it was a triumph without precedent. The celebration began, appropriately enough, on May Day. For Flynn, it was "the quickest settlement" she had ever heard of, and a rare moment of ecstasy. Afterward, she yelled over the sea of heads in the streets. "You've won a moral as well as a labor victory," she promised, adding that the time of an eight-hour workday and a three-dollar daily wage was coming. But Flynn left the workers with an admonition. "There were men and women in this fight," she screamed, her voice hoarse, "and at some time there may be an attempt to weed them out. You must defend those who fought this battle."

To young Isaiah, neither the triumph of the strikers nor the warning of the Rebel Girl was something to be forgotten.

＊

BY THE FALL OF 1916, AS AMERICA STRUGGLED TO AVERT ITS EYES FROM the spectacular carnage in Europe, Isaiah had taken on his first false identity. At a time when foreigners suddenly found themselves isolated and suspect, he revealed a desire to assimilate, in a hurry.

He changed his first name, becoming Cy, a variant of Ysai, the Yiddish name his parents had given him. Cy recrafted the name, creating a different ring—something novel, distinctly modern, and quintessentially American. It was a name that also bore the unmistakable aura of one of the heroes of the day, the legendary ex–Red Sox pitcher recently retired after twenty-two seasons, Cy Young.

It was not just a nickname. Even before he finished high school, Cy had turned from his father and mother, signaling a defiance that would only grow. It was as if he was determined to break with his ancestry, those generations of men, far-off and spectral, with Old Testament beards and long-suffering wives who bore children without end. Perhaps it had been only a question of time. His parents, after all, had led by example. Simon and Rena had come to the United States and remade themselves into good, naturalized townspeople of New England. They had distanced themselves first from the repression of czarist Russia, then from the strictures of the Lower East Side, where Jacob Riis's "other half" lived. Now Cy's turn had arrived.

He stepped firmly away from the Yiddish peddler and his homebound wife and moved, with a marked determination, toward mainstream America. By the fall of 1916, Cy had set himself a steep course. He would not only escape Willimantic but join the elite of America. He would try to win admission to the Ivy League. In the fall of 1916, he sat for the Yale Exams, the university entrance tests. Windham High enjoyed close ties with Yale, and a number of classmates, those with the right accent and religion, would move on to New Haven. Cy, though, was bound for a different destination.

Class of 1920, Columbia College.

CHAPTER 3

WAR

■ ■ ■

IN 1917, CY OGGINS ENROLLED AT COLUMBIA UNIVERSITY, A SOCIAL AND
intellectual citadel of the Ivy League. It was a time, if ever there was
one, when a great wave of change was set to break across America.
The country stood on the brink not only of world war but of mod-
ernism. The shift would be epochal, and its epicenter was New York
City. "They pour into New York from a thousand towns and col-
leges," rhapsodized Waldo Frank, critic, novelist, and chronicler of
the ascendant generation. "Inevitably, they are the artists and the
writers. For such are the men and women who desire to create a
world of their own to live in."

They came to New York to flee their fathers' world, the first generation in a long succession to do so. Seeking freedom in love and art,
they would end up struggling to keep pace with the tumult around
them. It was a time "of universal revolt and regeneration," wrote Max
Eastman, editor of the radical journal *The Masses*. Yet as Cy and his
classmates walked into the oak-paneled classrooms of Columbia,
they were already keenly aware of their unique, if accidental,
birthright. Their generation was only as old as the new century. And
it was coming of age at a propitious moment—"the just-before-
dawn," as Eastman wrote, "of a new day in American art and literature, and living-of-life as well as in politics."

CY WENT DOWN to New York, to the urban university on Morningside Heights, midway through the academic year. "February
entrants," as they were called, bore an unseen taint. Most often they

were Jews. Columbia was hardly alone in the practice. Across the Ivy League, Jewish candidates for admission had become so numerous that they were a subject of public debate.

The "Hebrew problem," as it was known, hung over the campus. Even as Cy settled into Columbia, it remained a source of tension, heightening a sense of alienation and exclusion. Given the number of prominent Jewish students on campus, it could hardly have been pivotal for the lithe, bookish boy from Connecticut. Over time, though, the isolation that Cy felt in college helped turn him away from the mainstream.

Nicholas Murray Butler, the president of Columbia, did not take the question lightly. "I suggest treating the candidate for graduation as one treats a candidate for admission to a club," he wrote to his dean in 1914. "That is, having his personal qualifications examined." At best, Butler was "a social snob of the first water," and at worst, a paranoid anti-Semite. By the time Cy enrolled in college, Columbia's imperious president enjoyed a reputation as the Bismarck of the Ivy League. With his silvery mane, burly physique, and unruly brows, he even resembled the German autocrat. Butler was also a politician of national stature. In 1912 he had been William Howard Taft's running mate in the presidential election. Faced with an increasing number of highly qualified Jewish applicants, Butler made use of the midwinter window. He could appear to keep the number of Jews down while filling the spaces of those students who had left campus by Christmas, either failing or quitting.

Although Cy joined the Class of 1920 a semester late, Columbia's admissions master, Adam LeRoy Jones, took note of his Yale Exams. Cy had aced the tests, scoring so well in English, math, history, Latin, and French that Jones granted him advanced standing. The additional credits gave the young man a head start, allowing him to keep pace with his class. All the same, the taint of his winter admission lingered.

On a campus rigidly divided by class and religion, Jews and Gentiles—WASPs, in the main—lived in different worlds. That, too, would change during the tumult of Cy's years at Columbia. As the borders of the social and intellectual circles on campus shifted, no longer were one's family and economic backgrounds the decisive markers. What mattered most, what determined a young man's friends, field of study, and above all his future was his politics.

FOR CY, IT BEGAN in his first days on campus. The Great War now loomed everywhere in America, even on the narrow horizon at Columbia. Since August 1914, the fighting had consumed Europe. The slaughter was without precedent. In the first six months of 1915 alone, more than a million men had lost their lives. In the summer of 1916, the British lost 60,000 soldiers in a single day. All the while, President Woodrow Wilson grew increasingly anxious, straining to keep the United States on the sidelines. In 1916, Wilson had run for reelection on the slogan "He kept us out of the war." He won, barely. But before long, "armed neutrality," the wishy-washy tack Wilson had followed for years, became untenable. Germany's declaration that it would resume submarine attacks two years after the sinking of the *Lusitania* forced Wilson's hand.

February 1917, the month Cy matriculated, marked the time "when the shadow of quickly impending war first fell across the path of our ordinary occupation," President Butler later recalled. For a nineteen-year-old from a Connecticut mill town, it was a singularly dramatic moment. First came the thunder from afar, the abdication of the czar in Russia. On March 17, Nicholas II ceded power in St. Petersburg. Then, on April 2, came the proclamation in Washington, D.C. President Wilson at last committed America to the war. "It is a fearful thing," Wilson told Congress, "to lead this great peaceful people into war, into the most terrible and disastrous of all wars, civilization itself seeming to be in the balance." The two events, coming within days, set the course for Cy's college career—and led him to look far beyond the narrow boundaries of academic life.

※

ON CAMPUSES ACROSS AMERICA, WILSON'S DECISION IGNITED INTENSE debate. The move to war, of course, affected young men more than any other group in the country. Yet nowhere did the battles prove as costly as at Columbia. During the war, the university underwent greater upheaval than any it had ever seen—or would again, until the student protests of 1968.

That spring, almost immediately, the fighting in Europe reshaped life on campus. For many in the United States, the bloodshed was distant, the battlefields remote locales with foreign names. For the students at Columbia, and at universities across the country, the war was a close and personal threat. It swept through Cy's class, overturning friendships and dividing classrooms. It also took the lives of a good many of his classmates.

Cy was, by all accounts, a gifted student. In his coursework that first spring and into the fall, he did well. He excelled in French, English, and philosophy. He also took a year-long course in psychology, "the new science," and survived physics, a requirement. By the winter of 1918, as he began his third term, he had settled on an ambitious track, a double major in history and English. Momentous events— politics on the world and local scale—would dominate his time in college, but Cy would not let his studies suffer. He completed the rigorous major ahead of schedule and with honors. The distractions, though, remained a constant lure.

Columbia College was still a small place, with no more than 1,200 undergraduates and a scattering of buildings. In its graduation photograph, the Class of 1920 seems a somber crew. Young men in white shirts, dark ties, and winter coats, they stand in just seven rows on the granite steps of Columbia's centerpiece, Seth Low Memorial Library. The war had winnowed Cy's class; only 237 students graduated with him. Many were absent on that snowy day—including Cy. It was as if he had lost whatever kinship he had once sought with the well-to-do young men of Manhattan. Whether or not he entered Columbia with passionate political stirrings, by the time he left, the Jewish boy from Willimantic was known—unabashedly—as a radical.

His classmates, in contrast, seemed to epitomize the allures of their generation. Cy was thrust into the center of a small circle of young men who, at a remarkable pace, would reshape the New York literary world after graduation. Richard Simon, half of the future Simon & Schuster, was among Cy's classmates. But Bennett Cerf was the one who dominated the class, and the campus. Cerf wrote "The Stroller," a column in the school paper, edited *The Jester*, the humor magazine, and held court each night in the dorm-room debates. In 1925 he would join Donald Klopfer, a younger Columbia alumnus, to found Random House.

Cy's class held not only the future stars of New York publishing but also its rebels. Matty Josephson, perhaps the generation's greatest muckraker, may have been the one Cy knew best. By 1934, with the publication of *The Robber Barons*, a scathing critique of America's first industrial titans, Josephson would gain fame. Cy and Josephson spent years together in the same classrooms; Josephson, too, majored in history and English. At Columbia, moreover, both were outsiders. Josephson—and another classmate who became a prominent left-wing writer, Joe Freeman—had come from Brooklyn and a middle-class Jewish home.

Matty Josephson never joined the Communist Party. ("I know I'm not virtuous enough," he once told a friend.) But long after Columbia, he did become one of the most prominent Marxists in American letters. In 1932 he helped draft a manifesto in support of William Z. Foster, when Foster ran for the third time as the Communist Party's presidential candidate. The self-taught son of an Irish father and an English mother, Foster was raised in Philadelphia but had worked since the age of ten in factories and packing houses across America. In Chicago, he had risen as the hero of meatpackers and longshoremen. Foremost among the party leaders, Foster stood up for the comrades in the lowest jobs, the slaughterhouses, mills, and docks across the country. In time he also became the party leader Cy admired most.

The Class of 1920 is notable for its members who soon found literary celebrity—the list also includes the novelist Louis Bromfield, the critic Kenneth Burke, and the writer William Slater Brown. Yet even early on, many of Cy's classmates gained an ability to absent themselves from the great events that defined the age. Even those who left campus early to serve "over there," volunteering for the Norton-Harjes Ambulance Corps, were instilled, as Malcolm Cowley wrote, with "what might be called a *spectatorial* attitude." It was a posture, however convenient, that could not have been further from the ideas and passion that had seized Cy.

·

LIKE THE MAJORITY OF HIS CLASS, CY WAS A DAY STUDENT, SINCE SIMON and Rena could not afford the extra expense of boarding. Each morning except Sunday, he rode the subway into the city, taking the new Astoria Line from its last stop, just opened, in Queens. Assuring himself that it would not be for long, he had moved to Long Island City, into the modest home, already crowded, of his brother, David.

A decade earlier, David Oggins had paved the way to New York. He had attended New York University and stayed on for law school. For the firstborn, an infant when his parents left Kovno, it was an improbable ascent. David had not only escaped the Willimantic mills but entered the professional class. By the time Cy went to live with him, David was running a fledgling solo practice downtown. He had rented an office on Nassau Street, one room on the ninth floor of the *New York Herald Tribune* building. His achievements could only have heightened expectations for Cy back home in Willimantic.

David, however, had long since parted ways with his past. In 1912, in Astoria, he married a Jewish Belgian girl, Sophia Trogheim. Cy had gone down from Connecticut with his parents and sister Betty for the wedding. David was twenty-six and Sophia twenty. They were not wed, though, as everyone at home on Center Street doubtless noted, in a synagogue. In time they settled into a colorless neighborhood that was distinctly Irish and decidedly middle-class. Number 428 Ditmars Avenue was a modest home, scarcely large enough for Sophia's younger brother and sister, who had followed her to the new country.

For Cy, given Sophia's siblings and David's ambitions, the home was claustrophobic. But until he finished college, he would have to make do.

Cy had entered a world far removed from the mills and spoolers, a realm of lofty ideas and blue blood. Herbert Hawkes, Butler's favorite Yale man and stalwart dean, served as his freshman adviser. John Erskine, who had established Columbia's Great Books course, taught him English literature from the Elizabethans to the seventeenth-century poets. George Odell, one of the day's great authorities on opera and theater, introduced him to Shakespeare. A legend of the New York theater world, Odell even lived on Broadway, in a hotel on West Forty-fifth Street. Odell, whose older brother was a former governor of New York, also served as Cy's adviser in his junior year.

Among the historians, Cy gravitated, as if by instinct, to two: Charles Beard, a brilliant young historian whose star was fast rising, and Robert Livingston Schuyler, the department's anchor. An expert on imperial history and the future head of the American Historical Association, Schuyler had earned his undergraduate and doctoral degrees at Columbia. He was also the eighth lineal descendant of Philip Pieters Schuyler, the Dutch settler who had arrived in Fort Orange, today Albany, in 1650. Cy took several courses with Schuyler, even asking him to guide his dissertation.

As Cy settled into the measured rhythms of academic life, the war hung overhead, threatening to cut short his studies. At Columbia, the war divided not only the student body but the university hierarchy. As Cy's first term came to a close, Butler laid down the law. His administration would stand foursquare behind the government in Washington. Dissenting voices, whether among the students or the faculty, would be silenced. "So long as national policies were in debate we gave . . . complete liberty of assembly, of speech and of publication to all members of the University," Butler announced on the eve of commencement in June 1917. "Wrong-headedness and folly we might deplore, but were bound to tolerate." No longer. "What had been wrong-headedness was now sedition. What had been folly was now treason."

He could not have predicted the troubles, but as Butler hemmed in the borders of university life and thought, he helped precipitate the turmoil to come. Columbia, he vowed, would become almost "a part of the apparatus of the Government of the United States for the preparation and training of men" for the war. There would be no place "for any person who opposes or who counsels opposition" to the law, or "who acts, speaks or writes treason." It was a warning to any in their midst who dared not to stand "with whole heart and mind and strength committed to fight with us to make the world safe for democracy."

On campus, the debate over the war soon left the realm of rhetoric. The student radicals began to stage rallies, and civil unrest threatened to break out. The war served as a recruitment drive for left-wing groups. The apologists for capitalism had new competition. Among the radicals, the only question was which program fit best: socialism, anarchy, or syndicalism. The students gave Butler a new nickname, Czar, and in time witnessed the end of their prewar liberties. Before Cy's first year was over, three Columbia professors, including Beard, were gone. The turmoil quickened the development of Cy's embryonic political consciousness. It also revealed, perhaps for the first time even to himself, an unquenchable desire for change.

Three events in quick succession marked the turn. In the first week of June 1917, as Cy prepared for his first exams, fireboats lined the Hudson. All along the river, they blared their horns, sounding the opening of draft registration. On May 18, Wilson had signed the new draft law. For the first time since the Civil War, young American men were required to sign up and serve. On June 1, Wilson vowed that anyone failing to register faced a year in jail. By the end of the first week in June, nearly 10 million American men had signed up.

Cy, though, was not among them. At Columbia, and across New York City, an antidraft movement had arisen and quickly gained force. It was brazen—and illegal. But the young radicals united in a student association, the Collegiate Anti-Militarism League. That spring New York police arrested three undergraduate members of the league for handing out antidraft pamphlets on street corners. In June, the case made the *New York Times*. One student, a Barnard senior, was "but a slip of a girl," due to get her diploma in days. Another was "a Hebrew with a respectable father on West End Avenue." And the third was Owen Cattell, a sweet-faced, well-groomed boy who happened to be the son of a Columbia luminary.

James Cattell had taught at the university for twenty-six years. A pioneering psychologist, he boasted that he had trained more practitioners in the new field than anyone else in the country. He had also long baited Butler and the overlords of Columbia. Cattell stood by his son, and even dared to hire Morris Hillquit, the Socialist leader and lawyer, to defend him. Soon he publicly challenged Butler. He wrote a letter on Columbia stationery to New York's senators and congressmen, arguing against sending American boys to Europe. The war, Cattell maintained, was not only immoral but illegal. When the *New York Evening Post* printed the letter, the trustees called for Cattell's scalp.

Harry Dana, a young literature professor, was also soon dragged before the board. H.W.L. Dana had famous roots: the "L" stood for the poet Longfellow, his grandfather. Dana, however, had a passion for radical politics. He was the one who bailed out the three students arrested in the spring. Butler issued a reprimand, but over the summer Dana stepped up his antiwar activities, attending pacifist rallies in Boston and New York. In the fall, Butler warned Dana that dismissal loomed, thanks to his "association with the most irresponsible, irrational and unpatriotic elements of the population."

On October 4, 1917, when Cy was only weeks into his second term, the Columbia trustees fired both Dana and Cattell. Still, the troubles did not end. In the classrooms and dorms, the students spoke only of the dismissals. "Purges," the radicals called them. Dana and Cattell had long been popular; now they became martyrs. Talk of a student boycott raged. But before anyone could act, another thunderbolt hit.

Within days, Charles Beard, the young star of the history department, resigned. For Cy, the departure of Beard, who would go on to become the dean of American historians, was the landmark. By 1917, every radical at Columbia worshipped Beard, as did thousands more across New York. The firings of Dana and Cattell, so bold a silencing of dissent, would only have reinforced Cy's loathing of the university's old guard and its self-affirming reflexes. But it was Beard's resignation that left a lasting impression. To the campus radicals, the historian's refusal to live by Butler's strictures had drawn a new line. It sealed their belief in the futility of institutional reform in America.

Beard did not quit over the war. He had, in fact, come out in favor of it. One morning in 1916, as the New York newspapers reported the sinking of a merchant ship by German submarines, Beard stood with eyes closed before his students and declared, "The history of the world was altered today." With the long face of a Roman philosopher, he relied on a natural flair for the dramatic. "It will now be impossible for the United States to stay out of the war. German autocracy will have to be destroyed." When Beard opened his eyes, they were full of tears.

Cy knew that Beard was not alone in supporting the war. He had followed John Dewey, the eminent philosopher and his Columbia colleague, in joining the interventionists. In a series of essays in the *New Republic*, which had taken a defiantly prowar stance, Dewey had even argued against conscientious objectors. At Columbia, the philosopher's acolytes—universally pacifist—were outraged. Randolph Bourne, who had graduated from Columbia four years earlier, led the counterattack. A dwarf hunchback, Bourne was the reigning polemicist of the day, hero to the junior radicals of his alma mater.

At Columbia, Bourne had been a devoted protégé of Dewey's. But in a pair of 1917 essays, "The War and the Intellectuals" and "Twilight of Idols," he turned on his mentor. "War in the interests of democracy!" Bourne wrote, "This was the sum of their philosophy . . . War was seen as the crowning relief of their indecision . . . Let us join the greased slide towards war!" Bourne's antiwar essays, to Waldo Frank, "marked the literary voice of young America, stirring at last against the iron course upon which the old America had bound it. Bourne found himself a leader of tens of thousands."

To Cy and his classmates, the battle between Dewey and Bourne came to embody the war on campus. It was not simply a generational chapter in the old struggle between fathers and sons. It was a fight for a new ideology, for a new American polity. To the radicals, who stood firmly behind Bourne, the winners soon became all too visible.

FOR CHARLES BEARD, the Columbia firings were the final straw. The dismissals posed a question not of patriotism or pacifism but of intellectual freedom. If the university's history department was the strongest in the country, the credit in large part was due to Beard. A Midwesterner who had taught at Columbia since 1904, he was not close to Cattell or Dana. Beard and his wife, Mary, herself a rising historian, were, however, passionate about politics. Both were liberals and, to the student radicals, rare kindred spirits.

In Beard, Cy and his classmates saw a scholar willing to challenge even the holy of holies. In his seminal 1913 work, *An Economic Interpretation of the Constitution,* Beard argued that the founding fathers had framed the Constitution as a "bulwark against democracy." Butler had once quipped that the ginger-haired historian was "redheaded on the inside as well as the outside." Columbia's president could stomach, if barely, liberal scholarship. Radical assemblies, however, were another matter.

At one gathering in 1916, Beard sat idle as a student yelled, "To Hell with the flag!" At Columbia, among both radicals and "patriots," as many of the conservative students called themselves, the protest was legendary. The historian was chastised but cleared of wrongdoing. Beard was too valuable to censure, let alone fire. But he was not too fearful to quit. "The university," Beard wrote in his farewell letter, "is really under the control of a small and active group of trustees who have no standing in the world of education, who are reactionary and visionless in politics, narrow and medieval in religion."

The day Beard quit, the radicals mobilized. They gathered in a dorm and debated tactics. They decided to stage a protest on the steps in front of the statue of Alma Mater. The stunt worked. Word of the resignation spread across New York and soon the country. The *Times* wrote an impassioned editorial, "Columbia's Deliverance," praising the move. On campus, however, Beard's departure, along with that of Cattell and Dana, left a void.

A chill set in. The days of feverish debate were over. To the radicals, the outcome was ominous. In the Columbia classrooms, just as Cy was beginning to find his footing and explore the intellectual frontiers of the day, the cost of one's words and actions had become patently clear.

The world now "stank of death," one of Cy's classmates later recalled. The Great War had come to dominate their time in college, even remaking the campus. In the fall of 1917, Cy saw the advent of the Student Army Training Corps, the ROTC of World War I. Dorms became barracks, and military officers had priority over professors for their choice of students. Undergraduates wore uniforms to class, and, steeling themselves for the call-up, marched shoulder to shoulder across South Field. By winter, Columbia's classrooms were half emptied. Hundreds had gone to the war.

All else now seemed trivial, superfluous. The debate over the fighting in Europe sharpened. Carlton Hayes, one of Cy's history professors, held the radicals spellbound in his lectures on "The Causes and Origins of the Present War." Hayes only strengthened their belief that the war was a product of "imperialism and militarism and nationalism," and that the fight for democracy was in truth only a struggle "for markets, colonies, and spheres of influence."

Cy held out for another year before facing the inevitable. He was torn, in all likelihood, between his duty to the law, his family, and his own beliefs. Students opposed to the war now risked being ostracized on two fronts. On campus, they were seen as traitors. At home, their parents—especially if they were Jews and immigrants—watched with alarm. During wartime, the fear held, dissent could bring nothing but harm to the family.

At the start of his second fall at Columbia, Cy took the train to

Connecticut. If in New York he could find an antiwar kinship of radicals, at home the new martial fervor had swept the town. In Willimantic, homes, clubs, and factories now flew "military service flags." The number of stars on the flags proudly declared how many family members or factory workers were serving overseas. A giant flag swirled over the American Thread headquarters. It had forty-one stars. The Willimantic Lodge 1440, Loyal Order of Moose, flew a flag with twenty-three. The Morrisons on Park Street had four sons in service, and Mrs. Owen O'Neill, apparently only for support, had erected a towering flagpole in the middle of her garden on Prospect Street.

On the morning of September 12, 1918, two months before the war's end, Cy joined the line of young men downtown. Nearly all were American Thread workers—Poles, Irish, and a few fearful Germans. At twenty, Cy at last added his name to the rolls.

THE GREAT WAR brought a split to the Oggins family, the first of many. The Oggins brothers, already separated by twelve years, would move further apart during the war. Throughout his years in college, Cy was living under his brother's roof in Long Island City. David not only gave Cy a room, he helped to pay his tuition—$150 a year, before it jumped to $250 in 1919. It was an extra expense that David, much later in life, came to regret greatly.

It did not take long for the momentous events abroad to redraw the lines at home. Cy's earliest political battles, whether in Willimantic or at Columbia, went undocumented. Even as a student, a budding scholar more intent on an academic career than a political crusade, Cy seems to have steered clear of the limelight. David, on the other hand, took public stands. And he made sure that they were entered into the historical record.

On October 20, 1919, the *New York Times* published a letter to the editor from Cy's brother. David was grateful to the newspaper for saving him from the temptations of Henri Barbusse, a French pacifist writer then in vogue.

BARBUSSE ON THE WAR—WAS THERE NOTHING MORE IN
THE STRUGGLE THAN SUFFERING AND DEATH?

To the Editor:
I read your article of the 17th inst. with reference to M. Barbusse. The arti-
cle came to my attention quite timely, for I was reading Barbusse's grim war
story. His book had begun to make me hate war, all wars, recent and remote.
But in the light of your article I reflected. The sinister propaganda therein
contained was revealed to me.

Barbusse's *Le Feu*, an unflinching account from the trenches in
Europe, caused a sensation when it appeared in English in 1918,
"translated from the 100th French edition," as *The Inferno*. In 1919, to
feed the demand among American pacifists, Barbusse wrote a sequel,
Light. The editorial that solicited David's gratitude had been unspar-
ing: "Henri Barbusse, thanks to the possession of something more,
though not much more, than ordinary literary ability, was able, while
the war was on, to make himself the pet of all the pacifists and
defeatists who read in French and English." Denouncing *The Inferno* as
"defeatist propaganda," the *Times* blasted his sequel as well. Barbusse
could write, the newspaper conceded, but so could "about four out of
five literate Frenchmen." David was thankful that the editorial had
opened his eyes, revealing Barbusse to be nothing more than "an out-
and-out defender of the Bolsheviki."

The dinner hour at the house in Long Island City could not have
been dull. On questions of history, or even the social and economic
forces of the day, David may have been willing to hear Cy out. The
first son, Russian-born and intent on slipping into the mainstream of
American life, he could play the practical foil to the family rebel. But
David, too, was passionate about politics—of a different stripe.

Soon after law school, Cy's brother had become a Republican.
Whether David was swayed by Teddy Roosevelt's progressive policies
or because he had left Willimantic a decade earlier than Cy and had
seen less of its grim conditions, he had grown staunchly conservative.
In fact, the summer after Wilson signed the draft law, David even

served on his local draft board. In July 1917, he was one of three men named to grant exemptions in his Queens district. His selection, in a heavily Democratic and Irish neighborhood, may have been mere charity. In the spring of 1915, when New York State held a constitutional convention, David had run for a delegate seat and lost. Democrats, not surprisingly, had taken all three seats allotted to his district.

In the fall of 1917, as Cy was preparing for his second round of Columbia exams, David ran again, this time for the state assembly. The matchup, as recorded in the *New York Times*, was hardly typical of the day: "David Oggins, (Rep.), age 32, born in Russia, lawyer, high school and N.Y.U.," versus "John Kennedy, (Dem.), Vice Pres., Amalgamated Meat Cutters and Butcher Workmen." The result could not have surprised many. The Irish butcher and local labor boss won in a landslide. David Oggins got 2,093 votes and Kennedy 6,453.

Twice defeated, Cy's brother only persisted. In November 1918, days before the armistice in Europe, he mounted one more campaign —now for state senate, running against another Irishman, Peter McGarry. An authority in the Irish neighborhood, McGarry was a Democrat with a following. He owned a bar. The Citizens Union, the League of Women's Voters of the day, handicapped the race: "The experience and training of David Oggins (Republican) lawyer, is not such as to justify his indorsement, in an overwhelmingly Democratic district, despite the fact that Peter G. McGarry, a saloon keeper, clearly indicates his unfitness for legislative office." The Citizens Union declined to endorse any candidate. David got 9,841 votes. McGarry won with 27,785.

The following year, David wrote to the *Times*. His letter revealed a turn away from his latent pacifist stirrings and, more significantly, a growing distrust of Bolshevism. His brother was not likely to have been troubled. To Cy, David's political career—serial disasters that failed to shake an immigrant's conservatism—offered a front-row seat to a farce. By 1919, the war in Europe had spawned a war at home. Within the Oggins family, battle lines were drawn as the stakes rose to a new, dangerous level.

Arrest night, February 20, 1939, The Lubyanka Prison, Moscow, USSR.

THE LUBYANKA:
1939

∎

HIS FACE THROBBED UNTIL IT WENT NUMB. WHEN THE GUARDS brought Cy into the room, he had already been hit more than once. They sat him down on the wooden chair and left him. For the first time since they had dragged him from the hotel, Cy sat alone.

Exhausted from the long line of prisoners, the night clerk went through the motions. The camera flashed twice—first a front-on and then a profile from the left. As the bulbs exploded, Cy did not blink. They had beaten him badly, not waiting until after the photographs were taken. One bruise circled his left eye. The other cast a shadow across the right side of his face from cheek to temple.

Cy still wore his suit coat. A herringbone tweed of ash gray, it pinched awkwardly at his shoulders. They had taken his tie already. The jacket and dress shirt beneath, its starched collar twisted open, made an odd combination. An outfit more befitting a street tough, it lent Cy a determined air, an unbending defiance that he may not have had.

On the grainy black-and-white mug shots, the clerk wrote Cy's real name as well as the Czech alias on the fake passport Cy had handed over in his hotel. The clerk's handwriting was clumsy, but the block letters below the portraits were large. With care, you could make out:

568. ЕГОН—ОГЕНС ХЕЙН-САЙ САМОЧ

Prisoner 568. A low number. But the new year was only seven

weeks old. The clerk made more than one mistake. Transcribed into English, the names he scribbled down made a bit more sense:

EGON—OGENS KHEIN—SAI SAMOCH

Clerical skills at the Lubyanka, as Russian historians like to remind the uninitiated, were never refined. After all, even the highest-ranking officers in Stalin's secret police rarely had an education beyond a few years in grade school in the hinterland. Maybe it was the hour, or the strange-sounding foreign names, but the clerk mixed up just about everything he could. He confused the first and last name of Oggins's alias, misspelled his real last name, got his real first name wrong, and botched his patronymic (a Russian's second name, which denotes "son of") beyond recognition.

Untangling the errors was easy. "Egon Hein" was the name in the false Czech passport that Oggins had used to register at the Hotel Moskva. The alias at first did not seem right. It sounded German, not Czech. But in time I saw how it had worked. Egon Hein would ring true as the name of a Sudeten German, an ethnic German born in Czechoslovakia. Oggins spoke fluent German and could pass as a European of indistinct origins. In the 1930s, the passports of choice among Soviet agents were Czech.

Later, in the Prague archives, the real Egon Hein appeared. Born in a rural village in 1915, he was far younger than Oggins. At the time of Oggins's arrest, moreover, the real Hein was studying medicine in Prague. He had never applied for a passport—he was too young and too poor to travel. His name, therefore, could be borrowed without fear. Moreover, the passport would be clean. If anyone ever checked, it belonged to a Czech who had never had trouble with the law.

"Sai Samoch" was a form of the truth. "Sai Simonovich" is how Cy's handlers had addressed him, in an odd blending of an American nickname and a Russian patronymic. The clipped gallop of sibilants sounded like air escaping a puncture. In the Lubyanka, he had heard it again. For years to come, the pairing would resound from the mouths of his tormenters.

LUBYANKA. FOR A LONG TIME the word had floated like a cloud that appears on a beautiful day to block the sun. Ever since Paris, Cy had not been able to help thinking of it. By 1939, at its mention even readers of American newspapers could conjure a foreboding image: the prison at the heart of the Soviet labyrinth of jails and labor camps. In the West, the Lubyanka had become a synonym for the entrance to hell. Stalin's secret policemen, though, called it "the Center," headquarters of the omnipotent guardians of the Soviet state. Prison and administrative corpus, it was both—a brutally efficient netherworld.

On February 20, 1939, Cy found himself inside the dark cluster of iron-shuttered buildings in the heart of Moscow. The Lubyanka consumed, as it still does today, the northern edge of the square that bore the name of Feliks Dzerzhinsky, the Polish revolutionary who founded the Cheka, Lenin's secret police and the first of many Soviet precursors of the KGB. By the time he died in 1926, "Iron Feliks" had built the Cheka into an apparatus of state control without precedent in history. The Romanovs had had the Okhrana to enforce the imperial will, and even Ivan the Terrible in the sixteenth century had had his *oprichniki*. But Dzerzhinsky's jackbooted *chekisty*, as the officers of the Cheka came to be known, took obedience and punishment to a new level.

The Cheka—ЧК, in the Russian abbreviation for the Extraordinary Commission to Combat Counter-Revolution and Sabotage— would be rechristened time and again. In 1922 it was renamed the OGPU, in 1934 it merged with the NKVD, and in 1946 it was consumed by the MVD. Eventually it became, of course, the KGB. During the final days of the Soviet Union, under Yeltsin, the KGB's domestic arm became the FSK, and most recently, after the Soviet collapse, it became the FSB. The name changes have never mattered. To Russians, the secret police today remain, as they were in 1939, *chekisty*.

Inside, the Lubyanka was a maze. It took months for new officers to find their way around. The main building, built in 1899 as the home of the Rossiya Insurance Company, was an imposing five stories of granite. In the early 1930s, three floors of yellow brick were added, and an annex of eleven stories, lavish by the standards of the day, was erected next door. Once inside "the main administrative building," as it was called by those who worked in its identical offices, visitors discovered a secret: the Lubyanka had a courtyard. Here stood a nine-story prison—the *Vnutrennaia*, the secret policemen called it, the Internal Prison. Built by the insurance company as a hotel for visitors from the provinces, the Internal Prison was reserved in Stalin's day for the USSR's most important political inmates.

The arrest had happened fast, in a blur. Cy had only glimpsed the night outside—the stream of snow and the lights in the small prim square in front of the Bolshoi. The men had bundled him into the back of the *voronka*—the crow, as Muscovites had taken to calling the Black Marias. Sometimes the NKVD disguised the vans, painting their sides with the words MILK or MEAT. By 1939, however, few in Moscow failed to recognize the crows that haunted the streets at night.

Inside, Cy could not sit. The back of the van was divided by wire mesh into windowless cubicles just big enough for a man to stand in. If they had picked up anyone else that night, he couldn't see well enough to recognize him. Cy did not have to stand in discomfort for long. The Lubyanka was two blocks from the Moskva.

By the time the doors of the *voronka* opened, Cy was in darkness. Two men hoisted him by either arm and took him in, stopping only at the receiving room. Cy stood as a clerk wrote down his name and the date and place of his birth. From the escorts, the clerk collected his passport. Then he told the American to remove his clothes.

New arrivals were "checked." One guard probed cavities while another scoured the clothes. They worked methodically from head to toe, seam to seam. The guards handed in for filing everything they had taken in the hotel: passport, wallet, watch, cigarettes, and money. Now they took his belt and shoelaces, and even cut the buttons from his jacket and trousers. Cy still could not understand Russian well, but the logic was plain to see. Suicide was a problem in the Lubyanka.

No one moved quickly here. The pace, by design, was glacial. Once the photographer had finished, the guards lifted Cy again. They took him along a corridor and up a wide stairwell. The corridors, he could see even on that first night, were cavernous. Windowless, they bent around the corners as if they had no end. The floor was covered with a chevroned parquet, which was washed each morning. Doors lined the hallways, but they were doors without signs, only numbers. The guards marched Cy upstairs, past the metal webbing. Here, too, wire mesh covered the spaces between floors—protection, of course, against jumpers.

That first night they took Cy to the *izolatory*, the solitary cells. He could not see how many there were; neither could he hear anything but muffled noise from within the thick walls. The guards opened a cell and led him inside. The bunk was narrow, a thin mattress on an iron cot bolted to the floor. He was given a sheet, a blanket, and a square pillow. A single bulb lit the room, hanging in the center of the ceiling. It, too, was encased in wire. Broken glass could open a vein.

The guards closed the door. It was heavy, ancient metal lacquered with decades of paint. A spyhole allowed his keepers to peer in. On the wall the contours of an old window, bricked over, were visible. The light was never turned off.

After a while Cy learned the rules. For seven hours each night, from eleven in the evening until six in the morning, he had to be in bed, but he was forbidden to sleep facing the wall. If he turned to the wall to shield his eyes from the bare bulb, the guards banged on the door. If he pulled the blanket over his head, they also banged. He had to show his head and hands at all times, even in sleep.

There could be no writing, either. Not even a word. Twice a day the guards checked the prisoners' mouths for papers. If they found any, the inmate would be sent to "the fridge," a bare cellar room equipped with fans to create constant drafts.

As the days passed, the realization dawned: they didn't starve any-one here; they only wanted everyone to be hungry, always. Inmates got two "meals" a day. Every day the guards would slide open the *kormushka*—a hole in the door covered by a piece of wood—and shove in the same thing: a watery soup (cabbage or fish, but never with much evidence of either), a chunk of black bread (maximum 500 grams), and a tin cup of black tea (never hot or strong) with one cube of sugar. New prisoners learned how to make it last: you balanced the cube in your teeth and drank the tea through it. Old-timers could make the sugar last for days.

*

"IF YOU SIT BEHIND CLOSED DOORS, ALONE WITH YOURSELF, YOU WILL without fail wander through the labyrinths of your memories," wrote Anna Larina, the widow of Nikolai Bukharin, the Old Bolshevik purged by Stalin in the spring of 1938. During her twenty years behind Soviet bars, Larina also "sat," as the Russians say, in the Lubyanka. "And if, moreover," she wrote, ". . . a gaping abyss lies ahead, and you sum up your life and come to the conclusion that a catastrophe has occurred and nothing can be done about it, then the need for memories expands beyond bounds."

Once the beating receded and the abrasions darkened to welts, Cy found clarity. He could not hear much. There was the chiming of bells—a church, against the odds, still stood not far from the prison. And the tapping, always insistent and indecipherable, on the far side of the cell wall. But as he sat in his cell, Cy could not help but return to the past. They had known no wants then, throughout their years in Europe. He and his wife had always had money, and he had always dressed with care and without regard to cost: a three-piece bespoke suit, watch fob, silver-handled walking stick, and, without fail, a black fedora. They had enjoyed every luxury, even time.

USUALLY THE GUARDS waited longer. Cy had counted only four days when they banged on the door. Two came in and took him from his cell. They marched him out and were joined by a third. There was a routine, he would learn, to walking the halls. Prisoners were escorted everywhere by three guards. One went in front, the second beside the inmate, and the third behind. At the turns in the corridors, small red lights were fixed high on the wall. As the escorted prisoner walked the halls, the lead guard would turn on the lights to indicate that a prisoner was in the corridor. He would also cluck with his tongue or tap his belt buckle. If an officer should appear, the guards would turn the prisoner to the wall. It was an elaborate procedure to keep prisoners from catching sight of the NKVD bosses.

No one had touched Cy since that first night. The guards had only brought the "meals." Now they led him downstairs, down to the first of the Lubyanka's two underground floors. They took him to a square room where the walls were covered with white tiles. An elderly woman in a smock greeted him. She was one of those Russian *babushki* he had seen everywhere, selling wild berries on the train platforms or bunches of wildflowers by the metro. Here the woman's job was to turn on the water. After a prisoner stripped, she gave him a shower.

Next came the haircut. Lice and rats were not as common in the Lubyanka as in ordinary jails, but the guards still maintained the rules. Hair was kept very short, nearly shaven to the scalp. The barber, a prison guard, had no razor (again, the fear of suicide), only clippers. The prisoners soon learned to measure out time by counting the haircuts. Rarely would two weeks pass before the guards returned them to the old woman and the barber.

Cy had suffered the fate of nearly everyone who entered the Lubyanka for the first time. New arrivals assumed that they would be informed of the charges against them. Someone would come, they imagined, with an explanation—a prosecutor, an investigator, a party functionary. But no one ever came. The prisoners were made to wait. They would lose sleep, weight, patience, and composure. Given enough time, they would also lose their sanity.

THE GUARDS LED CY down the same way as always, at the same leaden pace. The underground corridor, though, had doors. One after another, to the left and right. The doors were heavy, like the ones on the cells, but these had no peepholes.

The "comrade investigator," as the translator introduced the uniformed man sitting behind the desk, did not stand when they brought Cy in the room. He remained sitting. The office was small, lit by one light.

"Do you know where you are?" he asked Cy.

The investigator let the silence settle. Cy did not offer an answer. Rafail Alexandrovich Goldman was a man of stature in the Investigation Department of the secret police. A veteran NKVD officer, Lieutenant Goldman had years of experience in the Lubyanka. The translator, who had relayed the Russian to Cy in German, did not dare fill the silence. After a time, Lieutenant Goldman spoke again.

This is the heart of Soviet intelligence.

It was a script. A warmup repeated, almost without fail, in every first interrogation. One of Stalin's henchmen had devised the routine when the revolution first turned inward. Decades later, historians would analyze the structure and call it a masterful updating of the interrogatory tactics of the Spanish Inquisition. In the NKVD, however, the practitioners of this Stalinist craft did not know its origins. To them, it was called the Yezhov method, in honor of Nikolai Ivanovich Yezhov, the sadistic dwarf who invented the procedure during his tenure running the Lubyanka, from 1936 to 1938.

During Stalin's purges, more than a million innocent men and women were killed. At the height of Yezhov's reign, according to the most modest official statistics, at least 1.5 million people were arrested. Six hundred and eighty thousand were shot on charges of "counterrevolutionary activities" or "espionage." One of the most famous victims was Bukharin, the intellectual who had been a Soviet founding father and, in Lenin's words, the "golden boy of the revolution." Bukharin was also held in the Lubyanka. In March 1938, after a year of brutal interrogations and eleven months before Cy's arrest, he was executed as an enemy of the people.

Yezhov was a craven Stalinist and a sexual omnivore who devoured women, men, and boys with equal voracity. Under his reign, known in Russian as *Yezhovshchina*, the question of guilt disappeared in blood. But Yezhov saw the importance of keeping up appearances. Soviet law, even at the height of the purges, maintained an essential veneer of justice. The penal code of the USSR contained a clause unique in the history of jurisprudence: Article 58, Terrorist Acts Aimed Against Representatives of the Soviet Regime. Introduced in 1927 and last updated in 1937, Article 58 had fourteen subarticles intended to cover the range of crimes against the state: high treason, armed revolt, espionage, sabotage, terror, counterrevolutionary propaganda, and association with a counterrevolutionary organization.

The sub-subarticles had even greater elasticity, stretching to include "the suspicion of espionage." All the same, the NKVD was addicted to bureaucracy. Investigators had to fabricate a case—a job that demanded creativity, muscle, and time. Confessions, therefore, remained the first objective.

Yezhov had streamlined things. He designed a formula to entrap, with minimal effort, the prisoner in his own words. The accused would convict himself. He would be made to invent his crime against the state, build the case against himself, confess to it, and finally produce a list of accomplices to the crime that had never taken place.

The script was simple:

> *Investigator:* Tell me, why do think you were arrested?
> *Prisoner:* I have no idea.
> *Investigator:* (Silence)
> *Prisoner:* I should think you'd be able to tell me the reason.
> *Investigator:* (Silence)
> *Prisoner:* (Silence)
> *Investigator:* You are not ready. When you are, I'll be here.

With that, round one would end. The prisoner was returned to his cell. Sometimes persuasion was still required. More often, however, waiting did the trick. Anxiety could tear a person's mind apart. "Splitting" a prisoner, the jailers called it. In the end, the prisoners always asked to go back.

THE INVESTIGATOR SAT at the same desk. Before him lay a sheaf of papers. He untied the strings and opened the cardboard folder. He took out a document. It was a form several pages long, and at the top of the first page was a title in Russian: PROTOKOL DOPROSA, "Interrogation Report." The investigator spread out the form on the desk and spun it toward Cy. Then he took out a pen and placed it in front of the prisoner.

Police with seized papers from a raid on a Communist Party office in Boston, 1919.

CHAPTER 4

REVOLUTION

. . .

"POLITICS," ROBIN SAID, WHEN ASKED HALF A CENTURY LATER. "Politics was everything then. That must have been what brought Mom and Dad together." He was speaking of the years long before he was born, the years in New York of turmoil and hope following the Russian Revolution. "Politics was not just something you thought of once a year," he went on. "It shaped your whole life—who your friends were, where you lived, where you studied, where you shopped, where you ate. And, of course, where you worked."

Cy and Nerma were a most improbable couple. To outsiders, they could appear to be polar opposites. At first blush Cy seemed to be an Ivy League boy intent on a quiet life of books, as if a canyon separated him from Nerma, one of the Yiddish-speaking Bolsheviks of the Lower East Side. But to those in their circle, Cy and Nerma were nearly twins. In the early years, they remained in separate worlds, even as the cause exploded into life, spilling out of the pages of nineteenth-century European treatises and into the streets around them. Cy hovered at the edges of New York's young elite uptown, while Nerma lived downtown, amid factory girls and labor organizers. If Cy tried, at least on the surface, to etiolate his ancestry, Nerma did not stray more than a few blocks from hers.

They seemed a terrible mismatch. Cy towered over Nerma. It wasn't that he was particularly tall; he was not. But Nerma was very short. Like her parents, she stood scarcely four feet eight inches tall. What she lacked in height, however, she made up for in personality. Ever the center of attention, Nerma announced herself, and her politics, to one and all. Cy, even to close friends, could seem a cipher. Nerma was a speechifier. He was a scholar. She was a performer, he a thinker. To themselves, however, they were two of a kind. Cy and Nerma imagined themselves revolutionists in the making. Throughout their first years together, no matter where they went, they dreamed of one thing: the cause. They had no other cares—not money, ambition, or family. All their hopes were tied to the revolution.

Cy and Nerma were hardly alone. For the young men and women who rushed to join the movement after the birth of Soviet Russia, life did not extend beyond their small party circles. Lenin had risen in the East, and in New York the young radicals felt themselves far-flung comrades. They believed that at last their ideals would come to pass. "World revolution" was no longer a slogan but a plan. The new dawn would come first in the land of the Bolsheviks, then in Europe. They might not live long enough to see it—the struggle would demand sacrifices—but one day, perhaps even soon, the revolution would come to America, too.

When it came to street fights, Nerma was a natural. To friends, it seemed as if she had entered the world with her mouth open and her fists ready. Nerma was a political and sexual firebrand, a perilous combination of exhibitionist and renegade. She may have been born a fighter, but only as a young woman did she become a comrade. It was a transformation that began early on, in the years following her family's arrival in New York.

·

NOYME BERMAN HAD SET FOOT IN NEW YORK CITY, AGED ELEVEN, ON the first of June, 1909. By the time she and her family disembarked from the SS *Zeeland*, a little Russian girl with wild brown curls and no English, her name had already changed.

"Noima," as the portside clerk wrote it, was the Yiddish. In the old tongue, "Noyme" was the pronunciation for Nehama. Nerma, a rare name not usually heard beyond the borders of Bosnia, was an Americanization. The *Zeeland*, a British ship, had left Antwerp with 582 passengers. All but twenty-three were new immigrants from the German, Austro-Hungarian, and Russian empires, who filled the second-class cabins.

Nerma's parents, like Cy's, had come from the lands near Kovno. They, too, had left a shtetl. "Schipishke," the clerk had written. Unfiltered through her father's accent, it was Skapiskis, a Jewish settlement of nearly one thousand villagers at the edge of the Zarasai province on the western edge of the Pale.

Israel and Sheine Berman had reason to leave. Zarasai had suffered its share of misfortune—plague, fire, and Napoleon. Only after the province fell to the czar did the horizon brighten, as the Russians cut a road west from St. Petersburg and trade arrived. The Bermans' shtetl stood near the main route from Petersburg to Warsaw. Yet when Nerma's parents spoke of the old country, it was not of commerce. It was of Cossacks and pogroms, of the narrow borderlands between Russia and Poland and suffering the worst on both sides.

The ship had made a fast sailing—eleven days on the Atlantic. Unlike the Oggins couple, the Bermans came as older parents. Sheine—"beautiful"—was a popular name among Russian Jews. Israel and his wife, who adopted the name Sadie, came with four children. Nerma's brother Meyer was the oldest, listed as twelve years old. Chazan, another brother, was listed as nine, and Feige, another girl, as seven.

■

ON MY FIRST VISIT UPSTATE, ROBIN REMEMBERED SOMETHING. IN THE 1980s, after his mother had been living on her own for decades in New York, things had become so bad that she couldn't take care of herself. Robin and Ginny moved her up from the city to live with them. She did not bring much along, but a few years after Nerma's death, one of Robin's daughters made a discovery. "There's an old shoebox up in the attic," Robin told me. "Some things Mom dragged up from New York."

Nerma's shoebox held nearly a century of mysteries. On the second morning of my visit, a bright Sunday in early fall, Robin brought it down and with a dramatic flourish—"There it is"—thumped it on the kitchen table. The box held photographs of all sizes. A handful were in color, faded Kodacolor snapshots from the 1960s and 1970s. Most, however, were much older, yellowing black-and-whites from an unknown world. Their edges torn, many of the photographs were bent or cut. Some were so brittle they were breaking into pieces.

Robin and I spread out the photographs on the worn pine table. Arrayed before us, stretching three generations back, were more than a hundred images. The earliest date was 1915, the most recent 1980. As he sifted through the photographs, Robin fell quiet. It was not a nervous or empty silence but the kind one keeps out of reverence for the dead.

Some of the images caught my eye right away. A studio portrait of John Reed, for instance, with his crooked smile and typewriter at the ready. The Portland rebel had become America's most famous Red correspondent. In the years 1917 to 1920, the young radicals of New York City breathlessly studied Reed's dispatches from Petrograd, whether they appeared in Eastman's political monthly, *The Masses*, or, after the U.S. Post Office refused to mail the journal, in its successor, *The Liberator*. Reed was a rarity, an American hero revered by both the radicals on campus and their worker comrades downtown.

Not all of the photographs were so easily identifiable. Many presented mysteries that would take years to answer. A street scene in Asia. A villa in Europe. A private garden in Paris. Still others carried fragments of information: a name or a place or a date scribbled on the back. Nerma had written some of the notes, but most were in Cy's handwriting. More than one image showed him with an old Brownie around his neck. Cy was the photographer.

Several images were taken at political rallies. All across New York, street corners were political arenas, amphitheaters for agitation and propaganda. One photograph showed a mass of dark winter coats below the billboards at an intersection uptown. A crowd, nearly all men, milled about below a man standing on a soapbox. The street corner depicted in the photograph was at the northern perimeter of

Central Park. The speaker, the man with his fist in the air straining to capture the attention of the crowd at his feet, was Henry Jaeger, a leading radical of the day. On the back of the photograph, the penciling had faded but remained clear:

DEBS PROTEST MASS-MEETING
AT 110 ST & 5TH AVE, NYC
JAEGER—SPEAKER   APRIL 19, 1919

Eugene Debs had long been the great Socialist hope in America. In the presidential election of 1912, he had won 900,000 votes. In April 1919 he had been sentenced to ten years in prison for an anti-war speech made the previous summer in Canton, Ohio. In 1920, from prison, Debs ran again for the White House. He got even more votes then—913,664. No radical politician in America has ever commanded such broad support.

As the crowds swelled, so did the counterforces. The "White Cossacks," to the radicals, were the New York police. And their advance guard was the Gegan Bomb Squad, led by James J. Gegan, detective sergeant of the New York City Police. As the anti-Red forces closed in, using horses and nightsticks, the radicals took to the countryside.

The story of the retreat from the city was preserved in Nerma's shoebox. A stack of photographs showed a number of young people out in the country. One was a group portrait. The men wore suits and the women long, diaphanous dresses. Some were standing; others were lying in the tall grass of a sloping hill. The juxtaposition seemed intentional. These were city people who had taken refuge in nature. *We are young radicals*, the image seemed to say, *in search of an Arcadian dream.*

Even with her face cut off and only her stockinged legs showing, Nerma was easy to spot. She stood at the rear of group. Yet one woman lying in the grass in front of her also seemed familiar. She was short and round, with a mirthful smile. She wore oval wire-rimmed eyeglasses, and her unruly hair was in a loose bun. The reclining woman, impossible to identify with certainty, bore a strong likeness to one of the most famous Reds of the day, the Russian anarchist then living at 36 Grove Street in Greenwich Village: Emma Goldman.

There were portraits taken in the city, too: photographs of individuals, young men and women with hard-set eyes and solemn expressions. The backdrops were always locations downtown, anonymous and far from suspicious eyes—mostly rooftops. One, though, seemed different. It was a snapshot of young friends jostling together. Their faces were full of laughter and, it seemed, boundless hope. On the back of the photograph, Nerma had left a hint:

RAND SCHOOL BUNCH

AUGUST 1917

In the twenty-first century, the Rand School for Social Science is all but forgotten. Yet in the first decade after the Russian Revolution, the school was the center of radical teaching and Socialist thought in New York. The influence of the Rand, as it was known, reached far beyond its small corps of teachers and students. It not only taught political theory but mobilized the cadres for action. When Debs was arrested, the school organized the first protests in the city. It staged rallies and led a national movement for his defense. The Rand was also a critical link—perhaps the most important one—between Cy Oggins and Nerma Berman.

WHEN CHARLES BEARD left Columbia, he went downtown to the Village to help found the New School for Social Research. His former colleagues on Morningside Heights bristled, but Beard had long supported, albeit quietly, a far more radical cause. More than a decade earlier, the historian had helped to found the American Socialist Society, a group with aspirations of becoming the vanguard of the American Socialist movement.

On the evening of April 5, 1906, four of New York's most prominent Socialists—Morris Hillquit, Algernon Lee, William James Ghent, and Benjamin Gruenberg—met at Beard's home on West

123rd Street. That night Beard led them in drafting a blueprint for the Rand School. Hillquit, the preeminent attorney of the radical left, had recently lost a mayoral bid. Lee and Ghent were the authors of popular left-wing works. Gruenberg, the only one among the five without a book to his name, was a biologist. They had convened to establish the first academy for the enlightenment of the young laboring masses of America. In the 1890s, Beard, as a student at Oxford, had helped found the Ruskin School for "adult male workers." He and his colleagues now imagined a New York school that would take the Ruskin as its model. Education, not violence, they agreed, would provide the spark for radical social change. The revolution would begin in the classrooms.

The Rand School opened that summer, on the lower two floors of a brownstone at 112 East Nineteenth Street. By 1917, having lost the lease and outgrown its successor, it resettled near Union Square, so often the scene of labor rallies. The school moved into a stately 1885 building just off the square, 7 East Fifteenth Street. Five stories of stone beneath a red gabled roof and formerly the New York headquarters of the Young Women's Christian Association, it was promptly renamed the People's House. The school now had not only classrooms but a library, an auditorium, a bookstore, and a gymnasium. In the decades to come, battered by prosecutions, defections, and internecine warfare, its influence would wane. But the Rand had become a radical landmark and would endure for fifty years.

Nerma was not yet eighteen and was still living with her parents at 240 East Ninth Street in the East Village, when she enrolled at the school. Her brother Abraham attended as well. It was a young school; the vast majority of its students took correspondence courses or attended evening lectures. Nerma's class comprised no more than a few dozen students. Her teachers were among the most impassioned and charismatic leaders of the Socialist movement in America. In an age marked by protests and rallies, it was the police, not their professors, who set the path to adulthood for the students of the Rand. Mass arrests and political trials became the memories etched in their minds, the souvenirs they carried long after the tumult had ebbed. For Nerma, it would be a street-level education, an intensive course in radicalism and resistance.

SOMEWHERE AMID THE CROWDS, whether at a demonstration in Union Square, a rally in Madison Square Garden, or a debate in the Central Opera House on Sixty-seventh Street, Cy and Nerma stood together for the first time. Maybe it was in Pittsburgh in the spring of 1919, when thousands of Pennsylvania miners walked, helping to ignite the Great Steel Strike. Or that fall, in Washington Square, when the mounted police trampled a procession of radicals out to protest the American military intervention in Soviet Russia. Or perhaps the circumstances were less dramatic. Maybe Cy and Nerma simply met, as so many couples did in those days, at a dance.

If the days were filled with protests, the nights were dominated by "entertainments." It was an age when Freud's ideas exploded into an America still bound by nineteenth-century mores. *The Interpretation of Dreams*, published in English a few years earlier, had captured the minds, and libidos, of young men in Manhattan. Politics was part of the seduction. Liberation and contraception became the rage. "Women," cried Emma Goldman, "need not always keep their mouths shut and their wombs open!" Sex, in the name of free love, became a means of liberation.

For Cy and his classmates, the Rand School dances were a weekly fixture. Matty Josephson writes tantalizingly in his memoirs of a "young friend" who, in the early 1920s, when both were living in the Village, devised a clever scheme in his "pursuit of happiness":

He would go off on Saturday nights to the dances of the Rand School nearby, which were frequented by "Village" girls of Socialist leanings. "I would ask some girl there to dance with me," he confided, "and then bring the conversation around to the subject of Freud's sexual teachings, warning her about the evil effects of sexual repression and offering to interpret her

dreams. Sometimes it didn't work, but often they would come
to my room."

Just when and how Cy and Nerma met is lost in the margins of
history. It could have been 1918, as Cy wrote in Paris a decade later.
Or 1922, as Nerma said when all was already lost, when the men
from Washington knocked on her door. From today's vantage, however, it seems inevitable that once they had met, the two would fall
in love.

•

THE TURMOIL HIT FEVER PITCH IN 1919. ACROSS EUROPE, THE RUSSIAN
Revolution had roused workers and intellectuals, and the air of
expectancy quickly spread west. In New York, a new lecture circuit
had opened. Nearly every evening, it seemed, hundreds turned out to
hear tales "from the future," as the pilgrims who had journeyed to the
new Soviet Union returned to sing its praises.

Each day Cy and Nerma read the New York radical press for the
latest word on the great experiment unfolding in the east. But across
America, "the bourgeois press," the mainstream broadsheets, told a
different story: the rise of the Reds. During the war, labor stoppages
had been declared illegal. Now, though, the unions took to the streets.
From San Francisco to Chicago to New York, workers went on strike.
Suddenly, to the press, the public, and the government, the threat was
imminent. An army of "aliens," the headlines proclaimed, had laid
siege, and the foreigners, led by a vanguard of intellectual deviants,
were out to destroy the American way of life. The Red scare was on.

Then came the bombings, a political phenomenon: serial acts of
terrorism. On April 29, 1919, an explosive device tore off the hands
of an African American housemaid opening the mail of Thomas
Hardwick, a former senator from Georgia who had sponsored, in the
previous year, the Anarchist Act. Within days postal officials in New
York City intercepted thirty-four other bombs. Each was handmade
and addressed to one of the day's leading financiers and politicians,

John D. Rockefeller, J. P. Morgan, Jr., and Oliver Wendell Holmes, the Supreme Court justice, among them. The bombers, however, were undeterred.

On the night of June 2, A. Mitchell Palmer, Woodrow Wilson's newly appointed attorney general, was rocked from his sleep. A dynamite bomb had ripped off the front steps of his house in Washington. The bomber, almost certainly by accident, blew himself up as well. Little remained of him but the anarchist tracts found in the debris.

In the aftermath of the bombing spree, few in Washington bothered to make distinctions among the disparate stripes on the far left wing of American politics. Anarchists, Socialists, Communists, Russians, Italians, or Poles—they were all Reds. Communism, Palmer announced, was "eating its way into the homes of the American workman." "Tongues of revolutionary heat," the attorney general would later write, "were licking the altars of the churches, leaping into the belfry of the school bell, crawling into the sacred corners of American homes, seeking to replace marriage vows with libertine laws, burning up the foundations of society."

The war in Europe was over, but for the men in power, the time had come to wage a new campaign at home. They turned to an ambitious young lawyer with a bulldog scowl, a dutiful civil servant whose reputation had spread beyond the Justice Department. He had worked his way through law school at night, proven himself to be resourceful to a fault, and dressed so fastidiously that whispers of dandyism trailed him. John Edgar Hoover also had the right politics.

By the age of twenty-four, Hoover was already known as an anti-Red crusader. In July 1917 he had joined Justice, and he revealed an uncanny aptitude for personal advancement. His first job, as a filing clerk, was a $990-a-year position. Yet Hoover was soon promoted. He would head the new "Radical Department"—the General Intelligence Division, as he preferred it to be called—and oversee the effort to gather and systematize the federal government's intelligence on America's burgeoning radical movements. By November 1918, Palmer had named Hoover as his assistant. He would lead the government's war on the Reds.

The law enforcement sweeps that followed—"the Palmer raids"—
are often seen as the start of the anti-Red hysteria. In truth, the first
salvo came earlier. In March 1919, Clayton R. Lusk, a little-known
New York state senator, signaled a desire to lead his own campaign.
A conservative Republican from rural Cortland County, Lusk was a
graduate of the law school at Cornell who had served two months in
the legislature. Riding the jingoist, anti-immigrant wave, however, he
was named chairman of a new state legislative body to investigate the
"radical elements" of New York City. The Lusk Committee, as it was
soon nicknamed, had subpoena power, a corps of investigators, and
temporary quarters in the Prince George Hotel, just off Madison
Square. Lusk, acting by all appearances on his own initiative, was
ambitious—he would soon become the legislature's majority leader—
and hell-bent on quelling New York's troublesome Reds.

He struck first at Lenin's man in the city. Ludwig Christian
Alexander Karlovich Martens was a confidante of the Bolshevik
leader; the two had known each other since Lenin's prerevolutionary
exile in Switzerland. Since the beginning of 1919, Martens had served
as the first Soviet envoy to the United States. Fluent in English, German, and French, he could camouflage himself, and often did, but he
was Russian. Born in the south of Russia in 1875, he had joined Lenin
in St. Petersburg as a teenager. For his loyalty, he was rewarded with
the job of establishing the Bolsheviks' inaugural outpost in America.

In the spring of 1919, Martens opened the Russian Soviet Government Bureau at 110 West Fortieth Street, in the heart of Manhattan.
The Soviet Bureau, as it came to be known, was a modest office with a
grand agenda. On Lenin's command, Martens was to persuade the
Americans to lift their embargo on the USSR. In March he presented
his papers to Washington, but he was never accredited as a diplomat.
President Wilson made it clear that the United States would not recognize the Soviet state. Martens was left in limbo until June 12, when
Clayton Lusk selected the Soviet Bureau as his first target.

In the days that followed, New York City witnessed raid after raid
as Lusk's enforcers also visited John Reed's Socialist Left Wing office
on Twenty-ninth Street, the Wobblies' headquarters in New York,

and seventy-three district offices of the Communist Party across the city. At the office of the Left Wing Socialists, the police did not find Reed, but Lusk and his men were undeterred. They shifted their attention to the Rand School.

ON JUNE 21, 1919, a blue-sky Friday, a week before Wilson formally ended World War I at Versailles, fifty city police officers, state constables, and volunteers from the American Protective League marched along Fifth Avenue, shoulder to shoulder, two by two, passing in silence the ladies and gentlemen who were lunching in the sun-filled cafés. At Fifteenth Street, the procession turned right and marched down the north side of the street toward Union Square. Ignoring the crowds gathering at its edges, the men stopped only when they reached the People's House.

It was the biggest police raid in the history of New York City. Once the officers crossed the building's broad stone threshold, they were met by nearly a hundred students and teachers. At the head of the crowd was the Rebel Girl, the labor agitator Elizabeth Gurley Flynn, who had led the strikers in Willimantic. The police searched every drawer and file in the Rand, staying well past nightfall. When they finally left, they hauled out boxes of documents by the truckload. At the Prince George Hotel, the Lusk investigators, working alongside Russian translators, spent weeks picking over the haul.

Nerma Berman was still a student at the Rand when the police came. Among the mountain of paper seized by the Lusk Committee (preserved on ninety microfilm reels in the New York State Archives in Albany) is a handwritten card that records the details of her enrollment. Other Rand documents told of her role in the aftermath of the raid. A letter typed on school stationery, dated May 26, 1919, revealed that Nerma had not merely studied Marx and Engels at the Rand. In response to the Lusk Committee, she had led the counterattack, cofounding the Defense Committee of Students and Friends of the Rand School. The letter was an urgent plea addressed to the "local secretaries of the Socialist Party of the U.S." for contributions to the legal fund established for the school and its faculty. Nerma and two girlfriends, also students, were the sole signatories.

■

THE CAUSE, AS IF BY AN ACT OF TRANSATLANTIC WISH FULFILLMENT, had become real. It had fronts and flanks now, heroes and antiheroes. And in a city of soapboxes, the Rand School was a premier arena.

Charles Beard and his former Columbia colleague Harry Dana became sell-out fixtures at the school, drawing crowds to the People's House. Many among the Rand faculty, too, fervent speakers like Algernon Lee and the Russian émigré Alexander Trachtenberg, packed the lecture rooms. As the school's reputation grew, many of the biggest luminaries on the left—Helen Keller, Bertram Wolfe, Bertrand Russell, Carl Sandburg, and Upton Sinclair among them—spoke from its stage. One name, however, towered above all others.

Whenever Scott Nearing lectured, the Rand had to rent the hall nearby at the all-girls Washington Irving High School. A former professor at the Wharton School of Business, Nearing had become one of America's leading political renegades. His lectures at the Rand, on "The Human Element in Economics," lured more than a thousand students. Nearing was a noted economist, but his greatest gift was oration. He toured the country, often lecturing twice in a single day. In 1917 he debated the famed lawyer Clarence Darrow on his home turf in Chicago and held his own. They made such electric sparring partners, a grudge match (on the topic "Is the Human Race Worth Working For?") was later held at the Rand.

Part of the attraction was Nearing's background. Like Debs and Eastman, he came from Protestant stock. Although he was born into a wealthy family in Pennsylvania coal country, Nearing more closely resembled a hardscrabble farmer than an urban intellectual. It was not just a matter of his workman's khakis and old leather shoes. The majority of the Rand students were former street urchins, a step or two from the muck of the Lower East Side. Amid the chaos, the economist radiated an aura of sanity.

Nearing had taken a long route to radicalism. He lectured at the

Rand School as early as 1913 but had previously taught at Swarthmore and Wharton, at the University of Pennsylvania. In 1915, in a
case presaging the Columbia dismissals, Wharton fired him. Nearing
had dared to speak of "the breaker boys" in coal mines and the girls
in textile mills, condemning child labor in Pennsylvania. The state
governor took it as an attack; he had made his fortune in textiles.

By 1917, Nearing had moved on to Toledo University in Ohio, but
he was fired a second time—for speaking out against the war. Before
the year was out, he had returned to New York, joined the Socialist
Party and the Rand School, and become a cause célèbre. That year he
published *The Great Madness: The Victory of the American Plutocracy.* It was
only a pamphlet, forty-four pages long, but in it Nearing declared
that the new militarism was a plot perpetrated by the capitalist class,
denounced Liberty Loans as a rent-seeking sham, railed against Wilson's "un-American" draft, and quoted Bourne's "War and the Intellectuals." It was vintage Nearing:

> The two per cent of the people (one person in each fifty) who
> own sixty per cent of the wealth of the United States . . .
> believe that there are some things worse than war—the confis-
> cation of special privileges; the abolition of unearned income;
> the overthrow of economic parasitism; the establishment of
> industrial democracy. The plutocrats would welcome a war
> that promised salvation from any such calamities.

On March 22, 1918, the federal grand jury in New York indicted
Nearing under the Espionage Act of 1917, accusing him of "insubor-
dination, disloyalty, mutiny and encouraging resistance to the draft."
The Rand School, as the pamphlet's publisher, also came under
attack. The indictment did not charge the school but named its
underwriter, the American Socialist Society, the group that had met
in Beard's home more than a decade earlier.

Nearing's star could rise no higher. On the night of his indictment, he arrived at the Rand to lecture and was met with feverish
applause. He spoke of the British Labour Party and its readiness to

assume power. "Some of those who believe in democracy believe we ought to be ready here, so that when the system shows sign of going smash, there will be some body of people ready to take a hold." Throughout the spring of 1918, at mass rallies across the city, Nearing brought out the crowds. His talks attracted not only the Reds but the Browns, rival infiltrators and police spies. All too often the gatherings ended in fisticuffs. The Socialists were breaking apart, into left and right factions. That summer, at thirty-five and under indictment, Nearing decided to run for Congress from the Lower East Side. He ran on a bold platform—against the war, against American imperialism, and against the incumbent, a major in the Aviation Corps just back from the Italian front, Fiorello La Guardia. He lost in a landslide but soon won another victory.

Nearing's indictment paralyzed the Rand School. A guilty verdict, the administrators feared, could shut it down. The students had never imagined that the White Cossacks would strike so close. For Nearing, though, the case proved a bonanza. The courtroom was his biggest stage yet. After a first jury deadlocked, a second trial began on February 5, 1919. It lasted two weeks. In court, Nearing triumphed on rhetorical athleticism. *The Great Madness*, he said, was an attempt to answer "the greatest public question that had come before the American people . . . since the Civil War." The prosecutor could not keep pace:

> Q. And you wanted to persuade your readers to your own point of view about the war, didn't you?
>
> A. I wanted to present to my readers my opinion regarding the whole incident of the war, yes, sir.
>
> Q. And you did that for the purpose of persuading them?
>
> A. If they saw it my way, I expected them to accept it.
>
> Q. And you wanted them to accept it, didn't you?
>
> A. Yes.
>
> Q. You wanted them to believe this way, that this was an unjust war, didn't you?
>
> A. I wanted them to believe that this was a capitalist war.

> Q. And that it was an unjust war?
>
> A. As all wars are unjust, yes.

The Rand School made sure to print the trial transcript—all 249 pages.

THAT SUMMER, Nerma and her classmates again took to the streets. In the second week of July, with the school in danger of losing its charter, they staged a rally and faced off with the White Cossacks. This time the police climbed down from their horses and wielded clubs. In speech after speech that day, Rand lecturers railed against Lusk and the police who had ravaged the school. Norman Thomas, the Princeton-educated pacifist preacher, stirred the students, as did Algernon Lee, the school's director. Nearing, however, was the headliner. Within days his case was over. Debs, at sixty-three, had gone to jail. But on July 31, 1919, in a landmark decision in defense of free speech in America, the New York State Supreme Court found Nearing innocent.

In Washington, the Department of Justice was quick to react. On November 7, the second anniversary of the Russian Revolution, the government launched the first in a series of infamous operations— the Palmer raids. They should have been called "the Hoover raids." With Palmer's young assistant leading the charge, in eighteen cities across the country, the police, federal agents, and hundreds of deputies hired from private detective agencies arrived with clubs and guns, in paddy wagons and army trucks. In New York City, hundreds—some reports claimed more than a thousand—were dragged off to prison.

By year's end the federal government had scored its first triumph. On December 22, the United States deported 249 alleged radicals and illegal aliens. The most celebrated among them were the Russian-born anarchists Emma Goldman and Alexander Berkman. The police came before dawn, taking many of the deportees from their beds. Some were arrested at their homes; others came directly from prison. They were herded onto the USS *Buford*—"the Soviet

Ark," the reporters dubbed it—and sent on their way out of New York Harbor.

The pier was frigid that morning, but one resolute man in a heavy winter coat stood for hours. For Hoover, up from Washington to bid the Reds farewell, it was a moment to rejoice and linger before the flashbulbs.

•

WHEN 1919 CAME TO A CLOSE, CY WAS A SEMESTER AWAY FROM GRADU-ating. While Nerma fought for Nearing and rallied the radicals downtown, he had settled on a plan. Intent on an academic career, he would stay on at Columbia for his doctorate. Cy had even settled on a subject, imperial history. Empires—how they arise, develop, and fall—would form the course of his graduate study.

Among the few of his father's possessions that Robin had, things Cy had sent home or held in New York for safekeeping, was a 1922 set of George Louis Beer's history of English mercantilism. *British Colonial Policy, 1754–1765,* the first volume, appeared in 1907. It remains a classic. The frontispiece of Cy's copy identified the author as a "sometime lecturer in history at Columbia University." Beer was, however, in a unique position to explore the roots of British colonial economics: for a decade he had been a tobacco importer.

Robin kept his father's books on a shelf in his basement study. Cy's copy of Beer's first volume revealed how he had come to possess it. "With the compliments of the author," read the card glued inside the cover. Above and below, an inscription in a flowery cursive read:

AT THE SUGGESTION OF PROF. R. L. SCHUYLER

MRS. GEORGE LOUIS BEER

Beer had been a friend of Cy's professor, Schuyler. Cy's copy of Beer's second volume, *The Origins of the British Colonial System, 1578–1660,* contained not only notes in the margin—such as "Very imp.!"—but a sheet of notepaper. Folded neatly in half, the lined paper was filled with dark pencil writing. It was hard to read Cy's notes on Beer's colonial history without feeling the presence of an emerging Marxist. The long quotations jotted down by Cy cascaded down the page, front and back. Cy's reading of Beer seemed an awakening, his notes often echoing the Marxist rhetoric of the street radicals:

> *Though the religious motive figured very prominently in the writings of the day . . . it cannot be considered as one of the determining causes of the move-ment . . . The colonizing empires were mainly intent upon earning some return on their capital.* (29)

> *From the standpoint of the state . . . the colonizing movement was essentially an economic one.* (30)

> *In practice, virtually the sole connecting link between the settlers in America and the mother country was the proprietor, whether an individual or a corpo-ration.* (300)

Even before his matriculation at Columbia, imperial legacies had shadowed Cy. In the spring of 1898, the year of his birth, President McKinley had declared war on Spain after the USS *Maine* sank in Havana Harbor. The Spanish-American War had helped bring an end to Spain's empire and launch, with the conquest of the Philip-pines, America's own imperial ambitions. As Cy grew up amid the mills and factories of Willimantic, the colonialism that had domi-nated the nineteenth century was already ebbing. Yet by the time he graduated from Columbia, this age of predation and empire had ended. World war and the Bolsheviks had redrawn the map of Europe and the future of the lands to the east. The Romanovs and Hohenzollerns had fallen, and history, so it seemed to the young men of Columbia, was coming to a head. The age of revolution, Cy was certain, had arrived.

COLUMBIA HAD MARKEDLY changed him. So, too, had family tragedy. Simon Oggins died suddenly on the morning of December 13, 1918, at the family home on Center Street. He was fifty-five years old. The obituary in the *Willimantic Chronicle* was long, testifying to Simon's stature in town. "One of Willimantic's best known Hebrew citizens," Cy's father had retired at his usual hour "in good health and spirits." In the morning, however, at just after six o'clock, his labored breathing had awoken Rena. She had tried to rouse him but could not. The doctors, J. A. Girouard and T. R. Parker, came quickly but could do nothing.

Simon's heart had given out. The unofficial cause of death, though, was grief. In the great flu epidemic of 1918, Simon and Rena had lost Molly, their older daughter. She was twenty-five years old. Molly's death devastated Simon. He brooded over the loss, telling friends that the world would never be the same.

Between the summer of 1918 and the spring of 1919, the Spanish influenza had spread around the world, taking an estimated 40 million lives, including more than half a million Americans. The great flu was the worst epidemic ever to hit America. It was also another of the bonds that united Cy and Nerma. It had swept New York with an acute ferocity. On the Lower East Side, Nerma had also lost a sibling to it—her brother Abraham died the same year as Molly.

The loss of his father could only have sent Cy deeper into the cause. There was little to take him home to Connecticut. He was nearly alone. Rena had become a young widow but stayed on in Willimantic, and for a time took over the shop. In a few years, she too would leave, moving to the Bronx to live with Cy's surviving sister, Betty. David, the eldest, was now in charge. Cy could move out of his house once he had graduated.

Throughout the winter of 1919–20, New York roiled. The Palmer raids ignited a wave of protests unprecedented in the city's history, but it was not just New York. Across the country, demonstrations grew as workers and students responded to the hounding of alleged subversives. By spring the forces of law and order had discovered a case to justify their campaign. On May 5, 1920, two Italian immigrants were arrested and charged with the murder of a shoe factory paymaster and his bank guard in South Braintree, a workers' suburb of Boston.

Nicola Sacco and Bartolomeo Vanzetti were "a good shoemaker and a poor fish peddler," as Vanzetti told a reporter early on. They were also anarchists; both belonged to the Gruppo Autonomo, a Boston cell with intentions of toppling the state. When arrested, Sacco and Vanzetti carried loaded pistols but insisted they were innocent of the murders. Few historians, regardless of their political persuasion, believe that both men were guilty. Fewer still contend that they received a fair trial. For the radicals of New York, however, the arrests were enough. The aspiring Communists, Nerma and Cy among them, had found their martyrs.

•

ON THE FIRST SUNDAY IN JUNE 1920, COLUMBIA CELEBRATED ITS 166TH commencement, with nearly five thousand undergraduate and graduate students, family, and faculty crowding into the university gymnasium. It was a time to mark the victory in Europe. The First World War had become the "Great War." It was a triumph, Nicholas Murray Butler reminded the Class of 1920, not only of Wilson's promise to make the world safe for democracy but of the American way.

Cy sat in the center of the gym, caught near the alphabetical center of his classmates. As he listened to the speeches that day, he heard only patriotic peals of self-congratulation. It could not have been a comfortable afternoon. Butler had set the course of the day.

Colonel William Barclay Parsons, chair of Columbia's board, took the podium. Parsons, who had served in the war, pounded the lectern as he spoke of the university's share of the victory. Columbia's sons, he said, had heeded the call to serve the nation "when its fate was at stake." The university had lent nearly 8,000 students to the war effort, whether at home or overseas.

The "Captains of War," five men who had stood at the helm, received honorary degrees that day. Their faces were known to all Americans: Herbert Hoover, "who when Belgium lay bleeding," Butler said, "had organized the service for her relief"; Henry Pomeroy Davison, head of the American Red Cross; Rear Admiral William Snowden Sims, commander of the naval forces in Europe; and the commander in chief of the Expeditionary Forces, General John Joseph Pershing, known to fans and critics alike as "Black Jack" Pershing.

When General Pershing entered the gymnasium, the crowd leaped to its feet. As he stepped up to the dais to collect his degree, a roar went up. At the edge of the stage, Barnard girls "spelled it out" for the commander and snapped three staccato "Pershings" at the end of the cheer. Taken by the tribute, the general bowed several times and threw kisses in the girls' direction, his eyes moist.

Butler took the opportunity to offer guidance, not only to the graduating class but to the nation. "If indeed these be times that try men's souls, then they are good times in which to live," he said. "None but the weakling or the poltroon will turn his back upon the tremendous struggle to put civilization upon a new and yet stouter foundation." As Cy sat waiting for his diploma, Butler, a sterling example of the conservatism of the old age, now newly affirmed by the victory in Europe, hit a crescendo. "The call to men and women of capacity, of courage and of character is clarion-like in its clearness," he said, reveling in the chance to stand in for the president in Washington. "It is not a call to revolution; it is a call to hasten evolution."

Not all those gathered on that Sunday in the summer of 1920 shared the sanguine, patriotic vision espoused by the grandees of Columbia. In the streets of the city, not far beyond the university gates, the tide of radicalism was rising.

Cy and Nerma, ca. 1924.

CHAPTER 5

INTO THE NIGHT

. . .

THE KGB ARCHIVES, TODAY KNOWN AS THE ARCHIVES OF RUSSIA'S
Federal Security Service, the FSB, are considered among the hardest
in the world to gain access to. There was a time, in the first years after
the Soviet collapse, when they were opened a crack. Under President
Vladimir Putin, however, the archives were closed firmly again.

For years, as I followed the Oggins trail elsewhere, I weighed the
best approach. When I consulted a Russian historian, an expert in
the secret police under Stalin, his eyes grew wide. He saw an opportunity. "Let's make a legal case!" he said. "Force them to open the files
once and for all." When I went to see a retired KGB officer, a man of
stature in Putin's world, he warned against making noise. "You're better off making quiet inquiries," he said, before adding, "For a small
fee, I could try . . ." When I asked an American academic, a former
chairman of an Ivy League history department, he was blunt. "There's
no way in," he said, "unless you've got someone on the inside. You
have to get a mole."

In the end, the simplest route worked. The Lubyanka archivist
was not happy. The Oggins *delo* was bigger—much bigger—than
expected, and he wished he had been warned before kindly agreeing
to make photocopies. All the same, he pulled the file and kept it
locked in his safe. For weeks he picked over it, deciding what could be
told and what could not. The archivist complained, but in the end he
complied with the new law of the land.

Under Russian law, Robin had the right, as Cy Oggins's sole off-
spring, "to become acquainted" with his father's NKVD *delo*, the

state's case against him. Robin typed up a request and signed it, as the archivist requested, in blue ink. The letter was translated into Russian, notarized, authenticated, apostilled, and finally hand-delivered to the head of the FSB archives in Moscow. Within a month, the formal request and a bottle of Irish whisky worked.

In the spring of 2005, after nearly five years on the trail, I received the documents from the Lubyanka: 22 pages of what appeared to be a 162-page NKVD investigative file. Even these excerpts were expurgated; a number of lines had been ominously whited out. Some things, the archivist said, remained national security secrets and could not be revealed, even to the son of the man in question. Still, the documents from the archives, like Nerma's shoebox of photographs, were treasure.

■

CY JOINED THE PARTY EARLY, LONG BEFORE HE DEPARTED FROM NEW York. In 1920, after graduation, he moved out of David's house and left Queens. He took up residence, no doubt over his brother's warnings, in the heart of Greenwich Village, where the new Bohemia was taking root in the crooked streets south of Fourteenth. Nowhere in America offered greater opportunity to join the "proletariat of the arts." Nowhere else in the city could one as easily bypass the anti-Red police squads, the reactionaries uptown, still flushed with the victory in Europe, and Prohibition, the Eighteenth Amendment, newly enacted into law.

Cy settled into a furnished "hall-bedroom" on Perry Street, a cobblestoned block lined with twisting oaks and stately brownstones. Perry was best known then for Squarcialupi's, the Italian restaurant on the corner of West Fourth. John Squarcialupi, an "operatic baritone who had missed his career," catered to the young radicals. It was also a favored hangout for Malcolm Cowley and the setting for the bull sessions that gave birth to *The New Masses*, where John Dos Passos, Mike Gold, and Cy's former classmate Joe Freeman held court.

Cy moved into 68 Perry, a brownstone halfway down the block to Bleecker Street. He had a bed and a desk and shared a bath down the hall. The rent was cheap, no more than ten dollars a week, but 68 Perry was not just a boardinghouse for recent Columbia graduates. The five-story brownstone breathed with the ideas and passion of the revolution.

CY WENT BACK to Columbia. In the fall of 1920, without taking a break, he returned to get a doctorate in history. He embarked on the requisite years of coursework and, continuing a fascination with the collapse of empire, even began to settle on a topic for his dissertation. Spanish colonial history, he told friends, would be his theme. He intended to investigate the relationship between the death of Spain's empire and the postcolonial states born in its wake.

The Columbia historians had already taken note of Cy's achievements and invited him back for his Ph.D. No one in his family, however, seems to have shared their enthusiasm. Without their financial support, Cy was forced to turn to teaching. The university historians arranged a sinecure to keep him in the department. In 1921, Cy began to teach at Columbia. He was never a professor, as he would claim years later, only a history reader in the University Extension Division.

For Cy, the job was ideal. It brought him into direct contact with the men he admired most. Columbia was then expanding the program to help educate the city's new arrivals, the "foreign-born workers." Cy's "mature" students could not have differed more from the well-to-do sons of Manhattan who had dominated his college years. Far from the WASPs of Columbia, the extension students were largely East European workers, the new immigrants who filled the city's factories and sweatshops. Among the most popular courses were English and citizenry. Few of the students dreamed of a diploma. Most were interested, above all, in becoming naturalized Americans.

The extension program aroused controversy and the attentions of the Lusk Committee. In December 1919, James C. Egbert, professor of Latin and director of the division, had been called before the committee to explain the university's intentions. Most of the immigrant students, as the conservatives noted, were sent by the labor unions. The program, though, proved enormously popular. From 1919 to

1922, the numbers attending extension classes at Morningside doubled, from 6,213 to 12,096. To Cy, the students represented the party's dream, the true "student-workers."

Still, the salary proved less than ideal. Cy needed to earn more if he was to stay in graduate school. In the spring of 1922, he applied for a second job, to teach history in the New York public schools. He presented five letters of reference to the Board of Education. Four were from Columbia men, including Herbert Hawkes, Butler's stalwart dean, who had been one of Cy's undergraduate advisers, and Dixon Ryan Fox, a young historian who had recently published an acclaimed book, *The Decline of Aristocracy in the Politics of New York,* and who was the son-in-law of a Columbia historian, Herbert Levi Osgood. Cy had also reached back to Willimantic to enlist the support of Hyman Israel, his father's friend and the elder Jewish statesman of his hometown.

He got the job. He would teach night school—English to foreigners. The subject had changed, but his students, although younger, were most likely from the same pool as those in the Columbia extension program: the working poor of the city, the more determined members among the newly arrived and largely uneducated masses from abroad.

The teaching, though, did not pay enough. His brother was no help. Cy's relations with David had soured and their political divide had widened. Cy lost his brother's financial support. By the end of 1922, he had no choice. He would set aside an early dream and take a leave of absence from his graduate studies.

BY THEN NERMA BERMAN HAD BECOME KNOWN IN RADICAL CIRCLES. She was known as well to the Irish cops downtown. Although no record of an arrest exists, Nerma remained in the first ranks of the city's radicals throughout the early 1920s. She also traveled far and wide, going to the defense of comrades in Pittsburgh and as far away as Detroit. Whoever had to contend with the Reds from New York had likely come across her.

After all, Nerma stood out. She had a mop of curls, a lisping Russian accent, and a cackle for a giggle that punctuated her sermons. And when she spoke of politics, which was in most of her waking moments, the high-pitched words poured forth in an avalanche of assertion upon denunciation. Nerma was fashionable, fond of multicolored skirts, big-beaded necklaces, and flowing blouses. A tireless exhibitionist in politics and love, she caught the eyes of men and women. Inevitably, she managed to be in the center of the action and attention. A born performer, she seemed incapable of feigning only one state: serenity.

Scott Nearing was her first prisoner, but many followed. From San Francisco to Boston, Nerma helped a roll call of celebrated radicals who had been jailed in the name of rooting out sedition. The Rand School Defense Committee, a team of three students not yet twenty years old, had only been her start. By 1922, what had begun as an extracurricular vocation had become a calling.

Nerma had taken up a pen. Her columns appeared in the earliest editions of the *Worker*, the party broadsheet, which would become the *Daily Worker*. In the spring of 1922, the paper, then still a weekly, debuted a new feature, "Defense and Relief of Class-War Prisoners." The articles, pleas to free comrades in prison, were verbose screeds not easy to digest, but they soon became a fixture. And inevitably they carried a single byline:

> *Nerma Berman*
> *Secretary. New York Division*
> *National Defense Committee*

The accompanying address—Room 405, 80 East Eleventh St., New York City—doubled as the headquarters of the *Worker*.

Nerma's journalism, it seems, was limited to shrill calls to action. She excelled at two-thousand-word invitations to fundraising events—a dance, picnic, speech, or debate. She railed, in rotation, against the White Cossacks (the police), the False Prophets (the Socialists), and the Stool Pigeons (the law enforcement agents in the radicals' midst). Nerma had a talent, her comrades recognized, for raising money and rallying the cadres. It was a beginning with promise. Yet at the time no one could imagine how the expertise would become a necessity at the center of Nerma's fight for survival two decades later.

NO LESS ENERGETIC, no less driven by ambition and zeal, was a man almost Nerma's age who would prove a formidable opponent. J. Edgar Hoover now commanded an army of informants and agents. Teddy Roosevelt had founded the Bureau of Investigation, the BOI, in 1907 as a federal arm to root out state corruption. But in the years following World War I, the enterprising Hoover endowed the BOI with muscle, men, and a mandate. Hoover, not yet twenty-seven years old, had been rewarded. In 1921 he was made assistant director of the BOI, and in 1924 its director. By 1922 the BOI had moved into the radical circles of New York City. One of its agents, and perhaps more, had fixed on Nerma.

The investigation began, as many FBI cases do today, with a snitch. In retrospect, it was no surprise. Even among the unruly crowd at the *Worker*, Nerma was an easy target. Someone in her circle had turned, or been turned, and struck a deal with Hoover's men. As early as 1922, in a string of secret dispatches to Washington, the informant featured Nerma as a threat among the young Communists of New York.

"Nerma Bermann," the BOI's secret source warned, was on the organizing committee of the Young Workers League. She was leading a drive for closer ties with the Workers Party—the WPA, an aboveground political party established by the underground Communist movement in late 1921. During the spring of 1922, the warnings turned urgent. Nerma had been elected the leader of Group 7 in the Young Workers League, the source said. But in a matter of weeks, she pushed too hard. She demanded, at the top of her lungs, that the young radicals join the WPA, the aboveground party. Within a month she was shouted down. Group 7, the informant reported, voted to oust Nerma. She had lost her first battle.

Nerma, though, was not easily deterred. In May 1922 she got herself elected a delegate to the Young Workers League's national convention. Once again she pushed for the hard line. Nerma stood up and argued for, the informant explained to the BOI agents, "in effect joining the Third International," as the Comintern was often called. Hoover's men saw their source's point. In Washington, the Third International was the supreme threat of the day, the army of world revolution.

Nerma, however, did not have her way. Once again she was drowned out. "Resistance was encountered to this suggestion," reported the BOI informant. There were those among the delegates "who did not believe the underground methods recommended by Third International were applicable to conditions in the United States."

The Lusk Committee and the Palmer raids had drive the nascent American Communist movement underground. By 1922, all planning for the party's future took place in the strictest secrecy. All that spring, rumors swirled among Hoover's men that the Communists were preparing to convene another national assembly. Throughout the party, the cadres mobilized. So did the federal agents. The convention, the BOI knew, would take place soon. The location of the gathering, though, remained a strict secret, even among its participants, until the last minute.

On May 17, 1922, Hoover received a "very urgent" warning from his British counterparts. The message, conveyed by messenger and telephone, warned that a leader of the Third International, "recently organizing communist movement in Canada," was bound for New York for a "secret convention of American Communist Party." In Washington, the agents of the BOI had long been waiting to spring an ambush. That summer they got their chance.

In the third week of August, at a disused resort on the shores of Lake Michigan, the Communist underground held its last national "Unity Convention." For a week, nearly a hundred of the party elite, under the watchful eyes of a trio of emissaries from Moscow, lived in clapboard bungalows in the woods. The site was selected, in all likelihood, for its seclusion, and for the railroad depot in the nearby town of Bridgman. Trains ran directly from Chicago.

The Bridgman Convention, as it came to be known, would go down in the history of the American Communist movement as a landmark. The lakeshore conclave was the scene of hours of ardent speechifying. The debates, covering everything from famine relief to the "Negro question" to the fate of imperialism, ran deep into the night. There was also a good deal of merrymaking. One of the party leaders who attended, Ben Gitlow, wrote of the "sylvan scene" in the Michigan woods—an orgy of food, poker, and sex. Although Gitlow later toned down his account, the reports from Bridgman agree: the event was held in the utmost secrecy, and every precaution was taken to avoid infiltration. Guards were posted at the camp's edge. No one was allowed to leave early, and all personal and party documents were buried in watertight barrels on the grounds of the resort.

For the radicals, Bridgman could have been a disaster. Its disruption could have ended the Communist underground in America. On the morning of August 22, dozens of federal agents and Michigan state police raided the conclave. Hoover and his men had been tipped off. A BOI informer, codenamed K-97, had given the advance word. K-97, an Irishman from New Jersey named Francis A. Morrow, had been secretly working for the Justice Department since 1919. Known at the convention as Comrade Day, Morrow had become the central link in the BOI's network of spies and informants.

Seventeen men were arrested at Bridgman, including three of the party's top leaders: William Dunne, Charles Ruthenberg, and Charles Krumbein. Charged with being members in the illegal Communist Party, the accused claimed that they had gone to Bridgman only to chart the future of the Workers Party, not the underground Communist Party. To the Department of Justice, the case was closed. The Reds were lying.

The big catch, however, came the day after the raid. William Z. Foster, hero of Chicago workers and the man who led the faction that Cy and Nerma would join, had always insisted he was only a labor organizer. Foster had gained strength on the backs of the Midwestern unions. If the convention was in Michigan, the BOI suspected that Foster would be there. They were in the woods that night, waiting for him to arrive. But Foster eluded the net, leaving before dawn. He got as far as Chicago before the BOI agents caught up with him. The next afternoon Foster, too, was arrested.

BRIDGMAN WAS THE turning point. Nerma may not have been at the convention. Her presence is not recorded in the memoirs or reports of the trials that followed. But the debacle provided her first opportunity to rise to the national stage. In New York in the months following the arrests, she was the one who rallied the forces. On the first Friday evening in October, hundreds gathered at the Central Opera House on East Sixty-seventh to hear Foster and Ruthenberg, two of the seventeen men arrested at Bridgman, who had just made bail. Nerma ran the show. She booked the hall, lined up the speakers, and drafted the advertisements. The legal bills were multiplying. To bail out the defendants snared in the Michigan raid, Nerma needed an enormous amount of money, more than $100,000.

Bridgman also proved a boon to the party, an irony not lost on Nerma and her comrades. Before the arrests, the Communists had suffered from rising factionalism and declining membership. Worse still, they had lost momentum on the strategic front: among the ranks of urban workers. After the raid, though, the party could raise the specter of "government terrorism." Now there was a common threat—to free speech and free assembly—that could be used to unite the disparate recruits, the radical intellectuals and urban workers.

The assault in Michigan also gave rise to a new organization, the Labor Defense Council, or LDC. One of the party's first national grassroots organizations, it opened a bridge to the trade unions, and with its dues-paying members, the LDC also proved a reliable channel for raising funds. In 1925 the LDC would be subsumed by the International Labor Defense, a party creation that came to the fore in the 1930s in a series of celebrated legal cases that included the Scottsboro rape trial. By then, few recalled its roots. But Nerma Berman was among the founders of the Labor Defense Council.

Nerma's name had vanished from the pages of the *Worker* by February 1923. By April she had joined the new legal defense group. On

April 6, the LDC sent out a nationwide circular, an urgent letter asking for support. The defense council, the letter vowed, would aid not
only the Bridgman 17 but defendants in "other similar cases arising
out of the present attack upon the working class movement." More
than a dozen names, all among the party's luminaries, adorned the
letterhead. Foster was the LDC's national secretary and Eugene Debs
its vice chair. Elizabeth Gurley Flynn was a member, as was Earl
Browder, the future party boss, and Norman Thomas, the pacifist
preacher. One name, though, would be easy to miss: Nerma Berman.
Nerma had been appointed secretary of the LDC's main branch, the
New York office.

Another name on the letterhead stood out: Benjamin Mandel.
Nerma, and quite likely Cy as well, knew Mandel. A kindly man with
nervous tics, he was a leader of the Teachers Union in New York and
an activist in the local party apparatus. Using the party name Bert
Miller, Mandel was also the man who gave new recruits their first
party cards. The defense council was not the last time that Mandel figured in Nerma's life. Decades later, after Cy and Nerma's world had
turned upside down, Ben Mandel enjoyed a reincarnation under the
television lights in one of the ugliest spectacles of postwar America.

NINETEEN TWENTY-FOUR WAS THE POINT AT WHICH CY SLIPPED INTO
the shadows. He had stayed on Perry Street for years, until that spring,
when love and opportunity collided and the world suddenly, for the
first time perhaps since his childhood, seemed a place of promise.

It began with a stroll. Cy walked up to Fourteenth Street and
climbed the stairs to the New York headquarters of the Workers
Party of America. The WPA, since the 1923 dissolution of the underground Communist Party, now stood as the sole organized incarnation of the American Communist movement. A party functionary
—in all likelihood Ben Mandel, as Bert Miller—handled the paperwork. It was over in a few minutes. Cy walked out with a little red
booklet. The first page bore his name and his party number, and
stamped below was the red seal of the WPA, a hammer and sickle.

Nineteen twenty-four was early to join the party. Cy was a fore-runner, the documents from the KGB archives revealed. The Russian Revolution was only seven years old, and the Comintern just five. But Lenin was dead. After suffering a massive stroke, the last in an excruciating series, on January 21, 1924, the hero of Great October left the stage in Moscow. To the party loyalists in New York, he had left behind a command: "We must train men and women who will devote to the Revolution, not merely their spare evenings, but the whole of their lives."

Cy's belief in his ideals had only strengthened. But many of his fellow student radicals had moved on. After the war, one by one they turned into "good Republicans and Democrats." One classmate who had called himself an anarchist became a district captain for Tammany Hall; a "socialist" took over his uncle's shoe factory in Massachusetts; a "syndicalist" became a federal attorney. By the end of 1924, the party had only 3,434 dues-paying members in New York City. But they were the most devout, the faithful for whom Lenin's call had become a war cry.

At least one other Columbia student followed Cy into the party. Whittaker Chambers, disheveled and overweight even as an undergraduate, had enrolled at Columbia in the fall of 1920. In the 1940s, Chambers would become the most famous courier to emerge from the Soviet underground in America. The year that Chambers started college, Cy returned to Columbia as a graduate student. Whether they met in a party meeting or a classroom, Chambers and Cy knew each other. Moreover, Chambers's wife, Esther Shemitz, knew Nerma. Chambers, though, joined the party after Cy, in 1925.

THE TRANSFORMATION FROM Ivy League graduate to Communist radical was completed when Cy married Nerma, in 1924. On the afternoon of April 23, the couple went down to the city offices at the southern tip of Manhattan. In the new world where religion belonged to a bygone era, neither minister nor rabbi was present when they signed the papers, in the company of two friends, before the clerk in the Municipal Building. Cy was twenty-five years old,

Nerma twenty-six. On the marriage application, he wrote down his address as his mother's home. Rena by then had moved to the Bronx, to an apartment on Crotona Park.

In truth, even before they were married, Cy had left Perry Street and his bohemian bachelorhood. Typical of the new age, he had moved into Nerma's apartment at 308 East Eighteenth Street, which was (and still is) a drab brownstone on a narrow block between First and Second Avenues. It was spare and dark inside, but for Nerma it marked a significant step up. She had finally left the Lower East Side, but she remained deeply connected to its politics.

Cy had quit teaching. On the marriage papers, he wrote down a single word on the line marked "Occupation": "Research." He had stopped the classes at night and at Columbia. One year earlier, in 1923, he had changed jobs. He was hired by the Yale University Press to work in its New York offices. For any young scholar, it was a position to envy. It came with a good title, "research man," and a fine office at 522 Fifth Avenue, Room 829, overlooking Forty-fourth Street.

At twenty-five, Cy could be pleased with his success. He had married a genuine Communist, and each day he could stroll to work on Fifth Avenue. Even though he had been forced to give up on his doctorate, he could still imagine himself an aspiring academic. After all, thanks to his patrons at Columbia, he had been accepted into the American Historical Association—a select group in those days. Cy made sure to keep up with his dues. Even long after he'd left New York, each year a check for five dollars, the annual membership fee, would arrive. The job at the Yale Press, of course, was hardly a forward position in the trenches of the revolution. It would, though, prove an excellent cover.

Cy was hired to work on *The Pageant of America: A Pictorial History of the United States*, a sprawling historical series that the press hoped would commemorate, in a profitable fashion, the nation's upcoming sesquicentennial, in 1926. It was an ambitious project with a prominent profile. Ralph Henry Gabriel, a Yale historian, had assembled an eminent editorial board that included Arthur M. Schlesinger. In fifteen richly illustrated volumes, which would appear in succession from 1925 to 1929, *The Pageant* aimed to tell the story of America from

Columbus to Carnegie. One of the first surveys to feature photographs, its paramount achievement was a retrospective gilding of the origins of American industry and democracy. Volumes included *Toilers of Land and Sea, The March of Commerce, The Winning of Freedom*, and *In Defense of Liberty*. With embossed leather bindings and bald eagles printed on the inside covers, *The Pageant* was intended for the enlightenment of patriotic Americans.

For Cy, the job was ideal. He would have to learn to suppress his political leanings, but Oliver McKee, his supervisor, did not require him to sit in the office. He could spend hours on end two blocks away, in one of the world's great research libraries, the marble and granite main branch of the New York Public Library on Fifth Avenue. The research was painstaking. Volume V, *The Epic of Industry*, published in 1926, offered one example. Beneath a highly detailed map of "Bog and Swamp Ore Forges and Furnaces in Eastern Massachusetts, 1632–1776," the credit line read, "Drawn expressly for *The Pageant of America* by Gregor Noetzel, based on research by H. M. Ehrman and I. Oggins."

In a twist of history, the New York Public Library still holds traces of Cy's work on the Yale series. The library's Photograph Collection includes 7,669 photographs from *The Pageant of America* series, both published and unpublished. The images cover an extraordinary range, from corporate portraits of John D. Rockefeller and Henry Frick to Lewis Hine's photographs of immigrant workers. Among the photographs used in Volume V, several seem to bear a familiar handwriting, a dark, looping cursive. Many of the notations on the images appear to be Cy's. One print, however, offers unimpeachable evidence. In the margin of a photograph of a "Fourdrinier Paper Making Machine," there is a note, in the same handwriting, to the layout designer: "See Oggins."

Cy helped to collect the photographs. He may even have taken some of them. Among the photographs, especially in the "Unpublished" boxes, are bleak images of workers and their workplaces—blast furnaces and textile mills in New England, Italian steelworkers, Russian miners, young girls and old women in the mills, and heroic portraits of Eugene Debs and Bill Haywood, the Wobbly leader. Had Cy tried to recast Yale's celebration of America's past according to his own politics?

If at first the men at the press had no inkling of Cy's leanings, before long they had no doubts. Cy was unable to suppress his views. Even more than twenty years later, when Hoover's men called on the office, the office manager remembered them well. "According to Mr. RILEY," a New York FBI agent reported in a January 1947 dispatch to Washington, "OGGINS was married sometime during his period of employment at the Press and had the reputation of being a radical."

·

WHETHER OR NOT HE HAD MADE UP HIS MIND, CY HAD CLEARLY BEGUN his odyssey. He was moving, by turns cautiously and recklessly, toward a new life with Nerma, a double life with no assurances.

Almost from the start, Lenin had sent secret agents abroad. Long before the revolution, the Bolsheviks had understood the importance of espionage. Facing czarist persecution and police forces across Europe, they had mastered the black arts. For Lenin and his fellow Bolsheviks, exile was not only a political refuge, it was a school for tradecraft.

Werner Rakov, an ethnic German from a Baltic corner of the czar's empire, joined the Bolshevik Party in 1917. In the annals of espionage, Rakov is not well known. Of the hundreds of encyclopedic histories written on Soviet intelligence, only a handful mention him. Rakov, however, was an audacious pioneer. He was the first *rezident*, or chief of a Soviet intelligence residency, in America.

Rakov was born in 1898, the same year as Cy, in the German-speaking *gubernia* of Courland, today a part of Latvia. As a student, he became an associate of Karl Radek's, one of Lenin's closest comrades, and early on he served the USSR in Vienna, Berlin, and the Balkans. Werner was the youngest of three brothers. Nikolai and Paul were also spies of distinction, but young Werner made history.

At some point in early 1925—the exact date went unrecorded—Rakov slipped into New York City. Within days, he enrolled at

Columbia, under the name Felix Wolf. Wolf claimed to be a German exchange student intent on pursuing a graduate degree. In addition to German, he spoke fluent English, French, and Russian. At Columbia, he took only graduate courses in the philosophy and social sciences department.

The university archives reveal no trace of Wolf or Rakov, or of either of the agent's other known aliases, Vladimir Kotlov and Vladimir Inkov. The Moscow archives, however, contain more than 300 pages of classified documents detailing Rakov's biography and service to the Soviet state. Although he could pass as a German, Rakov was not sent to America as an emissary of the Comintern. Nor was he an agent of the OGPU. He was an officer of the GRU—the *Glavnoe razvedyvatel'noe upravlenie*, the name then, as now, of Soviet military intelligence.

By the fall of 1925, Rakov had founded the first Soviet spy network in New York City. Although Cy returned to Columbia often during this period, he had quit his studies by the time Rakov arrived. Did he know Rakov? Had the Soviet operative brought him into the underground? No archive in Berlin, Moscow, or New York yielded an answer. The truth remained beyond reach.

The path of Felix Wolf, however, could be traced. On May 24, 1923, the *Amerikanskaia torgovaia kompaniia*, the American Trading Company, better known as Amtorg, in the Russian acronym, had opened its doors in New York. Because Washington refused to recognize the USSR until 1933, Lenin needed a representative office in the United States. By 1925, Wolf was using the Amtorg offices on Thirty-seventh Street as an operational base. In the 1920s, the Kremlin's interests in America were pragmatic. Moscow did not imagine the country as a target for revolution but was keen to learn Washington's military and industrial plans.

Wolf did not remain in New York. He traveled to Chicago and Washington, D.C., before being abruptly recalled to Moscow in 1927. He was accused of Trotskyism and, a decade later, fell in the purges. In New York, though, even before he had left, the network that Felix Wolf started had taken root.

"CHIMNEY SWEEPS." "DOWNHILL." "Stony Point." The names were scrawled in faded pencil on the back of the photographs. Nerma had kept them for more than half a century. On a warm spring day in April 1924, the day after Cy and Nerma were married, they left the city. They went north to the Palisades, the woodlands that overlook the Hudson River. The black-and-white images told the story: Cy, metal canteen at his side, bending low on the rocky trail to pick wildflowers; an impromptu hearth, with an iron skillet on a circle of stones; the flattened grass of an afternoon of lovemaking.

The trip to the woods at first seemed like nothing more than a quiet honeymoon. Yet Nerma's shoebox held other photographs. On the following weekend, the Sunday after May Day, they went to the country again. This time their destination was Suffern, New York, just across the New Jersey line, along the southern edge of Harriman State Park. Then on Memorial Day they ventured out of the city once more. They took a ferry north up the Hudson thirty miles, to Stony Point. It was a rural patch that boasted commanding views of the river, an 1826 lighthouse, and the anonymity of a remote setting.

Cy and Nerma were taking steps. On May 24, Nerma went downtown and requested a copy of her certificate of arrival from the Naturalization Service. On June 13, she petitioned for citizenship. At the time, not all immigrants saw any need to become naturalized Americans. But Nerma was in need of a U.S. passport.

BY 1926, CY HAD lost all hope of returning to Columbia. The dissertation would be left unstarted, and the doctorate in limbo. While he became increasingly radicalized, his family seemed to be settling into the quicksand of the petit bourgeois. Betty had married Max Schneebalg, a German Jew with aspirations of becoming a dental technician. David had moved to a bigger house in Queens. David had married a second time. His new wife, Anna, was a Jewish woman born to Russian parents in New York. Their first daughter was now a toddler, and a second girl had been born that spring. With no financial support,

Cy made a sharp turn. He maintained his membership in the American Historical Association but decided to abandon academia.

Whether it was Felix Wolf or someone else who recruited him, Cy did not wait long to join the underground. Within two years of joining the party, he was selected for a mission—a clandestine trip to Europe. On August 26, 1926, he applied for his first U.S. passport, No. 281169. In the application he stated that he would "travel to Germany & France." By all appearances he went to Europe as a courier, surreptitiously bearing money, passports, or documents. By November 11, he had returned to New York, sailing aboard the SS *Majestic* from France.

Nerma must have been envious. For two years she had bided her time, filing papers in a Madison Avenue accounting office. The work was miserable, but at least the accountant, J.B.C. Woods, was a comrade. In 1927, however, Nerma severed all her party ties in New York. The preparation had paid off. Cy and Nerma at last received their orders.

This time they would go abroad together. In the third week of April 1928, just after celebrating their fourth wedding anniversary, Nerma applied for an American passport. She told the clerk that she was leaving the United States for "study and travel," that she'd be gone for "2 years" and would live in "England, France, Germany." On the application she also altered a few biographical facts. She changed the dates of her marriage, arrival in New York, and birthday. Nerma, it would seem, had recognized the possibility that the government might deny her a passport for her political activities.

The next morning Cy returned one last time to Columbia. He crossed the campus and ordered a copy of his college transcript. Within days Nerma got her first passport, No. 540387, and Cy his second. They had followed through on the advisories passed on from the men in Moscow. On the rare chance that anyone might check later on, they had made sure to apply for their passports, and pick them up, on different days.

Cy, however, had still not closed the last door on his life in New York. In the final days of April, he walked into the offices on Fifth

Avenue and told his bosses at the Yale University Press that he was quitting. His last day of work would be May Day, the holiday for workers around the world. Cy and Nerma had already booked a cabin. At age thirty, they would set sail on their first foreign adventure.

BEFORE LEAVING, NERMA wanted to see her best friend. Carrie Katz was a pretty, soft-spoken girl in her late twenties who lived in Brooklyn. She was the daughter of an Orthodox rabbi, but Carrie and Nerma had much in common. She, too, was voluble, a born renegade who felt constricted by the boundaries of the times. Above all, Carrie, like Cy and Nerma, was devoted to the cause. She was a charter member of the party, a fellow worker with Nerma at the Labor Defense Council, and a fellow "Fosterite." Like Cy and Nerma, Carrie was a loyalist of the William Z. Foster faction. Foster, in their eyes, represented the best hope for American labor. Unlike the sharp-tongued New Yorkers in their midst, the intellectuals who catered to the urban aesthetes, Foster had worked on the docks and in the packinghouses. He spoke from the trenches, not the pulpit.

Carrie Katz was not unschooled. She, too, had attended the Rand and, like Nerma, had sat at Scott Nearing's knee. Unlike Nerma, however, Carrie had written a scholarly essay under his tutelage. In the fall of 1923, Nearing had invited fifteen Rand students to join him in an unusual seminar. For three years the group met on weekends. The seminar, according to Nearing's design, would endeavor to discover the rules that govern social revolution. He dispatched the students to study the revolts, coups, and economic upheavals that had yielded revolutions around the world. The result of the quest was *The Law of Social Revolution*, a little red book the Rand published in 1926. Chapter 13, "The Russian Revolution of 1917," was written by Carrie Katz.

By then Carrie had fallen in love with a brilliant philosophy student, a fast-talking Brooklyn boy. They had married in March 1924, a few weeks ahead of Cy and Nerma. Her husband was short and stocky, with a trim mustache and a mop of dark curls. Even in those early days, he was known for his original mind. Decades later, long after the lines had been drawn and redrawn, fans and critics alike would look back and claim they had seen it then. "The philosopher of his generation," they would call him.

Carrie Katz had married Sidney Hook. By the time he died, in 1985, Hook was a legend—one of the originals, a 1920s leftist who became a cold war conservative. Along the way, he helped found the neoconservative movement that reshaped American politics at the end of the twentieth century. In the 1930s, Hook stood at the center of a group of young thinkers who argued ideas with such high-pitched passion, everywhere from Village parties to the country's leading journals, that they earned a collective title, "the New York intellectuals." They were young scholars and writers, Jews in the main, men like Eliot Cohen, Philip Rahv, Lionel Trilling, and Meyer Schapiro. Most were born in working-class families and gained fame as anti-Stalinist Socialists in the 1930s. In the postwar period, no other group of American intellectuals shaped the country's political debate more. Yet in the 1920s, Sidney Hook's wife, Carrie, knew Nerma, and Sidney and Cy were friends.

Hook had grown up in working-class Williamsburg, near the Brooklyn shipyards. At Columbia, where he enrolled as a graduate student in 1923, he relished his reputation as a street tough. Even in his twenties, his fame had spread in the city, from academic departments to radical circles. Hook, it was said, was not only a merciless debater but a philosopher who knew his Hegel and Marx better than any professor.

The aura grew. In the late 1920s, Hook became the first Jewish philosopher appointed to the faculty of New York University. By the 1940s, after the Nazi-Soviet Non-Aggression Pact of 1939, he was deemed a pariah by his old comrades. By then Stalin had cast out his archrival, Trotsky, expelling him first from the party, then from the USSR. In the 1930s, Hook became one of Trotsky's leading defenders in the West. In time he helped create a new political caste in America: the liberal anti-Communist.

It was, perhaps, an unparalleled political trajectory. To the end, Hook remained a divisive figure. To many in the old guard, he personified the turncoat. To others he defied categorization, being equal parts neoconservative icon and iconoclast. In his final years, though, Hook insisted he had never shifted left or right. He had remained, he said, a Brooklyn boy and a social democrat at heart.

IT IS EASY to see why Cy was attracted to Hook. When the two met, Hook was already considered the cleverest of the young leftist philosophers in the city. Not only were their wives friends, he shared Cy's singular passion—Marxism.

It is possible that Cy knew Sidney even before he met Nerma. They had overlapped at Columbia and had been taught by many of the same professors. Sidney had not been an undergraduate at Columbia, but he was working on his doctorate there from 1923 to 1928, when Cy was a graduate student as well. In June 1928, Sidney got his Ph.D. The previous year, with David Kvitko, a visiting student from Moscow, he had translated Lenin's *Materialism and Empirio-Criticism*. Published by Trachtenberg, the party leader and Rand teacher, it was an achievement Hook would later prefer to forget.

One weekend Cy and Nerma invited Sidney and Carrie to visit the Hispanic Museum uptown, on Broadway at 155th Street. As they walked through the exhibits, Cy told Sidney of his ambition. He had not quit Columbia, Cy said. He was still working on his doctorate. He was researching the roots of the Spanish revolution and would turn his findings into a dissertation.

Sidney, however, approached Cy from a distance. Like Cy, he was enamored of the revolution. But to him, Cy and Nerma always seemed an odd couple, one of the strangest in the movement. Nerma he could understand. She was nearly a twin of Carrie. But Cy remained an enigma. He never seemed comfortable with his surroundings, Hook wrote in a memoir years later. Cy was an intellectual who yearned to be with the masses, a scholar who believed that the revolution would arise only from the workers. "He came from a middle-class family," Hook remembered, "but had a fixation on the working class, whose virtues in his eyes were represented by Foster rather than by 'New York intellectuals.' "

ON THE LAST FRIDAY in April 1928, Cy rang Sidney. His voice was filled with excitement. He and Nerma were leaving, not just the city but the States. A trip, he explained, was in the offing. It was a stroke of luck, Cy said. He'd won a grant through the university for foreign study. "A foundation" had given the money to Columbia, Cy told Sidney, and he was the only one who qualified. He'd be gone for several months at least, "doing research." It was an opportunity that he and Nerma could not turn down. Cy said they would sail the following week. He kept the destination vague, although years later, Sidney insisted that Cy had told him that he and Nerma were bound for Latin America.

The news came as a surprise, but Sidney invited Cy to bring Nerma over to their place to celebrate. At the farewell dinner, on the eve of Cy and Nerma's departure, Sidney and Carrie rose to the occasion. The dining room table was crowded with food, and the talk ran late. The subject, as always, was politics. Whenever the couples got together, they spoke of little else.

As they sat together, their spirits soared. Cy and Nerma would be sailing on a tramp steamer the next afternoon. Cy had been lucky enough, he said cryptically, to use family connections to secure excellent accommodations. Sidney, on an impulse, offered to escort them to the pier. It seemed a nice gesture, but Cy declined. Nerma, whose eyes had been glowing all evening, could not resist.

"Why not?" she blurted out.

It was the end of the first week of May, a warm Saturday. Cy and Nerma agreed to meet the Hooks downtown, at the West Side piers. But early in the afternoon, just as Sidney and Carrie were about to leave home, Cy called with a change of plans. The couples would have to meet at a different pier.

Sidney and Carrie took the subway down to Chelsea but were surprised to find Cy and Nerma at the end of the street leading to the pier, far from the boat. It was too crowded at the pier, Cy explained. Too many people were pushing to load their bags, he said. The commotion would interfere with their goodbyes.

Instead Cy and Sidney and Carrie and Nerma went for a last stroll in the sunshine. They walked for so long that Sidney worried about the flowers Carrie had brought Nerma, which seemed to wilt in her hands. Cy saw the flowers and stopped. The couples exchanged farewells, and Cy and Nerma promised to write. They would all have a grand reunion, they said, in a few months, when the Ogginses came home.

ON SATURDAY, MAY 5, 1928, Cy and Nerma climbed aboard the *Leviathan*. As the horns blew, they stood against the wooden rail, watching the well-wishers onshore. A crowd had gathered to wave and shout farewell. Onboard were more than two hundred others, including celebrities from among New York's wealthiest: David Sarnoff, the founder of RCA, and the publisher Frank Doubleday and his wife.

As the giant ship sailed south along the North River and past the Battery, the steel and granite towers of Wall Street loomed large. Among the temples of American capitalism, there was only silence, nothing to portend the cataclysm to come. They sailed on past Lady Liberty, through the Narrows, and after a time entered dark waters. In a moment, as if someone had drawn a curtain, the ocean opened before Cy and Nerma, and the city at their backs vanished from view.

Café Josty, Potsdamer Platz, Berlin.

CHAPTER 6

A CHANGE OF SKY

■ ■ ■

THE ROOMS UPSTAIRS WERE ALWAYS LOCKED, BUT CY AND NERMA soon grew used to it. Cy knew, of course, it would not last. The villa was not a home. It did not belong to them, nor to the men who came to unlock the doors and, without fail, shut them behind them. The men from the Center, as Cy and Nerma had learned to call the Moscow headquarters of Soviet intelligence, had found the house and covered the rent. The Americans only lived there.

The villa in Zehlendorf was a contradiction. For Cy and Nerma, it was a façade that offered, for the first time in their lives together, a measure of stability. The house was large, three stories of carpeted elegance on a quiet street at Berlin's refined western edge. There was no traffic outside—no buses, trams, or passersby. Oddly, even in that first spring the villa gave the Americans a sense of pride and place.

Yet behind their newfound confidence lurked a suspension of disbelief. The money, clothes, antiques, evenings on the town, even Cy's hours at the university—it was all a veneer. Each was a fiction in a papier-mâché life, one lie layered upon another, and all fashioned by someone in an unknown office half a world away. Still, Cy and Nerma could forget all that. In thrall to their new buoyancy, they could look beyond the awkward truths of their new life. At least at first.

■

BERLIN WOULD BE THE BAPTISM. WHEN CY AND NERMA WENT ASHORE from the *Leviathan*, they stopped only briefly in Paris before boarding the overnight train east. On the morning of May 21, 1928, they arrived in the German capital.

With a surprising readiness, they slipped out of their old lives. In New York, Nerma had been the traveler, "the Communist fire-eater" dispatched to rally the comrades, whether the Jewish seamstresses downtown or German steelworkers in Detroit. Cy, however, had stayed out of the fray. He had been the scholar, waging war quietly on the page and in his own mind. In Berlin, they changed roles. Cy moved into the advance guard and Nerma to the rear.

It was gradual at first, a reversal by half-steps. Over time, however, as Cy traveled around Europe, the distance between them grew. Assuming the role of a bourgeois hausfrau, Nerma adopted a routine of domesticity. Cy, after receiving approval from above, took on the guise of a Young American Abroad—what in a decade's time would be called "a Hemingway hero." To all he encountered, he seemed an earnest traveler, a New Yorker of ample means and few cares.

Whether they knew it or not, Cy and Nerma were moving deeper into the underground. By 1928, Soviet intelligence had set down deep roots in Berlin. The Comintern had led the way. By the time Cy and Nerma arrived, the Comintern's OMS—*Otdel mezhdunarodnoi svyazi*, or International Liaison Department—was running a sprawling espionage network across Europe. Hundreds of foreign agents in state offices, newspapers, defense plants, and banks now reported to the OMS, and indirectly to Moscow. Many, like the young American couple newly arrived in Berlin, had been seconded from their national parties. A great number were intellectuals, students or would-be students, who had joined the Comintern to become foot soldiers in the new revolutionary army. Enlisting, they may have imagined themselves volunteers on the side of the righteous. However, they had joined, knowingly or not, a darker service. "Special work," they called it in those early days. The euphemism would prove opportune. It shielded the innocent, as many servants of the OMS surely were, from the blood to come.

By the spring of 1928, the OMS office in Berlin had outgrown its space. It had become one of Moscow's clandestine headquarters in the West, a busy hub for the expansive European network. Just off Unter den Linden, the tree-lined avenue in the heart of official Berlin, the office was hidden inside the Führer Verlag, at 131–132 Wilhelmstrasse. From the street it looked like a publishing house, a benign establishment amid the cluster of Western embassies and state offices. Inside, though, "a host of typists, couriers, translators and guards" busily manned "a dozen departments" for the OMS.

Only recently had the Comintern been forced to shift its clandestine tactics. Before 1927, OMS operatives had worked within the USSR's diplomatic missions abroad. But two raids revealed the risks of the practice. First, in April 1927, the Chinese police barged into the Soviet military attaché's office in Beijing, then known as Peiping. In London the following month, Scotland Yard ransacked the offices of ARCOS, as the Soviet trade delegation, as it innocently claimed to be, was known. The raids brought headlines, official inquiries, and international scandals. In England, Parliament even opened an investigation into Soviet espionage in the United Kingdom.

In Moscow the men who ran the secret network reacted swiftly. From then on, all OMS agents were to keep their distance from Soviet diplomatic missions. Embassies, consulates, and official offices of the USSR were off-limits. In place of the old ways, agents could now meet only in public places or at *yavki*, as safe houses are known in Russian. The *yavki* were designated residences where agents could not only meet but work. In time the Soviets had safe houses all over the world, even in Moscow. Anonymous locations, they could be an apartment overlooking a busy avenue or an abandoned farmhouse in a rural suburb. Apartments could be kept for rendezvous. Houses, though, were used for secret work, whether the task was routine or urgent—forging new "boots" or reproducing a report stolen off a general's desk.

The OMS followed strict guidelines in selecting the houses. Often they stood on the quiet outskirts of town, on a dead-end street or cul-de-sac. The preferred environs were remote, sparsely populated neighborhoods, but those sufficiently close to the headquarters downtown. Operational safe houses were run by agents with "clean" identities. If the residents were men and women who used their real names and real passports, police checks would quell any suspicion. The secret work, though, was performed at night, by others who came and went without a word. Vital to the success of the Soviet network, these *yavki* had to adhere to an exacting security regime. Above all, they could provoke no suspicion. In the ideal, they looked just like the villa in Zehlendorf.

CY AND NERMA QUICKLY shed the uniforms of their days in Manhattan, the proletarian outfits that made Nerma resemble Emma Goldman and Cy a peasant farmer. Nerma now took to wearing staid dresses and pleated skirts, while Cy wore bespoke three-piece suits, spats, and a gold watch fob. He grew his hair long, brilliantined it back, and added a distinctive pair of spectacles, thick round glasses of dark tortoiseshell. On his afternoon walks around town, whether on Unter den Linden or the dusty paths of the Wannsee, Cy donned a black fedora. And everywhere, it seems, he carried his most recent accessory, an elegant walking stick complete with silver handle.

The costumes were only half the disguise. As Nerma sank into a housebound routine, Cy adopted a dandy's avocation: dealer in objets d'art. The cover offered a number of advantages. As a well-to-do American connoisseur, Cy could now take short trips at a moment's notice, to Oslo one weekend, Copenhagen the next. He could also carry large sums of cash in an assortment of currencies without arousing suspicion. Best of all, the profession offered entrée to the intellectual quarters of Weimar. As an aspiring authority on art history, he would have cause to attend lectures on the subject at the University of Berlin, the Friedrich-Wilhelms-Universität, which stood on Unter den Linden downtown, directly across from the Opera. A former palace, it was an imposing stone edifice built in 1766 for the brother of Frederick the Great. To a Columbia graduate, however, its threshold marked a homecoming. Cy was returning not only to a safe haven but to the former home of Hegel, Marx, and Engels.

For Cy and Nerma, it was a spectacular start. If any country in Europe, to their hopeful eyes, met Marx's revolutionary conditions, it was Germany. The Weimar Republic, as Peter Gay has written, "was born in defeat, lived in turmoil, and died in disaster." For many West Europeans, the Great War was a memory. Germans, however, had to contend with its merciless aftershocks. In the winter of 1918–19, they had witnessed the tumult—the German Revolution, the historians called it—that sent the sailors into revolt and the kaiser into exile. The radical socialists Karl Liebknecht and Rosa Luxemburg had helped found the German Communist Party, the KPD, but their grand attempt to take power, the Spartacus Uprising of January 1919, had lasted less than two weeks and ended with Liebknecht's and Luxemburg's murders.

Berlin, like the rest of the country, still suffered the curse of Versailles. The loss of World War I had brought not only humiliation but a historic bill for reparations—$33 billion in 1921. The German economy, already in ruins, was ravaged by hyperinflation. Strikes erupted, followed by hunger riots. By the winter of 1923, a loaf of bread cost 428 million marks and Germans were burning banknotes for heat. The country had already crossed a threshold, opening the door to the plague known as National Socialism. The National Socialist German Workers Party had been gathering force in Bavaria since 1921, when an Austrian corporal and failed postcard painter had assumed the title Der Führer.

Berlin now lived under uncertain skies. As Cy and Nerma set out on their own, their hours in the villa fixed by the furtive strangers at work overhead and below, they saw the tumult firsthand. The city was a place where Nazi and Communist posters competed on lampposts, child prostitutes lined the Tiergarten, Reichstag deputies moved to lift the ban on homosexuality, and women of good upbringing, as Vera Nabokov confided to her husband, the young poet from Petersburg, arrived at work in government offices carrying pistols in their pocketbooks. The imperial landscape remained—Cy and Nerma toured the Kaiserschloss, the Siegessäule, and Sanssouci, Friedrich the Great's pleasure palace—but the staid capital of Kaiser Wilhelm had become a city of transgression. Nothing had prepared Cy and Nerma—not Marx, not the *Worker*, and certainly not the speakeasies of the Village. It wasn't just the politics. In art, music, and above all sex, Berlin stood alone in Europe, an intersection of the avant-garde and the illicit.

The sense of foreboding was strong, but the city could rise above the chaos, as if by levitation. In 1926, the year Hitler sent Goebbels as his *Gauleiter* in Berlin to revive the failing party in the capital, a Negro temptress from St. Louis seduced even the most jaded Berliner voyeurs. After Josephine Baker, wrote one survivor, "the women of Berlin were never the same again." The names would become mythic—Dietrich and Garbo, Einstein and Brecht. Even as Grosz, Kollwitz, and Dix memorialized the misery, jazz, or "yats," as the locals called it, filled the cabaret bars, and three opera companies competed nightly. Berlin, in Cy and Nerma's first year, saw the premier of *The Threepenny Opera* and Kurt Gerron singing "Mack the Knife" for the first time. The city had become the free capital of Europe. Tens of thousands of White Russians had arrived, and more would come. Berlin, however, could feign indifference for only so long.

Cy and Nerma may not have sensed it, but they had arrived in mid-prelude. Soon the fighting would come close. The Brownshirts would march into the Red districts, and Gerron, a Jew, would never sing in his own country again. In five years it would be over. The ugly tide would sweep Hindenburg and the old Prussians out. The Reichskanzler would rise, the Reichstag would burn, and the ideology, the most malevolent the world had seen, would triumph with a speed no one had dared imagine. But in the spring of 1928, to Communist revolutionaries, even foreigners and Jews like the American couple in Zehlendorf, Berlin was forlorn and desperate but expectant. Like Herzen's image of Europe after the 1848 revolutions, the city stood like "a pregnant widow." To Cy and Nerma, it was a revolutionary paradise.

•

LENIN HAD LONG SEEN BERLIN AS THE SHOWPLACE FOR WORLD REVO-lution. In 1921, the Comintern had proclaimed Germany the next country to undergo a proletarian revolution. That year the Commu-

nists staged an abortive uprising in central Germany, but the Kremlin had held fast to its dream, even in the face of abundant evidence
to the contrary.

Moscow in the fall of 1923 was "plastered with slogans welcoming
the German revolution," as Ruth Fischer, one of the earliest organizers of the German party, later recalled. Stalin had invited Fischer to
the Soviet capital, where she was surprised to hear the Soviets speak
of the German Communists in a pitch of celebration. Banners hung
across Moscow, brazenly predicting victory in Berlin: "Russian Youth,
Learn German—the German October Is Approaching!" The Soviet
forecast, though, proved illusory.

The martyrdom of Liebknecht and Luxemburg had been followed
by the failed uprising in Hamburg. In October 1923, Hamburg was
Germany's busiest port. More than 12,000 ships, the majority from
England and America, arrived annually. When the Communists
called a general strike, only a few hundred dockworkers took up arms.
Led by Ernst Thälmann, a bullet-headed former stevedore who was a
Hamburg native, the strikers attacked police stations across the city.
Within hours they were in bloody retreat and dozens had died. The
German revolution's spark had fizzled within three days.

The Hamburg revolt was a bitter defeat, but in its wake Thälmann
rose to the national stage. To Cy and Nerma, the burly Communist
embodied the Comintern's dream. By 1925, with Stalin's blessing,
Thälmann had taken control of the party and run for president. He
lost to Hindenburg, in the first of two failed campaigns, but gained
nearly 2 million votes. By the time Cy and Nerma went to Berlin, the
German party boasted a quarter of a million members and twenty-
seven daily newspapers with a circulation of 5 million. In the Reichstag, the Social Democrats still dominated—"Social Fascists," the Reds
called them derisively, for buttressing the patchwork Weimar coalition. Yet Thälmann now led the parliament's small but vocal Communist contingent of fifty-four deputies.

In the Kremlin, the German Communists were seen as among the
world's most dedicated. In Berlin, you could not miss them. All
across the city, they filled the cavernous meeting halls, the men in

soiled factory clothes in row after row. The air was thick with the smell of beer and tobacco, but visitors from lands farther west were struck by their sincerity and sense of purpose. In the city's black-collar districts, Moabit and Wedding to the north, the workers listened intently. On Friday evenings in Wedding they converged at Pharus Hall, a Communist landmark that rose above the grim dun-colored stucco tenements. Their faces were prematurely lined, their eyes dark and sunken, but they were not mere spectators. In New York, Cy and Nerma had read the stories. Now even from their hiding place they could see that the reports were true: the German comrades, more than any other working class in the West, were participants.

RED FRONT FIGHTERS, JOIN THE COMMUNIST PARTY! The giant red cloth, emblazoned with white letters as big as a man, covered the face of the enormous cathedral. On Whitsunday in June 1928, the German party staged a spectacular rally. Half a million workers flooded the streets. The Red Front fighters alone numbered more than 200,000.

Cy and Nerma had been in Berlin less than a month, and suddenly the city was aglow in a Communist bloom. Everywhere they saw red: red flags and banners in the air, red badges in lapels, and red ribbons on hats. The German workers, the masses whose sufferings they had heard so much about for so long, streamed downtown. The crowds were bigger than any Cy and Nerma had ever seen, far larger than any at the Union Square rallies in New York.

It was not the first time that the Red Front fighters, "the storm troops of the proletariat," as Berliners called them, had converged on the city. They had marched in the capital every year since 1924. Each time they wore gray uniforms, in the Soviet style, and caps featuring a single red star. The fighters came from across Germany, from the northern seaports, the Catholic south, feudal East Prussia, and the industrial belts in the Rhineland, the Ruhr, and Saxony. At their helm, basking in the midsummer promise of the day, stood Thälmann.

On that hot Whitsunday, the Red Front fighters set out early. They started marching from the north, in the city's working-class neighborhoods, where the locals had housed them for the night. As they made their way toward the center of town, their ranks swelled. By midmorning tens of thousands filled the streets. Girls appeared from *bierstuben* to pass pitchers of beer among the men. As they marched on, they sang of the revolution to come. By the time they reached the prim avenues of the professional class, the noise in the streets was impossible to miss. In the shuttered homes above, ladies and gentlemen awoke to the roar.

At the Lustgarten, the procession came to a halt. The giant green square, more park than garden, was the city's grandest stage. The centerpiece of official Berlin, heart of the kaiser's old empire, it was framed by landmarks: the Berliner Dom, the Protestant cathedral built to rival St. Peter's, on one edge; the Schloss, former palace of the Hohenzollerns, on another; the Altes Museum on a third side; the canal on the fourth. At least half a dozen avenues and bridges led to the square. Each was now overflowing with marchers. The police had come out as well. They stood arrayed on the cathedral steps, steel helmets gleaming, a dark phalanx of state power. Across the canal, hundreds more sat in trucks, rifles in hand.

The Lustgarten was a sea of red. The crowd spilled out across the square, along the length of the old palace, and down beside the narrow canal. There were so many men they clogged Unter den Linden, stopping all streetcars as far as the opera and the university. No document records that Cy and Nerma stood among the fighters, but it is hard to imagine them missing the chance.

When four o'clock came, at the buglers' call, the fighters fell silent. From the steps of the Altes Museum, a chorus broke into song. "*Brüder, zur Sonne und Freiheit,*" hundreds sang. "Brothers, to the Sun and Freedom!"

It was the anthem of the German Communists:

Brüder in eins nun die Hände, Brüder das Sterben verlacht!
Brothers, let's join hands. Brothers, let's laugh at death!
Slavery's ending forever. Holy is the final fight!
The tyrants' yoke is breaking, the powers that torment us so!
The blood-red flags are waving over the workers' world!

As Thälmann stood on the cathedral balcony, the voices carried overhead and out along Unter den Linden. Others rose to speak wherever they could, on pillars, statues, shoulders. The Red Front leaders invoked Sacco and Vanzetti, executed the previous year, the revolution in China, the uprising in Vienna, the strikes in France and America. They spoke rapturously of the future, of the providence to come, by the hand not of the divine but of the proletariat. The crowds listened, rapt, until the bugles sounded again.

In an instant, across the square the fighters raised their right fists and shouted out their oath, the words resounding against the stone walls of the old empire. Even after they had fallen silent, their last vow rang in the air.

"I swear," the sea had roared, "I will always and forever fight for Soviet Russia and for the world revolution!"

CY AND NERMA NEVER KNEW WHEN TO EXPECT THE MEN. THEY COULD enter the villa at any time. They were always men with accents, men in gray clothes, men from the east. They never had time for small talk, let alone news from the front. They rarely even spoke with the Americans.

The Russians kept the keys to the rooms upstairs and in the basement—the rooms that held the components of the secret workshop. Cy had seen the machines; there were many machines, a great variety, but each complex and modern. He, though, was never allowed to operate them. The Russians always did the work, stealthily, quietly, and on their own timetable. The Americans only had to keep up appearances.

Cy had been warned time and again: Never associate with Communists. Not American Communists and not German Communists. Not any. Once he had erred, and his handlers had fumed. It was an innocent accident. He had invited a fellow American home from the university, an architecture student from Buffalo. The two had drunk late into the night, and the American had burst into song. One selection, unfortunately, was the German Communist anthem, the song that had soared above the Lustgarten. The American was not a Communist. He had picked up the song from a German girlfriend. All the same, the Russians chided Cy. That the KPD's favorite march had resounded from the walls of the villa was worse than foolhardy. Cy could have blown the entire operation.

He and Nerma understood the rules and the reasons for them. They could travel around the city as they wished, but they could never browse in the Communist bookshops, read the Communist newspapers, or visit the Communist cafés. Above all, they were to avoid the Liebknecht Haus, the party headquarters. Named after the martyr of the Spartacus uprising, it was a massive building that filled a city block overlooking the Bülowplatz. Always draped with giant crimson banners and crowded with comrades from across Europe, it was the heart of Communist Berlin. To be seen there would mean certain exposure. Not only was the Liebknecht Haus under constant surveillance, it was rife with informants. The Americans could never reveal their politics, not even in a hushed conversation among themselves in the rear of an empty streetcar. Carelessness could cripple not only the Soviet network in the city but the underground movement across Germany.

To Cy and Nerma, the strictures, at least at first, did not seem unbearable. They could steer clear of "the parlor pink colony," the home district of many of Berlin's Socialists and Communists. They could live without the screaming matches at the Liebknecht Haus. And they could happily join the writers and painters at the celebrated café Schwannecke's, abstaining from the graveyard bar near the zoo, a beloved Communist dive. But after a time the silence became too much. Cy slipped.

It was not, at least at first, a mistake, a miscalculation, or a misstep born of human weakness. It was blind coincidence. Cy felt the stare first, and then after a moment he turned and made for the door. It was in vain. He knew that he had been spotted.

The American Express office in Berlin in 1928 was just off the Gendarmenmarkt, the city's most spectacular square. It filled the ground floor of 55 Charlottenstrasse. A lean granite building, it stood in the shadows of Max Reinhardt's Deutsches Theater and near the elegant landmarks that anchored the square on opposite ends, the French and German cathedrals.

Cy stopped by the office often. Few people had the address, but those who did—his mother, his brother, David, and his sister, Betty— were his only ties to the world at home. Columbia, too, sent the occasional letter. The American Express office, moreover, was a close walk from the university. Cy had made it a routine to wend his way by after lectures.

It was a chilly afternoon in autumn when the blood drained from his face. Cy had nearly made it to the door and out to the street when he felt the hand.

"Cy? Cy Oggins? What are you doing here?"

There was nowhere to run.

Cy turned and came face to face with the last man to see him in New York, Sidney Hook.

FIFTY-SIX YEARS LATER, Hook remembered it vividly. By then he was nearing the end of an epic political life. In the 1980s, Hook, once the devoted student of Marx and then the defiant defender of Trotsky, became one of the intellectual godfathers to the newest generation of American hard-liners. In 1984, at the age of eighty-two, he looked back on his battles and wrote his memoirs, *Out of Step*. He had a lifetime of war stories, and as many axes to grind. But his time in Berlin stood apart. Hook devoted an entire chapter to his meetings with Cy in 1928. "Encounter with Espionage," he called it.

Hook opted to disguise Cy and Nerma, giving them pseudonyms— Hilas and Magda. All the same, they were instantly recognizable. Later, among Hook's papers in the Hoover Archives, I found the original typescripts. In an early draft, he had crossed out their real names and scribbled in the aliases. The anti-Stalinist, it would seem, had a heart. Hook had elected to protect the Stalinists. Quite likely he intended to shield himself as well.

In 1928, Hook won a Guggenheim fellowship to study abroad. He and Carrie sailed from New York that June. They spent the summer and early fall in Munich and made brief forays around Europe. In October they arrived in Berlin and found a place in the center of fashionable Charlottenburg, at 69 Goethestrasse. Frau Rossteuscher, their landlady, was a widow who had a large flat and rented out rooms to students. It was an imposing art moderne apartment house, but the residents lent it the feel of a boardinghouse.

Hook, too, made a habit of visiting the American Express office. He was standing at the window cashing a check when he caught sight of "the figure of a man who seemed vaguely familiar."

Cy turned sharply away, but his profile remained visible.

"He was richly attired in an overcoat with a large fur collar," Hook writes in *Out of Step*. "He wore spats and carried a cane with a knobby metal head." The heavy tortoiseshell glasses threw Hook for a second, and his friend had gained at least twenty pounds, but all the same, he recognized Cy.

Cy went white. Sidney thought he might faint. But in a moment he recovered and, with a furtive look around, leaned in to whisper, "Meet me at five, tomorrow evening." He named a café on the Kurfürstendamm and rushed out into the street.

The café was only a few blocks from the widow Rossteuscher's. When Sidney arrived, Cy was already huddled at a table in a far corner.

Sidney could be foolhardy. Often he was pugnacious, irreverent, intellectually and socially blunt. He was not, however, naive. The chance meeting at the Gendarmenmarkt had stunned him, but he had interpreted the circumstances as best he could. Cy, he realized, was not engaged in "academic research." His friend, Sidney suspected, was "doing political work of some kind," but he did not have "the foggiest idea of its nature."

For Sidney, Berlin had been an awakening. The weather could be bleak, and the cityscape was not nearly as dramatic as New York's. But the politics electrified him. For the young philosopher—he had come to study Metternich, Hegel, Feuerbach, and Marx—it was a first trip to the barricades. In October, Sidney sent a postcard home to his parents in Brooklyn. "Politics," he wrote, "is to the daily reading fare of the German, what Sport is to the American. That's why the atmosphere here is more invigorating!"

Cy, too, had assayed the situation, weighing the risks of meeting his friend again. Perhaps he told himself he would throw Sidney off his trail, ward off accidental contact in the future. But Cy had ulterior motives. He missed the bohemian camaraderie, the give-and-take of New York, when he and his friends had argued late into the night, trying to measure the distance between ideas on the page and revolution in the streets. Cy also had another reason to see Sidney: he was desperate for news.

He and Nerma had come to Europe as agents of the Comintern. Eventually they would move deeper into the Soviet underground. In Berlin, though, they believed themselves to be fighting on behalf of the worldwide brotherhood. For Cy and Nerma, the Comintern, its strength and prospects, was not an abstract interest. Its future could determine the course of their journey and confirm their devotion to serve.

In Sidney, Cy saw opportunity. He would know the news. In Moscow that summer the Comintern had hosted its Sixth Congress. From around the world, party leaders had converged on the Soviet capital. The American party had sent two competing delegations, one led by Jay Lovestone, the other by William Z. Foster, the faction leader whom Cy and Nerma had supported since his days in Chicago. Lovestone and Foster were locked in a struggle for the party leadership. In Moscow, the stage was set for war. At stake was the future of the American party.

Even in Berlin, the factional war hung over their lives, but Cy and Nerma could not follow its every turn. Cy was desperate to know the scorecard. "What's happened at the congress?" he asked Sidney straightaway. Who was up? Who was down? And who was out?

THE SHOWDOWN HAD been long in coming. At winter's end in 1927, Charles Ruthenberg, then head of the American party, had fallen seriously ill. On his deathbed, he named Lovestone, then just twenty-nine, as his successor. The nomination enraged the Foster faction. In the spring of 1928, the Fosterites teamed up with James Cannon, the longtime chairman of the Workers Party, and set out to resist the new regime. Together with Cannon, a Kansan born to working-class Irish radicals, Foster imagined he would triumph. In May, Lovestone and Ben Gitlow decided to take their case to Moscow, hoping the Soviets could prevent a fatal rift. Bukharin, the Comintern general secretary at the time, was tasked with setting up an American Commission to mediate between the opposing camps—neither of which, as their stewards in Moscow liked to say, knew their Marx very well.

Trotsky, however, was Stalin's first concern. By the spring of 1928, Stalin had already taken care of his rival—or so he thought. Trotsky had helped lead the revolution and served as Lenin's war commissar through the civil war. With Lenin's death in 1924, however, Trotsky loomed as the chief threat to Stalin's hunger for total power. In November 1927, Stalin kicked him out of the party. On January 17, 1928, Trotsky, dressed in his pajamas, opened the door of his Moscow apartment and encountered a wall of OPGU officers. He did not resist as the secret policemen packed him off on the Trans-Siberian Express. He was exiled to Alma-Ata, capital of the Kazakh Soviet Republic. It was the beginning of an exile that would last more than a decade and end famously, in blood. With Trotsky banished to the Central Asian steppes, Stalin could turn to less pressing matters, like domesticating the quarrelsome Americans.

When the Comintern congress opened on July 17, 1928, the conflict between Lovestone and Foster took center stage within the marble walls of the Great Hall of Columns. The congress ran all summer. To the Americans, so absorbed in their fight, Bukharin seemed to run the show. Lovestone accordingly sought to curry his favor. Bukharin, though, had kept the competing Americans in the dark. He was in fact fast losing his own battle for power. Already his days, and therefore Lovestone's, were numbered. Only one man would decide which American faction would lose favor and deliver the final blow. But Stalin was biding his time.

BY THE SUMMER of 1928, when they sat together again, Sidney Hook and Cy Oggins had taken different directions. Their lives had already been shaped by divergent ambitions. Still, Hook felt for Cy. He related what little news he had heard of the congress. In his memoirs, Hook writes that he had asked his wife, Carrie, for the news. Carrie, he claimed, was the one who kept up on such matters. She not only followed the American party's internecine struggles but had maintained her membership even while abroad, transferring for the year in Berlin to the German party.

But Cy's curiosity was "insatiable." He seemed desperate to learn the latest from Moscow.

Earlier that summer, as it happened, the American delegation had come through Europe en route to Moscow. "By accident," Hook had met Alexander Trachtenberg and other party officials from New York who were heading to the congress. Hook knew Trachtenberg, who had published the Lenin translation that Hook had done with the Soviet exchange student David Kvitko the previous year. Trachtenberg and the others, Sidney told Cy, were in a "mood of exultant expectation that the Lovestone leadership of the American party would be sustained."

Cy knew little of the widening schism in the party. He told Sidney that he had heard that "the Bukharin group and all its sympathizers were under a cloud" but "knew no details." To Sidney, it seemed odd. Berlin in 1928 was home to more than 120 newspapers, covering the broadest political spectrum in the world. The Communist papers, moreover, were sold on nearly every street corner. Obviously Cy had not been reading them. At the time, though, Sidney did not know why.

They had shared half an hour of excited talk before Cy fell silent. In a moment, he confessed. "Sidney," he announced, "I am going to take you into my confidence."

What had begun as an innocent, chance encounter now took a dangerous turn. Sitting with Sidney in the rear of a café in the middle of Berlin's most famous avenue, Cy began to unfold a confession, or at least an admission, by halves, of the truth. The conversation, by all available evidence, went unrecorded in the anonymous offices on the Lubyanka square, the ones that stayed lit all night in Moscow. But all the same, within a decade the price of such recklessness would be plain. It could have cost Cy his life, and Sidney's as well.

Yet life in the villa in Zehlendorf had taken its toll. Cy fell prey to a need greater than his hunger for party news. He had to unburden himself. After all, Cy told Sidney, Nerma was "Carrie's best friend."

In his memoir, Hook replays the tumble of words that followed. "I know I can trust you," Cy announced, before saying that he was "doing special work for the Party." "I can't tell you about it," Hook remembers Cy saying, "but it's very dangerous for me to see you or anyone else I've known before. I must also keep away from anything political here in Germany."

Hook was a cold warrior long before the cold war. His memory could have been faulty, and he may have recast the conversation in a dark hue. Given his decades as one of America's leading anti-Communists, no doubt he did. However, the salient details of Cy's confession, as recorded in *Out of Step,* agree with all the available accounts.

To Sidney, Cy seemed depleted. His hours at the university—he told Sidney how he had been attending lectures—seemed the high point of his life in Berlin. Cy, at least in Hook's telling, had found himself trapped in a life not of his choosing.

As the two men sat and talked, they spoke of friends in New York. In response to Sidney's probing, Cy admitted that he'd never gone to Latin America and that he and Nerma had in fact sailed straight for Europe. He had since traveled all over the continent. Cy was exhausted, Hook writes, and complained of being weary "nigh unto death" and "damn lonely."

Cy knew that seeing Sidney again would pose a risk. Yet he realized that they would be frequenting the same places—the university, the American Express office, the libraries. He was bound to run into Sidney again. Before they parted, taking care to leave the café separately, Cy wrote down his friend's telephone number. He set a time to call the next day. He would be sure to phone, Cy said. That is, unless he and Nerma decided it was too dangerous to meet again.

Before getting up from the table, Cy made one request. Should Sidney not hear from him, and should they ever bump into one another again, he had to promise to do all he could to ignore Cy.

"Naturally," wrote Hook, "I was left in a state of great curiosity." That night he told Carrie the news. She could guess, correctly, that

Cy and Nerma were doing "special work" for the party. But Carrie assumed it was for the German party.

The next day, Cy rang at the appointed hour. Nerma had agreed that the risks were worth it. The two couples would meet for dinner at a restaurant downtown. It was a nice place, the kind of Berlin restaurant favored by wealthy foreigners and German businessmen.

Carrie and Nerma were overjoyed. For Nerma, it was a rare chance to catch up on the party circles in New York she had left behind. Cy, though, remained keen to hear whatever news he could from Moscow.

Sidney had made an effort to get the latest from the congress, and he did not disappoint. Lovestone's brief reign, he told Cy, was endangered. The Comintern bosses had reproached Lovestone and his followers for their hubris. The Fosterites were on the ascent. Cy and Nerma were jubilant. It was more than reason enough to celebrate.

They were all still eating when Cy abruptly left the table. In a moment he returned, explaining that he had made a phone call. It's okay, he said. "We'll go to our place for coffee."

The two couples piled into a taxi. When they arrived at the villa, the house was dark. Cy paid the driver and walked alone through the yard to the back. Soon he reappeared, opening the front door. "No one's here," he said. Only later did Hook put it together: Cy had called from the restaurant to make sure that his overlords were not at work in the villa. Assured that the house was empty, Cy invited everyone in.

■

BY 1928 THE CLANDESTINE ARMS OF MOSCOW HAD REACHED HIGH INTO the Weimar government. By the time that Cy and Nerma hosted Sidney and Carrie at the villa in Zehlendorf, Soviet operatives in Berlin moved with ease and, with rare exceptions, impunity. Moscow's spies stole state documents from a host of government chanceries, defense plants, chemical factories, and even the most secure offices of the German armed forces. During the Weimar years, the USSR and Germany carried on secret military relations. Despite the ban prescribed by Versailles, the Soviets offered the Reichswehr bases for training, and German officers were ferried to Moscow to help build a general staff for the Red Army. Information, however, remained at a premium. For the Soviets, the most coveted secrets nearly always fell within the same sphere: German military plans and industrial capabilities.

Cy and Nerma may never have known what work was performed under their roof at night. They had seen the complex and expensive machines that filled the locked rooms of their villa. But it is possible that they never even glimpsed the products the machinery churned out. Yet they could easily guess, and with a considerable degree of accuracy, at the range of possibilities.

The Soviets had become masters in the smugglers' trade of stolen information. The network extended far beyond Berlin, across Europe, and the goods moved swiftly. Documents could disappear one day from a desk or a file, be photographed or copied out, and be sent on to an eager readership in Moscow before dawn. At times the work was nearly impossible, and at others absurdly simple. Sometimes the information stolen was worthless. But sometimes it was priceless, as it would be in February 1933, when Stalin read Hitler's first speech to the leaders of the Wehrmacht two days after he gave it—in the secrecy of the Bendler Block, the German military headquarters. Sometimes the secrets were tapped out in the dark on a collapsible transmitter. Sometimes they were smuggled across borders by couriers. Often the contraband took the form of miniature photographs, tiny strips of black-and-white images, each no larger than a half-inch square, like the kind Cy printed and kept among his most treasured belongings for years.

The secret workshop in Zehlendorf may have been a factory for making fake passports or photographing state documents. Both would warrant the security precautions. But it is also possible that it was a production center for one of the Soviets' most ambitious—and harebrained—clandestine schemes of the interwar years.

IT WAS ALL STALIN'S IDEA. Years later, once the U.S. Treasury investigators and bankers had tied together the threads, they would figure that out. It was a reckless but bold undertaking, and only one man in the USSR could have launched it. Stalin had convened his spymasters to ask a simple question. Would it be possible, he wondered, to print U.S. banknotes? He did not have in mind a few dollars, but tens of millions. No one present in the Kremlin that day required further instructions. In the Lubyanka, the secret policemen set to work.

Decades on, historians would argue that the Kremlin had tried to destabilize the dollar by flooding the market with counterfeit currency. The real motive was less elegant: the USSR needed *valuta*, foreign currency. Stalin had taken a look at the state ledgers and feared that the great Soviet experiment would go broke. In the 1920s, the Kremlin had gone on a shopping spree, importing Western heavy machinery by the shipload. By 1928 the first Five-Year Plan threatened to deplete the coffers. Stalin was interested only in staving off disaster.

The Center's solution was simple: the Lubyanka would create a *valuta* department. The USSR would print its own $100 banknotes. The mission demanded a grand design, with agents penetrating foreign banks and governmental agencies across the West. From New York to Moscow and as far off as Shanghai, agents would join the task. But the operation was headquartered, as the sleuths from Washington and London learned after unraveling false leads for years and tracing $500,000 in fake bills back to their source, in Berlin—in 1929.

Were Cy and Nerma involved? The spy memoirs, court records, and once-secret archives in Berlin and Moscow yield no trace. They were in Berlin when the operation was developed. It is unlikely, although possible, that their villa was a production center for the counterfeiting. Yet Cy and Nerma almost certainly knew the two spies at the center of the scheme.

Nick Dozenberg and "Alfred" Tilton were among Moscow's earliest espionage agents in the United States. Both were Soviet military intelligence officers, and like their boss in Moscow, General Jan Berzin, Latvians. Dozenberg was sixteen years older than Cy. He had emigrated from czarist Russia in 1904 and, as an early activist among the Latvian workers in Boston, had helped found the American party. Dozenberg was recruited for clandestine work in the winter of 1927, only months ahead of Cy, and was soon transferred to New York. He had arrived in the city, on a Soviet stipend of thirty-five dollars a week, just as Cy and Nerma were preparing to leave for Berlin.

Tilton was much younger, only a year older than Cy. Yet he had recruited Dozenberg and now served as his boss in New York. Perhaps it was coincidence, but Tilton and his wife, Maria, had arrived in New York from France on November 2, 1926, two weeks before Cy returned from his first European assignment. And then in the spring of 1928, just as Cy and Nerma were settling into their villa, Tilton visited Berlin. The available evidence is scant, but it is difficult to imagine how Cy could not have encountered both men.

In retrospect, it is remarkable that the Soviets almost got away with the counterfeiting scheme. Even Walter Krivitsky, then the head of Soviet military intelligence in Europe, had gone to his boss, General Berzin, to complain of the risks. Krivitsky later fled to the West, but in the summer of 1930 he remained loyal and ready to risk his life for the revolution. "A few million dollars' worth of currency can accomplish nothing substantial today," he said, "except to damage the prestige of the state that prints them." General Berzin only replied with a question: "Didn't Napoleon print British banknotes?"

The scheme would have been absurd but for the quality of the notes. In New York, Dozenberg had procured—by means that remain unknown to this day—the paper stock used at the U.S. Mint. Even American bank tellers had trouble detecting the fake bills. Treasury agents in Washington later declared them "the most genuine-appearing counterfeits ever uncovered."

The Soviets had not only taken care to cover their tracks, they had exploited the chaos of the Weimar economy. By the fall of 1929, the Center had secretly bought Sass & Martini, one of Berlin's oldest private banks. Moscow used a front, a group of "American promoters" who claimed to own Canadian gold mines. Before long, of course, the Americans dropped out, and the bank's shares changed hands several times. In the end they came to rest with one Paul Roth, a former Communist deputy on the Berlin city council.

The money trail began on December 10, 1929, when $19,000 in false bills entered the Sass & Martini tills. The bank deposited them with Deutsche Bank, which in turn sent them on to the National City Bank of New York (the future Citibank). Soon counterfeit notes were trickling into the U.S. Treasury from Shanghai, Havana, Montreal, Bucharest, and even New York.

·

AS CY AND NERMA BEGAN THEIR SECOND SPRING IN BERLIN, THE TEN- sion spiraled higher. For the Communists, the Social Democrats remained the present danger. Fearful of attack on their left flank and eager to end the fight for the trade unions, the Social Democrats had become the party of repression in the capital. But each month, the storm in the south grew closer.

The Nazis, on a shrill voice and the promise of national resurrection, were on the ascent. In Berlin, Goebbels now sabotaged the Communists and Social Democrats—to him, they were all "Marxists," both rivals for the support of the working class and enemies to be eliminated. Hitler had long made his intentions clear. In the failed Munich beer hall putsch of November 1923, days after the bloody debacle in Hamburg, he had fired a pistol shot into the air and shouted, "The national revolution has begun!" The march on Munich had left more than a dozen Brownshirts dead and their leader jailed, but Hitler had used prison to his advantage. He emerged from jail at the end of 1924 and within a year published the first volume of *Mein Kampf.*

In the spring of 1929, the Communists were already endangered. In part it was their fault. They looked to the horizon and overlooked the widening gulf between their leaders, an intellectual clique in the capital, and the rest of the country. But then the Berlin police went on the attack. Months earlier the Social Democrats had banned Communist rallies. On May Day, though, when the party loyalists took to the streets anyway, the police stormed in. The violence lasted three days. Cy and Nerma witnessed the worst bloodshed in Berlin since the murders of Liebknecht and Luxemburg. More than thirty marchers were killed. *Blutmai*, Bloody May, as the Communists called the attacks, presaged the dark future.

WITHIN MONTHS the counterfeiting operation began to unspool. On January 23, 1930, while false $100 bills were beginning to surface in Berlin, the *Berliner Tageblatt* broke the story. Days before, the police had raided Sass & Martini, discovered that it was a Soviet front, and helped launch a worldwide investigation. Soon the scandal hit New York. The bills were flooding into U.S. banks as well. "Counterfeit $100 banknotes," the *New York Times* reported on January 30, "formed the topic of conversation today in banking circles and on the stock exchange." The extent of the scheme astounded investigators. Banks and shell companies across Europe, America, and even China were involved. Months passed as European bankers and U.S. Treasury agents joined forces with the intelligence services of half a dozen countries to follow the paper trail. Yet by then it was too late. General Berzin's men and women had passed more than $10 million in counterfeit notes.

Cy and Nerma had been in Berlin two years when the scandal began to fill the city's newspapers. In the first days of April, they made plans to abandon the villa in Zehlendorf. One morning Cy took the tram into the center of town, to the American Passport Office on Wilhelmstrasse. At the time, U.S. passports were valid for just two years. But on April 4, Cy had no trouble obtaining a new one, No. 730. He and Nerma repeated the procedures they had followed in New York. They took precautions, making sure to visit the passport office separately. Three days later, after enough time had passed, Nerma went to get hers.

By then the fear had settled in for good. Berliners could no longer avoid the Brownshirts. At the university, young Nazis heckled lecturers. Across Berlin, they manned the street corners and toured cafés, rattling collection boxes. That fall in the national elections, Hitler would obtain victory. In May 1928, the Nazis had received 800,000 votes. In September 1930, they polled 6.4 million. To the disbelief of sober-minded Germans, the 12-member Nazi contingent in the Reichstag would jump to 107 deputies. The march was on.

■

CY RAN INTO SIDNEY HOOK AGAIN, AT THE UNIVERSITY. WHETHER driven by loneliness or by intellectual hunger, Cy had decided to take the risk and break the rules. He started to attend Arthur Rosenberg's lectures on ancient history. Had they known, the men from the Center would have seethed. Until recently, Rosenberg had been among the most vocal of the Communist deputies in the Reichstag. In April 1927 he had quit the party, even daring to write an open letter to Stalin asking him to dissolve the Comintern.

For Cy, it was an opportunity he could not miss. Rosenberg had been forced to take a day job, teaching in a gymnasium. He lectured at the university only at night, and his talks were sparsely attended. Cy stood out. His "splendiferous attire"—suit, spats, and cane—"made him the most conspicuous member of the class," recalled Hook.

Rosenberg would soon write a seminal history of Weimar, but the university had forbidden him to teach contemporary German history. Cy believed that he was doing it anyhow. Sidney was not persuaded, but Cy was convinced that Rosenberg was teaching two courses at once, using Roman history "as a parable for modern times."

Throughout Sidney's year in Berlin, Cy saw him often. Nearly each week, as Hook remembers it, they got together. Each time the initiative came from Cy. He would call but never give his telephone number. They would meet with their wives in the city, mostly at out-of-the-way locales, and sometimes at the villa.

Sidney did have more news from Moscow. In the summer of 1928, his mentor from Columbia, the philosopher John Dewey, had visited the USSR for the first time. Cy would have been desperate to hear the impressions of America's most eminent philosopher. Dewey, moreover, had been in Moscow, by chance, during the Comintern congress. En route to Vienna, he wrote to his favorite student of his exhilaration:

July 25

Dear Sidney,

. . . It has been infinitely interesting here—a tremendous vitality—Something big is really happenning [sic]—of that I am sure, tho I don't understand things at all fundamentally, & am perplexed It would take a long residence & a speaking knowledge really to understand, but the perplexity is of a stimulating & not a depressing kind—It is immensely stimulating intellectually—to live in a country that has a definite philosophy of life—I feel that the theory is important more as a set of symbols, functions in a practical movement, than as the essential thing, & that the actual outcome may be something quite different from the symbolic formulations—Any way from my own standpoint I am sure I have been mislead [sic] by taking the theory too seriously, & not knowing what is going on in life—a genuine & significant rebirth of culture perhaps the greatest the world has ever seen.

Dewey was in good company. Cy and Nerma had heard and read such reports for years. In the Soviet experiment's first decade, many pilgrims from the West had told of the new "vitality," from John Reed and Arthur Ransome just after the revolution to Scott Nearing, Anna Louise Strong, and Maurice Hindus in the mid-1920s. In 1925, Nearing had visited the USSR and written, "I wish Greenwich Village could be toured around Russia for a few months. There is more actual construction of stations, factories, houses, etc. going on in Russia—twice over—than in any other country I have seen."

In New York, Cy and Nerma had watched as interest in the USSR soared. Even before the stock market crashed in October 1929, journals and newspapers were flooded with advertisements enticing enthusiasts to visit the Soviet paradise. One, placed by the travel department of the Amalgamated Bank, ran in *The Nation*:

GO TO SOVIET RUSSIA

Intellectuals, social workers, professional men and women are welcomed most cordially in Soviet Russia . . . where the world's most gigantic social experiment is being made—amidst a galaxy of picturesque nationalities, wondrous scenery, splendid architecture and exotic civilizations.

In June 1929, Hook, too, made the trip. He went to Moscow, he later said, less as a pilgrim than as a scholar, a philosopher keen to see nineteenth-century ideas come alive. Still, a postcard to his mother in New York, dated June 24, 1929, carried a distinct note of infatuation:

> *This is Moscow—bizarre and gorgeous—a city of startling contrasts—carrying ugly scars of the past and seeds of the future. Food is mean and clothes are rather shabby—but every brick, every road, every machine is a symbol of the new spirit. I have seen no Potemkin village. Just mingling with the people has enabled me to tap veins of enthusiasm that run deep under the surface of things. And just think of it! A country in which the red flag is the national banner and the International the national anthem.*

Sidney arrived in Moscow in the wake of the second and final battle between Lovestone and Foster. Given the stakes involved and his friend's thirst for news, it is hard to imagine that he would not have been eager to take the news home to Berlin and enlighten Cy.

By then the rumblings had made it to Berlin. The war for the leadership of the American party was over. In New York in March 1929, the Workers Party had held its sixth convention. At last, the Workers (Communist) Party of America dropped its mask, becoming the Communist Party of the USA, the CPUSA. The Comintern tried to install Foster as general secretary and failed. Lovestone had regained the upper hand, with 90 percent of the delegates backing him. After the convention, the Comintern summoned the American factions to return to Moscow. To sort out "the American mess" once and for all, Stalin convened a second American Commission, this time of his making. The commission had a dozen members. Eight were Soviets, and one was Stalin.

On April 12, 1929, the new American Commission met in the Comintern headquarters on Mokhovaya. For nearly a month the

Lovestonites and Fosterites engaged in a burlesque of charge and countercharge. By May 6, Stalin had had enough. The Americans would now see the Leader up close for the first time. Stalin had sat on the stage throughout the proceedings, behind the dais. Standing, he seemed comically short. He wore his peasant outfit—outsized burlap tunic and knee-high boots. His face was dark and pockmarked. His left arm, as the reports had claimed, was palsied. His mouth was small, half hidden beneath a bushy black mustache. And his eyes, as one of those present later recalled, glowed like the "yellow eyes of a mountain lion."

Stalin had bided his time. "Who do you think you are?" he shouted at the Americans. "Trotsky defied me. Where is he? Zinoviev defied me. Where is he? Bukharin defied me. Where is he? And you! Who are you? Yes, you will go back to America. But when you get there, nobody will know you except your wives."

It was a classic Stalin trump. He had turned on his allies and backed his critics. By day's end, the verdict was clear. Lovestone and Gitlow, who had come to Moscow buoyant, would be sent home and kicked out of the party.

Nineteen twenty-nine was the dividing line. By the end of the year, Trotsky was exiled from the USSR. The Wall Street crash should have swelled the ranks of the American party, but by 1930 it had only seven thousand registered members. At the same time the party leaders had divorced themselves from the rank and file of American labor. Foster, moreover, did not rise after Lovestone's fall. He now ruled the party but was captive to Stalin. The Comintern had hedged his power, imposing a secretariat of four. By 1929, Foster's most salient talent was obvious: his ability to toe the party line.

■

IN HIS MEMOIR, WRITTEN FROM A GREAT REMOVE, HOOK WAS CAREFUL to note that he felt no sympathy for Cy and Nerma, only pity. He saw them as victims of their own ambition. "We not only responded to their human need for companionship," he wrote. "We felt under positive obligation to see them." Cy and Nerma lived, as Hook remembered it, "in mortal fear." They were still "true Communist believers" but already seemed trapped.

During one visit to the villa, Nerma took Sidney and Carrie into her confidence. Years later, perhaps she regretted it. But on that night in Berlin the words poured forth. Maybe it was emotion, the elation of a spontaneous reunion so far from home. Nerma said how she yearned to return to the United States, to take her place again in the American party. Hoping to be sent back to New York, she had taken an enormous risk: she had become pregnant.

As Nerma laid out the details, the story brought tears. It was a horrible mistake, she said. Not the pregnancy—she and Cy had been married four years; it was time to have children. No, she said, she been wrong to tell the Russians.

In those days, the Center did not issue field manuals to agents. It was simply understood that children were discouraged. In the business of espionage, babies were seen as inconvenient accessories, demanding time and attention. Infants also made it hard to move on a moment's notice and, more important, difficult to escape the attention of strangers and the police.

Nerma had shared the news with their handlers before it was too late. Abortions were illegal in Germany. Even at the height of Weimar, Catholicism and conservative mores trumped the liberalism of the day. Every year, thousands of German women left the country to end unwanted pregnancies. The decision could not have been easy, but Nerma had followed orders.

Whether she underwent the operation in Berlin or was forced to travel outside, she did not say. But as her friends listened to the story, the toll of her sacrifice became clear. The young renegade, the voluble rebel who on the streets of the Lower East Side had always put passion above reason, now seemed captive. Nerma was no longer committed to the cause; it owned her. The years in Berlin had drawn a deadbolt across her old life, and there could be no return. Her future and now Cy's belonged to the Center.

One day Cy stopped going to Rosenberg's lectures. He had aban-doned the university, and his friends from New York. There would be no more visits to the villa, no more rendezvous on the Kurfürsten-damm, and no more telephone calls. Sidney Hook never saw Cy Oggins again.

Prisoners building the White Sea Canal, 1930s.

GULAG: 1940

■

CY HAD NOT HAD MUCH OF A TRIAL. AFTER HIS ARREST IN FEB-
ruary 1939, he endured nearly a year in the Lubyanka before
the OSO, the *Osoboe soveshchanie*, or Special Tribunal of the
NKVD, at last considered his case. On January 5, 1940, three
men sat behind a table in the Lubyanka and took up the first
matter of the new year, Case No. 85.

The NKVD tribunals were led by men in dark uniforms,
men with stony faces and leaden eyes. The officer who
spoke—this was his show—was the deputy chief of the
NKVD. He read from the stack of reports in front of him,
relating the salient highlights from the "investigation" of the
American prisoner, before coming to the charges: "espionage"
and "treason."

It was all, as Cy surely knew, just a formality. The interrogations had been an exercise in fortnightly absurdity. Rarely
had more than two weeks passed before the guards returned
and collected him again, leading him down to the interrogator's office. When the officer finished, Cy had yet to say a
word. His fate had been decided long in advance. After all, he
had given the NKVD men little to discuss. It was not the fault
of the interrogator. Lieutenant Goldman had tried his best,
but Cy refused to budge.

CY'S KGB FILE contains transcripts of their meetings. Lieutenant Goldman, like many of the officers in Stalin's secret
police, was Jewish. Yet he revealed little sympathy for the foreign prisoner. To him, Cy was a traitor. Evidence of a crime
against the Soviet state was irrelevant. In the months after Cy's

arrest, the two had formed an awkward routine. It was an interminable dance that had been rehearsed in the Lubyanka for years, and tragically perfected.

May 9, 1939, offered a typical performance. The guards came without notice to wake Cy in his cell and deliver him to Lieutenant Goldman.

"You were arrested for treasonous activities," the interrogator began, before asking flatly, "Which foreign intelligence service were you working for?"

Cy had heard the questions for months. He knew all the lines, the lieutenant's and his own, by rote.

"I never performed any treasonous activities," he said. "And I was never involved in any anti-Soviet organizations."

"Our investigation has already uncovered enough material to implicate you in treasonous activities," the interrogator went on. "We would suggest that you confess to the charges made against you."

"But I never engaged in any anti-Soviet work," Cy said.

"You're not telling the truth. We would recommend that you quit these stubborn denials."

"But I'm only telling you the truth."

"In that case," said Lieutenant Goldman, "during the course of our investigation we'll uncover the concrete facts of your treasonous activity."

"But you cannot have such facts," said Cy, "because I never engaged in any anti-Soviet actions."

On it went, for months. Cy always faced the same man, Lieutenant Goldman, and the routine never seemed to vary. To each accusation, Cy parried directly, and always in the negative.

Cy's KGB file, even what little of it the archivists released to his son, Robin, revealed the absurdity of the Soviet bureaucracy. The Lubyanka was a cavernous hall of mirrors and horrors. The interrogations, whether they lasted weeks, months, or years, inevitably led to a single result: bloodshed. The officers and guards paid little regard to logic, compassion, or even common sense. Yet even in the

Lubyanka there were rules, and no matter how absurd, the rules were obeyed.

Cy had been in prison for nearly two months when Lieutenant Goldman sought formal permission to continue his "investigation." On April 10, 1939, he passed the Oggins case up the chain of command to his boss. Major Nikolai Ivanovich Makarov, at thirty-three, had risen fast. A native of Leningrad, he spent his youth in factories before joining the secret police at twenty-two, in 1929. By the spring of 1939, when he considered Cy's fate, Makarov was one of the Lubyanka's most proficient interrogators, deputy chief of its Investigation Division. How many lives the major had already ended is unknown. The figure surely numbered not in the hundreds but thousands.

On the day Cy's file arrived on his desk, Major Makarov carefully reviewed it and scrawled his name across the first page, marking it "AFFIRMED." Two weeks later, Cy's pretrial detention was extended, "for further investigation," until June. In time the Lubyanka bosses gave the interrogators another six months, holding Cy until January 1940.

The interrogators had failed, but they succeeded all the same. For nearly a year they had tried to pry a confession from the American, without success. At the trial, the three NKVD officers of the Special Tribunal even heard the truth—"The accused has refused to confess." They learned, too, that "the investigation yielded no evidence to confirm the guilt of the accused." The admission, dutifully recorded in Cy's KGB file, was remarkable, but hardly an obstacle. Even absent a confession and any incriminating evidence, the tribunal had no trouble reaching a verdict.

It was a half-page document—two typewritten sentences—that foretold Cy's fate. "OGGINS, Isai Saimonovich," born 1898, "Jew, American citizen," was "to be sentenced to a term of EIGHT years for espionage." The term would begin as of the day of arrest, and the verdict was final. Stamped with the seal of the People's Commissariat for Internal Affairs, it was signed by the head of the secretariat of the OSO, the NKVD Special Tribunal, Ivanov.

Ten days later, on January 15, 1940, Cy was taken down to the interrogator one last time. He was not given an opportunity to speak, only a fountain pen. A prison translator read the verdict aloud and asked the prisoner to acknowledge that he was "familiar with the findings" of the tribunal. Cy picked up the pen and wrote his name with care, first in English, "I. Oggins," and then in Russian, slowly, in tentative Cyrillic, "Ogins, Sai Saimonovich."

AFTER THE GUARDS had returned him to his cell, Cy asked for a pen and paper. It was all he could do. Even in the Lubyanka they permitted letters. He would send a final plea to Vyacheslav Molotov, the Soviet foreign minister and Stalin's right-hand man. Hoping against hope, Cy weighed his chances. Molotov was a worldly man with an intelligent face. Countless others had written to the foreign minister in the past. If anyone would intervene on their behalf, they believed, Molotov would. It was not a question of mercy or clemency. The enlightened foreign minister would see right away that it was a mix-up, all a terrible mistake.

The next day, though, Cy awoke to find that the nightmare had darkened. The guards came early. Without any ceremony—no farewell to his keepers, no final words from his interrogator—Cy was taken from his cell. They did not bother to return his suitcase, the belongings that he had lost on the night they arrested him in the Moskva. In an instant, the Lubyanka was behind him.

The guards again threw Cy into the rear of the *voronka*, the crow. Where they were going, no one told him. In the rear of the paddy wagon, he could see only darkness. But by then the prisoner knew. He was heading to the station.

ON JANUARY 16, 1940, Cy was packed off from Moscow in an *etap*, as the shipments of prisoners were called. Nearly every day now the convoys left Moscow. Once sentenced, inmates were sent en masse from the capital in prison trains. The trains were specially outfitted: iron bars blocked the windows, barbed wire ran along the roofs, and guards rode at either end. Almost always they departed in darkness and headed east.

Cy was sent from Moscow in a special convoy run by the NKVD's Convoy Regiment No. 236. He was kept alone, locked in a separate prison carriage, in isolation. He was even assigned his own guard, the head of a convoy brigade, Comrade Tselyshchev. It was not simply because he was an American citizen. Cy had been designated an "especially dangerous prisoner."

From Moscow, the convoy headed south. As the train barreled on, the snow seemed to fall more heavily. At the stations along the way, even from inside the locked carriages, the prisoners could make out the routine: men and women swaddled in heavy coats walked the platforms, shoveling the snow as they went. Cy's convoy was headed for Ryazan, only a hundred miles southeast of Moscow. More often than not, the prison trains were given the rails at night. Soldiers, tanks, and heavy machinery took precedence. The trip, only the first leg of Cy's journey, took ten days. From Ryazan, the train headed for central Russia. As February neared, it arrived at the edge of the steppes, at Oryol, a town bounded by endless fields of wheat, now frozen white.

Cy could not see the city. The authorities rarely let the trains stand for long in the stations, and the guards kept the men out of sight and under lock inside the train, day and night. The guardians of the gulag did not consider it wise to let Soviet citizens witness their former comrades' departure for the labor camps. In all, the Soviets built 476 camps across the USSR. By the time Cy left the Lubyanka, nearly 2 million men and women were in prison or internal exile, and the NKVD provided the livelihood for 100,000 guards. A new saying, one rarely heard in public, had gained currency: "All of Russia was in camps."

Within days, once the word came, the train moved on from Oryol. Comrade Tselyshchev turned Cy over to Comrade Savalyev, a gulag officer, and together they now headed due east. Through the half-slats uncovered by iron, Cy could see the landscape slowly shift. This far from Moscow, the towns became settlements, and the fields in between were untracked swaths blanketed with drifts that rose above a man's waist. It was weeks before they reached the foothills of the

Urals, the spine of Russia. Once they had cleared the mountains, the train car filled with light—one long uninterrupted line of white.

They had arrived at last in Siberia. Jacques Rossi, the French survivor of the gulag, remembered it his whole life—"How beautiful the land of terror was!" Siberia, the prisoners now saw, was not only a place of persecution. The world's largest penal colony was also a land of ghostly beauty. The train hurtled on, sometimes coming to a sudden dead halt in the dark of a forest. Outside there were no sounds, no signs of life save the trees. On it went for weeks, before at last the air grew acrid and the horizon turned gray. At the outskirts of Krasnoyarsk, a grim city of smelters and factories at Siberia's western edge, the convoy came to rest. When the guards unlocked the carriages, the prisoners were rewarded with an unexpected sight—water. Before them darkly churned the Yenisei, the great river that begins near Mongolia and runs north to the Arctic Sea, nearly cleaving Siberia in two. It was late in the winter of 1940.

CY NOW FEARED the worst. From the banks of the Yenisei, smokestacks two rows deep belched black smoke across the water. Amid the mud and chaos, in the shadow of the metal plants that fed Stalin's war machine, tens of thousands of prisoners waited. Few stayed here long. Krasnoyarsk was not a final destination. It was a way station, swollen far beyond capacity, for the camps farther on.

By now rumor had turned to fact: the Moscow convoy was heading north. Even amid the squalor of the *tranzitka*, the massive transit camp that filled the eastern bank of the Yenisei, it was plain to see. The Yenisei would be their Styx. Cy's convoy would be piled onto one of the rusting barges that lined the river. From the *tranzitka* of Krasnoyarsk, the guards took only the Moscow convoys, the ones overloaded with the "special prisoners," soon to be known as "politicals," to the northernmost camps of the gulag archipelago, at Norilsk.

Whether at its birth in the 1930s or at its peak after the war, Norilsk inspired fear like no other place in Russia. Even in the darkened cells of the Lubyanka, the prisoners had spoken of it. The gulag had no shortage of horrors, but the camps of Norilsk—Noril'lag, they

called it for short—stood apart. Hundreds of miles north of the Arctic Circle, prisoners endured not only a camp sentence but a climate
unfit for human habitation.

The barge trip alone, nearly a month on the Yenisei from the
transit camp, was a torture that many did not survive. Cy suffered it
down below, in the hold. Beneath the waterline it was hard to sit in
the dark without praying for the journey to end. Suicide, however,
was rarely an option. Amid the mass of bodies, you could scarcely tell
one man's arm from another's leg. Hundreds were packed in close.
Each man got a *paika,* rations that consisted of a hard square of black
bread and a tin cup of watery bouillon. On good days, the soup might
hold a floating fishbone. With scant food and no windows, little separated day from night. It was not long before the men lost count of
the days. The guards on occasion threw down a *parasha,* but few of the
prisoners bothered to use the metal buckets. The stench grew
unbearable. They urinated and defecated in the dark corners.

The trip downriver covered more than a thousand miles. Rarely
did the small steamer pulling the barge chug faster than a few miles
per hour, and often, like the train, it would slow to a halt and anchor
at the river's edge for days. In the darkness of the hold thoughts
turned, almost inevitably, to the worst. In the Lubyanka, death had
seemed random. Cy had never known whom the guards would come
for, or when. Yet as the convoy edged north, a certainty neared.
Death would find them all, one way or another.

At last the barge reached Dudinka, the supply port for Norilsk
and a forbidding entrance to a veritable hell on earth. Emaciated and
exhausted, the prisoners emerged, struggling to put one foot in front
of the other. Their skin was gray with the pallor of prison. Their
clothes stank of sweat, urine, and excrement. Squinting at the sun,
they stepped slowly onto the planks. The dock, already rotting, felt as
if it could buckle. The men looked up and saw giant cranes studding
the steep embankment. For several years, in a feat of Soviet engineering, Dudinka received cargo ships. Stalin had ordered icebreakers to
open the Northern Route, the frozen seas separating the Yenisei
from Murmansk, the Arctic port to the west. Everywhere along the

riverbank, men wearing *telogrekas,* the thin cotton jackets of the camps, unloaded supplies. To the men emerging from the hold, it seemed that the docks were covered with crates.

The men of the Moscow *etap* formed a long line that snaked along the shore. Above them loomed a tower of steel: a statue of Lenin, silvery and gargantuan, that peered down on the ships. Standing front to back in the open air, the prisoners looked nearly identical and anonymous. It was as if they had already lost their features, and like a man caught between two mirrors, their faces seemed to repeat without end.

In Dudinka the authorities did the sorting. The bosses arrived from Norilsk to inspect the new *etap*. Every so often, as a clerk shouted out a series of numbers, a prisoner would leave the line. The numbers were stitched on the left side of his shirt. One by one, the men from the barge disappeared inside the building beside the pier. The processing could last for days. Every prisoner sent to Norilsk had to undergo a medical examination before he could enter the camps.

Stalin, far more than Hitler, appreciated the value of slave labor. Prisoners were sent to the camps not to die but to work. Lavrenty Beria, Stalin's secret police chief, who was given the task of running the gulag in late 1938, had devised a cynical formula. Prisoners would be sorted by their health and fed according to their work. By the winter of 1940, Cy's limp was pronounced. He could not hide it, nor did he want to. Inside the building, he was stripped naked. Once the exam was over, he was told to join the shorter line. For Cy, it would be a relief to be designated a second-class prisoner. He now stood among those who had been deemed unfit for hard labor.

He would, of course, still have to work. There were not enough *zeks* to keep pace, building factories, plants, offices, and apartment blocks to house the guards. But Cy would be spared the mines and quarries. The darkest horrors were reserved for the first-class prisoners, the ones who had come to Norilsk in the prime of their lives.

■

THE AMERICAN WAS ELEVEN YEARS OLDER THAN THE FRENCHMAN. CY and Jacques Rossi met early on in Cy's time in the Arctic. For a while, first in Dudinka and then in Norilsk, Cy and Jacques saw each other often. In Dudinka, foreign prisoners were kept together in a camp along the river just north of the growing town. Jacques had met other Frenchmen, two or three. There were other nationalities as well—Koreans, Afghans, even Japanese. But in 1940, there was only one American in the camps.

Cy was friendly, Jacques remembered half a century later, but not a friend. He was a comrade, another fallen member of the old brotherhood, yet somehow whenever time allowed and the Frenchman dared to probe, Cy always kept his guard high. The American did not want to tell stories—that was clear from the first. Cy told Jacques of his years in New York, of Columbia, the Village, and his wife. Details, however, rarely trespassed into their talks. There was no talk of his travels, associations, or loves. Even in the camps, he still looked stubbornly to the future. It was as if a cloud hung over the past, darkening Cy's memories. The American liked to keep to himself, and the others learned not to press him. Cy, it seemed, felt that to speak, even in the camps, even at the end of the earth when all around faced the worst, was to give himself away.

Cy and Jacques never knew when they would meet. Weeks would pass without their seeing one another. In Dudinka, some prisoners worked the piers and others the construction sites that sprawled across town. Whether they unloaded cargo or helped build apartment blocks for the guards, all prisoners worked in shifts around the clock. There was nothing else to do. At breakneck pace, the engineers of the gulag were building cities in the Arctic.

Cy had arrived in poor shape. He was gaunt and weak, and a mysterious ailment—"something to do with the nerves," he told Jacques—had stiffened one leg. Whether it was an injury or an illness, it had happened in prison or earlier. The leg slowed him, but Cy had lost none of his resolve. He knew well where he had arrived. For months Cy maintained his silence, letting Jacques and the others guess at his past, but he knew the odds.

"It's the end of the line," he told Jacques not long after they met. Somewhere along the journey east, in a cell or a transit camp, Cy had heard the stories. No one, they said, ever got out of the Norilsk camps.

When I spoke with Jacques, he could no longer remember the

month he and Cy had met, but he was certain it was "before the war broke out"—before June 22, 1941, the day Hitler turned against Stalin and discarded their 1939 Non-Aggression Pact.

It was the beginning of Barbarossa, the Nazi attack that stunned Stalin and left his generals staggering. On the war's first day, the Soviet air force lost more than a thousand planes. In Moscow, Russians learned of Hitler's about-face from loudspeakers in the streets, as Molotov announced the news on Radio Moscow. Stalin, who had refused to believe the warnings, had disappeared behind the fortress walls of his dacha in the woods outside the city. Fear seized the capital, and the unimaginable took hold: the Leader seemed vulnerable, and the Bolshevik experiment endangered. News of the attack even made it north of the Arctic Circle, to the prisoners who slept on wooden slats, three bunks high, in wind-bent barracks.

Cy, though, was imprisoned in a Stalinist miracle. Norilsk lies north of the 69th Parallel. Before the prisoners came, there was little around but the native peoples of the tundra, reindeer, and fields of snow, ice, and permafrost. No neighboring towns, railroad tracks, or roads. There were not even trees—at least, none that anyone from the "mainland," the rest of Russia, had ever seen. The tundra was dotted with dwarf pines, twisted stumps that grew no taller than a man. Winter lasted nine months a year, and the calendar was divided between polar nights and polar days, when the sun either never set or never appeared. Amid the white desert, few could expect to survive.

But Norilsk was not all guards, dogs, and watchtowers. The geologists' first settlement had long since yielded to an industrial labyrinth, a complex of mines, smelters, and camps. Since the days of Peter the Great more than two centuries earlier, the tundra was known to hold deep seams of coal. In the 1920s, Lenin's geologists had discovered precious metals—platinum and silver, nickel, gold, and copper. Before long, Dzerzhinsky, founder of the Cheka, the Bolshevik secret police and KGB precursor, set his sights on the far north. On May Day 1925, *Izvestia* printed his speech at the Sixteenth Party Conference. "The question of ferrous metals," Dzerzhinsky told the delegates, "is the most fundamental for our industrial economy." By 1935, Stalin had set forth a plan to raise the riches from beneath the permafrost. Following a blueprint both impossible and absurd, he ordered his engineers to build a city to mine the Arctic. Within months the first prison barge, with 1,200 men abroad, docked at Dudinka. In early 1939, a year before Cy arrived, Norilsk turned out its first copper and nickel.

When Cy was first led to his barracks, the Norilsk camps held more than 30,000 prisoners. The old shacks remained, long, lean barracks scarcely wide enough for four rows of bunks, but a small city had grown around the camps—whole blocks of apartments for the officers, guards, and their families, as well as schools, a hospital, even a single-runway airport. In time the prison labor force swelled to nearly 100,000, and Norilsk became the most prodigious metal producer in the USSR. Whether they worked aboveground, in the factories filled with the blazing heat of the gargantuan ovens, or belowground in the mines nearly a mile beneath the permafrost, all faced the same fate.

CY WAS EVENTUALLY thrown into a "mixed camp," where politicals and hardened criminals—thieves, rapists, and murderers—lived side by side. Only later, when Moscow ordered the "special camps" built after the war, did they sift out the politicals from the criminals. In 1940, among the political prisoners, Norilsk was home to an elite. Beria's secretary was there, as was the sister of Yagoda, the former head of the NKVD. So, too, was Blagoi Popov, the Bulgarian Communist accused with Dmitrov, the Comintern boss, of burning the Reichstag. Arrested in the fall of 1938, Popov had confessed but got fifteen years in the camps all the same.

As a second-class prisoner, Cy was exempted from hard labor. Thousands of *zeks* worked outside the camps. In all likelihood he was made to work in one of the service plants that fed the *Kombinat*—an electrical station, a uniform factory, or even the camp hospital. The particulars of how Cy spent his working hours are lost to history—or, more precisely, to the Soviet bureaucracy.

The guardians of the Norilsk gulag kept a camp card for every prisoner. The index cards were small but offered handwritten details of when and how each inmate spent his years in the camps. Half a century later, the Norilsk cards remained in Krasnoyarsk, locked away in the vaults of the regional headquarters of the Interior Ministry, the law enforcement body that eventually inherited the camps. Even more than fifty years after Cy's time in Norilsk, even after the fall of the USSR, the camp cards remained off-limits.

One Russian researcher, though, had seen Cy's card. Volodya Birger, an amateur historian and volunteer at the local branch of the Memorial Society, enjoyed rare access for a time to the ministry archives in Krasnoyarsk. Before the rise of Putin, when the premium on secrecy again set in, the officers had made a rare accommodation. They had allowed Birger to thumb through the Norilsk camp cards, more than 100,000 in all. He saw Cy's card but did not bother to copy it. A year later, when an official inquiry was submitted, the clerks at the ministry responded quickly. They had searched the Norilsk archives but not found any card for an American prisoner named Oggins. No such record, they replied, ever existed.

■

"IT WAS NOT A FAVOR," JACQUES RECALLED AS AN OLD MAN IN PARIS. "IT was a duty to keep a gulag promise." That was why, he said, "when I got out, one of the first things I did was contact Oggins's wife."

Jacques was one of the lucky ones, a veteran of Norilsk who survived and escaped the USSR. After Norilsk, however, he endured another seven years in a Siberian jail before Khrushchev revisited the crimes of Stalinism during the "thaw" of the 1950s. After Siberia, Jacques was sent to "internal exile," a purgatory that lasted another five years, in Samarkand, the ancient city in the Soviet republic of Uzbekistan. Looking back, he called his Uzbek years "the happiest times of his life." It was from Samarkand, in the mid-1950s, that Jacques had written to Nerma—"Norma Barron," as he called her then.

Even talking to Jacques, a fellow comrade and a fellow spy, Cy had never said he had served as a Soviet agent and never mentioned his work in Europe or elsewhere. He had only sought help from the

Frenchman. Fearing that his health would not hold and he would not survive the Arctic, Cy had gone to Jacques with a plea. "Get a message out," he told him. "If you can, get the word out that I am here."

Cy gave Jacques only the barest details. He told him that he was a professor of history at Columbia and that his wife, Norma Barron, of 874 Saratoga Avenue, Brooklyn, New York, must get an SOS from the camps. But Cy did not tell Jacques that it was not his wife's real name or her true address.

When Jacques sent a postcard to Norma Barron at the Brooklyn address, "something strange" happened, something that had always troubled him. "The wife wrote back," he said, "but she was confused." She told of "meeting me in Paris. But I'd never met her in Paris, or anywhere else. I had, in fact, never met Oggins before Norilsk."

It was a common mistake, Jacques said. "In the underground we all used aliases. It was easy to get mixed up." Nerma, he said, must have confused him with someone else. "Someone she'd worked with in that other life, in Paris."

Cy Oggins, Paris, ca. 1931.

CHAPTER 7

THE RED AND THE WHITE

■ ■ ■

Cy AND NERMA LEFT BERLIN IN A HURRY IN THE SPRING OF 1930. If either had harbored doubts before Berlin, they both now knew the terms of their engagement. Paris would mark a step deeper into the underground. By the start of the new decade, many of Cy's former classmates at Columbia had also moved to Paris. Most went to France seeking literary fame or free love. Cy and Nerma went under orders.

In Paris, Cy continued to play the part of the rich American abroad, only now he traded the Friedrich-Wilhelms-Universität for the Sorbonne. As in Berlin, he attended the university but did not enroll. He did, though, change profession. No longer was he an antiquarian. He kept up his studies in art history, but in Paris he became a writer—a ghostwriter, he would reply when asked what kind. For months on end, as he and Nerma settled into the French capital, Cy spent his days at the Bibliothèque Nationale, the national library. He was researching a book, or so the cover story went, on European agricultural economics. Somehow, though, the book, like the Columbia dissertation, never came into being. It remained a convenient fiction, an alibi that opened doors, or shuttered doubts, whenever it was necessary.

In Berlin, Cy and Nerma had proven their worth to the men in the Center. The Americans had not only kept silent but stayed obedient. Above all, Cy and Nerma had maintained the cover for the villa in Zehlendorf. Whether the agents had photographed classified documents, forged $100 bills, or both, the Americans ended their assignment in Germany without setback. On the train out that spring, as they passed the old Saxon barns and the fields gaining color, the forfeited pregnancy no doubt weighed heavily, yet in time they would remember Berlin with nostalgia.

In Paris the couple was given new responsibility and work. Even as they settled into Neuilly-sur-Seine, the prim *ville* just west of Paris, then a leafy suburb with more horses than residents, it was clear that Moscow would now demand all their time. By 1930, Stalin had grown obsessed with two primary enemies abroad: Trotsky, his former rival, and the leaders of the White Russian diaspora, the bourgeois antirevolutionaries who had fled the Bolsheviks and found refuge in Europe. More than 300,000 Russian refugees had resettled in France, the majority of them in the capital. With an aim to infiltrate émigré and Trotskyist circles as well as acquire French military and political secrets, the Center had operated a clandestine network in Paris for nearly a decade.

Cy and Nerma were sent to France on a specific mission. This time they would not merely provide a cover for other operatives. They were ordered to keep a vigil—no one ever used the word "spy"—on the leaders of the White Russian émigré community in France, in particular one vital branch of the fallen imperial family, the Romanovs.

■

WITH RESPONSIBILITY CAME A NEWFOUND CONFIDENCE. IN PARIS, CY and Nerma may have imagined themselves indispensable to Moscow. Or perhaps they merely recognized the obvious—that there would be no negotiation, no compromise, and no way out. Whatever the reason, this time they would go through with it. As their second spring in Paris arrived and the chestnuts of the Tuileries bloomed, nothing could force Nerma, at thirty-three, to terminate her new pregnancy.

Robin Simon Oggins, a baby boy with ginger curls, entered the world on the morning of October 30, 1931. He was born at the American Hospital in Neuilly, a few tree-lined blocks from where Cy and Nerma were living. It was and remains a famous hospital. During the Great War, the Harjes ambulance brigades, where a number of Cy's Columbia classmates had served, were headquartered there.

Although Robin never knew it while his parents were alive, Cy and Nerma gave him a middle name in honor of his grandfather, the Willimantic shopkeeper. His first name, however, remained a mystery. His mother always claimed it bore no significance. The name, she said, had come to her because their bedroom in Neuilly was "decorated with wallpaper covered with robins." Another of "Mom's stories," it left the son less than convinced.

"Robin," of course, could also have been a hopeful yearning, a desire to perpetuate the season of renewed warmth and possibility. After the abortion in Berlin, the birth of a child could have signaled a desire to break free. It could also have been the result of the Ogginses' new confidence, an ease in the underground that had been earned through the sacrifice. Or, perhaps, the name was chosen for its elasticity. "Robin" was androgynous. As Cy and Nerma traveled, the baby could be a boy one week and a girl the next.

More than seventy years later, Robin still got mail, especially from the U.S. government, addressed to "Ms. Robin Oggins." He never bothered to correct the error. Like most things from his remote past, "things that made little sense," Robin simply pushed it to a far corner.

.

CY AND NERMA ARRIVED IN PARIS AT A PROPITIOUS TIME. IN MOSCOW, the bloodlust would come later. The French capital, though, had already become the first battlefield of the Center's overseas war. If in Berlin Stalin sought German military and industrial secrets, in Paris the chief targets were personal. The city was the headquarters of the two groups at the top of Stalin's enemies list: the Russian Combined Military Union, the *Rossiiskii obshchevoinskii soyuz*, or ROVS, as it was known, and Trotsky's disciples, his followers around the world, whose numbers, to the great distress of the man in the Kremlin, had been rising in recent years.

By the winter of 1929, Stalin had decided that for Trotsky, the Kazakh steppes were too close to Moscow. In February, Stalin had Trotksy, along with his wife, Natalia Sedova, and his son, Lev Sedov, packed off again, this time on a boat for Turkey. In 1930 the Old

Man, as the Center had nicknamed Trotsky, had not yet made Stalin's hit list, but he and his entourage had the rapt attention of the OGPU. In Turkey, Trotsky stayed on the island of Prinkipo, today Büyükada. Yet he was only biding time, waiting for the French to allow him to go to Paris.

In the French capital, the ROVS, with nearly 30,000 members, had become the largest organization of White Russian officers abroad. Founded in Serbia in 1924 by General Pyotr Wrangel, the union brought together the rump White Army under the nominal leadership of the heir to the Romanov throne, Grand Duke Nikolai Nikolaievich. After the death of Wrangel in 1928 and the grand duke the following year, the officers' union moved its headquarters to Paris.

By 1930 the Center could no longer stand idle. That year—the year that Cy and Nerma arrived from Berlin—marked the advent of the Soviet practice of kidnapping enemies of the state. The first to disappear was General Kutepov. On January 26, a Sunday morning, Alexander Pavlovich Kutepov, the ROVS commander who had succeeded Wrangel, vanished from the streets of the seventh arrondissement. Amid the boutiques and cafés, a pair of OGPU agents stepped from the crowd and bundled the general into a waiting taxi. Nearby, a French policeman—a party member—stood watch, ensuring that anyone chancing upon the scene would think it an arrest. At home, the Center hailed the kidnapping as "a brilliant operation."

Kutepov, in truth, was an easy mark. He was blind to the political calculus of exile. During the civil war, he had courageously led his troops against the Reds, under the command of Wrangel and another famous White general, Denikin. Among the Russian diaspora in France, Kutepov served as a moral beacon and trusted guardian of the czarist past. But the ROVS was not a robust military operation. Informants and Soviet plants had penetrated the union, as they had penetrated the Liebknecht Haus. They had even infiltrated Kutepov's inner circle. Moreover, for a military man, the general was surprisingly naive. He imagined it possible to sit in his Parisian apartment and raise an anti-Bolshevik rebellion inside Russia. In the winter of 1929, only months before his kidnapping, Kutepov told his former commander Denikin, "Great movements are spreading across Russia! Never have so many people come from 'over there' to see me and ask me to collaborate with their clandestine operations." In fact, the emissaries were agents provocateurs dispatched by the Center.

Nonetheless, Stalin feared Kutepov. The goal of the operation was not "liquidation"; Kutepov would serve no purpose dead. Instead, Stalin wanted the general interrogated. But Kutepov never made it to Moscow. In a port north of Paris, he was packed onto a Soviet freighter, but in sedating him, his kidnappers used too much chloroform. En route to Russia, the general died of a heart attack at sea.

Four days after Kutepov's kidnapping, the Politburo met to review the state of the INO, the *Inostrannyi otdel*, the Lubyanka's foreign intelligence arm. The INO would gain greater scope and powers as the Soviet leadership now targeted three primary regions: Western Europe, the neighboring states of Eastern Europe, and Japan, the ascendant rival in Asia. In the intelligence blueprint for the decade to come, Moscow sought to disentangle and redirect its clandestine services. In time, the "organs" would be separated, streamlined, and refashioned into two main agencies, the OGPU and the GRU, the intelligence service of the Red Army. For the Center, it was an epochal shift. Lenin had focused on Western Europe—Germany, France, and England. Stalin now dreamed of a spy network without borders.

THE YEAR 1930 PROVED pivotal in the history of Soviet espionage overseas. It is not surprising, then, that Cy assumed a greater role in the underground that year, as Moscow expanded its clandestine operations around the world. Spying is one of the world's oldest professions, but in the 1930s the Soviets reaped an espionage harvest that remains unmatched. The decade that opened with the disappearance of one of the revolution's leading opponents would end with an ice axe driven into the head of one of its leaders. For the Center, it was a remarkable string of successes, and it was all due to the rise of the Great Illegals.

In Russian, a spy station in a foreign country is called a *rezidentura* and its chief officer is known as the *rezident*. Since its earliest days,

Soviet intelligence had deployed two subspecies of *rezidents*, "legal" and "illegal." *Legal'nye rezidenty* were spies who headed stations abroad but were tethered to a Soviet embassy, consulate, or trade office. *Nelegal'nye rezidenty*, the illegals, entered a country under a false passport and operated under deep cover, without a fictitious tie to a government office. The life of an illegal, naturally, was considerably more trying than that of a legal *rezident*. Illegals had to maintain a double life: their name, passport, occupation, and biography were all false. Since the early 1920s, the Soviets had dispatched illegals around the globe. But the "Great" ones stood apart. So remarkable were their accomplishments that the CIA in its earliest days made the study of the Soviet Great Illegals an essential part of basic training.

In the fall of 2001, after tracking Cy Oggins for more than a year, I traveled to northern Virginia to visit one of the Agency's first Soviet experts. He was eager to talk of "the beginning"—the days before the cold war. He was an old Russia hand who had entered the Naval Academy in 1942 and learned Russian there, one of the first midshipmen to do so. After serving in the Pacific Fleet during the war, he, too, had gone to Columbia. He was studying at the new Russian Institute and had progressed halfway through a dissertation on Russo-Indian relations when a recruiter arrived from Washington. In 1946, President Truman had created the Central Intelligence Group (CIG), which would pave the way for the CIA. Men who spoke Russian and knew Soviet history were in sudden demand.

The CIA man had a face that was long, outsized. Beneath the unruly strands of gray that shaded his broad forehead, his eyes were a milky blue, nearly opaque. He called himself "one of the dinosaurs," a survivor of the time "when intelligence wasn't yet a game within a game," and he knew a good deal of the untold history of Soviet intelligence in the West. He had not learned it at the CIA. His knowledge had come from the defectors, the Soviet spies whom he had debriefed over more than four decades of service. One lesson stood out. "Before the war the Soviets ran circles around us," he said. "The twenties, the thirties—that was their heyday. And the ones Uncle Joe Stalin had to thank for it were the Great Illegals."

The CIA man sat in an electric wheelchair. In 1955, just months before he was scheduled to receive the Salk vaccine, he had contracted polio. The chair was new, but he had mastered it. Whenever he went to get a book or a newspaper clipping across the room, it whirred loudly. He used to get into Washington with ease but had recently suffered two strokes. Now he rarely left the house. The condominium, one in a row of identical townhouses, was tucked off a highway that cut across the Virginian plains. Inside, it smelled of paint and linoleum. The living room was sparsely furnished but lined with books. In the kitchen, yet more books shingled the counters. The resemblance to Jacques Rossi's apartment in Paris, with its scholarly and spartan feel, was hard to miss.

He had a distinguished career. In the early 1950s, at a secret venue in West Germany, he ran the CIA's Defector Reception Center, the first stop in the West for Soviet citizens who managed to break through the Iron Curtain. From 1951 to 1973, he debriefed nearly every dissident from the USSR and every defector from Soviet intelligence. It was a defector who had given him polio. But it was not deliberate, he said. He and the defector had become friends.

The CIA man was a veteran of accommodation, a scholar with principles and enemies. In government, he did have one great ally: the diplomat George Kennan. He and Kennan were more than ideological comrades, the CIA man said. They had formed a kind of secret compact, a vow, as he put it, "to clear the mud from the windscreen." They had tried to sharpen Washington's focus on the "internal contradictions" in the USSR. The CIA man liked to talk of his kinship with Kennan, the accidental father of "containment," the doctrine of the cold war. It was as if he wished to say that he belonged to another era, a time when intellectuals counted for something in the Agency, when men with brains and knowledge fought America's secret wars.

When he invoked the Great Illegals, it was to speak of a lost tribe, a different class of spies. No police force or counterintelligence body in the West was prepared for their emergence. No one had ever played the game as they did, nor, he added, has anyone played it better since. The Great Illegals were men of intellect, languages, and endurance. They had come of age, to a remarkable extent, in the borderlands of Central Europe. Born between East and West, they were men without nations. They were devoted not to a homeland or to Stalin, or even to Lenin, but to the revolution.

IN MOSCOW, THE GREAT ILLEGALS were seen not as history but as heroes whose feats offered lessons in tradecraft. In the age of Putin, KGB veterans, even the most pro-Western, spoke of them in tones reserved for accomplished ancestors who had never been given their due. Few Russians knew their names, but many of their portraits adorned the "wall of honor" in the headquarters of the SVR, the Foreign Intelligence Service, as the KGB's First Chief Directorate was now called, in the woods of Yasenovo outside Moscow.

The Great Illegals numbered no more than a dozen men and women, yet together they formed the spine of an intelligence network that stretched from Europe to America to Asia. How many hundreds of agents, informers, and couriers they recruited will never be known, but the Great Illegals helped steal a generation of secrets. Contrary to the romantic notions of cold war novelists, the Soviets in the 1920s had no schools for secret agents. The illegals were chosen, as one of their number put it, "for their integrity, talent, and devotion." The best were also masters of seduction. They could ingratiate themselves in any company, whether their interlocutor was a visiting ambassador or a train-station prostitute.

Dmitri Bystrolyotov may have been the most dashing. He ended up in the gulag, sent like Cy to the camps of Norilsk. But he had served the Center with extraordinary devotion and skill. Bystrolyotov liked to claim that he was a descendant of the Tolstoy line and a distant relative of the great writer, but in truth he was born out of wedlock and no birth record survived. Among KGB veterans, Bystrolyotov is most fondly remembered for pioneering the honey trap—the seduction of a foreign target. A report in the SVR archives in Moscow noted his gift: Bystrolyotov "quickly became on close terms with women and shared their beds."

Richard Sorge, often called the Soviets' most accomplished spy, was another illegal with great charm. Born in Baku, the capital of Azerbaijan, in 1895 to a Russian mother and German father, Sorge was more German than Soviet. In World War I he served in the German army, was wounded, and earned a medal for valor. After the war, the labor unrest in Germany and his graduate work in Hamburg, where he studied Marx and Engels, led him to communism. In 1924, Sorge went to Moscow, where he was recruited for espionage. Not only could he pass as a German, but he possessed a magnetism that he never failed to exploit. In 1929, after serving in Europe and the United States, he was sent to Shanghai, where he built the Center's first reliable intelligence network as well as the foundation for a clandestine push into Manchuria. Sorge, however, is most celebrated for his years in Tokyo, where he posed as a Nazi reporter to penetrate the German embassy, earning in KGB circles the sobriquet "the spy of the century." Sorge kept Stalin informed with a string of intelligence coups, among them advance word of the Nazi invasion in 1941. Stalin, however, chose to rely on his instincts and not Sorge.

The Great Illegals were not all men of charisma and sex appeal. Some had to rely on intelligence. Walter Krivitsky, the spy who had dared to question Stalin's counterfeiting scheme in Berlin, could pass as Dr. Martin Lessner, an Austrian antiques dealer based in The Hague. Krivitsky was born Samuel Ginzburg in the town of Podwoloczyska in Galicia. He was one of six Soviet spies, childhood friends and future comrades, who emerged in the interwar years from the pastoral edge of the Austro-Hungarian empire, what is today western Ukraine. The other famous illegal from Podwoloczyska, whose career would nearly mirror Krivitsky's before his fall in a dark wood in Switzerland, was Ignacy Poretsky, alias Ignace Reiss.

The illegals could also be ruthless. Roland Abbiate, for one, was an assassin. Suave and dapper, he was born in Monaco but operated out of Paris during the years that Cy and Nerma were there. If the Americans met Abbiate in Paris, it would explain Nerma's strange reply to Jacques Rossi's postcard from Central Asia. She may have mixed him up with Abbiate. If so, Nerma could be forgiven for the mistake. In Paris, Abbiate went by the alias François Rossi. In Europe, they may have crossed paths with the Great Illegals. But in Asia, Cy would work for one of them.

To the CIA man, the Great Illegals had reshaped the "very nature of foreign intelligence." In the decade leading up to World War II, Soviet intelligence metastasized across Europe. The Center, in the name of fighting "counterrevolutionary sabotage," began to co-opt Comintern agents abroad. It was a hidden but lethal path. The Comintern's clandestine network, the OMS, started to rely on its foreign agents as secret liaisons to their national Communist parties. Before long, almost ineluctably, many were pulled into the ranks of the main secret services, the OGPU and the GRU. It was a burdensome promotion. Young Western idealists who had joined the Comintern to wage the good fight on behalf of the long-suffering masses now found themselves engaged in the black arts of sabotage and terror. The unluckiest few were even given the dirtiest jobs, mokriye dela—what spies term "wet work" and what others call murder.

"When you look back at the history of espionage," the CIA man said, "what's 'offensive' and 'defensive' is a slippery thing. Oftentimes, whether on the American side or the Soviet, the services will say they're only working on defense, when in fact they're moving ahead on offense." It was a catch, he said, "and a hell of a lot of unfortunates got caught in it."

In New York, Cy and Nerma may have imagined they were working for the Comintern. If in Berlin the doubts had somehow failed to surface, by Paris they surely knew. Cy and Nerma had been drawn into Stalin's OGPU.

■

NEUILLY-SUR-SEINE, COUNTRY PLAYGROUND OF PROUST AND BALZAC heroes, is bordered on the north by the Seine and on the south by the Bois de Boulogne. In the spring of 2005, the ville became a showcase for the political future and economic revival of France. Nicolas Sarkozy, a former mayor of nearly twenty years, was on the ascent and before long would become president. In April 2005, Sarkozy's old

Cy Oggins, Robin Oggins, France, ca. 1932.

neighborhood, its trees neatly pruned and sidewalks scrubbed, already seemed in a celebratory mood.

At first Neuilly did not make sense. It was a stretch, to say the least, to imagine an American student living here in 1930. Since the nineteenth century, Neuilly had been a preserve of the rich, a retreat for hunting, horseback riding, and picnicking. Moreover, it was far from the center. The métro did not even reach the *ville* in those days. For Cy to have settled in such a wealthy enclave, at such a distance from the Sorbonne, seemed foolhardy. The Sûreté Générale, the French intelligence service, was on the hunt. The Sûreté had studied the rise of Soviet espionage in Paris since the early 1920s, and no sentient investigator would have believed that Cy was simply another visiting American student.

Rue Chartran is today a ten-minute walk from the métro. A narrow street just one and a half blocks long, it curves sharply like a hook. Lined with elegant apartment houses, none taller than seven stories, and a handful of private homes, the street seems little changed from the years before the war. When I visited, it was the first weekend of spring. The air carried a damp chill, but everyone was out, bundled in sweaters and scarves, to purge their gardens of the remains of winter.

Madame Marise was furiously sweeping her brick walk, head bent behind a tall hedge. The leaves, wet and heavy, resisted her efforts. A short woman in her late seventies, she had an open, ruddy face. When interrupted, she just gestured across the street. "*La fille américaine,*" she said, repeating the words several times. At the townhouse across the way, the door stood ajar. A knock on the glass elicited a beautiful young woman. Whippet-thin, she wore jeans and a half-buttoned cardigan. Juliette spoke English without an accent. Her mother was American, her father French, and as luck would have it, she had just left Columbia with a law degree.

As Juliette translated, Madame Marise told of the old days. She avoided dates, ever careful not to betray the year of her birth, but described in detail how life had been on the rue Chartran in the 1930s. She had been born here. It was a cobblestone street then, lit at night by a single gas lamp on the corner.

Madame Marise spoke in rapid, clipped sentences that conjured up the distant past. In those days, she said, Neuilly was still a village. There were stables nearby, and horse trails throughout the woods. When her father, a successful merchant in the timber trade, built the house, only a handful of others had stood on the block. Number 12 — she pointed across the street — was the sole apartment building. Seven elegant stories high, it had two flats to a floor, and a heavy glass door laced with iron marked the entrance. Number 12 rue Chartran was the building where Cy and Nerma and Robin first lived in France. They moved into a garret apartment beneath the gabled roof. From the street, a set of four tiny windows and a narrow balcony were visible.

Madame Marise had lived here then but could not remember any Americans—no young couple from New York, no infant in a pram. Rue Chartran was now lined with apartment houses, but it was not much use exploring, she said. Hardly anyone from those days remained. "Everyone's gone," she said. "I'm alone here. Except, of course, for Monsieur Romanoff." Once again Madame Marise pointed. This time, though, she directed a long finger at the elbow of the street, to the house in the shadows.

THE HOUSE IN THE CORNER, Number 8, was a four-story red-brick *pavilion*, the Parisian version of a New York brownstone. Half a dozen names, carefully typed out, were taped across the buzzers by the door. Once grand, the house had long since been chopped into flats. One buzzer stood out. It read simply "M. R."

Monsieur Romanoff—the spelling was French—still lived at Number 8, but he wintered, and increasingly summered, in Spain, in a fishing village on the Costa Brava. Nearly a year, and a lengthy exchange of telephone calls and letters, passed before I returned to the rue Chartran. One morning in the spring of 2006, Monsieur Romanoff held up a hand against the bright sun, ushered me inside his house, and unwittingly unlocked the mystery of Cy and Nerma's mission in Paris.

Michel Fyodorovich Romanoff was a direct descendant of the dynasty that had ruled Russia for more than three hundred years. The paintings adorning the foyer told the story. The old oils hung in gilded frames above the marble floor. One wall was dominated by a large, lustrous portrait of a red-cheeked little boy wearing a uniform and carrying a sword: Alexander II. Known as the "czar liberator," the reformer who freed the serfs in 1861, Alexander II was killed by an anarchist's bomb in St. Petersburg in 1881. To his right, above the staircase, hung a formal portrait of Princess Paley, the radiant daughter of Alexander II's son, Grand Duke Paul.

The princess was Monsieur Romanoff's mother. By her desire and force, the family had come to Neuilly. Once the Bolsheviks took power, the Romanovs could not stay in Russia. "For Mother," Monsieur Romanoff explained, "there was no choice but France." Born in Paris, Irena Paley had lived there until 1913, when her family moved to Petersburg. In the kitchen, pastels of Russia, the onion domes and snow-blanketed convents of St. Petersburg, covered the walls. A single black-and-white photograph, a framed family portrait from 1910, hung near the sink.

Nearly eighty-two, Monsieur Romanoff had once been tall. Now when he stood, he seemed nearly cut in half, so badly had his spine become bent. Yet as he told the history of his family, the genetic inheritance emerged. His face was ruddy and angular, and beneath a steep forehead, his eyebrows were arched, his eyes pale blue. As he talked, his fingers, long and tapered, danced in the air, and even hunched over, he retained a regal air.

Monsieur Romanoff was a Romanov "on both sides." On his mother's side, he was the great-grandson of Alexander II, and on his father's the great-grandson of Alexander III. "That one," he said, pointing to the photograph on the kitchen wall, "is Father." The family portrait showed Grand Duke Alexander, his wife, Grand Duchess Xenia, and their seven children. Prince Fyodor Alexandrovich Romanov, Monsieur Romanoff's father, then a tall twelve-year-old, stood in a prim suit between his parents,

It was an admittedly complex lineage. Every time Monsieur Romanoff tried to chart the bloodlines, his memories became knotted. Both sides of the family, however, led back to czars. His paternal grandfather, Grand Duke Alexander Mikhailovich, an admiral who was known as Sandro, was the grandson of Nicholas I. Grand Duchess Xenia, his wife, was his first cousin. She was the daughter of Alexander III and the sister of Nicholas II, the last czar.

CY AND NERMA WATCHED the Romanoffs for more than four years. Princess Paley and her family had just moved into the house in 1930 when Cy and Nerma arrived on the rue Chartran. When Robin was born the following year, Monsieur Romanoff was six years old. Most of the time, though, he was boarding in Montcel, at a school near Versailles. Summers he spent in Biarritz, at the seashore among the White Russian émigrés. He had fond memories of his childhood and his parents' attempts to recapture the elegant past of Petersburg, but he, too, could not recall any Americans in their midst.

Cy and Nerma had gone undetected. The Center had chosen the assignment with care. Not only had they proven their trustworthiness, but as Americans they posed a minimal risk. On the rue Chartran, Russians would not have escaped notice. "Mother was always anxious," Monsieur Romanoff said. "She lived in endless fear of Stalin's spies. She knew Moscow was after her—it was a fact of our lives." If Princess Paley had heard Russian spoken on the street, "she

Prince Michel Romanoff with his father and grandfather in Biarritz, France, ca. 1934.

would have packed us up and fled the same day." But Cy and Nerma, as a well-dressed young couple from New York, made to seem even more innocuous by the arrival of a baby, could hover close.

For Cy, the exposure to imperial entitlement was a revelation. The Romanovs, accustomed to the palaces and parade grounds of Petersburg, were the antithesis of Cy's family, Jewish immigrants who had gone to America from the Pale. The Romanovs, even in exile, embodied the spirit of unbridled plunder that Cy had studied for so long and despised. Princess Paley, for her part, loathed the Bolsheviks, and in particular their secret policemen, those "pronounced Semitic" types, as she wrote in her memoirs, who had taken her husband and son.

Monsieur Romanoff spoke native French and English with an

American accent, but switched to Russian to explain the family trauma. "They barely made it out," he said. "In December 1918, my grandmother sent her two little daughters from Petersburg, when she knew it was the last chance." The girls were given fake passports with the names of the laundress's children and were smuggled out at night to Finland. The princess stayed on in Petersburg, hoping to save her husband, Grand Duke Paul. She fought long for his freedom, even winning a promise to intervene from Maxim Gorky, then the Kremlin's court writer. It was all in vain. In January 1919 the Bolsheviks murdered Grand Duke Paul, executing him in the middle of the night at the Peter and Paul Fortress. They also killed Princess Paley's son, Vladimir, who at twenty-one was known as "the poet among the Romanovs." He had survived the trenches of World War I but was killed when the Bolsheviks threw him down a mineshaft.

Monsieur Romanoff was eager to revisit the story of survival. His grandmother had fled Petersburg in 1919. The first Princess Paley left the USSR in midwinter, on foot. A count had approached her with a secret rescue plan, the work of the anti-Bolshevik underground in Finland. He offered a sledge, a horse, and himself as guide. On the frozen Gulf of Finland they encountered a blizzard. Covered in white, they were swept by the Bolshevik searchlights of the Kronstadt fort but escaped. All night they crossed the ice before reaching the Finnish coast.

Finland, though, soon became too close to Russia. The Bolsheviks were hunting for the Romanovs everywhere. In 1921, Princess Paley took her daughters and went to France. They first settled in the aristocratic Russian enclave in the sixteenth arrondissement but soon moved to Neuilly. The *pavilion* on the rue Chartran, built with stones reclaimed from a nearby village bombed in the Great War, seemed to offer a respite from the turmoil. In Neuilly, in a quiet corner far from the city, the Romanovs imagined they could regroup in peace.

Princess Paley loved Neuilly. The *ville* reminded her of Tsarkoye Selo, the czar's village outside Petersburg. "It was the country—the river, trees, grass, flowers," redolent of everything she had left behind. After a few years in France, she realized there would be no return to Russia. In the flood of refugees in Paris, however, she had found a calling. The White Russians were streaming in from all corners—from Belgrade, Bucharest, Berlin, even Shanghai. They arrived with no clothes or money, let alone work. "My grandmother could not sit and watch these wretched people," Monsieur Romanoff said. "The poverty was overwhelming."

In 1925, she founded *Le Comité de secours des émigrés russes*, the Committee to Aid Russian Émigrés. It would become one of the largest organizations of White Russians in Europe—and give the Center further reason to send Cy and Nerma to spy on the Romanovs. The OGPU and GRU tried to infiltrate the Comité time and again, and may well have succeeded. To the Soviets, the group was not only a threat but a source of vital information: its files comprised a virtual census of the Russian diaspora in France. By the time Monsieur Romanoff's grandmother died, in 1929, his mother had moved to Neuilly and taken over the leadership of the *Comité*.

Princess Paley, with her charity work and ties to the old imperial order, reigned as a doyenne of Russian culture in Paris. Her house, a living museum of the lost age, was often filled with émigré intellectuals—poets, writers, artists—and military men. General Efimovich, faithful aide-de-camp of the murdered Grand Duke Paul, was almost a member of the family. A Petersburg man, Efimovich was one of the best officers in the czar's army, an elegant gentleman who had lost everything. "Efimovich was the only one Mother could confide in," Monsieur Romanoff said, "the only officer she trusted." In Paris, the general devoted himself to the refugee committee.

Yet the most frequent guest was Nikolai Berdyaev. One of the preeminent Russian thinkers of the century, Berdyaev was best known as the author of *The Russian Idea*. A Christian existentialist, he was a voice of authority in the White Russian diaspora, a repentant Marxist turned anti-Stalinist. In the first years after the revolution, the Bolsheviks had tolerated the philosopher; Berdyaev was once arrested by the Cheka, interrogated personally by Dzerzhinsky, and let go. In 1922, however, he was exiled, traveling first to Berlin, then Paris. He settled in Clamart, a suburb to the southwest, where he soon founded an academy.

The philosopher, in Monsieur Romanoff's telling, sought Princess

Paley's help. Berdyaev had known French since childhood, but he and the princess worked together, often for days on end, on translations of his works. In 1931, Princess Paley finished *Le Marxisme et la Religion* and *De la Dignité du Christianisme et de l'Indignité des Chrétiens.* "The refugees were Mother's love," said Monsieur Romanoff. "But her work with Berdyaev was a mission, especially in the early thirties"— the years when Cy and Nerma lived nearby.

The rue Chartran was virtually unpeopled then. Only three houses stood on its eastern side: Number 12, where Cy and Nerma lived, a private house where Juliette's family now lived, and Number 8, the Romanoffs' *pavilion*. All three were united by an enormous garden in back, five acres of tall grass and plane trees that had once belonged to the local chateau. The garden had no walls, Monsieur Romanoff said. When the weather was fine, the neighbors would picnic beneath a giant chestnut tree. "Everyone came and went as they wished. It was open, shared by all."

Whether the Americans managed to get inside the house two doors down, attend Princess Paley's soirees, or mingle in the garden is unknown. At the least, Cy and Nerma recorded the comings and goings. They were able to keep a close watch, either from their narrow balcony, with its sweeping view of the street, the Eiffel Tower, and the city beyond, or during their daily walks behind the tall pram, up and down the sidewalk. Cy also recorded the neighborhood, from a variety of angles, on film. More than once he stood at the far end of rue Chartran and furtively photographed the *pavilion*. Nerma's shoebox had preserved the results, a collection of miniature black-and-whites, each printed no larger than one quarter of an inch square.

*

BY THE TENSE FALL OF 1933, CY AND NERMA SHOULD HAVE CLEARED OUT. While most eyes in Europe were on Berlin, where Hitler had swept to power at the end of January, Paris had become a city gradually paralyzed by strikes, corruption scandals, and a surging wave of antipathy toward immigrants, Jews, and above all Communists. Amid the political turmoil and labor unrest, the French Communists, long a latent force, were attracting the wrath of right-wing factions and the attention of the Sûreté-Générale. In July 1933, Trotsky had finally received asylum and was allowed to enter France. He stayed in Royan and then Barbizon, but he was not allowed to go to Paris.

The danger was nearing, but Cy and Nerma, whether out of stubbornness, blindness, or unyielding devotion, chose to ignore the signs. The Paris Préfecture, half a century later, admitted that it had kept files on the Americans: #1968684 for "Mr. OGGINS, Isaiah," and another for "Mrs. OGGINS, née BERMAN." Both, however, had been shredded before civilian eyes could see them. It was standard practice, a police archivist said. Files were routinely destroyed, "because of age." The prefecture, however, did offer other information—clues that pointed to Cy's return to Paris later in the decade.

The Sûreté records presented more of a tangle. In all, the archive comprised more than 2.5 million files, a trove of interwar surveillance of Communists and suspected Soviet agents in France. During the cold war, Western historians of Soviet intelligence who went to Paris left disappointed. For years they were told that the Sûreté files had been carted off during the war. "The French said they'd been stored on a barge on the Seine, which, by terrible luck, was bombed by the Germans," said Robert Conquest, the historian of Stalinism. No one believed the tale, he added, "because the Nazis had scarcely bombed Paris."

In Moscow, though, another version of the fate of the Sûreté records had long circulated. It was said that they had been taken from France during the war—first the Nazis had seized them, and then the Soviets. For years the Soviets denied that they had the archive. Even as general secretaries made gifts of its treasures to French prime ministers, Moscow refused to confirm the rumors. After the Soviet collapse, however, a deal was made. Beginning in 1993 and ending in 2000, the files, after being copied in Moscow, were repatriated to France. Yet by 2005, the Sûreté archives were again off-limits. "It's not only that they're classified," the clerk at the Archives Nationales told me. "The building is closed for asbestos abatement."

The Sûreté files may never be opened to the public. It is likely, though, that by the end of 1933, French intelligence officers as well as the Parisian police were surveilling Cy and Nerma. After all, the Soviet network in France had suffered a catastrophic exposure by then. Neither Cy nor Nerma was to blame. It was all the fault of another young American in Paris.

.

IN THE FINAL DAYS OF 1933, ROBERT GORDON SWITZ, A THIRTY-YEAR-old native of East Orange, New Jersey, received an anonymous telephone call at his apartment on the rue de la Chaussée d'Antin, near the Opéra. "Leave Paris at once," the caller said. "Or you'll regret it." The next day the police arrived at the American's door.

L'affaire Switz was a sensation—the first time, as far as anyone could recall, an American had been caught spying in France. It was also the first Soviet spy scandal in the country. In the following days, eight alleged accomplices were also arrested. As the investigation spilled into the press, Switz's story looked dubious. At first he claimed to have graduated from Yale, Class of 1917, but he had been born in 1904 and thus was too young for this to be true. He then claimed to be a Pan Am pilot, but he soon corrected himself, saying he was in sales, working for a U.S. firm dealing in scientific instruments. The company, when contacted, said that Switz was "a European representative" but had never sold anything.

The French police found nearly 50,000 Francs—nearly $3,800—in the American's apartment, which Switz could not account for. They also discovered letters from the French War Ministry, some bearing the minister's signature, and a number of uncracked eggshells, each precisely pierced at one end. Switz also possessed a set of classified documents from the French government. They had been captured on miniature film and rolled inside a cigarette. When the police burst in, Mrs. Switz, the former Marjorie Tilley, a twenty-two-year-old blonde who had graduated from Vassar, smoked the cigarette, negative inside, to the stub.

The Switz case made headlines, especially in the Communist *L'Humanité,* for more than a year. It came at a time when France careened from one political crisis to another; royalists, anti-Semites, right-wing Catholics, and fascists, emboldened by the rise of Mussolini and Hitler, all challenged the radical Socialist government of Camille Chautemps. To many, the fate of the republic itself seemed in the balance.

The Switz spy case also came at the height of the Stavisky affair, a far more damaging corruption scandal that roiled the Chautemps government. Alexandre Stavisky, a Russian Jewish émigré from Ukraine, was a serial swindler who amassed a fortune selling worthless bonds, in large part thanks to high-placed political patrons. Embarrassed by Stavisky, when the Switz arrests were first announced, leftists accused the French press of fostering anti-Semitism—many of the defendants in the spy case were Jews—and pandering to right-wing jingoism. But the Switz case was no hoax. It was the worst exposure yet to befall Soviet intelligence in Europe.

Cy and Nerma would have known the lead defendant, a lanky bohemian with an artist's goatee and a fondness for bow ties, as "the Aviator." Switz, whose father was a Russian émigré, had joined the GRU in 1932 and worked for the Soviets in New York. He and Marjorie lived in the Village at 12 Grove Street, a few blocks away from Cy's old brownstone on Perry. In New York, Switz had earned his pilot's license and run a secret darkroom in Brooklyn, where he photographed documents for the Center. In the United States, and in the Panama Canal Zone, he had enjoyed a string of successes before failure hit in the summer of 1933 and Moscow ordered him to Paris.

To the horror of the French Communists, the Switz case laid bare the scope of the Soviet underground in France. The courtroom grew crowded with defendants. Lydia Stahl, though, captured the most headlines and the public imagination. Baroness Stahl, as Janet Flanner, the Paris correspondent of *The New Yorker*, described her, was "an exceptionally bookish, art-loving private individual" whom the French police had watched closely since 1920. A baroness by an early, ill-fated marriage, Stahl "had pasted French fortification plans on her Paris flat's parlor ceiling and then pasted flowered wallpaper over them."

Stahl was a fabled Soviet spy. Born Lydia Chkalova in the south of

Russia, she had befriended John Reed in Finland, studied at Columbia (earning a master's in Chinese in the years after Cy left), and worked for "Alfred" Tilton, the GRU *rezident* in New York, in the 1920s. She had also visited Berlin when Cy and Nerma were there—a trip, quite likely, that she repeated more than once. In Paris, Stahl ran at least nine spies. Moscow had instructed the ring to steal French military secrets, including army mobilization plans and weaponry blueprints. The Soviets were particularly keen to get hold of the French formulas for the newest technology in warfare, chemical and biological weapons.

Moscow tried to dismiss the Switz case as trumped-up anti-Soviet propaganda. *Izvestia* noted that the spy case had hit at the height of the Stavisky affair and denounced it as a blatant attempt by the French right wing to divert attention from its involvement in the corruption scandal. The Stavisky case, however, did not end quickly. On January 8, 1934, the Russian swindler was found dead, shot either by his own hand or by the police. The fallout only grew. By the end of the month, Chautemps had resigned. The anti-parliamentarian camps, led by the paramilitary leagues, seized the opportunity. On February 6, street battles broke out in Paris.

The Aviator and his wife, meanwhile, did not hold up in prison. The French prosecutors only had to tip their hand and the Americans opted to talk. The police had fingerprints and two blond hairs, evidence found inside four rolls of miniature negatives that had mysteriously turned up one day at the French consulate in Geneva. The prints were Switz's, and the hairs were his wife's. Within days Cy and Nerma learned of more arrests. With each new round of indictments, the pressure on the Americans mounted. The Switz ring had included a French colonel and an engineer engaged in the manufacture of poison gas. Soon the police discovered caches of bomb-making materials, chemicals, and more state documents. By the spring of 1934, as six members of the ring confessed, the case exploded. In July thirty-two suspects were indicted and two hundred others placed under investigation. Of the indicted, the police managed to arrest twenty-two.

The eventual trial brought a turn that Cy and Nerma, and certainly their bosses in Moscow, could not have expected. The French magistrate warmed to the Switzes. "Two charming people," Judge André Benon called them in open court. "Americans in general," he said, "are not of a type to allow themselves to participate in such intrigue." In the end the ring was decimated, but the Aviator and his wife fared well. After sixteen months in jail, both were released. Within hours, in a small hotel on the edge of the Latin Quarter, Switz told a British reporter why and how he had become a Soviet spy. "I was tired of doing nothing," he said. "Tired of leading the life of a young man of easy money. I became immensely interested in the Russian experiment from a humanitarian point of view." He had been a true "Communist idealist," he said.

For months the French had interrogated Switz, who eagerly cooperated. "I was hesitant to give the names of all the people I knew," he said after his release. "But I am glad to think that in any case the police had them, so that I did not really betray them. That they all got what they deserve." The Aviator compromised, it was said, several hundred Soviet operatives working in Europe.

In Moscow, the Center was left with no choice. All operations in Paris were suspended. After the initial wave of arrests, many members of the underground had fled. Cy and Nerma, too, spent months out of France. In the winter of 1933 they traveled to Spain, staying far from view on the resort island of Majorca until the middle of summer. Perhaps they had received advance warning; that spring the French police were already closing in on the Switz ring. Certainly by January 1934, Cy would have known of the first arrests. From the press reports alone, he would know that the Aviator and his wife were in jail. He would also know, whether from his instincts or from his handlers, that they were likely to talk.

That summer, in the aftermath of the February riots, the French Communists made a historic concession. In June 1934, the Communists and Socialists formed an alliance to stave off the fascist tide. The United Front, it would prove a precursor to the Popular Front. For Cy and Nerma, though, there was little to celebrate. The Switzes remained in jail and talking. With the toll of *L'affaire Switz* threatening to climb higher, Neuilly was now off-limits.

The Sûreté had gleaned hundreds of leads from Switz, but he had not told all. His greatest secrets, especially the self-incriminating ones, he kept to himself. Still, Cy and Nerma could not know what the French had learned. Yet even by July, when prosecutors announced a second round of indictments, Moscow kept them in limbo. At some point that summer, Cy made it back to Paris, but only to pack up the flat on the rue Chartran. Then, on August 23, 1934, he returned to the American embassy and received a new U.S. pass-port—his fourth. Cy may not have known when he and Nerma would move on, but he had learned his next destination.

Autumn arrived early in Paris that year, but the Switz case dragged on and Cy and Nerma waited. With the threat of exposure hanging over them, it was impossible to work. For weeks they could do little but endure the torture of not knowing. Finally a reprieve came. On September 22, the couple, with their curly-haired toddler in tow, boarded the SS *Aquitania* in Cherbourg. Robin, not yet three years old, was on his way to New York for the first time. For Cy and Nerma, the fortnight's crossing would bring relief. Their European adventures, after more than six years, had come to an end. Or so they imagined.

Red Square, Revolution Day parade, 1941. Soldiers en route to the front.

BY DECEMBER 1942, THE BLOODSHED HAD BECOME AN EPIC: THE Great Patriotic War, as Stalin would call the struggle against Hitler. By then, World War II had long since recast East and West in an alliance of sudden necessity. The U.S. embassy in Moscow was nearly empty—the Kremlin had ordered the entire diplomatic corps evacuated that fall—when the men from Washington finally got the telephone call. This time, the Foreign Ministry official said, without warning or explanation, the American prisoner had finally arrived. After a long, nearly impossible journey to the capital from the camps of Norilsk, Mr. Oggins was ready to receive visitors.

On the morning of December 8, 1942, the temperature was far below zero when Llewellyn E. Thompson, Jr., and Francis Bowden Stevens, two young members of the U.S. diplomatic mission in the USSR, set out for the Butyrka Prison in the center of Moscow. A day earlier, Americans had marked the first anniversary of Pearl Harbor. The Soviets, though, had borne the brunt of Hitler's attack. The Wehrmacht had come to Moscow's edge, and only after a battle involving 7 million men had the capital survived. Now, five hundred miles to the southeast, even as the American diplomats sat in the embassy sedan while their chauffeur navigated the iced-over streets, the Germans were nearing their breaking point. In a city on the Volga named after the Generalissimo in the Kremlin, the worst battle yet—Stalingrad—raged.

Winter in Moscow is an annual siege, but the war had robbed the capital of its time-honored defenses. With scant coal for the furnaces, trams and trolleys carried wood across the city. The gas flickered on and off. Electricity was rationed. At night windows were draped with blackout curtains. Muscovites, desperate for news from the south, had grown anxious.

Outside the jail, swaddled women, young and old, crowded the frozen sidewalk. They carried parcels bound in newspaper—food, medicine, and letters—that they hoped, against the odds, would reach their sons, husbands, lovers. As Thompson and Stevens walked down the grim entranceway, opening their briefcases for the guards at every station, the women outside stood in silence. Their weary vigil seemed to mirror the mood of the city.

THE SECOND SECRETARY and the new consul were not keen on the assignment. The Butyrka Prison, built under the reign of Catherine II, was not a place for diplomacy. A sprawling aboveground dungeon, it was a glowering mass of eighteenth-century brick, turreted guard towers, and tiny windows thatched with iron. If the Lubyanka was famed for its bloody interrogation rooms, Butyrka was renowned for overcrowding. In airless cells built to hold a few dozen men, as many as two hundred prisoners fought for space. Mold covered the walls, fed by the steam from the leaky radiators. In Butyrka, said the prisoners who lived to tell of it, black bread turned white by day's end. The worst was the "kennel," a windowless hole in the cellar fifteen feet square where more than fifty men were forced to squat side by side without heat or fresh air.

Even in the guards' wing, where the NKVD officers politely received the Americans, the stench was present. The smell of thousands of men packed in close could not be contained. The lead man from the embassy, Llewellyn Thompson, better known as Tommy, had come to Moscow as an ascendant member of the young elite in FDR's Foreign Service. Tall and stiff-backed, to the Soviets he exuded an urbane, Ivy League air, but Thompson had been born in Las Animas, Colorado, a grasslands town of two thousand farmers and cowboys. Although his parents were not well-off, he had managed to attend the University of Colorado and then the Foreign Service Institute at Georgetown. At thirty-eight, six years younger than Cy, he was halfway up the State Department ladder.

He was also a veteran of the Washington wars over Soviet policy. Robert F. Kelley, a graduate of Harvard and the Sorbonne, had headed the State Department's Russian Division from its first days in 1924. Kelley brought together the Foreign Service's Soviet experts under one roof, built a large library, and filled rooms with files on the USSR. But in 1937, at the height of Stalin's terror, the division— home to the government's collective intelligence on the USSR—had mysteriously been shut down. It happened overnight. "One fine morning," writes George Kennan in his memoirs, Kelley was fired, his shop liquidated, and its "special files" destroyed.

Many would later argue that Kelley had come up against the new Moscow ambassador, Joe Davies. Known pejoratively among Foreign Service veterans as Mr. Marjorie Merriweather Post—his wife was the cereals heiress—Davies amused the Soviets and infuriated his staff by parking the family yacht, *Sea Cloud* (with its fifty-man crew), in Leningrad Harbor. In time, after his memoir *Mission to Moscow* became a Hollywood film, he earned shame as an apologist for Stalin. Kennan, for his part, kept his own counsel about the demise of the Russian Division. "I never learned the real background for this curious purge," he wrote, but not without adding, "There is strong evidence that pressure was brought to bear from the White House."

By the winter of 1942, Tommy Thompson had inherited, almost by default, one of the best jobs in the Foreign Service. In the 1940s, the diplomats lived and worked in an imposing pale yellow building, 13–15 Mokhovaya Street, adjacent to the Comintern headquarters and across from the Kremlin and the newly built Moskva Hotel. Among Muscovites, the embassy became an instant landmark. The *zhyolty dom*, they called it, "the yellow house." In Washington, though, it acquired a different nickname, "the school for ambassadors." George Kennan, Chip Bohlen, Loy Henderson—among the most capable men ever to serve in the Foreign Service—had apprenticed there.

Throughout the war Thompson anchored the embassy nearly on his own, even while the Germans bombed Moscow and it seemed in imminent danger of collapsing into rubble. In Spaso House, the vacated ambassador's residence, he took to walking around the giant chandelier, which swayed perilously when bombs landed nearby. For his safety, Thompson was instructed to take the ambassador's elegant Pierce-Arrow out at night and drive far from the embassy to sleep in it. But after one brutal December night on the streets of Moscow Thompson quipped that he would rather die warm at the hands of the Germans.

After the war, Thompson received the Congressional Medal of Honor for bravery. He also earned the envy of diplomats far senior to him. During the worst of the fighting around Moscow, he served as FDR's personal messenger to Stalin, often delivering presidential messages by hand. He would drive down to the Kremlin and negotiate his way past the guards and into Stalin's office. As he walked the Kremlin's endless corridors, Thompson tried to memorize the names on the doors, only to see them change each time he went.

His wartime service reaped rewards. Over the decades to come, Thompson would serve as the U.S. ambassador to Moscow under three presidents, Eisenhower, Kennedy, and Johnson. After the Cuban missile crisis, as Kennedy's chief Soviet adviser, he would be credited with staving off nuclear Armageddon. By virtue of his "very personal relationship" with the president and his brother, the attorney general, Thompson managed to assure Kennedy that Khrushchev, given the chance to save face, would back down. Thompson, Kennan would later write, was "the best man we've ever had in dealing with the Soviet regime."

On that midwinter day in 1942, Thompson arrived at the Butyrka Prison with backup. Franny Stevens, the new consul, was an eleven-year Foreign Service veteran who had arrived in Moscow only a few months earlier. Tall and mustachioed, he was a native of upstate New York with a string of postings: Prague, Warsaw, Paris, Riga, and Pretoria. Moscow, though, would prove the most daunting. Even getting to the USSR had been an ordeal. Stevens had come from Washington via Tehran and Baku in order to skirt the war.

The Red Army was battling the Germans to the south and west, and the fear of defeat was ever-present. With Christmas looming and almost no one else in the enormous embassy, Thompson and Stevens could not have been in a cheery mood. The invitation to

Butyrka, moreover, delivered at the last minute, and only after repeated requests from Washington, was unlikely to have stirred any dormant enthusiasm. But both men recognized that it was an opportunity almost without precedent.

The United States and the USSR, in signing a recognition treaty in 1933, had promised to notify each other within thirty days if a citizen from either side was arrested. The Roosevelt-Litvinov Agreement, as it was known, also required visits to detained citizens in jail. FDR had insisted on the provision. The Soviets, though, had never adhered to the agreement.

■

AT THE MOSCOW EMBASSY, IT WAS STANDARD PRACTICE AT THE START OF each year to send Washington a "consular list," a tally of every U.S. citizen known to reside in the USSR. In January 1943, the list totaled 169 persons, among them 56 government officials, 11 journalists, 30 students, 4 teachers, 1 missionary, and 1 American in the Butyrka Prison.

The U.S. government had learned of Cy Oggins's disappearance into the gulag only during the previous winter—nearly three years to the day after Cy's arrest. The State Department, unlike the BOI, did not maintain a single Oggins file. Dozens of reports, memorandums, letters, handwritten notes, telegrams, and ozalids (the photocopies of the day) pertaining to the case were among the department's disparate files. Still, the serpentine paper trail could be traced in the National Archives, and in the end it revealed the story. The first word of Cy's imprisonment had come from an unlikely source in one of the remotest corners of the Soviet Union. And it was urgently relayed to Washington, D.C., to the office of the secretary of state.

The news had come only thanks to the chaos of war. In the summer of 1941, when the first bombs fell in the nineteenth-century heart of Moscow, not far from Red Square, windows blew out and dogs turned wild with fear. In the Kremlin, panic struck. As the Nazis closed in, antiaircraft guns resounded across the city, even in the Lubyanka. Cy, Jacques Rossi, and tens of thousands of others were in

Norilsk. In the gulag, there was less food and more work. And yet, during the war, even the camps seemed to offer shelter.

By October 1941 the Nazis had seized Borodino, the site of Kutuzov's 1812 bloodbath with Napoleon, and the city of Kalinin, too, with its bridge across the Volga. The same day the First Panzer Division severed the railway to Leningrad. Moscow's lifeline was cut, and the Germans were at the city's western edge. Stalin ordered the government to evacuate the city. Only he, Molotov, and a handful of deputies would remain in the capital. Bridges and ministry buildings were mined. "Black snow" fell from the chimneys of government buildings as clerks frantically burned state documents. Nothing would be left for the Germans. Even Lenin, mummified in a granite sarcophagus in Red Square, was shipped out in a refrigerated train car.

The diplomatic corps was given four hours. By late evening, as a blizzard gained strength and the German guns grew louder, the staff of the American embassy and the press corps, including Cyrus Sulzberger of the *New York Times*, rushed to the Kazan Station. Chaos reigned. Kremlin guards held back the populace as the Americans joined the fleeing British, Japanese, Chinese, Swedes, Norwegians, Poles, Czechs, Yugoslavs, Bulgarians, Turks, Persians, and Afghans. The entire foreign colony was packed off to Kuibyshev, a city on the Volga six hundred miles to the southeast, then named in honor of an Old Bolshevik and today known again by its prerevolutionary name, Samara.

Moscow to Kuibyshev was an overnight train ride. The Americans were told to expect eighteen hours. The next morning when they awoke, they were surprised to discover that they had traveled a mere twenty miles. In the end, the trip lasted five days. It was not all misery. The train car that followed the diplomats' carried singers and dancers from the Bolshoi Theater. The Americans did not have "much in the way of food" but could offer "an excellent supply of liquor." Introductions were made, and by the time the train reached Kuibyshev, the compartments had mixed. The diplomats, "being young Americans," got "to know a fair number" of girls from the Bolshoi.

The life of the U.S. embassy in Kuibyshev during World War II is a little-known chapter in the history of U.S.-Soviet relations. Yet as a prelude to the cold war, it was a formative interlude. Before the war, Kuibyshev was an anonymous outpost in the Soviet hinterland. By the time the foreigners arrived, it had swollen to three times its pre-war size. By the winter of 1941, when it became the provisional capital of the USSR, more than half a million refugees had descended on the city. Peasants in sheepskins slept at the train station, while the streets, once dusty and quaint, had turned to frozen mud. Typhus raged, potable water was scarce, and famine threatened to decimate the local populace.

The American ambassador, Lawrence Steinhardt, an austere New York lawyer and early FDR patron, was less than enthused. The Soviets had given the Americans an old three-story schoolhouse to use as a temporary embassy. Flushing water was not available above the first floor, and the rooms were frigid. In the spring, months ahead of the Nazi attack, Steinhardt had been tipped off by an informant in the German embassy and sent his wife and daughter across the Baltic to neutral Stockholm. But even for a single man, Kuibyshev posed difficulties. It was a town, Steinhardt wrote to a friend, "where the Ritz Hotel has not yet been built, and where they have not learned of the existence of toilet paper—perhaps for the reason that there is not enough food to justify giving much thought to the former subject." Steinhardt did not last long. By November 1941 he was through.

The ambassadorship remained vacant until April 1942, when Admiral William Standley arrived. At seventy, Standley was a Navy hero who had retired five years earlier, only to be recalled after Pearl Harbor. He moved the ambassador's residence from the drafty rooms to Sadovia, "once the ornate and gingerbready town house" of a wealthy merchant. Not content with the offerings of the dismal local market, the admiral planted a garden in the yard of the residence. Standley complained to FDR that he had time on his hands, but he managed to read *War and Peace*, play bridge marathons, and hone his tennis skills, often playing with his NKVD minder, whom he grew fond of. A fervent golfer, he also had his men clear a driving range amid the tumult of the desperate city.

FDR had dispatched Standley to oversee Lend-Lease, the U.S. program to supply the USSR with more than a billion dollars' worth of materiel and supplies for the struggle against the Nazis. The admiral, though, soon realized that he would see little of Stalin and much of Andrei Vyshinsky, the purge trials prosecutor who had become Molotov's chief deputy. Before long Standley had taken a dislike to the Russians but struck up a friendship with the Polish ambassador, who lived next door, in similarly makeshift quarters. The warm relations, as the embassy records attest, led to an almost daily exchange of information and a mutual cause. When the USSR and Germany carved up Poland in 1939, tens of thousands of Polish army officers had been taken prisoner and disappeared into the gulag. Standley raised the question of their fate with the Soviets. Molotov did not enjoy the third-party meddling. To Standley's pleas on behalf of the Polish POWs, Stalin's foreign minister was terse: "There is always trouble where Poles are concerned."

The Poles, however, were grateful. It was only natural, then, that when a Polish prisoner of war walked into their embassy in Kuibyshev one day in the middle of the winter of 1942, the Polish ambassador would rush to tell Admiral Standley the astounding news.

•

THAT WINTER THE SOVIETS RELEASED HUNDREDS, IF NOT THOUSANDS, OF Polish officers from the gulag. "A general amnesty," Moscow called it. The prisoners were let out but forced to fend for themselves, without clothes, money, or papers. Somehow, many found their way south, along the Yenisei and across two thousand miles of ice and snow to Kuibyshev.

One carried an urgent, secret message from Norilsk. The letter, dated September 16, 1941, took five months to reach its destination. But its contents were relayed at once by coded telegram to Washington, D.C.:

THE LOST SPY 177

TELEGRAM RECEIVED

(MOSCOW)
KUIBYSHEV
DATED FEBRUARY 12, 1942
REC'D 1:40 P.M.

NUMBER 130, FEBRUARY 12, 1942,
11 A.M.
SECRETARY OF STATE,
WASHINGTON.

A POLISH CITIZEN WHO HAS BEEN RELEASED FROM PRISON BY SOVIET AUTHORITIES UNDER THE AMNESTY HAS ARRIVED IN KUIBYSHEV AND PRESENTED A LETTER DATED SEPTEMBER 16, 1941 TO THE POLISH EMBASSY WHICH CONTAINS A STATEMENT TO THE EFFECT THAT A MR. CY OGGINS, DESCRIBED AS A COLUMBIA UNIVERSITY PROFESSOR AND AN AMERICAN CITIZEN, ARRIVED IN MOSCOW FROM PARIS IN 1938, WAS ARRESTED IN FEBRUARY 1939 AND SENTENCED TO EIGHT YEARS IN PRISON. IT IS STATED THAT AT THE TIME OF WRITING HE WAS IN THE PRISON CAMP NORILLAG AT NORILSK, THAT HE WAS IN VERY POOR PHYSICAL CONDITION AND THAT HE WISHED HIS SISTER, MRS. BARRON, 874 SARATOGA AVENUE, BROOKLYN, NEW YORK INFORMED CONCERNING.

THE EMBASSY HAS NO INFORMATION REGARDING THIS INDIVIDUAL AND NO RECORD OF HIS CASE. IT IS ACCORDINGLY REQUESTED THAT THE DEPARTMENT ADVISE THE EMBASSY WITH RESPECT TO HIS CITIZENSHIP STATUS.

The Polish note repeated, nearly verbatim, what Cy had told Jacques in Norilsk. The biographical particulars, scant but telling, were identical. As Jacques spoke fluent Polish, it is likely that the Polish officer's note was another of the Frenchman's attempts to get the word out that Cy was in the gulag. The plea to the outside world, though, contained an error. Either Cy had not told the truth, or the

Pole had simply got it wrong. Mrs. Barron was not Cy's sister but Nerma's sister, Bessie Baron, who did in fact live at 874 Saratoga Avenue, Brooklyn, New York. Bessie was acting, wittingly or not, as Cy and Nerma's mail drop; in case of an emergency, they were to communicate only through her.

On April 15, 1942, Washington answered the telegram from Kuibyshev, sending a secret reply that summarized the State Department's findings on "Mr. Isaiah Oggins." The cable bore the notations of at least ten State Department officials, including Sumner Welles, the acting secretary of state. Replying to Kuibyshev, Welles, who had commandeered the department from the ailing Cordell Hull, wired a demand that the U.S. embassy should get the Soviets to confirm that Oggins was in the gulag. "You are authorized," he wrote, ". . . in your discretion to inform the Soviet authorities that the Embassy has heard that he is imprisoned at Camp Norillog [*sic*] in Norilsk and to request them to investigate the report and if it is true, to inform the Embassy regarding the reasons for and the circumstances attending his arrest, the nature of the sentence which has been imposed, and his physical and mental condition."

IN THE SPRING OF 1942, the U.S. embassy began its quest to see the prisoner. But the Foreign Ministry stonewalled the Americans. For the wartime allies, it was a remarkable standoff—and one that went entirely unreported. Only on June 15, after Standley had sent three diplomatic notes, did the Soviets even confirm that Oggins was in the Norilsk camps. Within weeks, Secretary of State Hull stepped into the case, cabling the embassy:

> Please take up this case informally with the Soviet authorities and since Oggins is an American citizen request permission for an American Foreign Service Officer to visit him as provided for in the 1933 agreement . . .
>
> Without at this time giving emphasis to the failure of the Soviet authorities, from the standpoint of commitments to the Soviet Government, to notify the Embassy of Oggins' arrest, you may, however, express some surprise at such failure.

An extended dance followed. The Soviets refused to answer for months. On July 3, Standley sent another request, and on September 11 added "a follow up note." Finally he received a reply. In Note Number 61, dated September 13, 1942, the People's Commissariat for Foreign Affairs reported that "Oggins is now in Moscow, that no objection is perceived to his being visited by a representative of the Embassy, and that the Foreign Office desires to know who will visit him and when."

Ambassador Standley cabled Tommy Thompson in Moscow and told him to pursue the matter. Standley was dispatching an embassy officer from Kuibyshev to Moscow to deliver the Oggins dossier, which contained what little information the State Department in Washington had been able to find on the prisoner. He asked Thompson to "seek an appointment with Oggins" and "please telegraph developments."

Washington had already grown anxious. On September 16, Secretary of State Hull cabled Kuibyshev a single line: "What is status Oggins case?" Within days, Thompson had heard a different story: Oggins, the Soviets now said, was not yet in Moscow after all. He was only en route. Thompson, now nearly alone in the Moscow embassy, sent a telegram to the ambassador in Kuibyshev reporting that "Foreign Office advises that Oggins has not yet reached Moscow but is expected in several days."

In the diplomatic correspondence, the lie is clear. The Soviets were stalling. All the while, for more than half a year, the best Soviet hands in the U.S. Foreign Service were kept in the dark. They did not know the identity of the prisoner—"a Mr. Cy Oggins, described as a Columbia University professor"—nor how he had ended up in the gulag. In the end, the Soviets made the Americans wait for nearly ten months simply to learn whether Oggins was still alive.

※

CY ENTERED THE ROOM SLOWLY, THE NKVD OFFICERS AT HIS SIDE. There were three of them, uniformed and armed. Two may have been prison guards, the pride of Butyrka, chosen for the honor. At least one of the officers, however, came from higher up, from the

Lubyanka. A meeting so rare would bear political significance. Even if nothing of import was said, no revealing words exchanged, a report would have to be made—and sent to the highest levels. In the Kremlin, they were waiting. Stalin may not have had any advance knowledge; Molotov had made the arrangements for the viewing. In time, though, before the matter of the American prisoner was over, the Leader would read a record of the conversation in Butyrka.

Cy moved with difficulty, even with a new cane. His leg had worsened in the camps but seemed to hurt less now. Perhaps the distraction was numbing. As he entered the room, Cy stared at the Americans. The reports of the meeting in Butyrka, on both the Soviet and the American side, do not reveal whether anyone had told Cy that he would meet diplomats, be given an opportunity to make his case. Yet he would have known that something extraordinary was awaiting him.

As the NKVD officers led Cy to a chair, Thompson and Stevens inspected the prisoner. Oggins stood no taller than five feet eight inches. His body appeared thin and his face haggard, but he bore no recent bruises. His brown eyes were rheumy, and his skin was sallow. His hair, cropped short, was little more than a dark gray stubble on his scalp. Forty-four years old, he had spent nearly four years in Soviet detention.

Thompson and Stevens were establishment men, diplomats steeped in a worldview very divergent from Cy's. They were envoys from Washington who saw virtue in expanding American influence abroad and curbing the Soviets' rise. But to Cy, after all the jails and camps, they were a relief. They were Americans, the first compatriots he had seen in years. At the same time, their appearance in the prison, sitting close now, across the table, could only have been a shock. Cy may not have had warning, but even if he did not know he would meet the diplomats, he entered the interview room with a feverish expectancy.

For months they had prepped him for the meeting. They had brought him, this time not in a fetid railway car, all the way from the

Arctic, and then kept him for weeks in the prison infirmary. For the first time in years, he had received treatment, medicine and rest. They had fed him, too, adding weight to his cachectic frame. Then today, in the dark early morning hours, he had been showered and shaved and his hair had been cut. Cy must have known that the meeting with whoever was coming to see him portended a turn of consequence.

Thompson, mercifully, kept his questions short. The interview was in English, and Thompson reported that he was "allowed complete freedom to question" the prisoner. But the diplomats knew well that he could hardly air any grievances in the presence of the NKVD men.

Thompson asked Cy about his health, and Cy answered that he suffered from a "nervous paralysis." It wasn't something that had happened in jail, he said. It was an illness from before the camps, something that had slowed him for years.

As Cy spoke of his illness, Thompson and Stevens heard an explanation. It was the reason behind the repeated delays. The Soviets had not wanted to show a prisoner in such desperate shape. They had brought Cy south from Norilsk in late August, but his treatment had required months. Throughout the fall, they had given him medicine and added weight to his cheeks and frame. As gaunt as Cy looked to the diplomats, the Soviets would never have shown a desperately sick man just delivered from the camps.

Cy, too, kept his words to a minimum. The temptation was great, but he held firm. He told the Americans, in quiet, measured tones, only the story of his ordeal: how he had not had a trial or a defense lawyer; nor had he admitted any guilt. That part was the truth, but it was not, of course, the whole truth. He wanted to save himself and to return to Nerma and their boy. But Cy could not, even if he wished, tell the Americans his entire story. Even to hint at it would endanger others. The war had come; the targets, at least for a time, had shifted, but the world that he had left behind lived on. In a café in Paris, a bookshop in Berlin, a train station in Madrid, wherever they convened, the underground still breathed. For all the delusion and collusion, betrayal and paranoia, the underground had survived. Cy could be sure of it.

In the years since he had vanished from the shadows, a generation of agents had been beaten, exiled, jailed, or made to disappear. In the West, as the bodies began to surface, the contours of the clandestine world had at last become visible. But not everyone had come aboveground. From Asia to Europe to America, agents still exchanged coded salutations and moved negatives, money, and weapons. The war had severed the party from its foreign arms, but the old networks, like phantom limbs, lived on.

TOMMY THOMPSON AND Franny Stevens, like many of the early Soviet experts in the Foreign Service, were clear-eyed diplomats. They had little sympathy for Americans caught in the thrall of the Soviet dream. They seemed to share an institutional indifference to the fate of those swayed. George Kennan, remembered today for his learned and humanist approach to diplomacy, may have inadvertently helped to shape the unwritten policy. In 1931, two years before the Moscow embassy opened, Kennan, then a young attaché in the Baltic listening post, wrote a secret memorandum that listed eighty-five "individuals residing in Soviet Russia, reputed to be American citizens but communist sympathizers." In the document Kennan cautioned that some of the Americans "might no longer be entitled to protection without the special approval of the Department." Kennan was only a junior officer at the time, but his memo's implication was ominous: the State Department should retain the right to deny help to American Communists, even if they were U.S. citizens.

Thompson began with the passport. Had Cy really used a forged passport to enter the USSR? It was true, Cy said. He began to explain but struggled to find the words. Yes, he had entered the country illegally. At the time, he said, he had not fully realized the seriousness. "Not feeling that I need return to the U.S. immediately, and feeling that I might not have another opportunity soon, I came to the Soviet Union to see the country . . . Not able to obtain a visa on my own passport"—he did not offer an explanation—"I allowed myself to be persuaded to come with a false passport." It was only a shortcut, Cy said, nothing more. He failed to mention, though, that the passport was Czech, and only later did the diplomats surmise that it had not been American.

What had happened to his own passport? Thompson asked. The State Department would need to know where it was. U.S. passports were sovereign property; they must be accounted for. "I left it in Paris," Cy said, "with good friends, with the idea that I would soon return to take it back."

Thompson and Stevens were not satisfied, but they knew it would be useless, under the circumstances, to probe further. They also knew they could have a second chance. Washington had instructed them to learn whether the prisoner desired to return home. If Oggins did, they were to ascertain if the Soviets would permit him to obtain a new U.S. passport.

Cy made his wishes clear: he desperately wanted to retain his U.S. passport. The prisoner's request did not surprise Thompson and Stevens. But the Soviets' response did: the chief NKVD officer in the room said he had no objection. The diplomats faced a problem, though. In jail, Cy had no identity papers. The State Department, Thompson and Stevens told the NKVD officers, would have to verify the prisoner's citizenship. And to do so, they would need photographs.

It was a rare request, perhaps without precedent, but the lead NKVD officer readily agreed. It would take time, he warned—the holidays were approaching—but the commissariat would make the photographs available. To the diplomats, it seemed a significant step forward. To Cy, it was an unimaginable concession. In his isolation, the offer raised his expectancy to unbearable heights. He may not have allowed himself to dream, but he knew the possibility now lay within reach. Whether it was fate, luck, or the political expediency of the wartime alliance, a miracle had occurred. The Americans were offering a way out.

As they stood to leave, Cy told the men from Washington that he "could not survive" in jail. "Please endeavor," he asked, "to keep in touch with me."

WHEN THOMPSON RETURNED to the embassy, his evening was only beginning. In recent days, the leaders of the United States and the USSR had kept him up late, exchanging communiqués. For months Stalin and FDR had engaged in a secret correspondence to coordinate the defense against the Nazis. The patrician FDR had little in common with the paranoid Soviet dictator, but he had come to respect Stalin as a strategist and to admire the endurance of the Red Army. Since June 1941 and the start of what he called "the Russian war," FDR had wooed Stalin, offering to send materiel, even planes and pilots, to the USSR. Stalin welcomed the aircraft but asked that the crews be left at home. From the beginning, the dance was awkward and doomed to end in disappointment.

The spring of 1942 brought a remarkable rapprochement. In May, Stalin sent Molotov to Washington, where he stayed at the White House. By December, though, both sides had grown frustrated. FDR was pushing hard for a secret meeting with Stalin and Churchill. Stalin, meanwhile, had demanded since the summer that the United States and Great Britain open "the Second Front"—a European attack on Hitler. FDR repeated his request to meet, switching the proposed rendezvous site from near Alaska to Africa, but Stalin refused. "Round Stalingrad, as well as at the central front, the battles are developing," he wrote. "Round Stalingrad we are keeping encircled a group of German troops and hope to finish them off." The Generalissimo would not leave the capital.

On the night of December 8, 1942, the day he had been to see Cy in prison, Thompson once again rushed to send the president an urgent telegram. Major General Patrick J. Hurley, accompanied by two other U.S. officers, had just made it to Moscow after a ten-day visit to Stalingrad. FDR was eager to read the report from the first U.S. military eyewitnesses to the battle. That night Thompson sent FDR a detailed and lengthy memorandum on the Soviets' progress in the south.

By then the Oggins case had been discussed at the highest levels in the State Department. No one knows if it was also aired in the White House. If it was, it is not hard to imagine the outcome. The

USSR and the United States were allies, and Lend-Lease, despite Ambassador Standley's public grumbling, was a success. The alliance with Stalin, however awkward and discomforting, was a national security necessity. By year's end, the Soviet leader had again made the cover of *Time*, becoming for the second time the magazine's Man of the Year. Stalin, *Time* said, "drank his vodka straight" and "talked the same way." A wartime scandal, much less the complaints of an American Communist in a Soviet jail, was not in either side's interest.

IN MOSCOW, THOMPSON was undeterred, all the same. On the following morning, he drafted a secret three-page memorandum on the visit to the jail. In the report, coded and cabled first to Kuibyshev, Thompson noted that the prisoner's health, even with the recent treatment, was failing. "My impression," he wrote, "was that Oggins is now fully aware of the advantages of American citizenship and that his health is such that it is doubtful whether he will survive the rest of his sentence."

Thompson's telegram was read in Kuibyshev by Loy Henderson, the veteran chargé d'affaires, who knew the Soviets as well as any man in the U.S. government. Henderson wasted no time in forwarding the news on to Washington. At one in the morning on December 11, 1942, he sent Thompson's message directly to Cordell Hull. The diplomats were only following the directives from Washington. The secretary of state made the decision: Oggins should be brought home, if only for interrogation.

·

ON JANUARY 9, 1943, AFTER RUSSIA'S LONG NEW YEAR'S HANGOVER, AND a month and a day after the first visit to the jail, the U.S. consul returned to Butyrka. After fifteen months in Kuibyshev, most of the embassy staff would soon move back to Moscow. On the second visit, though, Stevens went alone.

In Butyrka, the ritual reprised itself: the checks along the dark corridors, the guards, the silence, and then the prisoner. Like Thompson and Kennan, under whom he later served, Stevens was a rarity, an American diplomat who spoke and read Russian. He had been tutored by White Russians at the Sorbonne, and his wife was an émigré, born to a Polish father and an aristocratic Russian mother. Stevens's wife had stayed behind in Washington with their young son, but her view of the USSR—the fear of an exile—colored his thinking on the Soviets.

There were other influences. Before going to Moscow, Stevens had served under Ray Murphy, the chief of the State Department's "special unit," EUR/X. Murphy rarely appeared in the press, but he had been tracking the rise of Soviet intelligence for nearly two decades, since Cy's first days in the party. After Hitler invaded Poland in 1939, Murphy began to gather intelligence on the Nazi threat, and in 1942 he enlisted Stevens to help him assemble the documents into a 510-page book. Since they were working in such proximity, it is likely that Murphy's distrust of the Soviets rubbed off on Stevens.

This time the meeting with Cy was brief. Again he was brought in by the guards and seated across the table. Stevens had brought the passport application, and the NKVD officials had kept their word. It was perhaps the only time the NKVD ever made photographs for an American citizen's passport application. For the portrait (the original is preserved in the National Archives outside Washington) they dressed the prisoner in new civilian clothes. Cy wore an oversized dark suit coat, a white-collared shirt, and a black tie.

When Stevens had explained the six-page form to the officers, Cy was given a pen. Beneath the oath of allegiance, he added his signature, a heavy cursive in blue ink, the NKVD standard. Stevens glued the photograph to the application and after Cy had pressed an inky thumb to its upper right-hand corner, embossed it with the embassy seal. Later, Thompson would also sign the form, and Stevens would type in the biographical details. The State Department had found Nerma, but Cy gave them the names and addresses of his siblings, David and Betty.

The next day, Stevens, like Thompson, filed a report to Washington. Again the language was neutral, but he also seemed to favor sending Oggins home. "The impression gained from the NKVD officials who have been present at the interviews is that there will be little delay in releasing Oggins whenever the Embassy is prepared to issue him a passport," Stevens cabled. "And at that time it will be advisable for travel arrangements to be as complete as possible so that he may leave the Soviet Union with a minimum of delay."

Something from their encounter in Butyrka, it seems, had stayed with the diplomats. Maybe it was Cy's despair, or loneliness. It would scarcely have been possible to sit in the prison interview room and not feel his misery. Thompson, too, wrote of the urgent need to plan in advance, "before the eventual release of Oggins and issuance of a passport, since it will probably be impossible for him to obtain either food or shelter in the Soviet Union for more than a very short period after he obtains his freedom."

IN WASHINGTON, THE MEN IN THE STATE DEPARTMENT RELAXED. Everything appeared in order. The wartime alliance, it seemed, had softened the Soviets. No one could remember Moscow releasing an American prisoner, yet now the procedures for Oggins's return, or so they allowed themselves to imagine, were under way.

Across town, though, the investigation had already begun. The department had found Cy's consular file and unearthed his passport applications, renewal requests, and foreign registrations. The doubts soon gathered. On January 5, 1943, a State Department investigator forwarded a copy of Thompson's Kuibyshev cable to the FBI. He added a suggestion "that a check-up be made on Mrs. Oggins' activities in this country." "This Division," he wrote, "feels reasonably sure that Oggins was an agent of the Soviet Government." On March 8, one month after Stevens collected Cy's passport application from the Moscow jail, FBI headquarters sent an urgent memorandum to the Bureau's field office in New York City. The directive, ordering up an immediate investigation, came from J. Edgar Hoover.

Miliary barricade in a Shanghai street, around the time of the 1927 Communist uprising.

CHAPTER 8

JOURNEY TO A WAR

∎ ∎ ∎

IN THE FEARFUL AUTUMN OF 1934, WHEN CY AND NERMA LEFT PARIS, toddler in tow, and returned to New York, they found a country deeply changed. America during the six years of their European adventures had suffered the throes of the Depression.

On September 28, 1934, as Cy and Nerma disembarked from the *Aquitania*, Americans were still getting used to the new president and his "fireside chats." FDR had launched the First New Deal, a rush of urgent legislation to bring relief to those hit hardest by the economic crisis, but as Cy and Nerma made the rounds of their old comrades, it was everywhere apparent that the circle of dissent had widened far beyond the Communists and Socialists. The crash had been the costliest economic education in history, and distrust of Wall Street continued to run high. To many, FDR had brought the promise of change. But to Cy and Nerma, the crisis could only mean one thing: the storm was gathering.

CY AND NERMA STOPPED only briefly in New York before moving on to San Francisco. Still, they stayed in their old hometown long enough for a terrifying encounter. One day Sidney Hook reappeared in their lives, just as suddenly as he had in Berlin.

Hook was teaching philosophy at New York University and already on his way to joining the ranks of the country's foremost public intellectuals. In the United States that fall, the moment of truth for American Communists had yet to arrive. Stalin's purges were only beginning, and the show trials lay in the future. Hook, however, had left Carrie. The marriage had not ended because of an affair, or even a flirtation. It was a matter, Hook told friends, of irreconcilable politics. He had not only divorced Carrie but severed all ties to their former life.

Though Hook had once been close to the Communists, by the early 1930s he had moved sharply away, allying himself, as Carrie and her friend Nerma would say, with the devil himself—Trotsky. By 1933 he was corresponding with Stalin's rival, then still on Prinkipo. But he was not seduced into the enemy camp with his eyes closed. As Carrie held firm to the party, Hook turned to Trotsky and his followers, calling them years later "the black snake that could cope with the Stalinist rattlesnake."

The encounter must have come in the autumn of 1934, in those first months after Cy and Nerma returned home. It was a twist of fate so astounding that even late in life Hook remembered the meeting vividly. He had traveled down to the Lower East Side to visit a friend in one of the red-brick tenements of the neighborhood. When he rang the bell, someone mistakenly opened the door to the adjacent apartment. There stood Nerma, with a small child. She did not say a word, in Hook's telling. Whether from Carrie or another comrade, Nerma had learned of Hook's turn away from the party. She took one look at Cy's old friend before stepping back in shock and slamming the door.

∎

IF AMERICA IN 1934 REMAINED AT THE MERCY OF THE DEPRESSION, waiting on an economic godsend from Washington, San Francisco was a city at war. The waterfront, home port of nearly two dozen U.S. steamship lines, was among the world's busiest. Every month more than five hundred ships called, and in 1933 more than half a billion dollars' worth of goods crossed its docks. Yet in the years since the stock market crash, labor tensions had mounted, and in the summer of 1934 the longshoremen walked.

The San Francisco maritime strike of July 1934 lasted only a few days, but fighting broke out in the streets as unionists, strikebreakers, and police squared off. "Radical unionism," the city elders warned, had seized the chance to exploit the workers' plight and threatened "to close the Golden Gate." July 5, 1934, the day that saw the worst of the shooting, would be known as Bloody Thursday and reshaped Californian labor politics for decades.

Overshadowing the strike, however, was the growing specter of Soviet influence. Moscow had long been keen to recruit from among the ranks of the long-suffering men of the docks. The union leaders, an anonymous full-page advertisement in a local newspaper claimed, were "fomenting strife along Pacific Coast ports, in conformity with a general Communistic plan to Sovietize first the seaports of America and then the entire United States." Harry Bridges, the charismatic Australian of the International Longshoremen's Association, had led the strike. One of the few leaders of organized labor in the United States who called himself a Marxist, Bridges was pursued as a Communist by the federal government throughout his long career. The allegations of his party membership are still contended, but few of Bridges's defenders today deny the Soviets' interest in his union.

By early 1935, Cy and Nerma had entered the fray. In San Francisco, they settled on the edge of Pacific Heights, one of the city's exclusive neighborhoods. The small wood-frame Victorian apartment house at 3460 Sacramento Street had glass storefronts on the street level and eight apartments on the two floors above. The flat was by no means grand, but with twin bay windows facing the Pacific and the ocean breeze, it retained a feel of the city's earliest days.

San Francisco was celebrating its first centenary in 1935 and was fast becoming a city of ethnic neighborhoods, with the Asian immigrants of Chinatown, the Latins of the Mission District, and the Sicilians of North Beach. It was the Italians who dominated—the mayor was a florist named Rossi, and that spring a young man named Joe DiMaggio began his final season with the San Francisco Seals. But the city was also home to a burgeoning community of Russian émigrés, White Russians who had escaped the Bolsheviks and Jews who had fled the czarist pogroms. Cy and Nerma's apartment happened to be in close proximity to the Russian district. (Whether they chose it or it was chosen for them is unknown.)

By summer, though, Cy had already received his orders. On

August 13 he applied for his fifth U.S. passport, telling the clerk that he would travel to Japan, China, and India. This time he gave a false address—43 Cole Street, a house near Golden Gate Park. He also made sure to ask the clerk to cancel his previous passport, the one granted in Paris only a year earlier. Clean passport in hand, Cy embarked on the third leg of his odyssey.

In September 1935, after being in America for just one year, he set sail for China. Nerma and their boy would remain in San Francisco, as Cy now traveled alone. The trip to Asia would be his longest, and by far the most dangerous. Cy did not know it then, but he was not only parting with his family, he was leaving America for the last time.

·

THE SHANGHAI BUND, THE MOST FAMOUS WATERFRONT IN CHINA, loomed. Cy had crossed the Pacific on the *President Roosevelt*, stopping only briefly in Japan and Hong Kong. After the years in Europe and months of waiting in the United States, the great entrepôt of Asia at last stood before him.

It had been a long crossing, but not a lonely voyage. Nerma's shoebox again helped to tell the story. "On board the Pres. Roosevelt" read the inky scrawl on the back of the images. Cy had taken the photographs. On deck, a half-circle of Western women played volleyball and shuffleboard beneath a canopy of heavy nets. They were young women, wearing cardigans, pleated skirts, and large hats. At the edge, men in dark suits and hats sat on wooden benches along the rails, talking among themselves. Cy had sent the photographs, mementos of his journey, along with scenic postcards of Mount Fuji, home to San Francisco.

In the fall of 1935, all of Asia, along with anxious diplomats throughout the West, was watching Japan. The Japanese had embarked on a belligerent campaign of empire-building, beginning with the occupation of the vast northeastern province of Manchuria in 1931. The objective was clear: hegemony in Asia. Manchuria, which the Japanese promptly renamed Manchukuo, was rich in coal, magnesium, and iron as well as coolie labor, and had strategic importance.

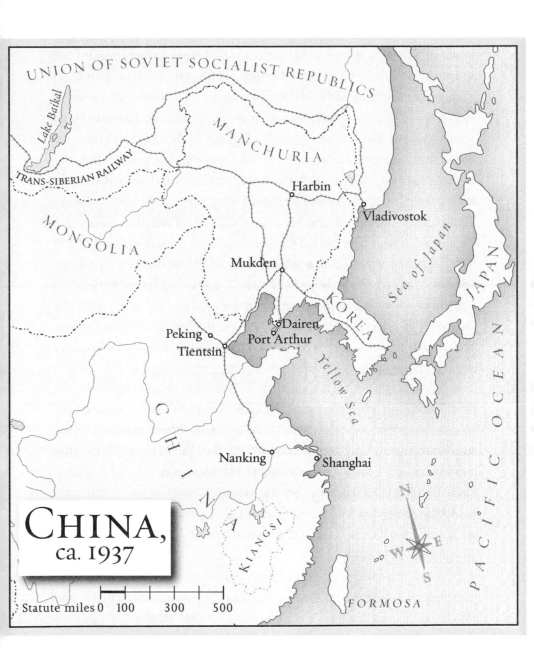

UNION OF SOVIET SOCIALIST REPUBLICS

Lake Baikal

TRANS-SIBERIAN RAILWAY

MANCHURIA

MONGOLIA

Harbin

Vladivostok

Mukden

Sea of Japan

JAPAN

KOREA

Peking

Tientsin

Dairen
Port Arthur

C H I N A

Yellow Sea

PACIFIC OCEAN

Nanking

Shanghai

KIANGSI

N

W   E

S

CHINA,
ca. 1937

FORMOSA

Statute miles 0   100   300   500

The Japanese right wing, though, dressed the imperial expansion in surprisingly modern political terms. In Tokyo, politicians and generals, dreaming of what a century later would be called "regime change," spoke of "liberation"—freeing the Chinese from the "white peril" of Western colonialism and the "Red peril" of Soviet communism.

Japan's militarization had been gaining momentum since the early 1920s, and Tokyo now stood squarely as Moscow's chief rival in Asia. Soviet envoys did not mingle with Japanese. But Cy did. Also on board the *Roosevelt* were a number of Japanese passengers. When the boat docked for a day in Kobe, he went off-ship and toured the city with a young woman named Kazuko Hiruri.

At some juncture along his journey, Cy may well have sensed a strange presence. If in Berlin it had been only a premonition, by Paris the threat had turned real. In France he had seen the consequences. Someone was watching him. Every move was being noted and, as his Lubyanka file would make clear, reported. Where Cy went with the Japanese girl that fall afternoon in Kobe, or what words they exchanged, was not recorded. The stroll, all the same, would come back to haunt him.

AS THE *ROOSEVELT* EASED toward the quay, the palisade of sky-scrapers rose on what had once been the Yangtze marsh. The Bund came close to resembling a Hollywood backdrop. As the ship came close to land, the landmarks—the Custom Tower, Hongkong & Shanghai Bank, Sassoon House, testaments to the city's colonial legacy—appeared along the riverbank. At the piers, junks clogged the waters. Crowded with new arrivals, the boats' prows were so squat and square that they seemed to sail backward.

Ashore, the dream dissolved into reality. Shanghai seethed with pilgrims and seekers—Chinese, Japanese, Europeans, Indians, and White Russians. Everywhere, evidence of the postcolonial chaos abounded. Since the 1860s the city had been sliced into sectors: the French Concession, the International Settlement, and the Chinese Municipality of Greater Shanghai, the largest of the three. The French ran their own sector, while the British and Americans had joined theirs to form the International Settlement. In 1935, the Set-tlement, as it was known, with more than a million residents, was the city's commercial and cultural center. The fight for China's riches—opium, cotton, and silk—was far from over. "Foreigners came to Shanghai," wrote an English reporter in 1935, "with two ends in view: to make money as quickly as possible and then to return home."

As Cy first toured the streets, he was confronted yet again with the legacy of empire. Shanghai, like no other city East or West, laid bare the colonial iniquity of the past century. A crossroads of foreign capital and native servitude, it was ruled by comprador traders, French merchants, British taipans, American bankers, and Jewish merchants with Baghdadi roots (the Sassoons, Hardoons, and Kadoories were the best known). Above all, it was a city-bazaar where opportunity was always for sale and the price ever negotiable.

To walk the Bubbling Well Road was to get lost in the mass of people bobbing in and out of the bookshops. One shop, the Zeitgeist, had recently been shuttered. Until 1933 it had been a Comintern front, where behind closed doors men and women born on the other side of the world had worked to usher in the new dawn. Along the Nanking Road, between the Cathay and Palace Hotels, the depart-ment stores—Wing On, Sincere, and Sun Sun—were as luxurious as any on Bond Street or the rue St.-Honoré. To the south, the French Concession was a labyrinth filled with rickshaws and walled with three-tiered villas, faux Tudor bungalows, and *shikumen*, the "stone-gate" houses, half Eastern, half Western, which reflected the sur-rounding mélange.

Farther on lay the old walled "Chinese city," a maze of squalor where even the locals got lost and few foreigners dared go. The streets and alleyways behind the tall stone walls reeked of poverty and overcrowding, yet the Chinese city seemed more vital than any other corner of Shanghai. "In no city, West or East," wrote Aldous Huxley after a visit a decade earlier, "have I ever had such an impres-sion of dense, rank, richly clotted life."

In a decade and a half it would all be over. The war would come, the government fall, and the Communists rise. Hedonism would subside in a sea of gray tunics, and the city's dance halls, opium dens, and singsong houses would lose out to state-imposed frigidity. Yet in the fall of 1935, as Cy walked its streets, Shanghai still seduced. It remained proud to be called, by locals and travelers alike, "the Whore of the Orient."

·

CY HAD LONG KNOWN THAT HE WOULD GO TO ASIA. AN AMERICAN IN China, especially one who was loyal, devout, and carrying a clean U.S. passport, was an asset of rare value. For years the Soviets had struggled to gain a clandestine foothold in the country. The Comintern's OMS and the Red Army's GRU had built networks in Shanghai and worked the northern front in Harbin, the city in the heart of Manchuria that was now home to more Russian refugees than Paris. In the late 1920s, Stalin had keenly watched China. When Tokyo occupied Manchuria in 1931, taking Japanese troops to the Soviet border, the Leader's interest had reached new heights. In the years that followed, though, Moscow's spies had suffered grave exposures. In the mid-1930s the Center redoubled its efforts, sending a new wave of Soviet agents, including an American, not yet forty but already accomplished, and, after nearly a decade in the clandestine world, well known among the bosses of the Lubyanka.

For Cy, the two years in China would mark the height of his espionage career. Asia would prove his most challenging assignment, not only because of the dangers of the arena. Traveling by himself, and with no want for money, the temptations would be many. In China, Cy could disappear and reinvent himself at will. Trader, writer, antiques dealer—he had to change masks often, effortlessly shedding addresses, occupations, and identities. In Shanghai and later, once he moved on to the north, Cy would have to rely on the skills of his European apprenticeship.

The Center had assigned him a mission that would put him at the center of the battle for China: running reconnaissance behind enemy lines, among the Chinese nationalists, imperial Japanese, and even the ascendant Nazis. To survive, he would need to trust his own tradecraft, and luck.

HE HAD BEGUN TO prepare back in Paris. Before leaving France, Cy had returned to his study of art history. In the Marais one day, he had stepped into Bonnardel's *papeterie* at 22 rue du 4 Sept. For two francs and forty centimes, he bought a small black moleskin notebook. In its pages, he took notes on the history of Asian antiquities. With care, he also sketched examples—vases, jugs, bracelets—dating from the Bronze Age to the Qing dynasty.

Robin still had the moleskin when I met him. The notes were in English, in Cy's dark, heavy handwriting. One subheading in French, "*L'Epoque Tcheou*," proved the necessary clue. In Paris, Cy had spent days pouring over the *Histoire des arts anciens de la Chine*—3,428 pages, with 476 color plates, in four volumes. Written by Osvald Sirén, a Swedish art historian and collector, it was a magisterial history of early Chinese art. Published in France in 1930, it soon became a classic.

Cy had reason to learn well. In Asia, his old cover as an antiques dealer would be convenient camouflage. On his travels, he did collect several works of art. Two Buddha heads now stood, nearly alone, on the mantle above the fireplace in Robin's house. Most likely Japanese in origin, they were made of gray stone. His father, Robin said, had brought them back as souvenirs. Cy had sent letters, too. Robin had kept the stamps—in time, their postmarks would help reveal his father's course across China.

Cy had sent home other clues, too. One was a blurry black-and-white photograph which, when enlarged, showed a street sign in Chinese and French. One afternoon in Shanghai, Cy had photographed a busy corner on the rue Wantz. One side of the road was walled with two-story stone houses, their wooden balconies jutting over the unpaved street. On the corner, three tradesmen, cobblers or tailors, sat at a makeshift worktable. An old canvas hanging on sticks half protected them from the wind and dust. On the right side of the frame, a little boy, no more than two years old, stood frozen in mid-step. With both hands cupped, he carried a small bowl. The men sat

Shanghai street scene, French Concession, photographed by Cy Oggins, ca. 1936.

in front of a red-brick building that was papered with announce-
ments, some in English. Young and old, they were bundled up in
heavy, old clothes. It must have been the winter of 1935.

Near the boy, three letters, C.M.F., were chiseled in stone at the
base of the building. *Concession Municipale Française* was the French
Concession, and the rue Wantz ran through its narrow center.
Named after an early architect of the district, the street stretched
four blocks, between the rue Lafayette and the avenue Joffre. From
where Cy was standing, it was only a short walk to the Chinese city.
For many Europeans and Americans, a tour of the squalor was an
obligatory field trip. Outsiders could visit in the afternoon and
return to the boulevards of the Settlement by sunset. For Cy, it
seemed, Shanghai's worst slum held more than curiosity. Teeming
with the native proletariat, it was the one district he yearned to
explore.

Cy had also taken several trips into the countryside. He walked
the mud roads where peasants pumped water into rusty buckets and
smiled. He photographed the villages where several families lived in
a single shack, a lean-to of rotting wood. He followed half-clad chil-

THE LOST SPY   199

dren chasing chickens. Judging from the scenes found in Nerma's shoebox, Cy appears to have traveled freely and widely.

He did not, though, miss out on the Shanghai nightlife. The *belle monde* flocked to the Paramount ballroom, but an all-night party reigned along the Settlement's rougher edges. Along the Fuchow Road, in establishments like Casanova's Del Monte's, and, on the shadier end, the Tumble Inn, the tea dancers—Chinese girls in cheongsams slit to the thigh and Russian girls in sequins—took a foreigner's hand for a dime. The Russian girls, as one pilgrim from the West wrote, suffered from a "listless depression" that showed through "their professional smiles." Cy made the tour, and even took up with an American dancer.

In all likelihood, Nerma never knew of the affair. Gundula Wood—the name hinted at Swedish roots—was a cabaret girl who worked in a dance bar. She had no interest in politics, Cy claimed years later when prodded by his interrogator in the Lubyanka—at least, none that he knew of. They met in the hotel; both stayed at the same place in the Settlement. How long the relationship lasted or how serious it was is unknown. Cy kept the details to himself.

But the news did reach the Center. Whoever was shadowing Cy was careful, and persistent, writing down where he went and with whom. Like the stroll with the Japanese girl, the affair with the American cabaret girl was duly recorded. Cy's indiscretion, however fleeting, would have a price—and it was rising.

·

A DOZEN YEARS EARLIER, LENIN HAD SENT A FAMED SOVIET AGENT TO China. Mikhail Markovich Borodin, a thirty-nine-year-old Comintern envoy and comrade of the father of the revolution, arrived in Canton in 1923. Born Gruzenberg to a Russian Jewish family in Byelorussia, Borodin had become a Bolshevik in his teenage years. He fought in the revolution of 1905, and after its failure spent more than a decade in exile in Chicago. In China, Borodin, with his outsized personality and fluent English, made fast friends—above all with Sun Yat-sen, the former doctor turned revolutionary who had founded the Kuomintang, the People's Party. Sun at the time faced warlord satraps on all sides and could scarcely hold his party together. Lenin worried about the "virginal naiveté" of the Kuomintang leader, but saw in his party the potential for a bulwark against imperialism in Asia. Chiang Kai-shek, then Sun's young head of staff and chief military strategist, was in Moscow on an extended stay when Borodin went to Canton in the fall of 1923. The exchange soon bore fruit: by 1924, Borodin had joined Sun's inner circle of advisers.

After Lenin's death, Stalin hoped to win over the Kuomintang, imagining that Borodin could bend both the nationalists and the Communists to Moscow's will. The Comintern instructed the Chinese Communists to seek an alliance with Chiang, but after the death of Sun in 1925, any rapprochement was doomed. On March 20, 1926, Chiang cut short the coalition between the Kuomintang and the Communists, and then, when Borodin was absent from Canton, staged his coup. Within a year, the alliance ended in the 1927 massacre of Communists and Borodin's humiliating retreat to Moscow. Stalin had gambled on forging a "revolutionary-democratic bloc" with the Chinese bourgeoisie, and lost.

The Soviet intelligence agencies only redoubled their efforts, sending a new wave of agents to China. In the late 1920s Shanghai became the operational arena of Richard Sorge, the Great Illegal, and his fellow spy and lover, Agnes Smedley. Smedley, the American writer and radical who had reported on Thälmann's Red Front Fighters in Berlin, had gone to China directly from Germany. In Shanghai she worked officially as a correspondent for the *Frankfurter Zeitung*. Sorge relied on Smedley to introduce him to her wide circle of Chinese friends, including several who joined his network. The Center had made progress in establishing a Chinese underground, but by the time Cy arrived, Sorge's old network was in ruins. Arrests and police raids had taken their toll.

The Settlement was blessed with a corps of British detectives, the elite of the Shanghai Municipal Police, the SMP. Their files, preserved in large part on sixty-seven microfilm reels in the records of the CIA at the National Archives, record the metropolis of vice in detail. The force resembled a racial pyramid, with Brits on top, Sikhs second, Russians third, and Chinese constables on the bottom. The SMP paid attention not only to the opium and sex trade but to the Soviet underground. A May 1933 report listed Sorge and Smedley as "suspected Soviet agents."

The SMP also caught a pair of Moscow's spies red-handed. On June 15, 1931, one Hilaire Noulens, "professor of French and German," and his wife, Gertrude, were arrested at 235 Sichuan Road, one of several flats they had rented in the city. The Noulenses first claimed to be Belgian, then Swiss, and gave the police three different names. In fact they were Russians—Yakov Rudnik, an OMS agent, and Tatyana Moiseenko, a GPU officer. By 1932, as the Noulenses sat in a Nanking jail, Madame Sun Yat-sen served as their liaison to the West. Willi Münzenberg, the Soviets' propaganda master in Berlin, was given the task of running a crusade to free the Noulenses, and their case threatened to become the biggest cause célèbre since the execution of Sacco and Vanzetti. International celebrities from Barbusse to Dreiser to Einstein, without knowing the Noulenses' true names, decried their arrests. In the end the couple was spared execution, but the scandal nearly closed down the Soviet network in China.

Three years before Cy arrived, in 1932, the Comintern, in the wake of the Noulens arrest, dispatched a small corps of replacements, most notably Otto Braun. The German Communist arrived in China with $20,000 for the Noulenses' defense, and soon moved on to Kiangsi, the remote province in the southeast where the Communists had set up a fledgling Chinese Soviet Republic the previous year. Investigating the Noulens case, the SMP learned of the Comintern's secret channel to fund its local comrades. "A sub-agency of the Communist International in Berlin," wrote the State Department official Robert Kelley to Secretary of State Harry Stimson in the summer of 1932, had fed nearly half a million dollars in one year to the Chinese Communists. The money, he added, was not for "trade union" work but for weapons.

For years, relations with China would frustrate the Kremlin. Stalin could not forgive Chiang, the strongman who had trumped him. "In general," he wrote to Molotov on June 19, 1932, "the Nanking government is comprised of *melkie zhuliki*," little hooligans. "But that does not mean, of course, we don't have to deal with these hooligans."

■

CY REMAINED IN SHANGHAI THROUGH THE SPRING AND SUMMER OF 1936. On July 21, he registered with the U.S. consulate. For a permanent address, he gave a second address in San Francisco, also near Golden Gate Park, 860 Arguello Boulevard. He wrote his real name but now listed his occupation as "free-lance writer."

One of the Center's primary concerns in Shanghai at the time was the *Voice of China*, a fortnightly newspaper that parroted the party line for the benefit of the English-speaking readers of China. Its first editor, who assumed the job in the weeks before Cy's arrival, was none other than Agnes Smedley. On September 2, 1935, Earl Browder, head of the American party, had written to Dimitrov, the Comintern chief, seeking approval for a plan "to assist Agnes Smedley, now in Shanghai, to publish an English language anti-imperialist newspaper there." Smedley had reported that "such a paper would be of great influence." Dimitrov, not surprisingly, was all for the idea. To shore up the operation, Browder dispatched two party functionaries from New York on a rushed secondment to Shanghai.

Manny and Grace Granich were in their forties when they set foot in China on January 31, 1936. Husband and wife, they were veterans of the early days in New York. It would seem likely, given the number of connections, that Cy and Nerma knew the couple. Grace had been Browder's secretary, and before that, Scott Nearing's. Manny's brother, Irwin, was better known as Mike Gold, a pseudonym he adopted after the Palmer raids. Mike Gold is nearly forgotten today, but the author of *Jews Without Money* was once hailed as "the Gorky of the Lower East Side." Gold was also the star columnist of the *Daily Worker* in the years that Nerma wrote for it.

Within months of their arrival, the Graniches had set up the Eastern Publishing Company. At first the venture appeared to be off to a good start, with the inaugural issue of the *Voice of China* appearing in March. Before long, though, problems arose—and the trouble was Smedley. She enjoyed close ties with the Chinese but was incapable of toeing the party line. Neither the Soviets nor Browder questioned her loyalty, yet as the warnings from the field mounted, Moscow replaced her. The job of running the paper fell to the Graniches, and they appear to have done it well. The *Voice of China*, wrote one British detective, was "radical to an extreme and violently anti-Japanese, it urged the people of China to unite and revolt against Japanese Imperialism."

It is conceivable that Cy contributed to the *Voice*. Its table of contents was littered with pseudonyms. Smedley, for instance, was R. Knailes, short for Rusty Nails, her Shanghai nickname. In the summer of 1936 the newspaper published a series of articles on the miseries of the Japanese-run cotton mills in China, a subject close to the heart of the boy from Willimantic. Within months, whether or not Cy was involved, the publishing venture came to a sudden halt. On November 30, 1936, the SMP raided the newspaper's offices. In Moscow, the alarm sounded, and the Graniches were forced into retreat. For the SMP detectives, four years after the Noulens case, Grace and Manny were the next target. The Settlement as a Soviet operational base was endangered. But by then Cy was gone. Just as he had in Paris after the Switzes' arrest, the American had moved on.

·

IN OCTOBER 1936, CY LEFT SHANGHAI, A CITY ENVELOPED IN ITS OWN political mists and social turmoil, and boarded a coastal steamer for the voyage north on the Yellow Sea to Dairen. Often the journey posed risks, with coolies packed into the hold by the hundreds and typhoons arising without warning. When the waves gained force and played havoc with the boats, sea captains would post guards at the holds, fearful that the coolies might break out in panic. Dairen lay only 550 nautical miles north of Shanghai, but if a storm hit, the voyage might last days.

Cy arrived in Manchuria at the height of Manchukuo, the Japanese name for Japan's puppet state in northeastern China. In the fall of 1936, travel to the region was tightly controlled. Germans and Italians were welcome, as Hitler and Mussolini were the only Western leaders to recognize the would-be state. Yet the boats from Shanghai hardly ever carried foreigners. Amid the traders crowded on board, there might be the occasional Western missionary, but rarely an American. Since Secretary of State Stimson had denounced the Japanese invasion in 1932, few U.S. businessmen dared to cross behind Japanese lines.

Dairen seemed an island at the edge of the world. In Moscow, where it was still called Dalny, Russian for "far away," the city was a conspicuous reminder of Russia's imperial reach and, concomitantly, its failures. Known today as Dalian, the port stood at the southern tip of the Liao-tung Peninsula, across the bay from Port Arthur, the lost prize of Russia's disastrous war with the Japanese in 1904–05. In 1898, the year of Cy's birth, Nicholas II had leased the peninsula from the Chinese and approved plans for a city at the terminus of the South Manchurian Railway, the extension of the Trans-Siberian. Yet after the Russo-Japanese War, Tokyo won the lease, acquiring both the railway and the port. By the time Cy arrived, Dairen was owned and operated by the Japanese company that made the trains literally run on time, the South Manchuria Railway Company.

Manchukuo held great promise: not only was it rich in natural resources, but it lay in close proximity to trading partners across Asia. It lacked only an autonomy movement. To lend their proxy state legitimacy, the Japanese had imported a son of the Manchus, Henry Pu Yi, the twenty-five-year-old heir to the dynasty that had ruled China from 1643 until the revolution of 1912. Pu Yi would gain fame as "the last emperor." First enthroned at age three, he had abdicated when the revolution came, and in 1917 was briefly made emperor a second time. The restoration, a short-lived dream

Emperor Pu Yi, Manchukuo Postage Stamp, 1935.

of a misguided Qing loyalist, lasted a week. Pu Yi, rescued by his English tutor, Sir Reginald Johnston, had lived in the intervening years under Japanese protection in Tientsin, the seaport near Peiping.

On November 15, 1931, the Japanese had delivered Pu Yi to Dairen, naming him Manchukuo's "chief executive." By 1934, in Shinto ceremonies that bound him to the sun goddess, the mother of the Japanese imperial dynasty, Pu Yi was made emperor for a third and final time.

•

WITHIN DAYS OF ARRIVING IN DAIREN, CY EMBARKED ON HIS FIRST trip across Manchukuo. He boarded a train for Harbin, the industrial city to the north, and was joined by a contingent of heavily armed Japanese soldiers—a precaution against the bandits who frequently attacked the trains. If a false calm pervaded Dairen, the "protected villages" offered a stark contrast. The Japanese had instituted a policy of "protecting" the peasants from rampant banditry by locking them away behind eight-foot-high stockades. The practice, tantamount to a quarantine, was a failure. As Cy traveled north on the Asia, the express to Harbin, the countryside laid bare the truths of Japanese rule. Poverty filled the landscape. Women washed clothes in the muddy streams, no matter the hour, while children, row after row of underfed bodies, worked the kaoliang, or sorghum, fields.

Harbin, once a remote village, was now a cosmopolitan city of 1,000 factories and more than 100,000 Russian émigrés. In 1935, after the USSR sold its stake in the China Eastern Railway to the Japanese, many émigrés returned to the Soviet Union, fearing the Japanese occupation more than the Bolsheviks. Yet in the winter of 1936, the *Kharbintsy*, as the local Russians were known, still predominated. Some carried "Nansen passports," papers issued by the Norwegian diplomat Fridtjof Nansen during his 1920s relief work, but others had only outdated czarist documents. In Manchukuo, both kinds of refugees were stranded. The Russians, wrote W. H. Auden and Christopher Isherwood on their "journey to a war" a year later, seemed a "fat, defeated tribe who lead a melancholy life of gossip, mah-jongg, drink and bridge . . . Their clocks stopped in 1917. It had been tea-time ever since."

Cy stayed a month in Harbin. He received his instructions from the Center and filed the requisite paperwork before returning south. In November 1936, Dairen posed considerable challenges for a Soviet spy. With fewer than 350,000 residents, it was everything that Harbin was not. Dairen was clean, safe, and uneventful. It had few European residents and only a handful of Americans, and all foreigners were required to register with the local authorities. Everyone, Japanese, Chinese, and Westerners alike, was monitored. Dairen, too, had a White Russian colony, but only a few hundred families. With the Japanese in charge and the local port and garrisons on a war footing, it was impossible for anyone to hide.

When Nicholas II envisioned Dairen as a czarist foothold in the Orient, he had, oddly, modeled it on Paris. The avenues were tidily laid out, their ends meeting in flowering *rond-points*. The main square was in fact an elegant roundabout, the Central Circle. Taking over in 1905, the Japanese only heightened the sense of self-importance. Imposing neoclassical buildings dominated the circle—the Yamato Hotel, the U.S. consulate, the Chosen Bank of Korea, Yokohama Bank, the Police Bureau, and the Administrative Building. Even Dairen's city hall tried to imitate a French state building: its mansard roof was decorated with *chiens assis*, the "seated dogs" of Parisian rooflines. Westerners were impressed. Will Rogers stopped by in 1931 and called Dairen "the most modern city and port you ever saw." Two years later, Peter Fleming, an English travel writer whose brother created James Bond, found it "a sort of Japanese Hongkong, very orderly and hygienic and up to date."

With rare efficiency, the Russians had laid out a tidy, segregated city. A bridge separated the "European Town" from the "Chinese Town," and the Japanese had only improved on the blueprint. In a region where most roads were reserved for oxcarts, Dairen boasted avenues lined with streetlights and sakura trees. Europeans drank the tapwater without fear, and at night the cab horses, for the horse-drawn buggies, were stabled outside town, to stave off the swarms of flies. The Japanese had also built modern facilities, including large schools and a hospital on a site cleared for a Romanov palace. "The general atmosphere of the place," wrote Fleming, "is suggestive of a garden suburb."

By the time Cy arrived, Dairen had seen a massive settlement campaign, with more than 300,000 Japanese "pioneers" displacing the Chinese natives. Shinto temples now stood amid turreted Russian homes, and the sunrise ceremonies, complete with loud chanting, awakened neighbors who had been born as far away as St. Petersburg. In seizing Manchuria, Tokyo had claimed a noble motive: Manchukuo would unite "the five races"—Japanese, Chinese, Manchus, Koreans, and Mongolians. The social blending, represented by the five colors of the puppet state's flag, promised a new Asian harmony.

To the Soviets, though, "the Manchukuo paradise" only masked Japan's imperial hunger. That spring, the *Voice of China* accused Tokyo of subduing Manchuria by "drugging the minds of the people with opium, weakening their resistance with propaganda, terrorizing them with armies, and destroying the economy of the country." The drumbeat of Moscow's anti-Japanese propaganda was impossible to ignore.

Soon events overtook the war of words. As the winter of 1936 set in, the tensions mounting in Europe reached Dairen. The Japanese generals had grown anxious, and the foreign powers, above all the Germans and Italians, placed their bets. More than ever, the Soviets hungered to learn Japan's secrets. In Dairen, Tokyo's plans were transparent. Everyone, it seemed, knew it was only a matter of time. War was close.

■

EVEN IN THE SECOND WEEK OF DECEMBER 1936, THE U.S. CONSULATE DISplayed few signs of Christmas. Stuart Grummon, the consul, was one of only two American diplomats posted to Dairen. A Princeton man three years younger than Cy, Grummon had joined the Foreign Service straight out of college. He had studied Russian in Washington, hoping for a post in the first embassy in the USSR, but had been sent instead to Haiti, then the Netherlands and China. A diplomat of the old school, he was courtly and reticent—and a friend of Cy's.

On December 16, Cy walked into the grand building on the Central Circle and registered as a foreign resident. The pattern continued. Cy gave his real name but listed yet another address, 345 Fulton Street, as his home in San Francisco.

He may have been hoping to see Grummon. In Moscow, when the diplomats later visited him in jail and asked who could verify his identity, Cy gave them one name: Stuart Grummon's. The consul, Cy said, could vouch for him if he cared to remember. It is not hard to imagine how the two men, Ivy League graduates of nearly equal age stranded in a remote corner of the world, would have welcomed each other's company. Grummon, however, was absent on the day Cy returned to the consulate. He was in Peiping, where he and his young wife were to spend Christmas, awaiting the birth of their first child.

As Cy filled out the usual paperwork, no one at the consulate had cause for suspicion. But if anyone had asked Shanghai to check the files, he would have seen that Cy had listed three different San Francisco addresses in a span of sixteen months. He also now claimed a new occupation. This time Cy wrote that he was in the employ of "Charles Martin & Co. of Harbin."

It was almost the truth. Cy had nearly given himself away, revealing the name of his underground boss, or at least one version of it, to the Americans.

Charles Martin does not figure in the Western accounts of Soviet espionage during China's turbulent years before the war. Sorge, Smedley, and Ruth Werner—a German Communist born Ursula Kuczynski, codenamed "Sonya" by the Soviets, and who died as Ruth Beurton—receive most of the credit. Charles Martin seemed, at least at first, another of Cy's inventions. But it was a clue, and it summoned an investigation.

When I asked, few historians of Soviet intelligence had ever heard of Martin. Similarly, among the oldest veterans, the retired officers of the KGB and the CIA, the name failed to elicit any recognition. The Library of Congress, the New York Public Library, the Hoover

Archives, and the National Archives yielded no further clarity. Only after months of searching did Charles Martin at last emerge.

A second clue floated up amid the sea of spy memoirs that appeared after World War II. The years following the victory over the Nazis saw the birth of a new best-selling genre in the West, the spy confessional. In the 1940s and 1950s, dozens of former espionage agents, eager to monetize their heroic exploits, wrote memoirs. As the USSR had shared in the Allied victory, many of the books were written by former Soviet spies, each of whom purported to tell the inside story of the rise of Soviet espionage in Europe before the war.

Charles Martin finally stepped out of the shadows, though, in a CIA book, *The Rote Kapelle: The CIA's History of Soviet Intelligence and Espionage Networks in Western Europe, 1936–1945.* Die Rote Kapelle, most often translated as "the Red Orchestra," was the Germans' name for the Soviet spy network that worked behind Nazi lines. After the war, historians and journalists amply chronicled the feats of the Kapelle agents, hailing them as heroes of the anti-Nazi fight. All too often, however, these accounts relied on self-serving memoirs of the ring's former members, many of who had also worked before the war—against the West.

At first the CIA study seemed to be of the same variety, an assemblage of excerpts from previous accounts, collated, declassified, and published privately in 1979. But *The Rote Kapelle* held a surprise: a biographical listing for one Charles Emile Martin.

WILMER, George. Aliases: CHARLES EMILE MARTIN, Lorenz, Laurenz and Dubois. Born 29 July 1889 in Petrograd, Russia. Reportedly, a Swiss of Soviet origin who spoke fluent German, French with a Marseilles accent, and Russian. He and his wife Elsa had two children, Erich and Galja. He was an engineer and photographic expert, supposedly from St. Croix, canton of Vaud. In 1939 he entered Switzerland. Martin lived at 32 Chemin de la Fauvette, Chailly, near Lausanne.

And another for his wife:

WILMER, Joanna. Aliases: ELSA MARIE MARTIN (née Maeder), Lora and Laura. Born 31 March 1899 in Leningrad. She was the daughter of Bartholomeo and Marie Nuenuksela. Married Charles Emile Martin on 31 December 1931.

The single clue had yielded several dozen more. Still, archives in Moscow, Paris, Berlin, Tokyo, Shanghai, and Washington offered little information. The corporate registration records of Manchukuo had long since disappeared. Charles and Elsa Martin had emerged briefly, but threatened to remain hidden forever—until they reappeared, in different guises, in one of the many memoirs of the Rote Kapelle.

Alexander Foote was a British spy who served in the Red Orchestra, without great distinction, until his arrest by the Swiss in 1943. In his 1949 memoir, A Handbook for Spies, Charles and Elsa Martin appeared as "Lorenz" and "Lora." Foote had encountered the couple in Switzerland, where they were living in a luxurious villa nestled among the hills above Lake Geneva. It was possible, of course, that the CIA gleaned all of its information on the couple from Foote. Yet if the Americans had learned of "Lora" and "Lorenz" from Foote's memoir, then the Swiss must have as well.

CHARLES EMILE MARTIN proved elusive, even to the best officers of Swiss intelligence. For forty-seven years, the Swiss Federal Archives had maintained the secrecy of its files on the Martins. In the fall of 2003, acting on my request, the Swiss declassified the dossier—all 325 pages. The mountain of documents, in German, French, English, and Russian—visas, consular registrations, identity documents, interrogation transcripts, surveillance records, court filings, police reports, and correspondence among Western intelligence services— told, in forensic detail, the Martins' story, or stories.

The Swiss authorities had investigated Charles and Elsa for nearly a decade. For years after the war, they watched the couple. They opened their mail and hauled them in for interrogations. Martin spun one ornate tale after another. Investigators in Bern, Lausanne, and Zurich chased names, dates, and addresses. They compared notes with colleagues in England, France, Italy, and the United States. The Swiss hoped to make a spy case, but in the end they settled for identity theft. On January 11, 1956, Charles and Elsa Martin were convicted of fraudulently obtaining Swiss documents and were sentenced to three months in jail. By fall, they were on a plane out of the country. The Swiss authorities, though, never learned their true identities. They only discovered that Charles Martin, like a lizard who sheds his tail each time he is caught, was a master at evasion.

CHARLES EMILE MARTIN liked to pose. He could be a wealthy Russian émigré, a Milanese industrialist ("Carlo Emilio"), or the illegitimate son of a poor Swiss widow. In truth he was Max (born Matus) Steinberg, a Ukrainian Jew from Belgorod-Dnestrovsky, a port town at the mouth of the Dniestr River on the northern coast of the Black Sea. Like so many of his comrades in the first ranks of the secret services, Steinberg came from a trading crossroads, a frontier between Europe and the East. Geography had blessed him with a taste for languages; his gift for subterfuge, however, was his own.

Max could have pretended to be Cy's twin. He stood no taller than the American and often claimed to be the same age. Yet the Russian was six years younger. He had a slight build, a thin, angular face, and inky black hair, which he wore swept low across the left brow. His eyes were dark brown, half hidden beneath heavy lids. Still, it was said that Max's gaze could be penetrating. He spoke native Russian, Ukrainian, and Yiddish and as a youth had mastered German and French with remarkable fluency.

Unlike Cy, Max tried his best not to stand out. He had a fondness for dark suits, plain neckties, and gabardine overcoats. Whether at a border crossing or an embassy reception, he could pass for a midlevel bureaucrat or an itinerant trader of unfixed European origins. Elsa, on the other hand, was striking. In Europe and in Russia, strangers seemed to remember her dark blond hair, large gray eyes, and weakness for furs and purses. But both were expert in the art of spying in plain sight, and as Charles and Elsa Martin, the Swiss personas they inhabited in China, they disappeared into history—almost.

The Manchurian assignment may in fact have been a reunion. By

1936, Max had already held a string of foreign postings, in Belgium, Romania, and Paris. It is possible that Max had served as Cy's boss in France as well. From the late 1920s to the early 1930s in Paris, he had run Operation Korridor, one of the Center's first attempts to infiltrate the White Russian émigré circles in France—a precursor to Cy's Romanov mission. By the time Cy arrived in Manchuria, Max Steinberg, aka Charles Martin, George Wilmer, Lorenz, Laurenz, Dubois, and no doubt many other aliases, was one of the Center's most accomplished and highest-ranking spies abroad. Max was an undiscovered Great Illegal.

MAX AND CY went to China to execute an ingenious scheme: not only would they make money for Moscow, but they would create a rare operational base behind Japanese lines. The plan, at once absurd and entirely plausible, was a great gamble. But the Center had deemed it worth the risk.

By 1935, everything was set. Max would pose as a well-to-do businessman, the Swiss partner of one Dr. Eugenio Carutti. In the files from the Swiss archives, the Italian seemed to be a Moscow impresario, a middleman representing a raft of Italian automobile companies in the USSR. With Dr. Carutti as a front partner in Europe, Max would launch an import operation in Manchuria, and Cy would be his lieutenant.

In the years following World War II, the Swiss tried to track down Dr. Carutti. They had only an address, Campagnia Commerciale Caproni, Piazza Paolo Ferrari 8, 20121 Milano. They sought the help of Italian intelligence and the Milan police, but it was useless. The Italian, it seemed, had vanished.

TO GET TO CHINA, Max exploited a loophole in Swiss consular operations. After the Russian Revolution, when thousands of Swiss citizens were caught in the USSR, the Swiss government offered to repatriate anyone whose citizenship papers had been issued before the Bolshevik takeover. Max had used two documents: a graduation certificate dated May 24, 1916, from the gymnasium of St. Catherine's, a Lutheran church in Petrograd, and a Swiss identity card for his "mother," Alice-Louise Martin, issued by the Swiss Legation in Russia in 1918 and extended in 1923 and 1928. Then, aided by the Swiss Red Cross in Moscow, he traveled to the Swiss legation in Warsaw. On July 23, 1935, he presented the documents and received a genuine Swiss passport. Elsa followed the same circuitous route to obtain hers. In the summer of 1935, the couple left the USSR, just as, half a world away, Cy and Nerma were preparing to part in San Francisco.

Charles and Elsa Martin appeared in Shanghai several weeks after Cy arrived. On November 21, they registered at the Swiss consulate, and the following day they obtained new Swiss passports. Within weeks they had boarded the train north to Manchuria.

In Harbin, Charles Martin established himself quickly. He rented a large furnished flat from one of the city's wealthiest landlords, a White Russian entrepreneur by the name of Chepitovsky. He opened an account at the local branch of the National City Bank of New York and deposited $75,000—an extraordinary sum for the day. Soon he rented a garage nearby. By mid-December, when he filed papers with the French consulate, the diplomatic proxy for the Swiss in Harbin, Charles Martin & Co. had been born.

·

MAX STEINBERG HAD BROUGHT CY TO MANCHUKUO AT A TIME WHEN the Japanese empire was well advanced on the road to war. As Cy settled into Dairen, the city had already lost its implacable calm. It now suffered the claustrophobic air of a closed town, and with each passing month the warning signs only grew stronger. Naval boats from Tokyo crowded the harbor, and new contingents of soldiers, troops of the Imperial Japanese Army, the IJA, filled the garrisons at the edges of town.

Among the Japanese occupiers, paranoia ran high. The case of Mr. Roth, an elderly Czech émigré and one of the wealthiest men in town, was well known. Born in the Carpathian mountains, he grew up speaking Hungarian but was fluent in English, German, Japanese, and, thanks to his time as a prisoner in World War I, Russian. The best linguist in Dairen, Roth was often called on to translate. The Japanese, though, accused him of being an American spy. They tried to make him talk, even drugging him and bringing in translators to take down his confession. But Roth spilled out his life story in his native Hungarian, a language none of the translators knew.

For years the social hub of Dairen was the Yamato Hotel, a drab hostelry on the Central Circle that was the town's finest. The hotel had seen its share of Soviet agents; Freda Utley, the English writer, was just one of many Comintern agents who had visited in previous years. The Yamato was run, like almost everything else in town, by the railroad company. Japanese girls strolled in its refined garden in kimonos while visitors gathered around the "talking machines," RCA radios, in the lobby. In the spring, the rooftop restaurant, where couples dined on white linen beneath Chinese lanterns, became Dairen's center stage. All summer the Yamato showed moving pictures on the roof. "Every Saturday Evening," the local newspaper advertisements promised, guests enjoyed "a movie program of Comedy, News and Sports."

To the thousands of pioneers sent from Tokyo, Dairen seemed the model of modernity. The native peasants, at the same time, subsisted on a single crop, soybeans. At the train depot in the port, newly built to great fanfare, a wall of bean cakes—dried wheels a yard long and stacked high by the thousands—stretched a mile along the pier. Dairen shipped steel, fur, wool, petroleum, and silk, but bean cakes remained the chief export. At night, even in the dark fog of the harbor, coolies worked the giant nets without relief, loading the cakes onto freighters bound for the pigs of Formosa.

To Cy, the posting, however exotic, brought isolation and loneliness. Yet even here, in this far-off corner of Asia, he could read of the turmoil in Moscow. The tensions in the Politburo, long hidden below the surface, had exploded into the open. In August 1936, Stalin had crossed a line that many of the faithful had believed he never would. Zinoviev and Kamenev became the first Old Bolsheviks killed in the purges. Zinoviev, as Cy well knew, had once led the Comintern. When Lenin fell gravely ill, he and Kamenev had joined with Stalin to form the party's ruling *troika* and rushed to help oust Trotsky. Now Stalin had returned the favor.

The *Manchuria Daily News,* the only English-language newspaper in town, announced the executions in giant headlines. For Cy, the *Daily News* was an unavoidable torture. An endless stream of anti-Soviet attacks, lurid and expansive, filled its pages. Often the reports were credited to "A Soviet Refugee." One such screed, an account of slave labor in the USSR, ran in the first week of November 1936 under a typical headline: "Whole of Construction Work in This Country Is Built Up on Sweat and Blood of Half-Nude Starving People Working Like Beasts."

At the same time, the newspaper sang the praises of the Fascists rising in Germany and Italy. Hitler and Mussolini by then had made up their minds. As late as 1935, German military advisers had stayed on in Shanghai, urging Hitler to back Chiang. Yet by 1936, the Nazis were pushing for a so-called anti-Comintern pact with the Japanese, a move Hitler envisioned as a hedge against Stalin. Now, when most representatives of American companies had long since decamped from Dairen, the Germans and Italians were left nearly alone to fight for the favor of the Japanese. In May 1936, the Nazis signed a trade deal with Manchukuo, and a year later they extended the pact. In the summer of 1937, Karl Knoll, Hitler's envoy to the region, arrived in Dairen.

In the final days of July 1937, the Railway Club hosted a garden party to mark the new era of German-Japanese cooperation. As the visiting Nazis and Japanese occupiers raised their champagne glasses, a handful of White Russian émigrés mingled in their midst. Overhead hung flags sewn for the occasion, bright yellow lotus flowers stitched onto black swastikas. The visitors from Berlin had delivered a selection of Nazi films to bring the evening to a rousing close. Throughout the evening, though, the dignitaries cast nervous glances at the sky. The war had come at last.

THREE WEEKS EARLIER, fighting at the Marco Polo Bridge had shaken Dairen. The bridge, less than twenty miles outside Peiping, was strategic, running alongside a vital railway line to the city. On the night of July 7, Japanese troops with blanks in their guns had gone on maneuvers in the area. At 10:30 p.m., the Chinese decided to shell them. None of the Japanese soldiers were killed or wounded, but at roll call, as the story has been recorded, one was missing. Believing that the Chinese had seized the soldier, the Japanese commander ordered an attack on the closest Chinese town.

The provocation, a pretext long awaited, proved sufficient. Prince Konoe, the Japanese premier, called for a "fundamental solution" of relations with China. Chiang Kai-shek responded in kind. "The only course open to us now," Chiang announced, "is to lead the masses of the nation, under a single national plan, to struggle to the last." The fighting on the bridge outside Peiping signaled the start of the Sino-Japanese War. It was also, in retrospect, the first battle of the new world war.

In Dairen in the weeks that followed, war preparations took precedence. As panic struck, all ships leaving for Japan were packed. Tens of thousands of Japanese civilians were eager to get out, and IJA ships crowded the sea lanes between Dairen and Tangku. "Dairen Scene Is Warlike," announced an anxious report in the *New York Times* on August 13. Hallett Abend, the newspaper's longtime China corre-spondent, had seen "six freights and gasoline tankers" in the Dairen har-bor, "flying red danger flags" and "unloading under the protection of a Japanese destroyer." The fighting, in Tokyo's plans, would be on a major scale, and decisive. The Manchukuo regime had requisitioned 123 Japan-ese freighters for the war. "At pres-ent," wrote Abend, "the Japanese are cocksure of and even jubilant over what they expect will be a quick and overwhelming victory."

The next day, the first bombs fell.

Manchukuo Airmail Stamp, airplane flying over the iron bridge across the Songhua River near Harbin 1936.

Bloody Sunday, the shocked expatriates would later call the horror they witnessed on August 15, 1937, in Shanghai. Bombs fell in the heart of the Settlement along the Nanking Road. The first reports blamed the Japanese, but soon the truth leaked: the Chinese had mistakenly bombed their own city. Crowds transfixed by the planes had filled the streets. Thousands were killed and injured. The floodgates had opened for all-out war.

■

IF IN THE GREAT WAR VICTORY HAD COME IN THE TRENCHES, THE NEW war would be decided in the air. Both the Chinese and the Japanese knew that. So did the Germans, Italians, Soviets, and Americans. Yet neither the Chinese nor the Japanese had much of an air force. For years the foreign powers had been vying with increasing audacity to supply them. Fighter planes, the warships of the skies, would take center stage in the battle for China—and in Cy and Max's operation in Manchuria.

Fiat was the giveaway. On August 6, 1937, a week before the first bombs fell on Shanghai, Cy went back to the U.S. consulate in Dairen. He walked across the Central Circle and went to see Grummon. He needed to renew his passport. This time, though, he made no mention of Charles Martin. Instead, on the registration documents he presented a new employer, "The Fiat Motor Company of Turin." Fiat, as the corporate historians at the company headquarters in Italy explained, once made more than cars. In the 1930s, the company ranked as one of the world's leading suppliers of airplanes.

The history of Fiat's relations with the USSR is no minor topic in the annals of international trade and Soviet five-year plans. Still, no historical account seemed to make mention of Fiat's dealings in China, let alone Manchukuo, in the 1930s. Moreover, as a quasi state empire, the company maintains an inviolate sense of proprietary knowledge. Fiat's historians were obliging but could find no record of a trade representative, American or otherwise, posted to Dairen. Similarly, the trail of Dr. Eugenio Carutti, the Italian who had appeared in the Swiss dossier of Charles Martin, seemed impossible to trace. The company had no record of any Carutti ever being in its employ.

Several Caruttis did appear, however, on various Web sites—a number in Italy, a few in Spain, and at least one in Argentina. One in Milan, "Dott. Ing. C. A. Carutti, Sr.," seemed promising. He was a *dottore ingeniere* and the founder of a company that manufactured heavy machinery. Carlo Alberto Carutti, eighty-four years old and in robust health, was eager to help. He spoke fluent English and German and had an art collection that he called his hobby—"about one hundred in all, including twenty Couberts, a few Cézannes, and a Monet." He also knew a good deal about his uncle Eugenio, the Carutti who had gone to Moscow in 1935, moved into the Metropol Hotel next to Red Square, and stayed for years, even throughout the purges.

CARUTTI'S ROLE in the Manchurian operation, like Max Steinberg's, had remained hidden for decades. The Swiss dossier, though, contained hints. Carutti, who left Italy after Mussolini's invasion of Ethiopia, had claimed to represent a raft of Italian companies abroad: Caproni, Breda, Alta-Italia, Isotta Fraschini Motori, and Fiat. All were connected to the automobile industry; all made cars or car parts. And yet one document in the Swiss files had leapt out. "Charles Martin & Co.," it reported, had "served as an agent for Fiat automobiles and Caproni airplanes."

Gianni Caproni had constructed his first airplane in a wooden hangar outside Milan in 1911. During World War I, his company produced a series of bombers for the Italian air force. Before long, Caproni planes were in great demand, even used by the French, British, and Americans. Soon, with the rise of Mussolini, Italian aircraft became showcases for Fascist engineering. Orders rose, and the planes got better—and bigger. By 1935, when Eugenio Carutti left Turin for Moscow, Caproni was making heavy bombers, the biggest and best in the world.

Eugenio Carutti, his nephew said, was not a medical doctor—the title was a relic of a legal degree. Uncle Eugenio, Carlo Alberto said, had been the commercial director of the Caproni aircraft company. The Center's scheme suddenly became clear: Carutti had been the front man for Cy and Max's operation in Manchukuo. The Soviets had used the Italian—with or without his knowledge, it was now impossible to know for certain—as the middleman for the Italian defense industry. Carutti's reach extended beyond Caproni. His nephew remembered his elegant car, a *coupe de ville* by Isotta-Fraschini, a company that made not only luxury cars but airplane engines. Breda, too, built attack aircraft, and Alta-Italia (Savoia-Marchetti's previous incarnation) made seaplanes. And Fiat, of course, also produced bombers.

It was an ingenious operation. The Center exploited the Japanese hunger in Manchukuo for airplanes, and the Italians offered a natural cover. By the time Cy and Max arrived in China, Mussolini was openly courting the Japanese regime. Soon Il Duce would follow Hitler's lead, sending an "Italian Fascist Goodwill Mission" to Dairen. The Center's plan was simple; the intelligence files from Switzerland even revealed pieces of it. The Swiss, when they arrested Martin, had discovered a prospectus for a new airline, "1 FIAT file concerning the Italo-Manchu Airline Company," as well as a stack of contracts with Caproni and Fiat, dated from 1935 to 1939. The Swiss dossier also contained a 1952 memorandum from J. Edgar Hoover's man at the U.S. embassy in London reporting the Swiss conclusion on Charles Martin & Co.: "The enterprise was involved in the sale of Fiat cars and Italian planes to the Manchurian government." Cars and planes. Cy and Max, working in tandem in Dairen and Harbin, negotiated, whether in earnest or not, the sale of Italian airplanes to the Japanese regime in Manchukuo.

It amounted to trading with the enemy, and it was a front operation with obvious allure. In Dairen, the Soviets were despised. Even with his flawless German and French, Max would have to stay in Harbin. But Cy enjoyed a unique vantage point. In February 1937, Dairen was home to fewer than 1,500 foreigners (the Japanese kept track). There were only 185 American men living in all of

Manchukuo. As an American representative of Italian defense firms, Cy had a front-row seat behind Japanese lines. He could follow the Nazi courtship of the Japanese, a quickening tango of great interest to the man in the Kremlin. He could track the White Russian émigré officers in Dairen, an increasingly restive and revanchist circle, including General Khanzhin, an old Cossack and Kolchak comrade long on the run, who would end up in due time in the hands of the Center. Above all, Dairen offered an inside view of Manchukuo's political, economic, and military affairs. Cy could learn Japan's colonial designs and forecast Tokyo's prospects for a southern drive along the eastern seaboard of Asia.

·

JAPANESE HISTORIANS STILL DEBATE THE REASONS BEHIND TOKYO'S NEED for a puppet state in China. Whatever the motive—a line of defense against the USSR, a colonial thirst, or an experiment in utopia-building—by the time Cy lived in Dairen, Manchukuo had become the staging ground for war in Asia.

In February 1937, the Manchukuo regime established its own air force. Thirty soldiers were selected to train as pilots at the Japanese air force base at Harbin. The force, however, had just one plane, an old French Nieuport fighter. Fighters and bombers soon arrived from Tokyo, but the force lacked a heavy bomber.

Cy and Max's operation in Manchukuo ran counter to the military histories of the period. On the eve of the war, the Soviets had aided the Chinese, not the Japanese. Stalin had lent bombers and pilots to Chiang's air force. Americans, too, had gone to Nanking to help. After 1937, the Texan Clair Chennault led a corps of U.S. civilian pilots who flew Curtis Hawks and Boeings for Chiang. Nanking hosted still other aviation advisers from abroad, even Germans and Italians.

Yet the Japanese had in fact struck a deal for Fiat bombers. In the final days of 1937, Tokyo purchased at least seventy-two Fiat B.R.20s, the aircraft that were known as Cicognas, Italian for "stork." The Japanese archives yielded a telegram detailing the deal.

Dated December 4, 1937, it was sent by the Japanese military attaché in Italy, one Colonel Watanabe, to the vice minister. "The aircraft now purchased are equal to three heavy bomber regiments," he reported. A twin-engine medium bomber, the B.R. 20 was armed with four Breda machine guns and could carry 3,528 pounds of bombs.

Charles Martin & Co., as the sole representative of Fiat in Manchukuo, may have brokered the sale. At the very least, Max and Cy would have made a good play at it, if only to keep up appearances. In Manchukuo, as Max casually told his Swiss interrogators one day, the airplane business "provided good insurance against any charge of espionage."

■

IN THE FALL OF 1937, MAX AND ELSA SUSPENDED THE AIRCRAFT OPERA-tion. They wasted no time in closing up shop and fleeing Harbin. They first tried to escape by boat, sailing from Dairen south to Shanghai. Before they reached Shanghai, though, the captain turned back. He had been warned, he said, of a typhoon. Later Max learned the true reason: the Japanese had sent a new wave of bombers over Shanghai.

Max and Elsa were forced to return to Harbin and head in the opposite direction: north to the Soviet border. Before leaving the city, Max went to the bank. Whether he and Cy had sold the Italian planes or cars, they had done something other than collect information. The Center had provided the down payment, but Charles Martin & Co. had made money. During the two years in Manchukuo, Max would later say, he had more than doubled his money. As he prepared to leave China, he transferred $17,982.97 from the National City Bank branch in Harbin to Paris. The remainder he removed in cash. With the fighting escalating fast, the station in Harbin was crowded. Few of the panicked Russian émigrés, however, dared venture north. Max and Elsa would board the train in Harbin and head for the Trans-Siberian. Somewhere, whether stuffed in their suitcases or hidden under their clothes, they carried the bundles of cash. Max left China with 200,000 Swiss Francs—no small amount in 1937, valued at more than $50,000.

Cy was nearly left behind. Max and Elsa had no time to close up the operation properly. Cy had to stay on to ensure that there would be no loose ends. Later, in the Lubyanka, he told his interrogator that he had barely escaped. Perhaps he was already ill. He never said what it was—an injury? a virus? a war wound?—but as he departed from Dairen, he may already have been suffering from the nervous condition that worsened in the gulag.

Cy, too, made it out by train. In October 1937 he went first to Harbin and then across the border to Blagoveshchensk, the Soviet town swollen with border guards. Headed north, the train crossed the forests and, as the taiga enveloped it, entered Siberia. He could not have been far behind Max and Elsa, and all three were now moving toward the same destination: Moscow.

The mission had taken its toll. Max and Elsa now had a small fortune tucked away for the future, but for Cy, suddenly everything came crashing down. Later, in the Lubyanka, he said that Manchukuo was impossible. First it was the Japanese's suspicions and then the bombs. The war had cut the operation short. The Japanese troops had moved south, beyond the Great Wall, with unprecedented swiftness. Soon they would reach Nanking and embark on six weeks of carnage. "The rape of Nanking," one of the worst civilian massacres of the century, would leave more than 100,000 Chinese dead and tens of thousands of local women raped. Within a year, as the Nationalists sought refuge in the central plains, the Japanese would have dominion over eastern China and more than 200 million Chinese.

Cy was fortunate to get out. At last he was headed west again. Winter had not yet come, but it would be a long train ride from the Far East, fourteen days inside a steel wagon at the best of times. Suddenly, with the rush and chaos of war at his back and ahead of him only the endless expanse of Siberia, Cy faced time—and silence.

As the days blurred and the train barreled on, Baikal, the great lake in the heart of Siberia, approached. Inside the narrow compartment, there was little to salve Cy's anxiety. Nerma and the boy were still in San Francisco. They would have to travel a good distance, for weeks, if not longer, to meet him halfway. Cy could not have known when he would get there, or even if he would. But as he sat on the Trans-Siberian hurtling toward Moscow, he at least could dream of where they would meet: in Paris again.

Parisians waiting at train station. October 3, 1938.

CHAPTER 9

THE STAMP MARKET

■ ■ ■

Robin was still a young boy, not yet seven, when Nerma took him back to France. Mother and son left San Francisco and sailed from New York on the *Ile de France*, arriving in the maelstrom that Paris had become in the middle of February 1938. In the wake of the Nazi ascent, Jews and refugees from the desperate corners of Europe now filled the city.

Cy had returned three months earlier. After the long train ride from China, he stopped off in Moscow, where, to his surprise, the debriefing was mercifully short. The men from the Center kept him only a few days. The bloodletting was on in full force, yet for some reason—Cy had no idea why—he was permitted to travel on.

During their second sojourn in Paris, the family lived in the sixteenth arrondisement, a district that thrived on status and the desire to maintain it. Rue Agar, however, the street where Proust had been born, was filled with a quiet anxiety that even its wealthy residents could not ignore. Cy and Nerma's new home, curiously, carried echoes of the old address in Neuilly. The apartment house at number 4 stood seven stories tall and was sandwiched between two stately moderne buildings. Rue Agar, moreover, resembled rue Chartran. It, too, was short—at one hundred yards, one of the shortest streets in Paris. And like rue Chartran, it was sharply curved.

"Rue Agar was shaped like an elbow," Robin recalled, "and our apartment house was right on the elbow." He had been young, but he could still remember highlights of the neighborhood. The cafés of the nearby rue la Fontaine and rue Gros. The stone church across the way, and the park next door. The place de Rodin up the hill, and the little bronze statue at its center. The bustling avenue de Versailles, the Seine below, and the Eiffel Tower across the bridge.

Every so often, "shards of memories" came to him. The carousel at the Jardin du Luxembourg, riding the wooden horses and "trying to get the brass ring." There was Miss Margery Eagle, an Australian woman who took him for long walks "but certainly wasn't a nanny." An office—either a doctor's or a dentist's—overlooked the grounds where the previous spring the Soviets and the Nazis had squared off at the 1937 International Exhibition. It was the advent of the wobbly, pusillanimous Daladier government. Paris was a city shrouded in fear, yet to a six-year-old boy the anxiety was invisible. For Robin, what remained most vivid after so many years was the stamp market. "And the feel of Dad's hand holding mine."

TO MANY IN PARIS, THE INSTABILITY THAT ROILED FRANCE THAT spring arrived with the flood of German and East European refugees. But to Cy and Nerma, the more urgent threat came from Moscow. In the late 1930s, the NKVD launched a war against itself. It was a homicidal flood that would leave Europe littered with corpses and a generation of fellow travelers adrift. In the underground, meanwhile, from Shanghai to New York to San Francisco, many among the most devoted wondered how it had all gone wrong. Others were too fearful to care.

Stalin had suffered *perebezhchiki*—literally, "runners to the other side"—before. But the losses had never been costly. Only one or two of the agents had spilled secrets, and in the West, moreover, few had paid any attention. The word "defector" only entered the English language a decade later, long after the USSR and the United States had ceased to be wartime allies. Stalin, however, foresaw the inevitable.

On June 20, 1937, eight months before Nerma and Robin's return to Europe, Alexander Barmine, a little-known Soviet chargé d'affaires in the Athens embassy, disappeared. When Marshal Tukhachevsky, the army chief, was purged, Barmine, a former pro-

tégé, had sensed the worst coming. He fled and soon turned up in the
United States, after visiting with the FBI.

Barmine was only the first in a long series of runners. In July,
Ignace Reiss, the Great Illegal from Podwoloczyska, lost his faith and
dared to write to the party's Central Committee denouncing the terror. He sent his farewell letter to the Soviet embassy in Paris, wrap-
ping it inside his Order of the Red Banner. Reiss had not only broken
the rules, he had dared to call Stalin a traitor to the revolution. "Up
until this moment I marched alongside you," he wrote.

> Now I will not take another step. Our paths diverge! He who
> now keeps quiet becomes Stalin's accomplice, betrays the
> working class, betrays socialism . . .
>
> Nothing will be forgotten, and nothing will be forgiven.
> History is harsh. "The leader of genius," "the Father of the
> People," "the Sun of Socialism" will have to account for what
> he has done . . .
>
> I intend to devote my feeble forces to the cause of Lenin. I
> want to continue the fight, for only our victory—that of the
> proletarian revolution—will free humanity of capitalism and
> the USSR of Stalinism.

By September 4, Reiss was dead, his well-dressed corpse found
outside Lausanne, along the highway to Geneva, riddled with twelve
bullets. In his fist the police found a strand of gray hair, and in his
pocket a Czech passport in the name of Hans Eberhardt and an
unused rail ticket to France.

The bloodbath spread quickly. Within weeks, on September 22,
General Evgeni Karlovich Miller was kidnapped in Paris. Miller had
taken over the ROVS, the White Russian officers' union, in 1930,
when General Kutepov, the hapless civil war hero in exile, vanished
from the same streets. Miller was entrapped with the help of a
NKVD mole: General Nikolai Skoblin, a flamboyant figure among
the officers, who ostensibly ran counterintelligence for the union.
Skoblin and his wife, the cabaret singer Nadezhda Plevitskaya, were

fixtures in the émigré circles of Paris. Their intrigues not only made headlines in France but inspired Vladimir Nabokov's first short story in English, "The Assistant Producer."

General Miller's kidnapping seemed a useless repetition of history. It was, though, only the first step in a complex plan. Stalin hoped to create the appearance of a conspiracy of Red Army generals and Gestapo agents working against him. It seemed an improbable cabal, but logic never stopped Stalin. A conspiracy among Soviet and Nazi officers would justify a purge of the Soviet army and security forces. At home the executions continued, and abroad the fear spread.

Sitting in the Café les Deux Magots in fashionable Saint-Germain one late September morning, Walter Krivitsky, the GRU *rezident* in The Hague, read the news of General Miller's disappearance. At the time, Krivitsky was in charge of Soviet military espionage in Western Europe. He was not only a close comrade of Reiss; the two had known each other since childhood. Moscow had handed Krivitsky a mission he could never fulfill: to kill his friend. Instead he had warned Reiss, sending him into flight.

Krivitsky knew his turn would come next. On October 6 he defied a recall to Moscow, failed to board his ship in Le Havre, and instead went into hiding in the South of France. Weeks later, Krivitsky sought asylum with the ill-fated Daladier government. On December 9, a new farewell letter appeared, this time in the *Times* of London. "For eighteen years, I faithfully and conscientiously served the Bolshevik party and the Soviet authority," wrote Krivitsky. Recent "events," however, had turned him. One of the highest-ranking officers of Soviet military intelligence abroad now threw down a gauntlet in the middle of Europe. The Leader, Krivitsky dared to cry out, had taken the revolution tragically off-course. "In the Moscow trials, especially in the secret trials, the best representatives of the Bolshevik Old Guard have been condemned as spies and agents of the Gestapo . . . Every fresh case, every fresh shooting," he wrote, "has shaken my faith more deeply."

AS CY SETTLED into the apartment overlooking the rue Agar and Nerma and Robin remained en route from New York, headlines spoke of the tensions mounting in Europe. But in Paris, among those in the Soviet underground, the Krivitsky defection reverberated the loudest. Then, in the middle of February 1938, a new sensation hit, causing tumult among the Russian émigré circles in France and Trotskyists around the world.

On February 16, at the nearby Clinique Mirabeau, a young Russian émigré registered under a fictitious name died suddenly. "Léon Martin, ingénieur," had entered the clinic on the cusp of his thirty-second birthday with acute appendicitis. *L'Humanité*, the Communist broadsheet, marked his passing with a four-sentence article. The death certificate, however, revealed the deceased's true name, Léon Sedov, and listed his parents simply as "Léon Sedoff, journalist, and Natalie Sedoff, without profession."

For Cy and for Nerma, who arrived with Robin only days later, it was grim news. Léon Sedov, as they surely knew, was Trotsky's sole surviving son. The cause of his death has been debated ever since. The clinic was run by Russian émigrés, and murder, whether by poisoning or by malign neglect, remains the most popular explanation. Trotsky by then had left France and since early 1937 been living in Mexico as a guest of the artists Diego Rivera and Frida Kahlo. That spring, Sidney Hook had even dragged John Dewey, at age seventy-eight, to Mexico to see him. But the Center's hunt was on in full force.

For the American agents in Paris, it would become increasingly hard to justify their participation in the underground. The revolution of Lenin had faded into the distant past and been replaced by a spiral of violence. The cause, it was fast becoming clear, was fed less by the bold tenets of Marx than by the paranoid vendetta of the man in the Kremlin. Nerma knew that the stakes had risen and that the underground itself was now at risk. She brought Cy the news from the States, where two Soviet spy scandals had spilled out across the front pages of the New York papers.

On December 10, 1937, an American woman who called herself Ruth Norma Robinson was arrested in Moscow, a week after her husband disappeared from their hotel, the National, right next door to the U.S. embassy. The man traveling as Donald Louis Robinson, the State Department figured out eventually, had been naturalized in New York City in 1934 as Adolph A. Rubens. "The Robinson-Rubens affair," as it became known, made headlines for more than a year. But only after the fall of the USSR, when the KGB archives opened briefly, did the true identity of Robinson-Rubens emerge: he was Arnold Ikal, a long-serving GRU agent. Like his colleagues in New York, Tilton and Dozenberg, as well as the former GRU chief in Moscow, General Jan Berzin, Ikal was Latvian. He and his wife also worked closely with Tilton and another Soviet agent whom Cy and Nerma knew, Whittaker Chambers.

The Ikals had been recalled to Moscow in the fall of 1937, within days of Cy's departure from Manchuria. In New York, Ikal was known as the genial "Richard," and in Moscow as "Ewald." His wife was Ruth Braman, née Boerger. Ikal would long be remembered among veterans of the New York underground for his good looks and rare managerial skill. In the United States, he had run, among other projects, a false passport ring. The Ikals had worked on the team cobbling "boots" at the New York Public Library. The scheme was brilliant, and simple. In those years anyone applying for a U.S. passport only had to send a birth certificate by mail. The crew at the library would search recent obituaries in newspapers from across the country, looking for notices of deceased children. When the dates of death approximately matched agents' birthdates, they would write to the state's records division for a copy of the birth certificate. The copy was then sent to the Passport Office as proof of citizenship. The ploy rarely failed. In this fashion, Ikal is said to have produced "100 to 150 passports."

Nerma knew that the Ikals were not the only ones who had been purged from the New York underground. On December 18, 1937, the *New York World-Telegram* stirred a second spy scandal, breaking the news of the disappearance of Juliet Stuart Poyntz. Poyntz, a tall, big-boned native of Omaha, was fifty years old and no common foot soldier. A founding member of the CPUSA, she boasted an academic pedigree rare in the party: she had graduated from Barnard and Oxford and taught for a time at Columbia.

Poyntz had not been seen for six months. One evening in June she had received a call from a former lover at the hotel where she'd been living, the American Women's Association Clubhouse, two blocks south of Central Park on West Fifty-seventh Street. Poyntz put on her hat and coat and went to meet him in the park. She left her passport in her desk, her clothes neatly folded, and the light on in the room. She never reappeared. For years rumors circulated that her body had been buried in the Village, behind a brick wall. The case went unsolved, but important details did emerge. In the years before she vanished, Poyntz had left the aboveground party and become a clandestine Soviet operative—"an agent in New York for the receipt of military and naval intelligence" from, among other sources, the Brooklyn Navy Yard.

Cy and Nerma, as much they may have wished to do so, could no longer avert their eyes. When they finally rendezvoused in Paris, at last they could speak in private of the defections. First Reiss and Krivitsky had fallen in Europe, and then, from the old New York underground, Poyntz and the Ikals. Cy may have crossed paths, if not worked, with Ikal, and Nerma is likely to have known Poyntz, first at the Rand School, then at the ILGWU. Poyntz had been a director of the Rand and head of its Labor Research Bureau when Nerma was a student. Later she was also a leader of the Ladies' Garment Workers' Union, helping to organize Local 25, the Ladies' Waist and Dressmakers' Union in New York. Nerma at the time was also an activist in the local.

In Paris, the toll mounted. Before long, Rudolf Klement, the thirty-year-old German leader of Trotsky's new Fourth International, a vain attempt to build an anti-Stalinist counterinsurgency, also disappeared. The French police fished a body from the Seine and tentatively identified it as Klement's, but the corpse was headless, and no one could be certain. All the same, the German was never heard from again.

To many of Cy and Nerma's comrades across Europe, the trail of bodies augured the death of the underground, the disappearance of an entire generation of believers in the Soviet experiment. Yet in Moscow, the successful "operations" only emboldened the Center. In the spring of 1938, when Cy and Nerma were living on rue Agar, Stalin decided to up the ante. In his hunger to silence his old rival, the Leader launched his most ambitious clandestine operation. It would not be easy, and certainly not secret, but Stalin had deemed it essential to assassinate Trotsky.

For Cy and Nerma, the vengeance wreaked by the bosses in Moscow foretold the end of the campaign. The idealism that had led them into the trenches would endure. Their hope in the "bright future" would not waver. But the masquerade, in the tense Paris spring of 1938, at last came to a close.

Before May was out, Cy was gone. Robin was not yet seven. In adulthood he had only a fractured memory of it—no sense of a quarrel, a separation, or even a departure. He and Nerma were left alone in the apartment. Soon illness and his mother's distractions would overtake his life, yet in the spring of 1938, Robin had little to fill the emptiness left by his father's absence. "I saw my father very little during my lifetime," he said during one of our first conversations. "He was always traveling to other places. And much of the time that he *was* around, I was too sick to be moved."

The string of illnesses had begun in San Francisco. In 1937, either in the spring or the summer, Robin had climbed out of the bay window on Sacramento Street and fallen from the fire escape. The accident left him with a broken right hip, so that one leg was slightly shorter than the other. For years Robin walked with a rolling gait. Then there was a case of whooping cough—"caught, or so I was told, from our landlady in San Francisco." In France the cough worsened, and Robin endured stays in "a series of sanatoria." Much of the time that Cy was in Paris, Robin was away.

Still, Robin's father had given him a pastime that would be a lifelong pursuit. "When Dad was in the Far East and we were in San Francisco, he'd started me off with stamp collecting," said Robin. The stamp market was the last thing he remembered from that spring in Paris. "Dad was there with us, and though I didn't see him very much at all, he did take me down to the stamp market." It may have been the only thing the son remembered ever doing with his father. "We went together. I can recall walking with him there, among the sellers, very clearly." Robin would forever remember the feel of his father's hand holding his own hand. "And then—he was gone."

Summer came, and as the days grew longer, Europe stood yet again before the abyss of war. Cy had left his wife and son and was headed into the East again. He had set a course, in the face of logic and the rising tide of violence, directly into the darkness.

.

AT THE SAME TIME, CHARLES MARTIN, CY'S BOSS DURING THEIR CLAN-destine operation in China, was desperately trying to forge an alibi. Max Steinberg, the Great Illegal behind the Swiss alter ego, had run in the opposite direction. As his former American agent crossed into the USSR, Max was quietly pursuing a plan to use his Swiss papers to resettle in Switzerland.

It had been quite a journey from China. After escaping Manchukuo, Max and Elsa stayed in Moscow at the Hotel Metropol. At the Metropol, two NKVD officers came visiting. They wanted to know why Max had rushed to leave Harbin and shut down Charles Martin & Co. in such a hurry. Somehow Max satisfied them with his answers. After eight days, he and Elsa were allowed to leave Moscow.

First they traveled to Paris, then on to Milan. Max returned to Europe, he would later say, with the hope of restarting the plane business. For months he traveled across Eastern Europe and the Baltics with Dr. Carutti, the prodigious broker for the Italian defense companies. Carutti's contacts seemed endless; even the Estonian defense minister, General Laidoner, was keen to buy Caproni bombers. Business looked promising, but before long the operation in Europe proved untenable. As tensions rose, no one wished to do business with Italian companies.

Max and Elsa spent their first year after China apart. In the summer of 1938, Elsa rented a flat in Zurich in her own name, at 22 Mythenquai. Meanwhile, Max first tried to make Italy his new base, registering on July 18, 1938, as Charles Martin at the Swiss consulate in Milan. By the fall of 1939, though, he had joined Elsa in Zurich, where he opened an account with the National City Bank in New York and transferred into it more than $12,000. Max seemed blessed with fortuitous timing. He opened the New York account on September 9, eight days after the German invasion of Poland.

In the months after the outbreak of the war, Max and Elsa retreated to their secluded home in the hills above Lake Geneva. Elsa bought the Villa Regina-Margarita, at 32 chemin de la Fauvette in Chailly, outside Lausanne, in late 1939. Max arrived soon thereafter. Of the dozen books written about the Red Orchestra, several assert that Max and Elsa were turned in Switzerland—that they became double agents for the Nazis. This claim is unfounded. Max and Elsa, it was true, did try to disappear in Switzerland. They moved into the elegant villa and set up house in the hopeful belief that the Center would not find them. For a pair of veteran illegals, it was a surprisingly naive proposition.

•

BY THEN NERMA AND ROBIN HAD ESCAPED FROM PARIS. "THE EXODUS," Robin called his mother's rush to leave France and survive the Nazi onslaught. His health had only deteriorated, and Nerma had parked him for months on end in the care of others. By the summer of 1938, Robin's hip had healed, but the cough had become severe asthma. There was another illness—the doctors called it "shadows on the lungs." Robin was never certain, but it may have been tuberculosis. He was taken first to La Bourboule, a famous spa in the Auvergne, today advertised as the "premier pediatric clinic" in France. In winter, after spending the fall in Paris, he was sent to a school in the elegant skiing village of Gstaad in the Swiss Alps. The Ecole Alpine Polygala was remote and small, with only ten boys and five girls.

From Gstaad, Robin sent letters to Nerma, never longer than a paragraph or two. He wrote to her in Paris, and sometimes in Zurich.

Throughout the time that he was boarded out, Nerma, it seemed, traveled across Europe. As the months passed, Robin's handwriting grew clearer, stronger. He told of his days—"Yesterday the big ones went skiing but i stayed at home. Today I went luging in the garden" —and of the school's upcoming celebrations—"They have a day when a man named Saint Nicholas comes and in the night he puts oranges and penuts in our shos." At times he addressed both his parents. It was clear, though, who was writing back. By the middle of March 1939, Robin asked his mother a single question: "Will you ask Daddy to send me a letter?" It was the plea that anchored many of his letters, even the two-line note he had written, at six, before leaving San Francisco. Cy, however, remained in the East, traveling, or so Nerma believed, somewhere remote and unknown.

At some point in the first half of 1939, Robin's tour of Europe's finer children's resorts, schools, and spas was interrupted. Nerma collected him from Gstaad, and together they traveled to Cannes. They were not in the South of France long before he suffered another severe bout of asthma. He remembered recovering in Grasse, the small town in the hills above Cannes on the Riviera.

As Nerma and Robin, an American Jewish mother and her son, shuttled around France and Switzerland, anxiety crested throughout Europe. In the wake of Kristallnacht, when the stormtroopers destroyed storefronts and synagogues across Germany and Austria in November 1938, the Nazis had signaled their intention to reinvent anti-Semitism, this time on a continental scale. In the following months, paranoia and dread had surged across Europe, as hundreds of thousands of desperate Jews fled across borders. By late summer Nerma and her comrades faced a new threat, an unexpected about-face from their own leader.

On August 23, Stalin and Hitler stunned the world, not to mention loyal ideologues and faithful fellow travelers, with their Non-Aggression Pact. Stalin, in the eyes of leftists, had allied the USSR with a nation that was evil incarnate. Molotov-Ribbentrop, as the accord became known, for the Nazi and Soviet foreign ministers who signed it, instantly paved the way for Hitler's invasion of Poland and seizure of the Baltic states, and in time the division of Europe. For many in the underground, even the most stalwart among the Center's agents, the deal was the last deceit. Around the world, Soviet sympathizers rushed to abandon the cause.

Not Nerma. She remained, through it all, resolute in her faith. Privately, perhaps, she was devastated, but she revealed no sign of doubt. Cy could easily slip into the shadows forever, but Nerma held firm. Even as the Nazi threat loomed unchecked, with the Fascists now joining hands with the Soviets, she did not dare question the wisdom of the Leader in Moscow.

By the late summer of 1939, Nerma could wait no longer. Robin was then living at yet another sanatorium, Chez Nous, a *pension des enfants* in Megève, the French resort town in the Alps. He later had trouble placing it, but knew it had been near the Italian border. The memory of how everyone had feared the Italians, so close by, was vivid. There was another reason Chez Nous was fixed in Robin's mind: he was still there, and nearly eight years old, "when the war came."

One day in the first week of September, without notice, his mother arrived from Paris to collect him. They left for Paris on the train the same day. As Robin remembered the journey across the breadth of France, he raised the question himself. He had no idea how Nerma had known to come get him, and no notion who could have warned her. But it was not the first time he had wondered about the origins of his mother's knowledge. "As I got the story," he said, "my mother had heard from Dad. He'd told her, 'Get out of Europe.' "

■

AT THE SAME TIME, THE CENTER REGAINED CONTACT WITH MAX AND Elsa. Sitting in Switzerland, Cy's old boss did not know the aim of the mission, nor could he refuse it. Moscow had tracked him down with a singular purpose: to force him to participate in the Soviets' boldest clandestine operation yet, the assassination of Trotsky.

In August, Ramón Mercader del Rio, a young partisan of the Spanish Civil War, born in Barcelona but raised in Paris, and his mother, Caridad, an aristocratic devotee of the cause, sailed from Le

Havre to New York. According to the plan, another Soviet agent, their immediate superior, "Tom," was soon to follow, but at the last minute he required new travel documents. Tom was living in Paris on a Polish passport but was in danger of being mobilized into the French army. He would need not only a clean passport but a U.S. visa. By 1939, however, with waves of refugees desperate to cross the Atlantic, such visas were nearly impossible to obtain.

The men at the Lubyanka assayed their options and tracked down the old illegal, the man who had run the Center's American agent in Manchuria. Nerma remained in Europe, but the purges had depleted the underground in France. Max, who had revived the cover of Charles Martin, was deemed the Center's best conduit to the American consulate in Paris. Lev Vasilevsky, the NKVD *rezident* in Paris, dispatched two loyal agents, men not known for their mercy, to pay a visit to Max in Lausanne. The meeting, by all accounts, was less than cordial. Max came armed with a pistol, fearing the worst. Yet by the end of his talk with the agents from Paris, he had caved.

The men handed Max a passport—French or Iraqi; sources vary—in the name of a Syrian Jew and ordered him to get a U.S. visa as soon as possible. Whether by bribery, negligence, or courtesy of a mole in the consulate, Max managed to secure the visa within weeks. The bank account he soon opened in New York City was almost certainly a second step.

Tom, the Jewish refugee now headed for America, was Naum Eitingon, an NKVD henchman of many names—General Kotov, General Leonov, Comrade Pablo, Leonid Naumov, Pierre, and Lyova. To his friends and closest comrades, Eitingon was simply Lyona, the nickname for Leonid. One of the most accomplished spies in Stalin's secret services, Eitingon, who had served in Shanghai in the 1920s and Spain during the civil war, was tasked with overseeing the murder of Trotsky.

Max knew Eitingon but had not recognized his passport photograph. For the mission to New York, Tom had grown a mustache and altered his hairstyle. Eitingon arrived in the United States in October 1939, two months after the start of the war, and promptly set up an import-export office in Brooklyn. The office would provide legal cover for Mercader, the Spaniard who had preceded Eitingon to New York and was now traveling as Frank Jacson, a Serbian engineer with a Canadian passport, to see the Old Man in Mexico.

•

WHETHER THE WARNING HAD COME FROM CY, THE CENTER, OR A SYM-pathic friend with rare clout, it was not luck that saved Nerma and her son. She had waited for Cy to return as long as she could. Leaving Europe, she knew what Robin could not: that she might be leaving Cy as well. Somehow, however, Nerma managed to book two tickets on the SS *Washington*, which sailed from Le Havre on September 9, 1939.

Once the boat crossed the Channel and reached Southampton, the U.S. ambassador in London, Joseph Kennedy, ordered it held for a day to take on an additional ninety-one passengers. They were Americans rescued from the SS *Athenia*, a British liner bound for Montreal that the Germans had torpedoed on the first day of the war. Ambassador Kennedy's twenty-two year-old son, Jack, had lobbied for the delay. On September 7, JFK, on leave from Harvard, had gone to Glasgow to see the survivors of the *Athenia*. The following day the ambassador cabled a warning to Washington. His son had reported that the rescued Americans were "in a terrible state of nerves and that to put them on a ship going back to America for seven days without a convoy or some kind of protection would land them back in New York in such a state that the publicity and criticism of the government would be unbelievable." The ambassador offered a suggestion: with German submarines lurking close by, any ship sailing to the United States would require an escort by British boats.

On September 12, the *Washington*, one of the biggest ocean liners the United States had ever built, departed from Southampton overfilled with passengers. "There were people jammed in wherever you looked," Robin said. With a capacity of 1,100 passengers, the ship was carrying 1,746, clearly most of them with exceptional connections, for this was no longer an ordinary Atlantic voyage. They bunked down everywhere—on the decks, in the corridors, in the gymnasium. The crew even drained the swimming pool and lined it with cots. Seventy-six women slept on makeshift beds in the Palm Garden, the drawing room where the orchestra normally played at teatime. Robin slept in a cabin with four men, while Nerma shared a room with three women.

Sailing from England in the days after the *Athenia* was sunk, all on board suffered a heightened state of anxiety. To show that the *Washington* was a neutral American passenger ship on the high seas, the crew painted the sides with an enormous Stars and Stripes and the ship's name in giant white letters. At night, in the darkness of the ocean, they floodlit the U.S. flag fluttering above the top deck. Among those crowded on board were Ambassador Kennedy's wife, Rose, and three of her nine children—Bobby, Eunice, and Kathleen. The writer Thomas Mann, who had emigrated to the United States the previous year and had urgently cut short a return trip to Europe, was also on the liner. Mann wrote to his brother Heinrich of having endured the voyage "amid the throng of 2,000 persons who spent the nights on improvised cots in public rooms transformed into concentration camps." Also on board were the actor Robert Montgomery, the tennis stars Don Budge and Bill Tilden, the theologian Reinhold Niebuhr's wife and their two young children, and more than two hundred Mormon missionaries "ordered home from the war zone."

The voyage would prove historic. The *Washington*, swollen with human cargo, was the first American refugee ship to leave Europe since a torrent of bombs had destroyed Europe's twenty-one-year peace.

New York City, from the SS Washington, *ca. 1939.*

CHAPTER 10

TRUTH WILL WIN

. . .

NERMA AND ROBIN LANDED IN NEW YORK ON SEPTEMBER 18, 1939, homeless and penniless. For months they shuttled from one place to another. Robin was not certain whether they stayed with friends or strangers. He remembered an apartment uptown, "near the park"—Central Park—but could not recall the addresses or the names. But as she drifted, Nerma left behind a trail of documents—forms, applications, and questionnaires filled out in offices across the city. The records tell of a forlorn return and a desperation to shape a new life.

In the fall of 1939, mother and son lived briefly on West 91st Street, just by the park. Soon they were living at 64 West 108th, before moving up to 143 West 113th, in what remained of Jewish Harlem—the same building where Cy and Nerma had lived in 1928, before their sojourn in Berlin. All the while, throughout those first months back in the city, Nerma collected mail in Brooklyn, at her sister Celia Cohen's house.

For Robin, that first summer back in the United States stood out. He was not yet nine, and it was in essence the first summer of his American childhood. From June into the winter of 1940, while Nerma "had no permanent residence," Robin was boarded out with a family in Pennsylvania.

She may have found the place through a comrade. Nettie Samberg had also sent her son, Yank, there. A 1934 issue of the *Daily Worker* yielded a photograph of Nettie Samberg. Like Nerma, she was a labor activist and a street fighter from the early days. Robin remembered walking with her on the Lower East Side one day and passing a line of strikers. When a scab crossed the line, Nettie spit in his face. The mothers rarely visited, however.

The following summer Robin moved on to Martin's Farm, a dairy farm in Huguenot, New York, just across the Pennsylvania border. Nerma agreed to pay Mrs. Merle Martin thirty dollars a month to host Robin.

Mrs. Martin complained—the money was late, or never came— and Robin needed new trousers. "I have been patching them to keep him going," she wrote to Nerma. Robin stayed on at the farm through most of the summer of 1941. Each morning he walked to school in Huguenot, a two-room schoolhouse with eight grades, four in each room.

By the start of 1941, Nerma had settled in Greenwich Village. She moved into an apartment at 8 Barrow Street, a three-story building off Sheridan Square. She had still not found stable work, but the flat was large; she could sublet two rooms and cover the rent. The lodgers, Nerma would later tell the FBI, brought in eighty-eight dollars a month. She did not know, though, that the men from the Bureau were already watching two of her purported lodgers, Angela Guest and Ruth Jerusalem, two women who had recently escaped the conflagration in Europe and were deemed close enough to the cause to warrant investigation.

FOR ROBIN, those first years back in the States held fond memories. "There's really only one reason for the nostalgia," he said on one of my trips upstate. "Baseball." Robin learned that for a dollar twenty, he could spend the day at Yankee Stadium. "The subway cost a nickel," he said, "and a grandstand seat was a buck ten." Robin's first game was the last game of the 1942 season at the Polo Grounds. It happened to be "a scrap game"—not a make-up game, he explained, but a wartime promotion: anyone who brought at least ten pounds of scrap got in for free. Robin carried an old tire.

He was nearly eleven years old then, and on weekends, at least once or twice a month, he stayed in Brooklyn with Bessie and Joe, his

aunt and uncle, at their place on Amboy Street in Brownsville. Bessie
Baron, Nerma's elder sister, was much older. Joe had spent decades
working for the post office and had lost his house in the Depression.
He did not seem "particularly happy" to have his nephew trespass on
their weekends. Robin could not recall many details from the return
to New York, but he knew when the weekends in Brooklyn had
started. It was before "Mickey Owen dropped the third strike," he
said, referring to the Brooklyn Dodgers catcher who was blamed for
the Dodgers' loss in the fourth game of the 1941 World Series. The
Yankees had trailed in the score at Ebbets Field but had come back to
win. "I heard that game," Robin said, "at Bessie and Joe's."

The more Robin told of those first years back in New York, the
more the FBI files made sense. At first Nerma's decision seemed odd,
more than foolhardy, even suicidal. To judge from their lack of
money, the underground had abandoned her. But Nerma, it
appeared, had not abandoned the underground. While Cy remained
mute and far away, she was preoccupied with an unknown pursuit.
Robin, at least, had no idea how his mother spent the hours when he
was at his aunt and uncle's, "from Friday afternoons till Sunday nights."

FOR NERMA, the return home was a time of anguish. In October 1939
she opened an account at the Corn Exchange Bank at Ninety-first
and Broadway with $900. By the following June, it was empty. Even
two years later, she was still without an income. She had gone to ste-
nography school and learned typing and shorthand, and she did get
work. She tried office filing for a war relief group, social work for a
Jewish agency, and even selling hosiery, but she could not hold down
a job. For a time she received aid from the Jewish Social Community
Service on 164th Street, but she kept moving from job to job. By the
start of 1942, Nerma had sixty-nine cents in her bank account. On
January 15 she went to the Welfare Department on Broadway and
filled out the long application. She was near-destitute, she admitted
to the clerk, and exhausted from searching.

Nerma could no longer afford the place on Barrow. In October
1942 she and Robin moved into an old brownstone at 322 West Fif-

teenth Street. The apartment was three flights up, on the top floor—
the cheapest place in the building. "It was not," said Ginny, Robin's
wife, "a pleasant place." There were four rooms: two big rooms, a
storage room in between that had no natural light and little furniture
except an old steamer trunk, and one other room, "a tiny little one at
the north end," which became Robin's bedroom. The toilet was in
the hall, but Nerma still managed to let out one room.

That fall Robin won a scholarship to the City and Country
School, a private grammar school in the Village with famous Progressive roots. For the first time he went to the same school two years in
a row. But he was bullied and without recourse. Nerma, meanwhile,
discovered that there were few people in New York whom she could
rely on for help.

Cy's brother, David, for one, would not listen to her entreaties.
David had his own worries. One reason his first marriage failed
may have been his wife's inability to have children. His second
wife, Anna, had blessed him with two daughters, Muriel and
Diana. By the time Nerma and Robin returned to New York,
David's girls were already teenagers. He was still a solo practi-
tioner, living and working in Queens, and now could not even
provide for his own family. David, moreover, wished to have little
to do with Nerma or his brother's boy. Robin could not recall ever
meeting Muriel and Diana. In fact, he remembered seeing his
Uncle David only once, at the wedding of his Aunt Betty's daughter. It was after the war, probably in 1946, "the year 'Rum 'n Coca-
Cola' was a hit." At the wedding they played the song, and Robin
could still recite the lyrics.

David, the Republican lawyer, had never recovered from supporting Cy during his Columbia years. By all accounts, he also never
wavered in his conservative politics. As a gray-haired man of fifty-six,
David had registered for the draft in the so-called old man's registration of April 1942. Still smarting from the money wasted on Cy,
David now refused to listen to his brother's wife and her radical
views.

Nerma faced far greater obstacles. Cy had not been heard from since the spring of 1938, and the four years of silence were likely to have convinced their old comrades that he had been purged. If the old members of the New York underground knew that Cy was in the gulag, Nerma would be considered radioactive. Only her closest and most daring friends would now see her.

Still, as she struggled to find a new life with Robin, Nerma could only guess at Cy's fate. She had witnessed the toll in Europe—the spies who had vanished and the bodies that had surfaced. She felt the fear and knew its source. And yet she had no idea whether Cy was alive or dead.

.

"MY MOTHER DIDN'T REALLY TALK ABOUT MY FATHER MUCH," ROBIN said once, early in our conversations. "The story was that he'd been lost in the war. But I never heard how and why." When Robin was still a young teenager, Nerma did once tell him the truth: that Cy was imprisoned in a "concentration camp." She did not elaborate, leaving the boy to imagine his father in the hands of the Nazis.

One day after the war, though, Robin made his own discovery. He opened the old steamer trunk that Nerma had left in the storage room, the dark room in the middle of the flat on West Fifteenth, and found the story that his mother was too fearful to tell him. It was a long trail of correspondence between the State Department in Washington, D.C., and Mrs. Nerma Oggins of New York City. At last, as a teenager, Robin learned the truth.

When I called Robin from Moscow for the first time, he read me a letter from the State Department's assistant chief, Special Division. It was dated March 4, 1943—two months after the men from the U.S. embassy had visited Cy in the Butyrka Prison.

My dear Mrs. Oggins:

I refer to previous correspondence concerning your husband, Mr. Isaiah Oggins, who is imprisoned in the Soviet Union. The Department is in receipt of a report from the American Embassy in the Soviet Union to the effect that the Soviet authorities have indicated that there will be little delay in releasing

*your husband at such time as he is furnished with a passport, it being under-
stood that he would have to be repatriated promptly.*

The official went on to tell Nerma that the department would grant
her husband a new passport, "valid only for his immediate return to
the United States," but that she would have to cover the cost of his
return and "prepay his passage" to the United States.

Five days later, on March 9, 1943, Nerma received an urgent
telegram from Sumner Welles, then in his final days as FDR's acting
secretary of state. As Robin read the words on the phone, his voice
was empty of emotion.

> FUNDS REQUIRED TENTATIVELY ESTIMATED AT TWELVE HUN-
> DRED DOLLARS BUT FURTHER AMOUNT MIGHT BE NEEDED
> ACCORDING TO CIRCUMSTANCES AND TYPE OF ACCOMMODA-
> TIONS AVAILABLE WHEN YOUR HUSBAND IS READY TO PROCEED.

On April 17, Nerma mailed a check to Washington for $400. It was
all that she could manage to scrape together. Eleven days later, after a
frantic search, she sent another $50. She sent the money with a des-
perate plea for a loan, $800 to make up the balance.

Nerma waited two months. On June 22, she at last received an
answer. The State Department letter was three sentences long. As
Robin read it on the phone, his voice began to quiver.

> Competent Soviet authorities have informed the Embassy that
> they cannot reconsider your husband's case. It is therefore
> impossible to obtain his release at this time.

Along with the letter, the State Department had enclosed a check,
refunding Nerma her $450.

Robin called the letters "all strict bureaucratese," but to him the
correspondence had made the story of his lost father terrifyingly
clear. "They dared to make my mother pay his way out," he said. "You
gotta understand—this was a woman making twenty-five bucks a

week." Nerma had managed to come up with $450 and $10 for a telegram. "That was it," said Robin. "The government just let Dad sit in a Soviet jail and rot."

◼

EVER SINCE ROBIN HAD FOUND THE LETTERS IN THE TRUNK, HE HAD believed that the U.S. government was complicit in the circumstances that led to his father's death. It was a tragic, tidy story—and, given the times, it seemed to make sense. After all, on Capitol Hill, just as Robin discovered the letters, the Red-baiters were gaining force.

The crusade was long in coming, but on the eve of the war the jingoist fears had found momentum. In May 1938, as Nerma and Cy parted in Paris, Congress had created a Special Committee on Un-American Activities. Known as the Dies Committee, after its thirty-seven-year-old chairman, the ambitious Texas Democrat Martin Dies, it soon became a national platform for conservative anti–New Dealers. Established as a temporary committee to investigate seditious propaganda—primarily the alleged ties among German Americans, Nazi groups, and the Ku Klux Klan—the Dies Committee in time evolved into the infamous HUAC, the reporters' shorthand for the House Special Committee on Un-American Activities. By 1945, HUAC had become a standing committee of the House.

In the first years after the war, America savored victory. Senator Joseph McCarthy had yet to become a celebrity, and Edward R. Murrow had not yet found a cause in combating the excesses of "the junior senator from Wisconsin." It would be years before the hunt for Reds seized the country's attention. But Nerma was already transfixed by the events in Washington. She knew one of the men at the center of the congressional investigations. An old comrade, he had become the source of her most urgent fears.

IN THE EARLY 1920S, when Cy and Nerma were newly married and starting out in the party, Ben Mandel was known in the New York wing as Bert Miller. A onetime high school typing teacher, he had been a leader of the Teachers' Union in New York before becoming a party activist. As Miller, Mandel had signed Whittaker Chambers's first party card, and for a time he ran the business office at the *Daily Worker*. Nerma, though, had known him earlier, from their days as leaders of the Labor Defense Council. In 1923, in the wake of the Bridgman raid, she and Mandel served together on the national board of the LDC.

Mandel, as dramatically as anyone in America, embodied the turn, so pervasive in the 1930s, from Communist to anti-Communist. It began in 1929, when Stalin overthrew Lovestone and his followers and Mandel was kicked out of the party. Within a decade he had joined the anti-Red crusade. He worked first for the Dies Committee, leading its research squad, before graduating to HUAC. In time, as the hunt for subversives grew and his star rose, Mandel helped to orchestrate many of the investigations and purges of the McCarthy era. But already in the summer of 1941, when his name first emerged in press reports, Nerma was stricken with fear. McCarthy's shameless opportunism still lay in the future, yet she had seen the early parade of witnesses. It was not hard to see how the turncoats would fall into line. Sooner or later, Mandel would name her.

SINCE HER FIRST months back in the States, Nerma had feared the worst. The trail from Europe—those cowardly former comrades, as she saw it, who had betrayed the revolution—would eventually lead to New York. The defectors, in fact, were already encircling her. The Aviator, the erstwhile Soviet agent Robert Switz, had returned to New York and was particularly eager to spill his secrets. After their release in France, Switz and his wife, Marjorie, had fled to Eastern Europe. Yet since 1938, the Switzes had been back in the States and singing to the FBI.

Another of Cy and Nerma's erstwhile allies had turned against the USSR, too. The strange, heavyset man, a would-be writer with a double chin, a facile literary touch, and dreams of grandeur, had also been at Columbia in the 1920s. Whittaker Chambers had not yet testified, but he had begun to talk. On September 2, 1939, the day after the Nazi invasion of Poland, Chambers flew to Washington and met with Adolf Berle, the assistant secretary of state, who was close to FDR. Berle, a powerful New Dealer from New York, served as the State Department's intelligence liaison. Chambers, who had broken with the party the previous spring, had come to unburden himself.

After dinner, over coffee at Berle's elegant home, Chambers spoke for hours. He outlined the history and depth of the Soviet underground in Washington. And he named names. Berle jotted notes on a piece of paper, and later that night typed them up in a four-page memorandum that he entitled "Underground Espionage Agent." Berle included a question: "Note: When Loy Henderson interviewed Mrs. Rubens his report immediately went back to Moscow. Who sent it? Such came from Washington." Berle's notes would not surface for years, but among the names he wrote down that night was that of Alger Hiss.

At the same time, Nerma had witnessed, along with the rest of America, the illustrative descent of Walter Krivitsky. In December 1938, Krivitsky had arrived in New York, accompanied by his wife and five year old son. The following spring he came in from the cold. He published a series of articles in the *Saturday Evening Post* charting the rise of Soviet intelligence abroad, from Stalin's counterfeiting scheme in Berlin, to the Center's role in the Spanish Civil War, to the bodies of Trotskyists and former Soviet agents that had surfaced across Europe. Krivitsky's "exposés," however, were notable for an absence of detail.

Remarkably, the U.S. government had all but ignored the defector. In January 1939, when Krivitsky went to Washington, few officials saw him. A high-ranking veteran of Soviet military intelligence had finally walked in, but Hoover and his men paid him scant attention. Only three State Department officials bothered to debrief Krivitsky. One was Ray Murphy, the Irishman who had tracked Soviet intelligence since Cy's earliest days in the party. Murphy met with Krivitsky several times, in particular to probe the two New York mysteries, the Robinson-Rubens case and the disappearance of Juliet Poyntz.

By the fall of 1939, Krivitsky was refashioning his *Saturday Evening Post* articles into a book. In October he testified before the Dies

Committee. In January 1940 he returned to England, to see MI5. The British debriefing, extensive and expert, was done by his MI5 handler, Jane Archer—a former secretary whom Kim Philby would call one of the best officers "ever employed by MI5." Krivitsky soon left for Canada, and returned to New York later in 1940.

Ever since his open letter to Stalin, Krivitsky had known his fate. In New York, he lived under an assumed name. It was a shock, all the same, when a maid discovered him dead in the Bellevue Hotel in Washington, D.C., just blocks from the Capitol, on the morning of February 10, 1941. Krivitsky had been shot through the right temple. His body lay on the bed, shoes off. A .38 caliber revolver lay nearby, and three notes, in German, English, and Russian, were on the bedside table. Krivitsky was scheduled to testify again, to HUAC.

The police ruled it a suicide. The FBI at first declined to investigate. Chambers, who had befriended the former Great Illegal in America, remembered a saying: "Any fool can commit a murder, but it takes an artist to commit a good natural death."

.

ROBIN HAD TROUBLE REMEMBERING MUCH OF HIS ITINERANT ADOLES-cence, but he never forgot the letters and telegrams that he had found hidden in Nerma's old trunk. They lingered as he grew older, the only evidence of his father's demise he had ever come across. Even when he went to college and on to work, marrying and becoming a father himself, the correspondence from Washington, cold and distant as it was, remained the heart of his father's story. The letters seemed unimpeachable affidavits in the prisoner's defense, and proof of the U.S. government's callous neglect.

But Robin had made a false deduction. There were, in fact, two trails of paper in Washington. The first comprised letters and telegrams sent between Nerma and the State Department. The second was internal to the Foreign Service: the top-secret memorandums and dispatches cabled between the U.S. embassy in the USSR and Washington. Unlike Moscow, no single agency in Washington kept an Oggins file. The CIA reported that its archives held no trace of the case. The FBI had no records of an investigation of Isaiah

Oggins, only of his wife. The State Department records at the National Archives presented a maze. Over time, though, the pieces came together. The department's collective response—dispatches and consular records from Moscow and Kuibyshev, Washington and New York, Shanghai and Dairen, Berlin and Paris—vastly extended the paper trail that Nerma had saved in her trunk. The U.S. government's response to the discovery of an American prisoner in the gulag comprised more than a hundred pages of declassified documents, stretching from 1942 to 1948.

THE NEWS CAME FIRST to Greenwich Village, as it turned out, via a telephone call. Until March 1942, Nerma had not known—contrary to what her former bosses in Moscow would later contend—that Cy was in the gulag. One month after the Polish POW walked into the Polish embassy in Kuibyshev, a Mrs. Kinsey of the New York office of State's Passport Division called Nerma with the news. *Your husband,* she said, *is in jail in Russia, and he is ill.* That was it.

On July 31, 1942, Nerma appealed to Washington. She sent a two-page handwritten plea to the "Chief, U.S. Passport Division." From the letter, it was clear that she had not heard from Cy since Paris and that she had not known of his imprisonment. She demanded to learn the charges against him, his sentence, and the state of his health.

On October 17, Nerma wrote again, asking the department to deliver a message to Cy. She enclosed $2.50 for the cable, twenty-five words long:

OGGINS
CAMP NORILLAG NORILSK
U.S.S.R.

ROBIN FINE REMEMBERS AND ADORES YOU GET WELL HIS SAKE
COURAGE WRITE 322 WEST 15 STREET N.Y. CITY LOVE NERMA

By December 1942, Molotov had entered what was becoming a high-level case. It was Stalin's foreign minister who had instructed the Lubyanka to permit the American diplomats to visit Oggins in jail. Next came Tommy Thompson's cable to the wartime embassy in Kuibyshev. On December 11, the news—"Oggins wants to go home"—was forwarded to Washington.

Then, on New Year's Day 1943, Nerma received a miraculous present: a letter from the State Department that included a message from Cy. It was the first that she had heard from him in four and a half years:

> I received your message and am happy to know that you and the child are in good health. I should appreciate your doing everything you can to make it possible for us to be together again and I am looking forward to that time.

Within days, on January 9, came the second jail visit, when Stevens returned with the passport application. Two days later, the diplomats in Moscow sent their dispatch to Washington summing up their preliminary conclusions. They enclosed a new message from the prisoner to his family:

> I send my deepest love to you and Robin and urgently request you to make every possible effort to assist me for I need all your help and love.
> Your keeping in touch with me regularly would be appreciated .

Cy's messages had restored Nerma's hope and given her new momentum. On March 3, 1943, she sent another plea to the secretary of state, Cordell Hull. Yet within a day, the letter from the department's assistant chief, Special Division, arrived, warning of the need to prepay Cy's passage home.

BY THAT TIME, the State Department had already begun its investigation. Days after the Polish POW brought the news from the Norilsk camps, a clerk in the Records Division in Washington began to dig for "Cy Oggins," as the telegram from Kuibyshev gave the prisoner's name. On February 17, 1942, the clerk reported to the Political Department that he had "searched this name in our indexes and files without success." He looked elsewhere: the Columbia University

Register for 1937–38, the Bronx telephone directory for the prisoner's sister, and "several other sources of information," all "with negative result."

The clerk did, though, uncover an Isaiah Oggins. The next day the department sent Cy's passport file to the New York field office and asked the special agents to pick up the trail. T. F. Fitch and Daniel H. Clare were two Irishmen long familiar with the clandestine maneuvers of Soviet agents in the United States. Tommy Fitch, the chief special agent, had helped crack the Robinson-Rubens case and flown to Oregon in 1939 to take Cy's former colleague the forger Nick Dozenberg into federal custody. A postal inspector long before he joined State, Fitch had exposed innumerable cases of passport and mail fraud. Dan Clare, a Massachusetts native who had graduated from Colgate in 1925, had worked for years as a corporate investigator downtown, until the Depression closed his small firm. As World War II approached and the federal authorities sought investigators to root out seditious foreigners, Clare had joined Fitch in the field office. Together, they would spend much of the 1940s chasing suspected Communist spies and German saboteurs across New York.

Fitch and Clare began their search at Columbia. They inquired at the university offices about a professor of history named "Ogins." They also checked the city directories. They went to an address in Brooklyn—432 Amboy Street—looking for the woman named in the telegram from Kuibyshev as Oggins's sister, Mrs. Barron. They found Bessie Baron and learned that she was in fact not Cy's sister but his sister-in-law. Bessie in turn led them to Nerma.

By April, Fitch and Clare had done their job. The department had formed an early conclusion about the mysterious American in the Moscow jail. On April 15, 1942, Sumner Welles sent a secret telegram to the Moscow embassy detailing Oggins's tangled passport history. He ended the cable with a warning:

IT IS POSSIBLE THAT HE HAS BEEN ACTING FOR YEARS AS AN AGENT OF A FOREIGN POWER OR OF AN INTERNATIONAL REVOLUTIONARY ORGANIZATION. NEVERTHELESS IT IS BELIEVED

THAT IN VIEW OF HIS AMERICAN CITIZENSHIP AND OF THE
SOVIET AGREEMENT IN 1933 TO INFORM THIS GOVERNMENT OF
THE ARREST OF AMERICAN CITIZENS, THE FAILURE TO REPORT
OF HIS DETENTION SHOULD NOT BE IGNORED.

The word "possible" in the first sentence had been crossed out with
a red pencil. In its place, someone—most likely Loy Henderson, the
veteran Russia hand who read the cable—had written "probable."

Cy Oggins, in the eyes of the U.S. government, was not to be
trusted. The secretary of state had sent the diplomats to see Oggins
in jail with their eyes wide open. By January 5, 1943, days before
Stevens would see Oggins for the last time, the State Department
had reached a decision. "It is believed," wrote an unnamed official in
the Political Division, "that the attached case of Isaiah Oggins should
be taken up with the FBI, with the suggestion that a check-up be
made on Mrs. Oggins' activities in this country. This Division feels
reasonably sure that Oggins was an agent of the Soviet Government."
It was the nod that put Hoover's men on the case.

·

ROBIN NEVER KNEW THE OTHER HALF OF THE STORY—THE BAILOUT.
Three weeks after the FBI began an investigation, on April 1, 1943,
four of the top Soviet experts in the Foreign Service gathered to consider helping "Mrs. Oggins." Before the meeting was over, they would
take a straw poll on whether or not the department should advance
Nerma a loan of $800—the balance of the estimated cost of bringing
her husband home.

The four officials who met in an oak-paneled office of the East
European Division were Chip Bohlen, Loy Henderson, Freddy Reinhardt, and Bartley Gordon. All had served in Moscow, and all except
Gordon would become ambassadors. There were few men in Washington who could better judge the gravity of the case. Bohlen and
Henderson, above all, could guess the fate that awaited an American
prisoner in a Soviet jail. After the war, Henderson would be shunned
as a cold warrior and packed off as ambassador to Iraq. His sober view

of the USSR, however, was formed from the inside. He had been in the Butyrka Prison. On February 11, 1938, he was the diplomat who visited Ruth Robinson, the American arrested after her husband, the spy Ikal, "disappeared" in Moscow. Bohlen, too, had witnessed Stalin's terror. In 1938 he attended the Moscow show trials when Bukharin was sacrificed, along with nearly two dozen other Old Bolsheviks. Bohlen was considered suave and unflappable, a diplomat's diplomat. But the trials had shaken him. As he wrote in his memoirs,

> With obvious relish, [Gen. Vasily Ulrich] intoned the names of the defendants, followed, in eighteen cases, with the refrain: "To be shot, to be shot, to be shot." It took more than an hour to read all the sentences, and by the time of the last "to be shot," I felt that the top of my head was coming off. I could not go to sleep easily for almost a month after that.

The four men weighed the consequences of their decision with care (the handwritten notes from the meeting are in the National Archives). The vote, surprisingly enough, was unanimous. Nerma would be loaned the funds needed to get her husband, a suspected Soviet agent, to Washington.

In the following days, Nerma sent the two checks—one for $400, then one for $50. On April 30 she mailed another letter to Washington, asking that a message be cabled at once to Cy:

> HAVE COURAGE. TRUTH WILL WIN. I AM SENDING FOUR HUN-
> DRED DOLLARS TOWARD THE COST OF YOUR RETURN TRANS-
> PORTATION. GAIN STRENGTH FOR THE JOURNEY. ROBIN IS FINE.
> WE ARE BOTH WAITING AND HOPING. LOVE.

On May 9, after the long May Day holiday, the Commissariat for Foreign Affairs sent a brief diplomatic note to the U.S. embassy. In it, Molotov delivered the sudden and stunning about-face: "The competent Soviet authorities do not consider it possible to reconsider the Oggins case."

Perhaps it was the war, or perhaps it was negligence, but the news was slow in getting to Barrow Street. In the USSR, Joseph Davies, the former ambassador, had arrived on a "second mission to Moscow." FDR had sent Davies, ever the sunny optimist on Soviet affairs, as an emissary to strengthen his ties with Stalin. On May 23, Stalin hosted him at an epic Kremlin banquet. Davies had come to premiere *Mission to Moscow*, the faux documentary based on his preposterous but best-selling memoirs. The first Hollywood film to cast the USSR in a rosy light, it was a product of Davies's well-endowed ego and a U.S. propaganda effort to inspire domestic support for the Soviet war effort and win over Stalin. Davies himself introduced the film, assuring viewers that "no leaders of a nation have been so misrepresented and misunderstood as those in the Soviet government during these critical years between the two world wars." Stalin appeared pleased with the gift from the West; he returned the favor, announcing the dissolution of the Comintern, the outmoded agency of world revolution, during Davies's visit.

Admiral Standley, the current ambassador, who also attended the Kremlin screening, could only fume. Bypassed and humiliated by the White House, Standley threatened to resign. Only on June 10 did the ambassador finally forward the news about Oggins—now more than a month old—to Washington, which in turn relayed it to New York.

On June 23, Nerma opened a letter and read, below the familiar gold seal of the State Department, that "competent Soviet authorities have informed the Embassy that they cannot reconsider your husband's case. It is therefore impossible to obtain his release at this time."

·

NERMA FELL INTO AN ACCELERATED DESCENT. SHE NEVER LEARNED OF the department's decision to lend her money. Instead she laid the blame on the men in Washington, accusing them of complicity in her husband's imprisonment. Hers was not a simple grudge but an all-consuming fear of officialdom, particularly of the American variety, and a loathing of bureaucrats wherever she encountered them.

Throughout the early 1940s, Nerma floated from menial job to menial job. It was years before she managed to hold a regular position, as a secretary at Worth Hardware, a wholesaler on White Street, downtown. She stayed on for more than a decade, but Robin never saw the office. While he was at university in Chicago, he went home only once a year. By then she was "already on her way."

The secrets that had long haunted the family tore Nerma apart. "It was the fear," Robin said. "She'd insist to you that someone was after her. She was forever stuffing things in books. Letters, photographs, notes, bits of paper. She had things hidden all over the apartment." Robin could not have known it, but his mother had cause to be afraid. The men from the Center were watching her, even in New York. So, too, were Hoover's agents. The FBI was opening her mail, tracing her telephone calls, and keeping a watchful eye on her correspondents and contacts.

Meanwhile, word about Cy Oggins's fate spread among the survivors of the old underground. *The Gremlins of Lieutenant Oggins,* a picture book of an odd sort, was published in New York in the spring of 1943. It arrived, and was advertised and reviewed in newspapers across the country, at the height of the war—more than four years after Cy's arrest in Moscow, one year after Nerma learned the news, and two months after the FBI launched its investigation. *The Gremlins* was a mock-epic poem written by Irwin Shapiro. A strange relic, it seemed to defy explanation.

The title, of course, could have been a coincidence. During the war, gremlins, "those funny little men who play pranks on airmen," had become a feature of American popular culture. Shapiro's was one of three gremlin tales to appear that spring. Weeks earlier, Random House published *The Gremlins,* a fable of RAF gremlins written by Lieutenant Roald Dahl and accompanied by Walt Disney's drawings, while Dutton published *Listen, Hitler, the Gremlins Are Coming.* Lieutenant Dahl, the future author of *Charlie and the Chocolate Factory,* had flown Tiger Moths in Africa during the war and never written a children's book before. At first Shapiro's *Gremlins* seemed only an imitation of Dahl's book, but it was filled with hints too strong to ignore.

Lieutenant Oggins, for instance, was Sam Tilden Oggins. When read as a coded message, Sam stood for Cy, and Tilden for Alfred Tilton, the Soviet *rezident* in New York in the 1920s. Lieutenant Oggins, moreover, was "a long lanky lean sort of chap," and the gremlins employed the secret methods of the underground in their endeavors. They intercepted "radio messages" and used "shortwave" for "code messages." One breed of Shapiro's gremlins, "the sly Whispersnitches," even boasted "long crafty fingers adept in the arts of snitching and filching maps, papers and charts."

The plot, too, seemed to mirror Cy's odyssey. Lieutenant Oggins was an aviator, a bold young American who yearned to fly high—to "*outfly* any flyer that's flown." Above all, he wanted to show his wife, now left alone back home, that he was "a hero." Lieutenant Oggins was an ace pilot, but the gremlins cut short his flight home. Surrounded by Messerschmitts, he had turned his plane around. Lieutenant Oggins imagined that he was heading west, but he had lost his maps and his compass had failed. He crashed in Germany. Captured by the Nazis, the pilot was "held for a court-martial," denied an attorney, charged with "having committed, innumerable times, awful, deplorable, reprehensible crimes; of ruining the plane with which [he was] trusted," and now faced an unknown fate "in some foul concentration camp."

Shapiro died in 1981, at age seventy. Only one reference book, *Contemporary Authors*, offered a biographical sketch. Born in Pittsburgh, he was "an artist, poet and writer, with a strong interest in American folklore." There was no mention of family, nor of anyone who might recall his early days in New York, in particular his politics. Shapiro wrote more than forty books, many of them for Golden Books and nearly all after *The Gremlins.* Some were patriotic tales, with heroes from Davy Crockett to Daniel Boone. Others, like *Joe Magarac and His U.S.A. Citizen Papers* and *John Henry and the Double Jointed Steam-Drill*, seemed to carry radical undertones.

Shapiro, though, had not always written for children. In the late 1920s, he studied painting at the Art Students' League of New York. At the time, Esther Shemitz, the future Mrs. Whittaker Chambers, also attended the school. Their transcripts revealed that they had even taken the same course—life drawing, taught by the noted muralist Thomas Hart Benton; but so had dozens of other students. During the Depression, Shapiro sold shoes, set type, worked in a camp and in a factory. In the 1930s he helped translate two Hungarian novels and tried his hand at drama and film criticism. A former colleague, a writer who shared an office at Golden Books with Shapiro after the war, remembered his wit and humor but nothing of his politics.

At last shadows of an earlier radicalism emerged. The theater archives of the New York Public Library yielded the only known typescript of a thirteen-page play by Shapiro, *90 Percent of the People.* Written on a union grant in 1938, the play was leftist agitprop, a crude attack on isolationism. In the same singsong rhymes he would employ in *The Gremlins,* Shapiro argued for entering the war, fighting fascism, and lifting the arms "embargo on Loyalist Spain." The play was bound in a collection of sketches—all social justice dramas—produced by the New Theatre League. An alliance of leftist dramatists that included Clifford Odets and Irwin Shaw, the league was well known in the history of American theater. It not only helped speed the arrival of Stanislavsky on Broadway, it was a Communist front.

The discovery quickened the search for a link to Cy Oggins. The Social Security Death Index listed Shapiro's card number and place of death, and for twenty-four dollars, the county clerk of West Palm Beach, Florida, photocopied and forwarded his will. The will offered the name of the writer's only son. Jonathan S. Shapiro, however, is not an uncommon name in the United States, and the probate filings did not include any contact information other than a P.O. box in upstate New York. Two years would pass before a telephone number emerged.

One morning early in 2007, more than six years after my discovery of Lieutenant Oggins, Jon Shapiro told me of his parents' past. "First thing you should know," he said, "both my parents were Communists." For years the Shapiros did not dare speak of it, but Irwin and his wife, Edna Richter, had been deep in the party. In the 1930s, Edna served as the Moscow correspondent for the *Daily Worker.* Irwin,

too, had been a fervent believer but had muted his activism in order
to work. "My father kept his politics under wraps," Jon said. "It wasn't
something Golden Books would've liked to hear." Yet on the eve of
the war, the Shapiros had turned their backs on the USSR. The terror, the show trials, the pact with Hitler—whatever it was, said Jon,
"my parents saw the truth, thanks to Stalin."

Shapiro was not the only gremlins fabulist who had obscured his
past. During the war, Lieutenant Dahl secretly served British intelligence. His *Gremlins* was also agitprop, part of a directive "to try and oil
the wheels between the British and American war effort." Shapiro's
tale was indeed written in code. It was an attempt to speak to the
believers now adrift in the clandestine world. The gremlins are out
there, Shapiro warned, and eager to bring you crashing to earth.
Abandon the cause, implored the hidden subtext, if you wish to get
out alive.

·

FOR ALL AMERICANS, THE EARLY 1940S WERE YEARS OF WAITING AND
yearning for a war of horrific force to end. For Robin, they were also
years of awakening. When he suffered from his mother's black dogs,
he would escape to the public library down the block and find solace
amid the books. He could make friends in the Village and play ball in
Washington Square. But for much of the time during those years,
whether in the city or at camp in the country, Robin was on his own,
left to imagine where his father had gone.

On July 17, 1944, Nerma once again asked the State Department
to cable her husband. On July 22, Cy would turn forty-six years old.
She enclosed $5 to cover the cost and economized on words:

BIRTHDAY GREETINGS CY ROBIN FINE IN SUMMER CAMP I AM
WORKING COURAGE WAR SUFFERING EVERYWHERE IT MUST
END LOVE NERMA

Nerma had returned to her first occupation: prison relief. She
not only routinely lobbed volleys at the State Department, but time
and again she petitioned the Soviet consulate in New York. She

may have protested too loudly. At winter's end in March 1945 came the accident.

To Robin it was a routine affair. But at thirteen, he was nearly killed. For years already he had been roaming the Village by himself after school. It happened in an instant. He was jaywalking across Eighth Avenue, a block from home, when a taxi slammed into him. His skull was fractured and his kidney and spleen were ruptured. At St. Vincent's Hospital, the doctors did not talk of survival.

"Could've happened to anyone," Robin said as he told me of his injuries. Nerma, he added, did not pursue a legal case and settled for $2,000 out of court. Robin was still hindered by a limp, but that was the legacy of the fall in San Francisco. His was an eventful early medical history, Robin realized. The series of accidents and injuries revealed the legacy of an absent mother. To Nerma, though, in her fear and isolation, it may have seemed a sinister warning: the possibility, not unheard of in the underground, that someone might use a child to keep his mother silent.

ALL THAT WINTER and spring, as the European war drew to a close, FDR's health was in sharp decline. On April 12, 1945, while at the Little White House in Georgia, the health resort Roosevelt had built for polio treatments, the president suffered a massive cerebral hemorrhage and died. Two weeks later, in a concrete bunker fifty feet below the Chancellery building in Berlin, Hitler took his own life. The Soviets had reached the German capital. American GIs liberated Buchenwald and Dachau, and the British Bergen-Belsen. In New York, the horrors of the Nazi camps dominated the front pages. By summer's end the war was over, and in October the UN charter was ratified. Peace, Nerma imagined, would bring reunification.

Robin stayed in the hospital for three weeks, but by fall he was ready for school. He finished City and Country that year and at thirteen headed across town for the afternoon shift at Stuyvesant, the high school on East Fifteenth Street that was still all boys then. Nerma had tried to provide Robin with a home and a first-rate education. Stuyvesant, the "manual trade school for boys" founded in

1904, was one of the best and most competitive public high schools in the city.

All the while, Nerma kept writing to the men in Washington. Her targets would shift as the officials came and went, but Mrs. Oggins in New York City maintained her campaign. On March 3, 1947, she anxiously wrote to the new secretary of state, George C. Marshall. Marshall, only a month on the job, was about to embark on a trip to Europe and Moscow. Not until June would he announce America's undertaking to rebuild Europe.

Nerma begged Marshall to raise the Oggins case with Stalin. It is "now almost 4 years since I have had any news of my husband," she wrote. This time, Robin added his own voice to his mother's plea. At fifteen, he still did not know the truth, but he, too, wrote a letter to the new boss of the State Department:

> Dear Mr. Marshall
>
> I have not known my father very well but the impression I got during the years (few) I knew him was that he was one of the straightest and cleanest men that ever lived. I know dad must be innocent, he could never do anything bad. Is it fair then, that he should be taken from his wife and child and thrown into a prison far from his native land? No it is not. I beg you to use all the power at your command to right this wrong. To by this act relieve my mother of the great burden of not only working and keeping house but of trying to be both a mother and a father to me. To relieve my father from suffering and be put back with family and friends. And to give me a fathers companionship. In the name of God Mr. Marshall. I implore you to do this.
>
> Sincerely yours,
> Robin S. Oggins

Robin had no memory of the letter, which lay for decades among the files of the National Archives. But he did know of its result. From Washington there was only silence.

■

That March, State Department investigators paid a visit to the top-floor flat on Fifteenth Street. The agents asked polite questions and did not stay long. They were interested to learn how it was that her husband had ended up in the gulag. Nerma somehow kept her composure and found the answers to send them on their way. For years, however, the FBI considered returning to interview her.

The Bureau was not only interested in her husband. Throughout the 1940s, Nerma's name appeared in FBI investigations in New York. It seems to have arisen first in 1940, amid allegations that the Soviets had penetrated the Brooklyn Navy Yard, then a critical munitions plant. During the war it cropped up in a variety of cases, and then in 1946 yet again, as the Bureau tried to unravel the tangle of allegations made by Igor Gouzenko, a Soviet cipher clerk who had recently defected in Canada.

The FBI was curious, above all, about Nerma's choice of friends. Ruth Domino Jerusalem was a German writer who had fled the Nazis and come to New York, at age thirty-two, in the summer of 1941. Angela Haden Guest was an Englishwoman from a distinguished family. Ruth and Angela may well have been friends even before they came to New York. Both had worked the partisan frontlines in Spain as nurses during the civil war, and both, although they did not advertise it in New York, had strong ties to two men who had gained fame fighting for the revolution. By the summer of 1946, Ruth and Angela were rooming together in New York, and both were under FBI investigation. Hoover's men believed, rightly or wrongly, that both women had once lived at Nerma's.

Ruth Jerusalem was a writer and poet who taught at Bryn Mawr and elsewhere and was later published in *The New Yorker*. To the FBI, though, she was the "reported wife of Gerhard Eisler." Before the war, Ruth had been married to an Austrian Communist doctor and writer, Fritz Jerusalem, and although there was no evidence that she had in fact later married Eisler, the FBI was acting on an informer's tip. Gerhard Eisler was not well known in the first years after the war. But by

1947, after he was arrested for passport fraud and contempt of Congress, he became notorious. Eisler was the brother of Ruth Fischer, a German Communist leader ousted from the party in 1925, and Hanns Eisler, a left-wing composer who worked in Hollywood in the 1930s. He was also a longtime Comintern agent and for much of the 1940s, the *rezident* in charge of Soviet military intelligence in the United States. In 1949 Eisler would make headlines by jumping bail and fleeing aboard a Polish ship, the *Batory*. He eventually resurfaced in East Germany, where he long served as the state's chief propagandist.

Nerma's other reported lodger was Angela Haden Guest—"Angela Ida Marjorie Judith Carmel Haden Guest," in the FBI files. Angela, or Angel, as she was known in Spain, came from an English family known for its politics. Leslie Haden Guest, her father, was a doctor who served as a leading Labour MP from 1923 to 1927. "A theosophist with a fiery temper and a considerable libido," Bertrand Russell called him in his memoirs. Russell and Haden Guest had traveled together to the USSR, leading a delegation of Labourites in the spring of 1920. The group met Lenin and Trotsky and were feted wherever they went. Few of the Englishmen went home convinced of the shining Soviet future, but Russell and Haden Guest were the gloomiest. "Everyone is afraid to speak," Haden Guest wrote of the Soviets in the *Fabian News* that summer. In time he moved to the right, and in 1927 he broke with Labour for a decade.

Baron Haden Guest, as he became on his retirement from the House of Commons, had five children. Angela was his sole daughter. In New York, she went to college, studied medicine, and in time married an American and joined the World Health Organization. By 1946 she was joined in the city by a brother, Peter Haden-Guest, who had been appointed to run the Information Secretariat at the UN.

Angela's older brother, though, had died years earlier, at twenty-seven. David Guest, as he preferred to be known, was one of the first English martyrs to the cause. A Marxist theoretician and a mathematician with promise, he went to Spain in the spring of 1938. In July, after crossing the Pyrenees on foot, he was shot through the heart in the battle of the River Ebro.

Yet in 1947, his legacy lived on. David Guest had entered Cambridge in 1929. His tenure at Trinity College had begun with the Wall Street crash and closed with the rise of Hitler. It was a time, a classmate wrote, when "over five-sixths of the earth's surface there raged an economic crisis without parallel in the history of capitalism." At Oxford and Cambridge, socialism was the vogue. Guest, however, was one of the few students who took to the streets. In London he joined the strikers in Battersea. In Germany for a term, he was arrested at an anti-Fascist rally and spent two weeks in jail. By 1931, Guest returned to Trinity "with a hammer and sickle emblem prominently displayed in his coat." Angela's brother founded the first Communist cell at Cambridge.

It was quite a circle of comrades. Kim Philby joined as treasurer, and soon they added a second-year Trinity student, Donald Maclean. Guest also initiated another Trinity boy to Marxism-Leninism, Guy Burgess. In time, two more Trinity undergraduates, Anthony Blunt and John Cairncross, would find their way to the party, and the underground. David Guest was not one of the Cambridge Five, the Center's most celebrated Western recruits. But he was one of their earliest inspirations. His ghost would follow them for decades.

Angela was never known to be a Communist. In Spain, she did not even see her brother. She only received his effects—scarf, copy of Virgil, and little wallet, "pierced by the bullet" that had entered his heart. In Nerma's FBI file, however, an informant had marked her as a member of the British party, an allegation that remains uncorroborated. She was also reported to be a regular at the meetings on Bleecker Street in the Village, the monthly gatherings of the party's Sacco and Vanzetti Club. Above all, Angela was suspect by association. In the summer of 1942, according to the FBI files, she was collecting her mail at Nerma's place on Barrow Street. Robin remembered her clearly. "Angela and Mom were friends," he said. "At least she was around an awful lot."

FOR NERMA, the first years after the war had not brought peace, only anxiety. The furies, real and imagined, gained force. There had been interludes of quiet, but by the summer of 1947 the FBI again drew close.

On June 2, two agents knocked on Alger Hiss's door at his office in Washington, D.C. The former State Department official was just six months into a new job as head of the Carnegie Endowment for International Peace. The agents asked Hiss about charges that he was a Communist and whether he knew a man named Whittaker Chambers. Hiss replied that he was not a Communist and had never heard of Chambers.

Three days later, on June 5, Max Steinberg, as Charles Martin, opened a second account at the National City Bank in New York and transferred $500 into it. On June 26, a call was placed from Watkins 9-6054, a New York number registered to a flat on Fifteenth Street, to Lafayette 1690 in Boston. It was one of only five toll calls Nerma made from April 1 to October 11 of that year.

The FBI tracked the call. It was placed to an attorney at a Boston firm across the street from Faneuil Hall. This time the field agent in Boston got it right. "Page 3 of referenced report," he wrote, "indicates that an individual named 'BARTELETT' was the individual listed on the toll tickets of subject, having called this number on June 26, 1947. It is therefore possible that this individual is identical with CALVIN PAGE BARTLETT."

If Calvin Page Bartlett was not yet well known, Hill, Barlow, Goodale and Wiswall was—the firm was among Boston's finest. Arthur D. Hill, a former district attorney, was one of its founders. Hill was best known, though, as the FBI noted, for having taken on the toughest case of the century: the last appeal of Sacco and Vanzetti. The anarchists had spent seven years in jail, proclaiming their innocence to the end. Throughout the years, the judicial system, even while revealing its faults, had ratified its own errors. The final appeal was doomed. Hill had assumed the defense when no one else would, weeks before Sacco and Vanzetti's execution on August 22, 1927.

Cal Bartlett was three years younger than Cy. The son of a Republican governor of New Hampshire, he had gone to Yale and Yale Law.

In 1947, Bartlett was one of six partners at the Boston firm and not one known as a hero of lost liberal causes. He would gain prominence, however, during the height of the McCarthy hysteria for taking on cases that others would not accept.

For Nerma, it had been her longest campaign, five years of letter-writing and searching for aid among the survivors of the old underground. Despite all her efforts, she did not even know if Cy was alive. The call to Bartlett was telling. Fear had given way to panic. Whether for herself, her husband, or someone else, it was not clear, but Nerma was looking for a good lawyer.

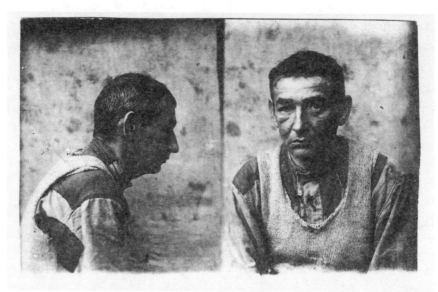

Cy Oggins, Moscow, ca. 1947.

EXECUTION

■

WHEN CY WALKED INTO THE ROOM, HE HAD BEEN BEHIND barbed wire for more than eight years. Outside, the Moscow air was heavy and wet. The building stood in the center of the city, anonymous and silent, with no plaque adorning its entrance. It was a narrow side street, filled on weekdays with passersby, officers and comrades going to and from their offices in the shadows of the Lubyanka. As they navigated the sidewalk, they were blind to the goings-on behind the gray cement.

It was in the middle of the summer of 1947 when Cy was taken from his prison cell for the final time. He was led down a corridor and into a white-walled room devoid of features and nearly empty of furniture. It would be the last room in the labyrinth.

Cy knew that the odyssey had come to its end. He had learned, only too well by now, how the Soviet bureaucracy worked (or did not), how the machine, at once intricate and impervious, rolled on. Arrested in his hotel room on the top floor of the Moskva on February 20, 1939, Cy had been sentenced on January 5, 1940, to a term of eight years. The Soviets had rules—laws that, however absurd, would be strictly obeyed. By the beginning of 1947, Cy knew that his journey through the prisons and camps, eight years that had taken him from the Lubyanka to Norilsk and back to Moscow, was nearly over. When February ended, he was overdue. But the knowledge that his term had passed did not bring comfort. For months Cy waited, through the spring and into the summer.

THAT MORNING THE MEN had come. Release had arrived. Only one final medical examination remained. Standard procedure, the guards said, before freedom.

It was, of course, a ruse.

Cy had been taken not to a medical clinic but to Laboratory Number One, the *Kamera*, as it was called by the few secret policemen who knew of its existence. Founded in 1938, the *Kamera,* or chamber, would be described after the empire had fallen and the lines had been redrawn, as a "toxicological laboratory." In practice, it was an experimental death chamber.

Laboratory Number One was hidden inside the squat square building at 11 Varsonofyevsky Pereulok, one block from the Lubyanka. Today iron bars remain on the windows. The building is an exclusive medical clinic for the Russian Security Service, the FSB. In 1947 it was the preserve of Dr. Grigory Moiseevich Mairanovsky, a colonel in the Medical Corps of the NKVD, and the executioner of choice in Stalin's court.

Cy entered the laboratory thin and weak. His shoulders were stooped, his neck was bent, and his eyes had been darkened by the years behind bars. What torture he had endured in the camps and jails would go in secret with him.

Mairanovsky, professor of pathophysiology and director of the laboratory from 1939 to 1951, personally administered the shot. Born in 1899, a year after Cy, Mairanovsky had also been a student during the revolution. He had graduated from university in Tbilisi, the Georgian capital in the Caucasus, in 1919 and gone on to Moscow, earning a medical degree in 1923.

The doctor was an unsavory character even by the standards of the secret police. He had a thick brow, wide-set reptilian eyes, and outsized ears that protruded at right angles. He was, though, an expert. Mairanovsky has been called Stalin's Mengele. A biochemist with a professional interest in poisons, he was appointed to head the laboratory by the bosses of the Lubyanka. More than half a century later, his name would appear in newspapers across the West amid the speculation that followed the poisonings of the Ukrainian president Viktor Yushchenko in Kiev in 2004 and the former KGB officer

Alexander Litvinenko in London in 2006. Mairanovsky pioneered the Soviet use of poison as a traceless means of execution. His preferred subjects, it was said, were foreign prisoners. He nicknamed them *ptichki*, birds.

ISAIAH "SAI SIMONOVICH" OGGINS, as the Lubyanka clerk wrote out his name and filed away his case, was killed by means of lethal injection. The poison was curare, a brackish resin extracted from tropical plants of the genus *Strychnos*, used even today in South America; tribal hunters tip their blow-darts with the poison to paralyze their prey. Curare delivers an insidious death. The toxin works itself into the body by constricting every muscle, including the heart. Within minutes the poison arrests all motor nerves, the avenues that send impulses from the brain and spinal cord to the muscles.

The chief symptoms, as Mairanovsky later cataloged them for a Soviet interrogator, were

loss of voice and strength, muscular weakness, prostration, labored breathing, cyanosis and death with symptoms of suffocation while retaining complete consciousness. Death was excruciating, but the man was deprived of the ability to shout or move while retaining complete consciousness. Death of the "patient" ensued within ten to fifteen minutes after a sufficient dosage.

It was a cruelty beyond words. As Cy gasped for air, his heart gave out. Mairanovsky termed it "an experiment," a test to see whether the poison could be detected after death. When the doctor read the autopsy report, he was pleased. No trace was discovered.

It was not an execution; it was state-sponsored murder. Only months before, in May 1947, Stalin had banned capital punishment. But the American prisoner could not be released. The men of the Lubyanka, the Foreign Ministry, the executioners themselves—all had only heeded the Leader's cue.

Stalin and Molotov, 1949.

CHAPTER 11

THE NOTE TO STALIN

■ ■ ■

THE PENTAGON'S INTEREST IN THE KGB ARCHIVES WAS A WELL-known matter of public record. "The Note to Stalin," as I came to call the document that would help unlock the Oggins case, was not. And yet, the note had come to Washington straight from the hands of Boris Yeltsin.

On September 23, 1992, the new Russian president was in a buoyant mood. A year had not passed since the Soviet Union had been relegated to the ashcan of history. Yeltsin still basked in the glory of the "Second Russian Revolution," a cuddly bear beloved by Western leaders. As he entered the presidential office, he bussed Malcolm Toon, the American diplomat, on both cheeks. Toon, a career Foreign Service officer and blunt hard-liner on Soviet affairs, had served three tours in the USSR, in the 1950s, 1960s, and finally, as ambassador, 1970s, under Presidents Ford and Carter. The former diplomat was tall, with a shock of white hair and an easy old-school manner. Toon had long ago retired to play golf in North Carolina. Now, at seventy-five, he was back in the Kremlin on another mission to Moscow.

Yeltsin had summoned Toon on short notice, along with Robert Straus, the Democratic power-broker from Texas then serving as the U.S. ambassador. It was early in the autumn, but the air outside was chill and the leaves had begun to turn. The Kremlin office, newly refurbished with Swiss furniture and gilded chandeliers, seemed to glow.

Yeltsin held a dossier. He had survived the most trying year of his life, as Russia witnessed its greatest upheaval since 1917. There had been bouts of depression and drinking. The triumph had never been assured. Now at last, in his hands, he had something to offer. Russia's new president lifted a page and began to read. As he quoted from the document, his voice flooded with emotion. The Americans sat transfixed.

It was a file recently retrieved from the archives. The prisoner, Yeltsin said, was an American, who, even though innocent of the crimes he had been charged with, had been killed. Here at last, he added gravely, was evidence of the crimes of the past: a U.S. citizen executed without cause on Stalin's personal orders.

The Americans were dumbfounded. Only Toon found words. Those were indeed very bad times, he said.

FOR YELTSIN, the meeting in the Kremlin marked a turning point, a threshold of sorts to a new era. Fourteen months earlier, he and two fellow presidents of former Soviet lands had met at a Politburo chalet in the Belarussian woods and moved to dissolve the USSR. Within days, among the men who stormed the Kremlin, the questions began to swirl: How to begin anew? How to wipe the slate clean? Talk arose of the need for "a case"—a trial to air the sins of the past. Yeltsin engaged a team of lawyers and historians to prepare a case against the Communist Party. They dreamed of a ban, in perpetuity, on the party.

The Oggins case was to be prime evidence. The trial, however, never came off. Yeltsin feared the pendulum of retribution. He and many of his comrades were tied to the old ways. Yeltsin was born of the system, and for decades, long before his joust with Mikhail Gorbachev, he had enjoyed the privileges of a party boss. Soon the prospects for a show trial faded, and before long economics trumped ideology. The new Russian state, suffering the Soviet hangover, was deeply in debt. The Yeltsin government needed Western friends and grateful patrons more urgently than it needed to eliminate the threat of a Communist restoration.

In his first months in power, Yeltsin baited the Americans. He dropped hints that U.S. prisoners of war from World War II and the

Korean War might still be in the USSR. Rumors soon flew of Vietnam veterans trapped behind the Urals. In the United States, a squall of protest grew. To quell the uproar, in the spring of 1992, Presidents George H. W. Bush and Yeltsin formed the U.S.-Russia Joint Commission on POW/MIAs, to "seek to determine the fate" of the servicemen missing on both sides.

In June 1992, Yeltsin came to the United States on his first presidential trip. On June 15, en route to meet President Bush at the White House, he gave an interview aboard Air Russia to the NBC anchorman Tom Brokaw. As the cameras rolled, Yeltsin upped the ante. "Our archives have shown that it's true," he told Brokaw, of the stories about American POWs from Vietnam. "Some of them were transferred to the former USSR and were kept in labor camps. We don't have complete data and can only surmise that some of them may still be alive."

Bluster or blunder, it was a Yeltsin masterpiece. The Russian president's claim led the evening news, and the American public was outraged. Congress demanded action, with John McCain and John Kerry, Vietnam veterans, clamoring the loudest.

As the talk of American POWs in the USSR overshadowed the summit, the White House launched an initiative. In the Rose Garden, President Bush announced that he was dispatching Ambassador Toon to Moscow. He called the search for the missing soldiers "the highest priority for our administration and I know for every American." Yeltsin stared at the television cameras and vowed to do all he could. "We shall try to investigate each and every case," he said. "All the information will, of course, be handed over to the American side." Bush declared himself confident of his new partner. The Russians, he said, "will get to the bottom of it."

IN THE KREMLIN fourteen months later, on that fall afternoon in 1992, Yeltsin did not host the American envoys alone. By his side sat a stolid man in a military uniform. To Ambassadors Straus and Toon, General Dmitri Antonovich Volkogonov seemed the model of a Soviet officer—bushy eyebrows, square shoulders, medals strung across the chest. At sixty-four, Volkogonov was a *glasnost* hero, a military historian and celebrated biographer of Stalin and Trotsky. In the Kremlin, he deferred to Yeltsin. But the general was the one who had spent months in the KGB archives and the most closely guarded vault, the Presidential Archive, which held Stalin's personal papers. Volkogonov, whom Yeltsin had named to head the Russian side of the POW/MIA commission, had searched for American POWs and found Oggins.

Yeltsin relished the chance to hold the ambassadors spellbound. He turned the pages of the Oggins dossier slowly, letting the horror sink in. Quoting from the documents, Yeltsin spoke of the "cynicism" of the case. Stalin's henchmen had a word for such murders, he said: "*Likvidatsia.*" His face registered revulsion. The American prisoner, he said, had been "liquidated."

"The hiatus between the truth and the story that was put out," Yeltsin went on, "shows how much untruth and how many lies existed between our countries." It was, he assured the Americans, "a cold war habit" that "we are overcoming."

．

THE NOTE TO STALIN IN FACT WAS A REPORT, MARKED "TOP SECRET," TO the Soviet leader and his foreign minister, Molotov, from Viktor Semyonovich Abakumov, chief of the MGB, as the KGB was known in the spring of 1947. Abakumov, whose prominence and bloodlust remain greatly underappreciated, was plucked from obscurity after purging the southern town of Rostov in 1938. Younger than the men who rose through the ranks with Beria, as a sadist he was their equal. In *The Gulag Archipelago*, Aleksandr Solzhenitsyn records how Abakumov was "not averse to taking a rubber truncheon in his hands every once in a while" for confessions. His deputy was even more diligent; he would take care to roll out "a dirty runner bespattered with blood" over a fine Persian rug in his interrogation office.

Tall and handsome and only thirty-nine years old that spring, Abakumov, like his rival, Beria, was a sex addict. He kept a lavish apartment for trysts and was linked to dozens of women, including the émigré actress Olga Chekhova. The playwright's niece, Chekhova was a darling of Hitler's and, according to numerous accounts, an NKVD informant. Abakumov also grew obsessed with the film star Tatiana Okunevskaia after Beria raped her. When she dared to refuse him, he banished the actress to the gulag.

Stalin, however, trusted Abakumov. During the war he had run the counterespionage division SMERSH, short for *Smert' shpionam*, or "Death to Spies." And in the postwar years, as head of the MGB from 1946 to 1951, Abakumov served with unforgiving distinction.

Three pages long, the Note to Stalin resembled bureaucratic Swiss cheese. A censor had cut out words and entire paragraphs. More peculiarly, many words had been written by hand in the spaces between typewritten phrases. Standard practice at the uppermost heights of the Soviet bureaucracy, it was a stenographic secrecy that revealed the depth of the paranoia. Although the Kremlin and the Lubyanka carefully vetted their typists, even they were not allowed to know the contents of such ultrasecret documents. In the final instance, the most sensitive words were written in by hand.

Translated into English, preserving the lines whited out and words written in by hand (in italics), the Note read:

COPY

TOP SECRET

COPY NO. 4

COUNCIL OF MINISTERS OF THE USSR

21 MAY 1947

NO 2773/A

TO COMRADE STALIN, I. V.

TO COMRADE MOLOTOV, V. M.

I am reporting to you on the following:

In April, 1942 the *American* Embassy in the USSR, by a note addressed to the Minister of Foreign Affairs of the USSR, reported that according to information possessed by the

Embassy, the *American* citizen *Oggins, Isai* is imprisoned in a camp in *Norilsk*. On behalf of the *State Department*, the Embassy asked for a report on the reason of his arrest, the term to which *Oggins* was sentenced and the condition of his health.

In connection with the insistences of the *American* Embassy, on the order of Comrade MOLOTOV, two meetings took place, on 8 December 1942 and on 9 January 1943, between Embassy representatives and the sentenced *Oggins*. During these meetings, *Oggins*   told the representatives of the *American* Embassy that he was arrested as a Trotskyite, who had illegally entered the Soviet Union on someone else's passport, in order to contact the Trotskyite underground in the USSR.

In spite of such a declaration, the *American* Embassy in Moscow repeatedly raised the question with the MID [Foreign Ministry] of the USSR regarding the review of the case and the early release of *Oggins*, forwarding *Oggins'* letters and telegrams to his wife, who lives in the *USA*. They also informed the MID of the USSR that they recognize *Oggins* as an *American* citizen and are prepared to repatriate him to his homeland.

On 9 May 1943, the *American* Embassy was told that "the competent Soviet authorities do not consider it possible to reconsider *Oggins'* case."

On 20 February 1939, *Oggins*

was in reality arrested on the charges of espionage and treason.

During the investigation, these allegations were not confirmed, and *Oggins* did not plead guilty. However, a Special

Tribunal of the NKVD, USSR sentenced *Oggins* to 8 years in the ITL [prison labor camps], counting the term from 20 February 1939.

the appearance of *Oggins* in the *USA* might be used by persons hostile to the Soviet Union for active propaganda against the USSR.

Therefore, the MGB, USSR considers it necessary *to liquidate Oggins, Isai, informing the Americans that Oggins, after meeting with the American Embassy representatives, in June 1943 was returned to the place of internment in Norilsk, and there, in 1946, died in a hospital as a result of aggravated tuberculosis of the spine.*

We will ensure that the archives of the Norilsk camp reflect the course of Oggins' illness, and the medical and other aid rendered to him. Oggins' death will be recorded officially as an illness by autopsy and burial certificates.

Given that *Oggins'* wife

is in New York, and has repeatedly inquired at our consulate for information about her husband, and knows that he was arrested,

we consider it useful

> *to summon her to the consulate and inform her of the death of her husband*

I request Your instructions.

ABAKUMOV

WITHIN HOURS of Yeltsin's meeting with Ambassadors Toon and Straus, the Russian news agency TASS put out a two-paragraph item on the murder of an American prisoner under Stalin. In the United States that night, ABC News broadcast a report that an American named "Augins" had been killed in Moscow during Soviet times. The next day, the *Washington Post* ran the first of two stories reporting that "Oggens" had been executed on Stalin's personal orders. On September 25, 1992, the *New York Times*, in an article on Volkogonov's discoveries, listed "Isaiah H. Oggins, born in Massachusetts," as among the cases emerging from the archives.

That fall, General Volkogonov came to Washington. On November 11 he testified before the Senate Select Committee on POW/MIA Affairs, chaired by Senator Kerry, and reprised the story that Yeltsin had told the Americans in the Kremlin. Oggins was an innocent man, Volkogonov said, falsely accused and wrongly convicted of espionage, who had served his term only to be killed when he should have been released. The American, he assured the senators and reporters, was murdered "because he had seen too much." Stalin, Volkogonov testified, had feared what Oggins would tell the American government about the gulag—the camps and the horrors he had witnessed.

The official story ended there. Yeltsin and Volkogonov had reopened the case with dramatic flourish, only to close it again.

On January 14, 1993, President Bush received Ambassador Toon in the Oval Office. Long-standing members of Washington's patrician elite, the two spoke as friends. The president was eager for good news to tell the families of American POWs and MIAs, but Mal, as he called Toon, had none. The ambassador could only hand over a thin folder from Moscow—a few dozen documents on the fate of Americans who had died in the USSR. The Oggins case overshadowed all others.

Bush listened intently and thanked Toon. "You're doing the Lord's work," the president said.

■

"LIKVIDATSIA, OF COURSE, INVOLVED RISKS," SAID ANATOLI. "BUT WHAT else could Stalin do?" It was early in the second term of the Putin reign. We were sitting in a half-lit Swedish café on the northern edge of Moscow, and Anatoli Sudoplatov was explaining why his father had killed Cy Oggins.

Pavel Sudoplatov was one of Stalin's longest-serving intelligence officers and most loyal assassins. Sudoplatov *père* called himself "a professional revolutionary." In 1919, as a twelve-year-old in Ukraine, he had run away from home and joined the Red Army. By fourteen he was working for the Cheka. A decade after his death, his colleagues called him "Stalin's Terminator." Sudoplatov had overseen the Oggins murder.

After World War II broke out, Stalin had called Sudoplatov to the Kremlin and named him head of the *Osobaia gruppa,* the Special Group, a Lubyanka department that would carry out assassinations and sabotage behind Nazi lines. He in turn enlisted his trusted number two and co-conspirator in the murder of Trotsky, Lyona Eitingon. The Oggins execution was the work of three old friends. Mairanovsky administered the shot. Eitingon accompanied the "patient" to the laboratory. Sudoplatov took care of the paperwork—and the body.

Anatoli was Pavel's only surviving child. At fifty-nine, he had black hair that was graying at the temples, and his square jaw was fading into his jowls, but there was no mistaking the resemblance. Father and son had been close in many ways. Anatoli, though, had earned his reputation as an author and professor at Moscow State for decades. Trained as a demographer, he was expert in the history of Soviet intelligence. His knowledge was encyclopedic, sparkling with names, aliases, dates, and operational details. As he spoke, I understood why he had chosen the restaurant. We were the only patrons.

Anatoli was no fan of the new Russian president. But in the age of Putin, his compatriots were coming around. He had become a talking head, appearing on televised roundtables and the radio. "At last peo-ple appreciate," Anatoli said, "the sacrifices made by the greats of Soviet intelligence."

A dozen years after the Soviet collapse, Stalin had finally found his place in history: savior of the Russian people. He had forged the USSR into a military-industrial giant, defeated Hitler, and kept the Americans at bay. The terror, the years that had sent as many as 20 million Soviets to camps, jail, or death, was now deemed worth the price. In a recent poll, more than half of the respondents agreed that "on balance, Stalin did more good than bad for the country."

THE LEADER DIED on March 5, 1953, at the age of seventy-four, four days after an all-night bacchanalia with his Politburo cronies at his dacha. Officially, the cause of death was cerebral hemorrhage, but Stalin's closest drinking partners had left him to die. Beria, who had been among the inner circle to the end and who later claimed to have played a hand in Stalin's demise, moved swiftly into the power vac-uum. Molotov returned as foreign minister, and Georgi Malenkov became prime minister. Beria sought to rise highest: he again took charge of the state security apparatus.

Yet within months, Beria, too, fell. Arrested in June 1953 and charged with an array of crimes from terrorism to the rape of a sixteen-year-old girl, he was sentenced and executed before the year was out. In December, the Soviet press announced that Beria and his accomplices had been "in the pay of foreign intelligence agencies" and had conspired "to seize power and liquidate the Soviet worker-peasant system for the purpose of restoring capitalism and the dom-ination of the bourgeoisie."

Beria's demise, with inevitable momentum, brought an ignoble end to Sudoplatov's career. Along with Eitingon and many others of the former elite of the NKVD, Sudoplatov fell within weeks. On August 8, 1953, the old partisan, master spy, and architect of the murder of Trot-sky was greeted by a knock on the door in the middle of the night.

IN THE AFTERMATH of Stalin's death, an unfamiliar leniency ruled Soviet officialdom. As the predators became the prey, few among the

Lubyanka's former elite were executed. Many were interrogated and tortured by their own old methods before receiving long prison terms. A large contingent found themselves packed off to the *Vladimirsky tsentral*, the famous prison in the town of Vladimir, a half-day's drive from Moscow. Like Butyrka, the jail was built in the late eighteenth century under Catherine II and resembled a small castle. In the 1950s its cells held many of the USSR's most politically sensitive prisoners.

They were called the *Berievtsy*, the Beria Men. The Vladimir prison housed a number of NKVD generals who had served the fallen security boss, but Sudoplatov and Eitingon were among the stars. So, too, was Mairanovsky. The doctor who had run Stalin's laboratory of death had not survived the loss of his protector. In 1953, Mairanovsky was sentenced to ten years in jail—not for murder, but for illegally storing "strong-acting chemicals" outside the workplace. Mairanovsky betrayed his former employers with remarkable ease: he turned against Beria (shot in 1953), against Merkulov (shot the same night), and against Abakumov, the secret police chief who signed Oggins's death warrant (shot the next year).

The Beria Men were almost all NKVD generals, heroes too regal to walk the yard with commoners. Sudoplatov joined Eitingon in Vladimir in 1958. Both had been spared execution. Eitingon was sentenced to twelve years and won early release in 1964. Sudoplatov did not get out until 1968.

By then a new caste of prisoners had arrived: the dissidents. Revolt Pimenov was a Leningrad mathematician, and Anatoli Marchenko a construction worker born to illiterate parents. Marchenko would spend nearly half his forty-eight years in Soviet jails, camps, or exile. Both he and Pimenov were jailed for anti-Soviet agitation. At Vladimir they joined Boris Menshagin, a lawyer who served as burgermeister of Smolensk during the Nazi occupation—and had the bad luck to have learned of the Soviet slaughter of thousands of Polish officers in the nearby Katyn Forest. Menshagin, arrested for treason, set a Soviet record: sentenced to twenty-five years, he spent all but two in solitary confinement.

Pimenov, Marchenko, and Menshagin wrote memoirs, and each

singled out one prisoner in Vladimir. They did not always get his name right, or his past, but they remembered him clearly. He was slight, not tall, and yet a formidable figure in the prison. He would walk "the Box," the high-walled inner courtyard open to the sky and snow, with the Beria Men, but he also managed to signal his distance from them. As they walked the yard side by side, hands at the back, he followed just behind. Miraculously, he had preserved from the outside world a sense of entitlement, and a wardrobe to match. He wore a general's *papakha*, a tall lambskin hat, and a heavy woolen coat, "which hung on him like a greatcoat." The solitary figure was Max Steinberg.

CY'S BOSS IN China had ended up in the same prison as Sudoplatov. For a time, handler and hangman even shared a cell. Max and Elsa had returned to the USSR from Switzerland in the fall of 1956. To their surprise, they were not shot on sight. For three months their former colleagues watched them squirm, before taking pity. On January 26, 1957, Max and Elsa were arrested at the Balchug Hotel in Moscow and charged with "betraying the Motherland." They were spared the death penalty, according to Sudoplatov, only because Steinberg managed to return "the money given to him for operational purposes in 1937." On March 15, 1958, the Military Collegium of the Supreme Court of the USSR sentenced Max to ten years. Elsa received five. Elza Vasilievna Shutker, as her prison record revealed her to be, was a Latvian born the same year as Max. The two, the Vladimir files made clear, were not husband and wife—only comrades, illegals, and perhaps lovers.

In his first years at Vladimir, Max was shuffled among the Beria Men in the hope that he would get them to talk. The jail was dank and forever freezing. Yet his fellow prisoners remembered Max's cell as a "luxury apartment," with warm blankets and a tablecloth. Even in jail, Max wore his tailored European suits and kept up, via *L'Humanité* and *Neues Deutschland*, with the Communist news from abroad.

Max also won a reprieve. The telegram came on New Year's Eve 1965. Someone—a daughter, according to one account—petitioned for his release, and the Supreme Court reduced his term to time served. On January 8, 1966, Max moved to Moscow, to a small flat in the Textile Workers District, on the city's industrial eastern edge. Whether he rejoined Elsa, who had been released in 1962, after serving fewer than four years, is unknown. She, too, had resettled in Moscow, but like Max faded into obscurity.

PAVEL SUDOPLATOV FOUGHT for twenty years to clear his name. "Things were not easy—we had little money, few friends," said his son, Anatoli. "Almost all of his comrades abandoned him. But Father never gave up."

Even from his cell in Vladimir, the former spymaster could see the changes accreting. Max and Elsa were not the only ones to get out. By the end of 1961, Mairanovsky, too, was freed. He moved back to the Caucasus, to run a chemical institute in Makhachkala, the capital of Dagestan, where in 1964 he died—a Jewish Mengele in a Muslim Soviet republic on the shores of the Caspian.

In 1965, after Khrushchev's ouster, Anatoli's father appealed from jail to the Soviet leadership to reopen his case. For years the USSR's highest legal authorities refused Sudoplatov's request without bothering to offer a reason. Finally they gave one: the Oggins case. In his plea from prison, Sudoplatov admitted that he had taken part in four state-sanctioned executions—"eliminating the enemy during wartime," as he put it, by "extraordinary means." The authorities countered that it would be impossible to review his case without first reconsidering each of the executions. "And that was impossible," said Anatoli, "because the American's case could not be reopened." His father's file, he said, included a letter from the military prosecutor's office, dated August 19, 1969, that declared the Oggins matter "sealed."

Only in the final days of the USSR, once the end of everything that he held dear had come, did Pavel Sudoplatov find relief. He claimed to have received official "rehabilitation," the Soviet form of grace. The letter from the military prosecutor, Pavel Boriskin, came in the months after the failed coup of August 1991, on the eve of the dissolution of the USSR and two days before the prosecutor's retirement. Although the legality of the declaration remains a matter of debate, Sudoplatov's pension was restored. To celebrate, Sudoplatov did what a generation of retired KGB men have done since: he wrote his memoirs.

Special Tasks: The Memoirs of an Unwanted Witness—A Soviet Spymaster proved an audacious act of self-justification and, as was to be expected, a highly contentious historical source. In his memoirs, Pavel Sudoplatov revisits the Oggins case. He resorts to the Eichmann defense: he was acting on orders. He also claims that in unearthing the case, General Volkogonov obscured the truth. Oggins, Sudoplatov writes, was not killed because of what he could tell about the gulag. Neither was he killed because the Soviets suspected him of being a "Trotskyist agent," as Abakumov had reported to Stalin. The Russian edition of *Special Tasks* is more revealing:

> The West by then was sufficiently well informed about the gulag, and the reasons for eliminating Oggins were not so simple as were written in our newspapers . . . In fact, Oggins arrived in the USSR on a false Czech passport—not a word about this appeared in the papers. He did in fact sympathize with Communism and was a secret member of the American Communist Party. Oggins was also a veteran agent of the Comintern and the NKVD in China, the Far East, and the U.S.

Oggins was killed, in Sudoplatov's telling, because he had become a double agent. The Kremlin, he goes on, feared that Nerma had gone to the FBI. "She attempted perhaps on behalf of American counterintelligence to revive our agent network in America that had been disrupted since 1942," he writes. In the Lubyanka, the toll was seen as great. "Our security services were of the opinion that her work with the FBI had already caused serious damage to our operational positions in the U.S. and France."

The executioner, in the end, felt no remorse. "Today, recalling this man," Sudoplatov writes, "I feel sympathy. But then, in the years of the cold war, neither we nor the Americans ever considered the moral aspects of liquidating dangerous enemies such as double agents."

■

THE PICTURE AT LAST WAS COMING CLEAR. SUDOPLATOV'S REVELATION of the motive, Abakumov's précis of the case to Stalin, Volkogonov's gift to Yeltsin—all seemed to unwrap the mystery. The trouble was, though, each version was wrong. The truth was lost in a cascade of misinformation, disinformation, and lies.

Oggins was not a double, nor even a Trotskyist. Nerma had not gone to the FBI; the agents had come to her. She had even lied to them, telling the FBI that Cy had "abandoned" her and Robin in Paris that last spring. Cy had taken to "philandering," Nerma told the agents, and she had no idea where he'd gone, or why. Decades later, General Volkogonov had also misled the investigators from Washington. Stalin had killed Cy not because he feared releasing a gulag witness, nor because he believed the American agent had been turned. The Lubyanka interrogater had baited Cy with reports of his liaisons with "foreign spies"—the Japanese girl on the boat from San Francisco, and the American dancer in Shanghai. But the truth was far simpler.

It had come down to Max Steinberg. "If Oggins worked for Steinberg in China," Anatoli said, "it makes perfect sense."

Max Steinberg had tried to quit. He was a *nevozvrashchenets*, "one who failed to return." He was, in fact, one of the highest-ranking spies to try to trick Moscow. By 1939, Steinberg had risen to the rank of lieutenant-general. In his memoirs, Sudoplatov ranks him among the most important defectors, "the people who were in charge of our operational networks in Western Europe—[Alexander] Orlov in Spain, Krivitsky in Holland, Reiss and Steinberg in Switzerland."

When Max had tried to flee, Cy would have been among the first hauled in. "A roll-up," the old CIA man in Virginia called it. He explained how such things played out. When a Soviet intelligence officer was tripped up—or switched sides—the Center went after every agent in his control group. Guilty by association, they were removed from the field. And, almost always, eliminated.

If Cy was arrested because of Max's refusal to "return to the village," he was killed because of HUAC. "Consider the time," Anatoli said. "If Oggins got out, it would have damaged much more than

Soviet prestige." He was thinking of McCarthy and the anti-Communist crusade. In 1947, the hearings on Capitol Hill were daily headlines. The hunt for Reds was hitting fever pitch.

The Soviets had only dangled the American prisoner. They allowed the embassy men to see Cy in jail only because they wanted to learn what Washington knew of him and to see if Washington would take him back. The State Department had said they would, as early as 1943. The Americans had not only signaled their desire to repatriate Oggins; for years they demanded news of his health and status. The Soviets had never intended to let Cy return to the United States, but four years later, by the spring of 1947, Stalin had to act. The American prisoner could be forced to testify before the television cameras in Washington. The Kremlin had spy networks—in America, Europe, and Asia—to protect.

On January 7, 1948, the Soviet Foreign Ministry informed the Moscow embassy of the death of an American citizen in a jail in the town of Penza. "A second-category invalid," the prisoner had died nearly a year earlier, the death certificate claimed, from "a paralysis of the heart on the grounds of acute sclerosis of the coronal artery coupled with a paroxysm of angina." The autopsy had further revealed, it was reported, a tumor on the bladder, yielding the "supplementary diagnosis: 'papuliferous cancer of the bladder.' " Isaiah Oggins, the ministry added, had been buried in a local cemetery in Penza, the one reserved for Jews.

The news took months to reach Nerma. The U.S. government, though, should not have had no trouble locating Cy's wife. The FBI had tapped her telephone for months in the previous year, and agents were still opening her mail. The letter finally arrived in the first days of June 1948, but Robin never read it. Nerma did not keep the announcement of Cy's death. It mattered little, as neither the death certificate nor the burial report was accurate. Both were merely spectacular examples of Soviet fabrication.

CHAPTER 12

AFTERLIFE

■ ■ ■

N O WORDS OF SOLACE OR CONSOLATION COULD POSSIBLY HELP. The photographs made it all terribly plain—the pain, the loss, and the futility. Robin sat in the kitchen, staring at the images on the table. Ginny had already gone to bed; he and I were alone. I had gone again on a weekend visit, this time to deliver the package from Moscow, the documents from the KGB archives.

The men in the Lubyanka had adhered to the letter but not the spirit of the law. The archivists of the secret police files had allowed only a glimpse into the Oggins file. Even in releasing the documents, they, too, had tried to black out the truth. But the archivists had done something else, something gratuitous and extraordinary. Something that made no sense.

If the search for Cy Oggins had begun with a rumor in the Arctic, it ended with the image of a broken man in front of a bare cement wall. The clerks had included two small photographs, originals. Of all documents raised in my search, none was more chilling. Black-and-white mug shots, they showed Cy from the front and the right side, the same positions he was photographed in more than eight years earlier, on that first night in the Lubyanka. The defiance, though, was long gone.

Cy wore a *zek*'s tunic, patched and repatched with black rags, and over it a threadbare sweater, its arms and neck cut off. Beneath his dark eyes, the bruises were now sculpted welts. The wall behind him was pockmarked with dark blotches, stains that suggested blood. These were the final photographs, taken, it seemed, in the last hours.

Ginny had confessed it the first time we met. "You know," she leaned close to say, "Robin's wanted this his entire life. To know what happened." In the years since, she had suffered a string of ailments. Her legs were weak, she used a wheelchair, and her mind, once scholarly and exacting, was going. Ginny hardly ever spoke now. She was slipping away. With his wife upstairs in bed, Robin and I sat in silence, an emptiness broken only by halting sobs.

IN THE FALL OF 2002, after more than forty years of teaching, Robin retired. At seventy-one years old, he had ended his career as an associate professor. "It's just the price of doing my own thing," he told the reporter from the campus newspaper. The valedictory article noted that Binghamton was losing one of the "foremost experts on medieval falconry," a long-serving professor who did not have "such rosy academic roots." The reporter quoted a colleague, a fellow historian, who called the failure to reward forty years of service with a full professorship "a kind of slap in the face." But Robin, he added, had gone "his own way," "at his own speed." "He was not going to be intimidated."

When I ventured upstate one last time, I found Robin in a good mood. The classroom was his love, but he had looked forward to time outside it. There was reason to celebrate, too. Quietly, in his way. *The Kings and Their Hawks: Falconry in Medieval England,* the book begun a lifetime ago, was at last out. An elegant volume with 13 color plates, 709 footnotes, and a 38-page bibliography, it was published, in an ironic turn of history, by Yale University Press, his father's American employer. "The first broad history of English royal falconry in medieval times," Yale called it, "a book that draws on forty years of research."

Robin had started it in Chicago. In 1950, he had left New York and his mother. Even after dropping out of high school, he'd scored well on the entrance exams and been rewarded with a place at the University of Chicago. He graduated from the university's Great Books program. Then came the job on the railroad, the nights as a towerman above the Baltimore and Ohio tracks. Like his father, Robin seemed drawn to the world of the blue-collar worker, the proletariat. It was a job that made his mother proud. By 1955, he was back in graduate school and hit his "stride at last."

Robin had been living in a basement room in a professor's house when Ginny moved in. She had entered the university at fourteen and took a room in the attic. They were married in 1956 and within a year Ginny was pregnant. Robin returned to the tower. The late 1950s were a struggle. He tried his hand at whatever he could find. He worked the quiz shows—*Twenty One* and *College Bowl* on TV, and wrote answers for Mike Wallace's *Question of the Day* on CBS Radio. By 1962, with three children in tow, they had moved to Binghamton.

The more Robin spoke of his life after New York, the more I heard a need for definition, to know the precise nature of things. Dates, timetables, distances, weights—all were benchmarks to frame history. He would call on objects, too—the slides and stamps. Robin was a collector, an assembler and organizer. In the kitchen, a low shelf within arm's reach of the table held fat reference books, including medical and household manuals, how-to's and buying guides, cookbooks and bird books. In his basement study, rows and rows of metal drawers held thousands of slides of cathedrals, castles, medieval illuminations, images of old London, and a shelf of binders held the stamps. Each was labeled, ordered, and readily summoned. Having survived a childhood unmoored by lost memories, he kept the buoys close by. The stamps above all were treasure, a passion handed down from his father.

As often as he could Robin went on long walks. He took me out on his route, a disused rail line that had become an asphalt path for bikers and walkers. Rails for Trails, the program was called. Robin approved of such reclamation projects, making use of something no longer in use. He clipped a pedometer to his belt. As we walked, the ticking at his waist kept pace.

The town had changed so much, he said. It was no longer the place he and Ginny had moved to. In the 1990s, IBM had laid off thousands, and not much but Wal-Mart and a giant mall had moved in. Chain stores had flooded the valley floor across from the hillside. The population was dwindling. Doctor's offices and physical therapy clinics lined the main road.

Robin wasn't worried. It was a good life. He'd had sabbaticals to study the kings and their hunting. He'd had his students, his children, and most of all Ginny. In retirement, the search through his parents' past had proved a welcome diversion. Robin was always eager to hear where I'd been, what I'd found. Yet whenever I took the files upstate, he seemed reluctant to study them. He was relieved, of course, to learn that the U.S. government—"the folks I've paid taxes to all my life"—had not deliberately "let Dad rot." But the search, from the beginning and throughout, was not his.

There were days, of course, when Robin still wondered, when he thought about what his father—and, yes, his mother—had done.

He had gotten a call once, a few days after General Volkogonov testified before Congress. On the phone was a man from the State Department.

Was there anything he could do? the official asked.

Robin requested only any records pertaining to his parents.

A manila envelope soon arrived. Inside were his mother's and his own passport records. As for his father's, the man from the State Department sent his regrets. "We have been unable to locate any record of your father," he wrote.

INSIDE THE HOUSE, neat rows of videotapes, television versions of John le Carré thrillers, stood on a living room shelf. In all the hours we spoke together, Robin never once used the word "spy." Slowly, over the years of conversations, I had taken away the comfort of ambiguity. But Cy Oggins's son found refuge in history.

"They were radicals," Robin said as we walked that day. "They were believers. They were young and maybe they were naïve, but everyone they knew was in that political whirlwind—the fight for the masses. You could still imagine you could make the world all over again." Robin could set his parents' desire in the historical context. He could understand how it all began and, of course, how it ended. But one question lingered: "How could they be so blind?" After the 1930s, the purges, the show trials, and the invidious Hitler-Stalin pact, how could they have not seen the horror coming?

Nerma, Robin knew well, was not one to retreat. I was not so sure. After he and his mother returned to New York in 1939, she had done something strange. Nerma never spoke out. The woman who spent her youth trying to get political prisoners out of jail never went public. She did not go to the press, did not protest at the Soviet embassy, did not even seek relief in Washington—contrary to what Moscow heard—until the State Department called her in 1942. Nerma had not seen Cy for four years. Still, she kept silent. An American prisoner in the USSR would have been front-page news. The publicity and consequent political pressure may have been Cy's best defense. But Nerma had held her silence.

Why? I had a guess: Robin. To step forward and make a case would have put her young son at risk. I had offered him an excuse, but Robin would not take it.

"Not a chance," he said. "Mom didn't keep Dad's arrest quiet for my sake." To go public would have been an admission, he said, that everything she had ever believed in, ever fought for, was wrong. "It would have been betrayal."

Like Hook. Sidney Hook was always the turncoat. "He'd betrayed the movement," Robin said, "and Mom never forgave him." Sidney, for his part, never saw Cy or Nerma again, not after the strange, chance sighting in the tenement in the 1930s. On occasion he did pick up rumors. Cy, he would hear, had kept traveling for decades, and once someone reported a sighting of him in Iran.

Robin would doubtless have preferred to embrace the idea that Nerma had kept silent for his benefit. But he could not. His mother had never broken ranks. To the end, Nerma remained embalmed in her impervious idealism. "She didn't need to protect me," Robin said. "She needed to protect the cause."

He was less certain of his father. He had always wondered if he had stayed devout to the end. Cy was arrested late; 1939 was after the worst purges. In the eighty-two-page chronology I had assembled, there was, however, a window—a possibility that he had in fact seen the signs and wanted to get out.

Cy left Paris in late May 1938 and, according to the official documents, entered the USSR on June 1, only to be arrested on the frigid evening of February 20 in Moscow. That left a gap of nearly nine months in the timeline. It seemed unlikely that his handlers would have kept him in the Moskva Hotel for so long before arresting him.

The window opened wider when I found a letter from Japan. Nerma had kept the old blue-tissue aerogram among her mementos. Dated February 15, 1957, it was sent by a Japanese professor of Russian literature. Misao Naito, a military translator during the war, had shared a cell in Siberia with Jacques Rossi, the French survivor of Norilsk. The two became best friends. In 1957, Naito had just been released, but Rossi remained in the USSR. It fell to Naito to send the message. He got the years wrong, but delivered a plea, via Rossi, from Cy:

Mr. Oggins was captured by Russian M.G.B. (Ministry of State Security) in Moscow in 1937 and was thrown in a Moscow prison. In 1938 Mr. Oggins was sent to a frozen desert Norrilsk [sic] which lies on the river of the Enisei. At that time there was going the construction of a new industrial center on the Far North. I met him working in that building of a new city.

Mr. Oggins was suffering from the disease in his leg. Mr. Oggins begged me to communicate to his wife that only the Washington Government could save his unfortunate situation, in which he fell down, traveling from China for Paris.

He asked me to write "only the doctor of Washington could help me in my illness."

By it he wanted to mean abovementioned. In that year, 1938, Mr. Oggins disappeared. Where could he go? I don't say. But I consider as my duty to fulfil his wish.

Dear Mrs. Oggins! I'm sorry it is all that I can say about your husband on the grounds of Jacques Rossi's telling. As the nearest friend of Jacques Rossi, now I must fulfil a wish of him in my turn, delivering a message of your dearest husband in 1938.

> *always yours,*
> *Misao Naito*

The letter from Japan raised two mysteries. "The doctor of Washington," the first, may have been Cy's attempt to tell Nerma whom to contact in the old underground. The second, though, was more intriguing: the possibility that Cy had been headed west and not east, "traveling from China for Paris," when he was arrested in Moscow.

Cy's words from Norilsk offered a more probable version of events. The nine months between his departure from Paris and his arrest in Moscow were filled by a return to China; Cy had left Nerma and Robin in Paris because he had been ordered back to Manchuria. He had entered the USSR in June 1938 but traveled beyond Moscow, to Dairen. By the time he was back in China, the war was raging. Max and Elsa, now in their Swiss refuge, were nowhere to be found. Facing a suicide mission, Cy may have grabbed his old Czech passport and fled for Paris and his family.

There was further evidence. In the accounts that followed General Volkogonov's disclosure of the Oggins case in 1992, contradictions surfaced. Vladimir Vinogradov, a KGB archivist, let slip a detail that erased the gap in the timeline. "Oggins had come to the Soviet Union," he said, "to work for a commercial concern in 1939, but was arrested a short time later"

The puzzle of Cy's final months of freedom could include a return to China and a longing for his wife and son in Paris. It was a sentimental notion, but one impossible to rule out. Max Steinberg had tried to get out. His American agent may have wished to follow suit.

·

"YOU CAN NEVER ESCAPE FROM YOUR HISTORY ALTOGETHER," WROTE Sonya, aka Ruth, born Ursula, the German spy who had served in China and England and was one of the Soviets' best. "If a nightmare haunts my sleep, the enemy is at my heels and I have no time to destroy the information. If I find myself in new surroundings, I am forever discovering hiding places for illegal material. I cannot bear to see parents saying goodbye to their children on railway stations."

Toward the end, Nerma lost her mind. First came the paranoia, then the prescriptions. The FBI played its part, too. On February 10,

1949, Special Agents Thomas G. Spencer and Francis X. Plant interviewed Whittaker Chambers's wife, Esther, in the Baltimore FBI
field office. The interview continued on the following day at the
Chambers's farm in Maryland, site of the soon-to-be-famous pump-
kin patch.

Mrs. Chambers, when asked about "Nerma Oggins (née
Berman)," told the men that she had known her in New York in the
1920s. They had worked together at Norman Thomas's pacifist journal, the *World Tomorrow*. Esther took care to add that Nerma had not
worked there long—and that "because of her extreme radicalism, she
(CHAMBERS) had opposed any re-hiring of OGGINS by the
magazine."

The two women may have known each other elsewhere. Esther
had gone to the Rand School and worked as a bookkeeper at the
Ladies' Garment Workers' Union. She remembered that Nerma had
worked at the International Labor Defense and at Local 25 of the
Garment Workers' Union. And before the FBI men left the farm
that day, Mrs. Chambers recalled something else—she had also
known Mrs. Oggins's husband.

The FBI had long maintained an interest in Nerma. In case after
case, leads real and imagined would circle back to her—a phone number in the notebook of a Soviet spy nabbed in Manhattan, a report
from the intelligence officer at the Brooklyn Navy Yard, a cable from
the Bureau's man in Paris. At times the agents would unseal her mail,
and at others they would track her friends and associates. The investigations would suddenly arise, only to recede just as quickly.
Throughout the 1950s, after Burgess and Maclean fled to Russia,
Hiss went jail, and the Rosenbergs were executed, after the lands of
Eastern Europe fell under Soviet domination and the United States
lost its nuclear monopoly, the FBI kept the case open. In the end,
though, after more than thirteen years of periodic investigations, the
men from the Bureau went to see Nerma only once.

On March 1, 1957, two agents from the New York field office
arrived at the top-floor flat on Fifteenth Street. They were working
one of the big spy cases then fast unfolding and had followed a thread

to Nerma's door. Unlike the State Department special agents who had come a decade and half earlier, the FBI men were not particularly interested in Nerma. A short, fifty-nine-year-old widow of an American Communist lost to the gulag did not pose a Bureau priority. Still, the agents had pulled her file, and when Nerma proved surprisingly "cooperative," they seized the chance to revisit her "past activities."

In the agents' eight-page single-spaced report there is no mention of coffee or tea. But the interview must have lasted hours; Nerma for the first time detailed her life story on the record. She began with her birth in the hinterland of Russia and marched on through a breathless rendition of her life's turns and travails. She took care, though, to leave out vast swaths of her travels in Europe. She refused to name anyone she had met overseas, and, when asked point-blank, coldly "denied ever engaging in any espionage activity." In the end, Nerma kicked the agents out, but not before they had exhausted their long list of questions. It was as if the encounter, another perilous junction in a long life of duplicity, had been a welcome relief.

IN 1965, AFTER THIRTEEN YEARS, Nerma quit her job downtown. She left Worth Hardware as soon as she could get her union pension, at sixty-seven. She would live another two decades on her own in New York. In 1968 she left the place on Fifteenth Street and returned to her old neighborhood, the Lower East Side. A low-income, union-subsidized residency for seniors, Nerma's last home in New York stood in the shadow of the Williamsburg Bridge, a few blocks from her family's first stop in America.

By then, fear had taken her and chaos had set in. "She was fading," said Robin. "The place was a mess. Cockroaches on the table, papers everywhere, the works." Nerma became captive to an array of medications, "lithium not the least among them." She installed a chain lock and deadbolts, dreading the day the men would return. But there was "something else," Robin said, something that gnawed at her.

Nerma had rarely told her son the truth about his father. Of her time with Cy in Europe she said little, and even less of his journey to

China. Yet once Nerma had opened up. "She always felt very bad about it," Robin said. "That she hadn't gotten Dad out—and that she'd gotten him into it." It was the guilt, he said, that weighed the heaviest. "That was her burden, and it was overwhelming."

IN THE AFTERNOON ON that last Sunday, Robin invited me to see his mother. I half imagined that he meant the remains he had spoken of earlier in the day. After Robin and Ginny had moved Nerma upstate in the 1980s, there had been one long year at the house, then another five or six in assisted living, before a nursing home in a quiet, pastoral setting nearby.

On January 27, 1995, amid the company of the lonely and very aged, Nerma died. Nearly ninety-seven, she had outlived Cy by almost fifty years.

In the basement, among the filing cabinets filled with slides of cathedrals, castles, and medieval illuminations, a box held her ashes. "We never really decided what to do with it," Robin said. The ashes, however, were not what he had in mind. He led me to the living room, turned on the television, put a disk into the machine, and left.

The Elders, shot in 1971, long before the days of handheld video, was forty-four minutes long. A young crew, a lanky, shaggy-haired interviewer and two film students on a grant, had descended on the seniors' residence. "We were looking for people who weren't just old but wise," said the producer when I found him. "We were looking for ordinary people who had had remarkable lives."

Robin retreated to the kitchen and sat facing the picture window, flipping through the sports section of the newspaper. But when Nerma's voice—shrill, laced with a lisp, and floating the Slavic consonants of her youth—filled the room, he was listening.

The crew had toured the building. They filmed a class of seniors painting and a resident demonstrating calisthenics. Yet Nerma dominated. She was short, stubborn, and breathless. Her hair was gray but still curly at the edges. She wore a pair of oversized horn-rimmed glasses, a big-beaded necklace, and a boxy cotton housedress, something akin to a Canal Street dashiki.

After the first question, the interview became a monologue. Given a soapbox after so many years, Nerma could not contain herself. The film was grainy, shot in black-and-white. But in the half-light of her unadorned apartment, Nerma seemed to glow. She spoke in cascading paragraphs and betrayed a compulsion to elaborate on the self-evident.

At the time Nerma was seventy-four years old, but when she chose to unfurl her distant past, it was easy to imagine the young rebel in the trenches of the good fight. You could almost see her at work: at a mass rally in Union Square, among the Rand School bunch, with the strikers in Pittsburgh, working the dance halls for Sacco and Vanzetti, taunting the White Cossacks, denouncing the Lovestonites, rallying the Fosterites. All the while, she kept talking, ever the revolving top, and the firebrand still.

Nerma expounded on longevity and its travails. Religion and its illusions. High art, from the Louvre to a recent discovery of her own "inherited sense of color." South African politics, a new cause, and her cousin the Labour M.P. But amid the proclamations, one phrase came to the fore: "the community." The Negroes, the masses, the unions, the schools, the seniors, even the criminal element—they were all the community. "I was always an internationalist," she said. "The community is my friend, and my love, and my hope. My hope is that it will lead to a better world."

Nerma still had her mind then, yet she clung to her false ideals. Had she not, her life, or what remained of it, would have cruelly unraveled, her beliefs and dreams hollowed out by the twentieth century's sadistic monsters. Nerma could not let go of the slogans of the past. The mind-numbing pabulum of the party, like mantras from a bygone era, remained her only solace.

"All my life," she went on, "I have worked for improvement of poor people. In my youth I was very active in the revolutionary movement. I had my disillusions, but I'm still working for the needy and the people that really need help. And I see a better tomorrow.

"I don't sit home and worry about the angel of death," she said. "I'm an optimist. I have in senior years developed a new philosophy—

what's the use of worrying? I take every day as it comes and look toward a performance, whatever it be." She did not "dwell on the end." "Because the end is—well, I'm not religious and not terribly good, so I can't have the solace of heaven. And the idea of hell is not too hot. Or it may be too hot."

On she marched.

"I was married once," Nerma said, "to a very interesting man."

She paused and drew in half a breath, as if to lower the last veil, before she caught herself.

"But he died young."

ACKNOWLEDGMENTS

∎

MY GREATEST DEBT IS TO ROBIN OGGINS. FOR SEVEN YEARS, CY Oggins's son endured questions, and more than a few unexpected answers, with patience. Robin's hunger for the truth not only emboldened my search, his candor, trust, and exacting sense of history made this book possible.

To support the research and writing of this book, I had the great fortune of winning two fellowships, one from the National Endowment for the Humanities and the other from the Dorothy and Lewis B. Cullman Center for Scholars and Writers at the New York Public Library. From the fall of 2005 to the spring of 2006, the grand library at 42nd Street and Fifth Avenue became a second home. I could have found no better place. Although a number of the holdings' works on American communism have suffered the abuse of sectarian partisans —volumes gone "missing" or pages razored out—the library was the locus of much of Cy Oggins's own research in the 1920s, and as I discovered, remains the repository of the *Pageant of America* photographs he helped to collect. In a glorious office overlooking the lions, I wrote the first draft of this book.

Jean Strouse, the Cullman Center's indefatigable director, Pamela Leo, and Adriana Nova kept me on track, and despite the best efforts of my fellow fellows, hard at work. One hundred thirty-seven miles of shelves fill the old Croton Reservoir, but thanks to the Cullmans' generosity, and the Center's three muses, the library has midwifed a new generation of books. I am indebted to the entire NYPL staff, but above all Paul LeClerc, its president, David Ferriero, director of the Research Libraries, and their colleagues, H. George Fletcher, Wayne Furman, Nancy Kandoian, Edward Kasinec, M. Rassoul Sambe, and David Smith. My gratitude, as well, to the Mrs. Giles Whiting Foundation for supporting my year at the library.

Sadly, many of America's campuses and Internet communities of historians remain rent by the old debates. Yet in this work I pursued a staunch neutrality, and perhaps because I was born in the age of Kennedy and Khrushchev, I could draw on sources from both sides of the cold war barricades, people who may not speak to one another. Tony Hiss, the writer and son of Alger Hiss, offered his insights early on, while Alan Weinstein, the National Archivist and author of *Perjury*, made available unpublished material. Tim Davenport, master of the Early American Marxism Web site, was an enthusiastic guide, while Jerrold and Leona Schecter, Pavel Sudoplatov's American coauthors, shared their knowledge of Soviet intelligence. Peter Filardo and his colleagues in the Robert F. Wagner Labor Archives at the Tamiment Library in New York offered kind help, while Herb Rommerstein, the author and former HUAC investigator, searched his legendary files.

Around the world, throughout the serpentine research of this book, hundreds gave of their time and expertise: historians and gulag survivors, archivists and librarians, accidental witnesses and descendants of the players in the Oggins odyssey. My research took me to Russia, Germany, France, England, and, electronically, Argentina, China, Italy, Japan, and Switzerland. I am grateful to have met and spoken at length with four remarkable men who have passed away: Donald Jameson, James L. Lewis (a code clerk in the wartime U.S. Embassy in Kuibyshev who transmitted many of the Oggins cables), Jacques Rossi, and Anatoli Sudoplatov. George Kennan, as well, not only offered encouragement but graciously answered queries about the Oggins case.

My thanks, too, for their time and memories, to the relatives of those who played a role in the Oggins story: Eugenio Carutti (grandson of Dr. Eugenio Carutti), Carlo Alberto Carutti (Carrutti's nephew), Richard Clare (son of Daniel Clare), Anthony Haden-Guest (nephew of Angela Guest), Franz von Hammerstein (son of Kurt von Hammerstein), Caroline Rand Herron (granddaughter of George Herron and Carrie Rand), John Hook (son of Sidney Hook and Carrie Katz), Dr. Ernest Hook (son of Sidney and Ann Hook),

Debra Kalish (granddaughter of David Oggins), Arthur Kornberg (nephew of Carrie Katz), Alice Kramer (granddaughter of Nicholas Dozenberg), Robert Leder (former son-in-law of David Oggins), Beth Leder-Pack (granddaughter of David Oggins), Tatyana Lengyel (daughter of József Lengyel), Sherry Miller (daughter of Llewellyn E. Thompson, Jr.), Judy Nelson (daughter of Stuart Grummon), Gottfried Paasche (grandson of Kurt von Hammerstein), Michel Romanoff, Andrew Romanov, Martin Schneebalg (cousin of Max Schneebalg, Cy Oggins's brother-in-law), Doris Scott (daughter of Thomas F. Fitch), Jonathan Shapiro (son of Irwin Shapiro), Nick Stevens (son of Francis Stevens), and Llewellyn Thompson (nephew of Llewellyn E. Thompson, Jr.).

Thanks, as well, to the veterans of the Moscow diplomatic corps, former foreign service officers or code clerks, in addition to James Lewis: James McCargar, Isaac (Ike) Patch, Ace Rosner, Vladimir Toumanoff, and Thomas P. Whitney.

Wherever I went, I found enormously generous and expert guides:

In Willimantic, Tom Beardsley, former scholar in residence at the Windham Textile and History Museum, helped trace Cy Oggins's earliest years in the Thread City. At my first email from Moscow, Tom, a Yorkshireman who toured the USSR on a coal miners' junket in the 1980s, came headlong to my aid.

In New York, at the Columbia University Archives, Marilyn Pettit was an early and essential ally, chasing queries with gusto—a custom that Jocelyn Wilk ably continued. Bill Santin, in the registrar's office, searched his files time and again. Cleo Paturis, longtime partner of James T. Farrell, not only spent a memorable afternoon talking of Sidney Hook but opened Farrell's notebooks for me. Jordan Auslander, ghost chaser extraordinaire, provided navigational tips at the Municipal Archives and "repositories of the dead" near and far. At the Art Students League, Stephanie Cassidy found the transcripts of Irwin Shapiro and Esther Shemitz, and at the South Street Steamship Museum, Dan Trachtenberg charted the path of ocean liners in 1934. In addition, in ways small and large, Roger Alcaly, Vadim Birstein, Helen Bodian, Jeffrey Frank, Neil Gordon, Lucy

Lehrer, Robert McCaughey, Susan Mesinai, George Packer, Jim Rasenberger, Alex Star, and Sam Tanenhaus were sources of assistance and encouragement.

In Chicago, Bill Duff, the veteran FBI agent and biographer of Theodore Mally, and Marvin Makinen, biochemist and expert researcher of the Wallenberg case, went to great lengths to share their knowledge and materials.

In Washington, D.C., Kai Bird and Robert Dallek, two of our finest historians and biographers, lent encouragement from the start, steeling my courage in the first years of research. Yuri Koshkin, as ever, was an invaluable reserve of knowledge and insight. Eric Lewis shared his father's extraordinary letters and photographs from the USSR of the 1930s. Regina Gorzkowska, Oleg Kalugin, and Stephen Schwartz listened to questions and offered careful answers. Seymour Hersh pointed me to Jim Lesar, one of the best FOIA lawyers in the United States, and Gus Russo, a pro at prying documents from the FBI. David Wise, the country's sharpest writer on the CIA and its foibles, kindly offered leads. At the US-Russian POW/MIA Commission in the Pentagon, James Connell, Major Timothy Falkowski, and Al Graham extended every professional courtesy, as did Lieutenant Mary Olsen of the Defense POW/Missing Personnel Office. Natalya Miromanova offered early assistance, while Shawn Dorman of the American Foreign Service Association posted a notice that bore remarkable fruit, and Misuzu Nakamura translated the introduction to the Japanese edition of Jacques Rossi's memoirs. Thanks, too, to Max Friedman, Marcus Raskin, and Saul Sanders for their time and assistance.

At the Library of Congress, John Haynes, a leading historian of American communism—and Soviet intelligence's malignant influence—was an unstinting source of leads. At the National Archives, Sally Kuisel and Ed Schamel were gracious, diligent, and essential. John Taylor, an archivist who turned eighty-seven in 2008, and has served the public for sixty-two of those years, shared his unparalleled knowledge of the CIA records, including the remarkable files of the Shanghai Municipal Police.

At the Woodrow Wilson International Center for Scholars, Lee Hamilton, public servant without rival, and Blair Ruble, stalwart director of the Kennan Institute, remained great sources of encouragement. Janet Spikes, Dagne Gizaw, and Michelle Kamalich of the Center's library provided early, invaluable assistance. Christian Ostermann, director of the Cold War History Project, offered leads in the East German archives. Thanks, too, to the Association for Intelligence Officers (AFIO), Rowena Clough of the National Cryptological Museum Library at the NSA, and Richard McKee of the Diplomatic and Consular Officers, Retired (DACOR).

In Boston, Carl Sapers kindly shared his memories of his colleague Calvin Bartlett.

In Moscow, Denis Babichenko, Vladimir Bobrenev, Svetlana Chervonnaya, Ilya Gaiduk, Oleg Khlevnuik, Nikita Khrushchev, Vladimir Korotaev of State Military Archives, Galina Kosabova, Katya Lebedeva, Anna Masterova, Vera Obolonkina, Nikita Petrov, Igor Tavrovsky, and Semyon Vilensky extended vital help, as did the late Vladimir Birger in Krasnoyarsk and Svetlana Ebizhants and Alla Makarova in Norilsk.

In Paris, Dmitri Sezemann shared memories of the Russian émigré circles of the 1930s and his parents' years in Stalin's secret police. Celestine Bohlen, Dr. François Condroyer, Manon Loizeau, Françoise Mandelbaum-Reiner, Natalie Nougayrede, Juliette Riviere, Nikita Struve, Arkady Vaksberg, and the editors of *Russkaya mysl'* offered insights and hospitality. In the Bibliothèque nationale and the archives of the Paris police, Donna Elveth was a meticulous researcher.

In Berlin, Ben Aris, Klaus Dettmer of the Landesarchiv, Elisabeth and Wolfram Fischer, Heiner Klemm, Heike Schmidbauer, Tim Trampedach, and Ernst von Waldenfels offered kind help. In Munich, Freddy Litten, one of the keenest sleuths among historians of Soviet intelligence, offered pointers to an amateur and saved me, time and again, from blundering. Markus Wehner shared his files on the Rakov brothers, treasure from the days when the Russian archives welcomed Western scholars.

In Prague, Sonia Skyvarova provided careful assistance to root out the real "Egon Hein."

In Bern, Urs German of the Schweizerisches Bundesarchiv took up my search and made it his own—to extraordinary effect. Urs refused to believe that "Charles Martin" (aka Max Steinberg) could have been tried in Switzerland, and returned to the USSR, without leaving a trace in the Swiss archives. After checking and rechecking, Urs discovered the invaluable Swiss dossier on the Martins.

In Tokyo, Akira Takizawa led me through the Japanese archives to the telegram recording the Caproni bombers from Italy, and Chris and Etsuko Bjork generously translated the archaic diplomatic language of imperial Japan. In Shanghai, Jason Cai discovered the modern name of the French Concession street where Oggins wandered, and Noam Biale, an able assistant, photographed it.

Great thanks, too, to James Billington, the Librarian of Congress, for allowing me to camp out at the Kluge Center. And to John Dunlop, and his colleagues Natasha Porfirenko and Dale Reed at the Hoover Institution, for a similar month of research in 2003. Thanks, too, to Diane E. Kaplan at the Sterling Library at Yale, and for permission to publish materials, Dr. Larry Hickman of the Center for Dewey Studies at Southern Illinois University, Dr. Ernest Hook, and David King, assembler of the world's greatest private archive of Soviet photography.

To the historians and biographers not named elsewhere, gratitude for advice and encouragement: Konstantin Akinsha, Christopher Andrew, James Barrett, Bernd-Rainer Barth, Arnold Beichman, Todd Bennett, Miranda Carter, John Chapman, Robert Conquest, Emil Draitser, the late Theodore Draper, John Fox, Paul Freedman, Tom Grunfeld, Jacquelyn D. Hall, Peter Huber, Maurice Isserman, Gary Kern, Mario Kessler, Harvey Klehr, Robert Lichtman, Lynn Mally, Julia Milkenberg, Rana Mitter, Reinhard Müller, Hayden Peake, Mark Peattie, Todd Pfannestiel, Christopher Phelps, Vladimir Pozniakov, Ruth Price, David Roessel, Clifford Rosenberg, Michael Rosenthal, David Roskies, Anthony Saich, Steven Solnick, François Thom, Frederic Wakeman, Alan Wald, Eric Weitz, Sean Wilentz, Andreas Wirsching, Tom Wirth, and Vladislav Zubok.

To all my fellow fellows at the Cullman Center: great thanks. Every member of our class contributed, knowingly or not, to this book—from the medievalist Ray Scheindlin decoding Nerma Oggins's Yiddish scrawl (in Hebrew letters on the back of a photograph) to Edmund White discoursing on the *"chiens assis"* of Dairen's rooftops. The novelist Joseph O'Connor and the historians Rebecca Shanor, Kirk Swinehart, and Judy Walkowitz helped me stay on course and half-sane.

Thanks, as well, to Mark Franchetti, Tom Hulce, Lauren Kim, Julia Rask, and Mark Richards for their unflagging enthusiasm. I am grateful, too, to my agent, Valerie Borchardt, and her parents, Ann and Georges, for their continued support.

Great thanks to the friends—who else?—who slogged through an early draft and offered essential critiques: Charlotte Bacon, Catherine Barnett, Peter Carwell, Rob Jenkins, Ed Kline, Mary Morrissy, and J. Peder Zane.

To Bob Weil, editor and friend, I owe a debt I can never repay. Bob has grown used to starring in authorial acknowledgements—and rightly so. He is not only an obsessive idea man and dazzling line editor, but a peerless champion of books. I remain in the debt of all at W. W. Norton, in particular Jeannie Luciano, Bill Rusin, Tom Mayer, and Lucas Wittmann. In shepherding this work, Tom and Lucas, young men of many talents, were models of enlightened efficiency.

My greatest thanks I reserve for Mia, and our girls, Oona and Sasha—without whom I'd no doubt have finished this book in half the time, but without whom I could not breathe.

APPENDIX: ARCHIVAL DOCUMENTS

1. Arrest order from the NKVD—Peoples Commisariat for Internal Affairs—for Isaiah Oggins, February 20, 1939. (FSB, Russian Federation)

2. First page of prisoner biographical report for Isaiah Oggins, completed February 24, 1939. (FSB, Russian Federation)

3. State Department telegram, April 15, 1942, from Sumner Welles, acting secretary of state, to the U.S. Embassy in the USSR, summarizing Oggins's passport file. (NARA)

4. "The Note to Stalin"—memorandum from Minister of State Security Viktor Abakumov to Stalin and Molotov, May 21, 1947, reviewing the Oggins case and setting forth the plan to liquidate the American prisoner and to falsify the record, reporting his death by natural causes. (TFR documents, Pentagon)

5. Excerpt from FBI field report, New York office, on Nerma Oggins, dated August 31, 1943. (R.O. Papers)

6. Italian police registration, July 18, 1938, for Charles Martin, aka Max Steinberg. (Swiss dossier)

7. Memorandum, dated July 9, 1952, and stamped "GEHEIM" (secret), from J. A. Cimperman, legal attaché, U.S. Embassy in London, to Bundespolizei, Bern, Switzerland, on the Soviet scheme to import Italian aircraft to Manchuria. (Swiss dossier)

| 1. |

СССР

РОДНЫЙ КОМИССАРИАТ ВНУТРЕННИХ ДЕЛ

ОРДЕР № 2643

Февраля дня 193 9 г.

Выдан _____

Государственной безопасности

на производство

в. _____

Ареста и обыска

Хейн Эгона, он-же

Оггинс Исай (Сай) Саймонов

рес *Гостиница, Москва, ком. 1035*

одный Комиссар Внутренних Дел СССР

ник Второго Отдела
равления НКВД СССР

авка: *35*

1ᚴ

СССР
НАРОДНЫЙ КОМИССАРИАТ ВНУТРЕННИХ ДЕЛ
Главное Управление Государственной Безопасности
ПРОТОКОЛ ДОПРОСА

К ДЕЛУ № ....

193_9_ г. _Февраля_ мес. _24_ дня. Я, _Ст. Следователь_
(должн., наимен. органа, фамилия)

Сл. части .... допросил в качестве _обвиняемого_

1. Фамилия _Оггинс - Хейн_

2. Имя и отчество _Исай_

3. Дата рождения _Июль 1898_

4. Место рождения _Виллиматик Америка_

5. Местожительство _Москва гост. Москва_

6. Нац. и гражд. (подданство) _Американец, Американский_
подданный

7. Паспорт ....
(когда и каким органом выдан, номер, категор. и место приписки)

8. Род занятий ....
(место службы и должность)

9. Социальное происхождение _сын продавца_
(род занятий родителей и их имущественное положение)

10. Социальное положение (род занятий и имущественное положение)

   а) до революции _служащий_

   б) после революции _служащий_

11. Состав семьи _жена Берман-Оггинс Норма. Франция, Париж_
(близкие родственники, их имена, фамилии, адреса и род занятий)
сестра - Ревека Оггинс ; брат- Давид - Нью Иорк, Америка
сын 7 лет - Робин Оггинс

PREPARING OFFICE
WILL INDICATE WHETHER

Collect
{ Full rate
  Day letter
  Night letter

Charge Department:
  Full rate
  Day letter
  Night letter

Charge to
$

TELEGRAM SENT

Department of State

Washington,

April 14, 1942.

Secret

15

11 pm

TO BE TRANSMITTED
CONFIDENTIAL CODE
NONCONFIDENTIAL CODE
PLAIN AIR
PLAIN

AMERICAN EMBASSY,

KUIBYSHEV.

173

361.1121/34

This cable was sent in confidential Code.
It should be carefully paraphrased before
being communicated to anyone.   SC

Your 130, February 12, 11 a.m.

An American passport, no. 14160 San Francisco series, was issued at Washington on August 13, 1935 to Mr. Isaiah Oggins who was born on July 22, 1898, apparently at Willimantic, Connecticut, of naturalized American parents. On December 16, 1936, he registered with the American Consulate at Dairen, Manchuria, stating that he was a representative of Charles Martin and Company of Harbin. On August 6, 1937 the passport was renewed for two years at Dairen. At that time he stated that he represented the Fiat Motor Company of Turin, Italy. The Department's information indicates that he subsequently went to Paris and thence proceeded in 1938 to Moscow.

It is possible that he has been acting for years as an agent of a foreign power or of an international revolutionary organization. Nevertheless it is believed that in view of his American citizenship and of the Soviet agreement in 1933 to inform this Government of the arrest of American

PREPARING OFFICE
WILL INDICATE WHETHER

Collect
Full rate
Day letter
Night letter

Charge Department:
Full rate
Day letter
Night letter

Charge to
$

TO BE TRANSMITTED
CONFIDENTIAL CODE
NONCONFIDENTIAL CODE
PARTAIR
PLAIN

TELEGRAM SENT

Department of State

Washington,

-2-

citizens, the ~~failure to~~ report (of) his detention ~~cannot~~ ~~neither not~~ be ignored.

You are authorized, therefore, in your discretion to inform

the Soviet authorities that the Embassy has heard that he

is imprisoned at Camp Norillog in Norilsk and to request

them to investigate the report and, if it is true, to inform the Embassy

regarding the reasons for and the circumstances attending

his arrest, the nature of the sentence which has been

imposed, and his physical and mental condition.

Welles

Acting

КОПИЯ 284
Совершенно секретно
экз.№ 4

СОВЕТ МИНИСТРОВ СССР

" мая 1947 года
№ 2773/А

товарищу   С Т А Л И Н У   И.В.
товарищу   М О Л О Т О В У   В.М.

Докладываю Вам о следующем:

В апреле 1942 года американское посольство в СССР нотой в адрес Министерства Иностранных Дел СССР сообщило о том, что по имеющимся у посольства сведениям американский гражданин Оггинс Исай находится в заключении в лагере в Норильске. Посольство по поручению Государственного департамента просило сообщить причину его ареста, срок на какой осужден Оггинс и состояние его здоровья.

В связи с настояниями американского посольства, по указанию товарища МОЛОТОВА, 8-го декабря 1942 года и 9-го января 1943 года состоялось два свидания представителей посольства с осужденным Оггинс. Во время этих свиданий Оггинс сообщил представителям американского посольства, что он арестован как троцкист нелегально в'ехавший в Советский Союз по чужому паспорту для связи с троцкистским подпольем в СССР.

Несмотря на такое заявление американское посольство в Москве неоднократно возбуждало вопрос перед МИД СССР о пересмотре дела и досрочном освобождении Оггинс, пересылало письма и телеграммы Оггинс его жене, проживающей в США, а также сообщило МИД СССР, что признает Оггинс американским гражданином и готово репатриировать

TFR 18-20

2.

его на родину.

9-го мая 1943 года _американскому_ посольству было сооб щено, что "соответствующие советские органи не считают воз можным пересматривать дело _Оггинс_ ."

20 февраля 1939 года _Оггинс_

был действительно арестован по обвинению в _шпионаже и предательстве._

В процессе следствия эти подозрения не нашли своего подтверждения и _Оггинс_ виновным себя не признал. Однако Особое Совещание при НКВД СССР приговорило _Оггинс_ к 8-ми годам ИТЛ, считая срок заключения с 20 февраля 1939 года.

появление _Оггинс_ в _США_ может быть использовано враждебными Советскому Союзу лицами для активной пропаганды против СССР.

Исходя из этого МГБ СССР считает необходимым Оггинс Исая ликвидировать, сообщив американцам, что Оггинс после свидания с представителями американского посольства, в июне 1943 году был возвращен к месту отбытия срока наказания в Норильск и там, в 1946 году, умер в больнице в результате обострения туберкулеза позвоночника.

В архивах Норильского лагеря нами будет отражен процесс заболевания Оггинс, оказанной ему медицинской и другой помощи. Смерть Оггинс будет оформлена четырьмя болезни, актом вскрытия трупа и актом погребения.

Ввиду того, что жена Оггинс находится в Нью-Йорке, неоднократно обращалась в наше консульство за справками о муже, знает, что он арестован, — считаем полезным вызвать ее в консульство, сообщив о смерти мужа.

Прошу Ваших указаний.

АБАКУМОВ.

FEDERAL BUREAU OF INVESTIGATION

Form No. 1
THIS CASE ORIGINATED AT NEW YORK CITY   NY FILE NO. 100-45923 IV

REPORT MADE AT	DATE WHEN MADE	PERIOD FOR WHICH MADE	REPORT MADE BY
NEW YORK CITY	8/31/43	8/16,17/43	b7C

TITLE: MRS. NERMA OGGINS, alias Norma Jermann

CHARACTER OF CASE: SECURITY MATTER (R)

SYNOPSIS OF FACTS:

Subject born 4/20/98, Vologda, Russia. Subject entered U. S. 6/1/09 and was admitted to citizenship 9/18/24 in the U.S. District Court, SDNY. Married ISAIAH OGGINS 4/29/24 at N.Y.C. and was deserted by husband in May, 1938 in Paris, France. Subject resides with one child, born in France 12/31/31. Subject's Social Security number is [   ] Educated in U. S. and France. Subject has resided at numerous residences in N.Y.C. and has record of intermittent employment. Preliminary investigation reflects no indication of subversive activities. Subject presently resides at 322 West 15 Street, New York City. No known criminal record, N.Y. Description set out.

REFERENCE: Bureau File 100-191369
Bureau letter dated August 9, 1943 to the New York Field Division.

DETAILS: At New York City

This investigation was instituted as a result of a letter from the Bureau which advised that the State Department had reported to the Bureau concerning certain activities of ISAIAH OGGINS who was felt to have been engaged as an agent of the Soviet Government. As a result of this information, a preliminary investigation was requested of the activities of the subject.

It was ascertained by the writer that an extensive file

APPROVED AND FORWARDED: E. E. Conroy
COPIES DESTROYED
COPIES OF THIS REPORT:
5 Bureau
4 New York

31 SEP 1 1943

Cognome e nome .... M a r t i n , Charles Emile ...... No. .... M/ 961

Professione .... Ingegnere

Luogo e data della nascita ...... Pétrograde il 29 luglio 1899

Comune d'origine ...... St. Croix .... Cantone .... Vaud

Nome del padre .... - - .... Nome della madre ...... Alicenée Martin

Cittadinanza originaria dei genitori .... svizzera

Cognome e nome della moglie .... Mäder Elsa Marie

Luogo e data della nascita .... Pétrograde il 31 marzo 1899

Comune d'origine .... Cantone ....

Luogo e data del matrimonio ...... Bartolomeo e di Anne Marie nata Njunuksela

Cognome e nome dei genitori ...... Petrograde il 31 dicembre 1931

Marito: Pas. No. 380432/4463 del 22.3.1935 da Varsovie

Carte di legittimazione: Moglie: Pas. 380431/4462 22.3.1935 da Varsovie

Indirizzo : _Di Eugenio Carnelli junior Ding. C.Martin_

..... _Compagnia Commerciale Caproni Piazza Prati Ferrari, 8_
Via Durini, 24 _Milano_

18 LUG. 1938

Ch. Martin

Data :

Firma :

THE FOREIGN SERVICE OF THE
UNITED STATES OF AMERICA

EHEIM

Amèrican Embassy, London W.1
1 Grosvenor Square

9. Juli 1952

*Copie de l'original
à été envoyée à m.
Decosterd, Lausanne.*

9. AOÛT 19

11 AOÛT 1952
18. Aug. 1952

Bundespolizei,
Bundeshaus,
Bern/Schweiz.

– 7. AUG. 1952

(1952?)

Als ich in der zweiten Hälfte März 1951 in Bern war, erkundigte ich
mich bei Ihnen ob Charles und Elsie MARTIN, welche in Lausanne wohnen, schon
befragt worden seien und ob es weitere Entwicklungen gegeben habe inbezug auf
unsere Untersuchung gegen diese Personen.

Auf Ihren Vorschlag nahm ich Kontakt mit Inspektor A. Ritschard und
Hrn. Charles Knecht in Genf, am 1.April 1952; diese schlugen ihrerseits vor,
dass ich Brigadier Decosterd in Lausanne aufsuchen solle, da seine Abteilung
den Fall behandle. Ich habe daraufhin gleichentags mit Brigadier Decosterd
Fühlung genommen und den Fall mit ihm diskutiert. Während der Unterhaltung
erklärte er, dass Charles MARTIN einen Brief von der National City Bank (NCB)
of New York erhalten habe, worin angezeigt wurde, dass der Saldo seines Kontos
12.27 Dollars betrage.

Ich erklärte mich bereit, durch meine Organisation Erhebungen machen
zu lassen betreffend die Transaktionen auf seinem Konto bei dieser Bank und
ich habe soeben einen vertraulichen Bericht erhalten, worin erklärt wird, dass
MARTIN im Jahre 1937 ein Dollarkonto bei der Mandschurischen Zweigstelle, in
Harbin, der NBC unterhielt. Während dieser Zeit hatte MARTIN sein Quartier im
Nebengebäude der NCB in Harbin und betrieb eine Agentur für Fiat-Autos und
Caproni-Flugzeuge unter der Firma Charles MARTIN & Co. Das Geschäft in Harbin
wurde im Juli 1937 geschlossen. Ebenfalls im Jahre 1937 unterhielt MARTIN ein
Dollarkonto bei der Shanghaier Zweigstelle der NCB und identifiziert sich als
einer der Partner von Charles MARTIN & Co. Diese Gesellschaft befasste sich mit
dem Verkauf von Fiat-Autos und italienischen Flugzeugen an die Mandschurische
Regierung und behauptete, ein Kapital von $ 75.000 zu besitzen. Das Geschäft
mit der Regierung von Mandschukuo kam nicht zustande und die Gesellschaft wurde
im Spätjahr 1937 in Shanghai aufgelöst; der ganze Saldo von $ 17,982.97 bei
der Shanghaier Branche der NCB wurde an die Zweigstelle Paris transferiert.

Am 9. September 1939 eröffnete ein Charles E. MARTIN, Mythenquai 22,
Zürich, Schweiz, ein Konto bei der NCB of New York, 55 Wall Street, New York
City, mit einem Einlagedepot von $ 12,002.98, welches aus dem Transfer von
MARTINS Konto bei NCB Paris bestand. Dieses Konto ist noch immer offen in den
Bankbüchern. Während der letzten 1 1/2 Jahre war keine Aktivität zu verzeichnen.
Der Saldo auf 1.Januar 1951 betrug $ 25.77 und wurde reduziert um $ 4,50 pro
Quartal bis zuletzt $ 3.27 im Konto verbleiben. Das Konto wird abgeschlossen
sobald die nächsten Quartalsbankspesen fällig sind.

Am 5.Juni 1947 eröffnete MARTIN ein zweites Konto bei der NCB New York;
er gab seine Adresse als: Chemin de la Fauvette 32, Lausanne, Schweiz. Dieses
Konto wurde eröffnet mit einem Transfer von $ 500 von der Union Bank of Switzer-
land. Das Konto wurde am 29.März 1948 geschlossen, der verbleibende Saldo von
$ 476.00 an Charles E. MARTIN, Lausanne, Schweiz, transferiert.

Es versteht sich, dass diese Informationen auf streng vertraulicher
Basis gegeben wurden. Ich würde es schätzen, wenn Sie diese an Brigadier
Decosterd weiterleiten würden mit dem Ersuchen, keine weitere Verteilung vor-
zunehmen, da dies unsere Quelle gefährden würde, deren Empfindlichkeit Sie ja
mit Banken in Ihrem Lande erfahren haben.

./.

NOTES

ABBREVIATIONS

ADST:	Association for Diplomatic Studies and Training, Arlington, Virginia
FRUS:	*Foreign Relations of the United States*, Office of the Historian, U.S. Department of State
FSB:	Archives, Federal Security Agency, Russian Federation, Moscow
Hoover:	Hoover Archives, Hoover Institution, Stanford, California
HUAC:	Archives, House Committee on Un-American Activities, in NARA-DC
LOC:	Library of Congress, Washington, D.C.
NARA-CP:	National Archives, College Park, Maryland
NARA-DC:	National Archives, Washington, D.C.
NARA-NY:	National Archives Northeast Region, New York, New York
N.O. FBI Files:	Nerma Oggins FBI Files, from central files and New York field office
NYPL:	New York Public Library, New York, New York
PRO:	National Archives (Public Record Office), London, England
RG:	Record Group
RGASPI:	Russian State Archive of Social and Political History (formerly RTsKhDNI), Moscow
RGVA:	Russian State Military Archive, Moscow
R.O. Papers:	Documents and correspondence in the possession of Robin S. Oggins
SISS:	Senate Internal Security Subcommittee; Archives, NARA-DC
SMP:	Shanghai Municipal Police Files, in Records of the CIA, NARA-CP
Swiss Dossier:	Federal Archives of Switzerland (Schweizerisches Bundesarchiv); Fond: E 4320 (B) 1990/133; Vol. 133, C.12.5200
TFR:	Task Force Russia Files, U.S.-Russia Joint Commission on POW/MIAs, Pentagon

CHAPTER 1: "THE AMERICAN PROFESSOR"

10 *"The American professor"*: Interview with Alla Makarova, Norilsk, Aug. 8, 2000.

10 *"Microfilms in heels"*: Interviews with Jacques Rossi, Paris, Oct. 13, 2000, Apr. 18, 2001, Aug. 31, 2001.

CHAPTER 2. THREAD CITY

18 *"the Thread City"*: For the history of Willimantic, I have relied on interviews (Jan. 28, 2001; Aug. 14, 2005) and correspondence (Jan. 20, 2001; Jan. 23, 2001; Feb. 5, 2001) with Thomas R. Beardsley, as well as his published writings: "Willimantic: Textile City," *Connecticut History* 42, 2 (Fall 2003): 97–104; *Willimantic Industry and Community: The Rise and Decline of a Connecticut Textile City* (Willimantic: Windham Textile & History Museum, 1993); *Willimantic Women: Their Lives and Labors* (Willimantic: Windham Textile & History Museum, 1990); Beardsley with Roberst Asher, "Voices of Willimantic Textile Workers," *Connecticut History* 42, 2 (Fall 2003): 159–86.

18 *a dollar a day*: By 1912, the year of the Willimantic strike, the women workers, based on their skill, were earning three rates: $10, $9, and $6 a week. *Willimantic Chronicle*, Apr. 26, 1912, p. 1.

19 *the shtetl of Abolnik*: Also known as Bolniki or Balninkai in the Ukmerge District, Kovno. Additional information can be found on a Web site for researching Jewish genealogy in Lithuania, www.jewishgen.org.

19 *Melamdovich*: Also spelled Malamdovich. Simon Oggins's father was Meyer Melamdovich, his grandfather Mendel Melamdovich. The name Oggins may have arisen from the Russian Jewish surname Oginz, spelled variously, which appears in the records of the Vilna region of the period.

20 *"renounce and abjure"*: Naturalization Certificate (Superior Ct. N.Y. Co.), Simon Oggins, Apr. 23, 1898, Bundle 546; Record No. 1, Records of the Immigration and Naturalization Service, Record Group 85, NARA-NY.

24 *"You've won a moral"*: *Willimantic Chronicle*, Apr. 26, 1912, p. 1.

CHAPTER 3. WAR

27 *"They pour into New York"*: Waldo Frank, *Our America* (New York: Boni and Liveright, 1919), p. 177.

27 *"universal revolt"*: Quoted in Thomas Bender, *New York Intellect: A History of Intellectual Life in New York City, from 1750 to the Beginnings of Our Own Time* (New York: Knopf, 1987), pp. 230–31.

28 *"I suggest treating"*: Robert McCaughey, *Stand, Columbia: A History of Columbia University in the City of New York, 1754–2004* (New York: Columbia University Press, 2003), p. 266.

28 *"a social snob"*: Ibid., p. 266.

29 *60,000 soldiers*: Geoffrey R. Stone, *Perilous Times: Free Speech in Wartime* (New York: Norton, 2004), p. 136.

29 *"when the shadow"*: N. M. Butler, speech at the Alumni Luncheon, Columbia University, June 6, 1917.

29 *"It is a fearful thing"*: Woodrow Wilson, *War Messages*, 65th Cong., 1st Sess., Senate Doc. No. 5, Serial No. 7264 (Washington, D.C.: 1917), p. 8.

30 *no more than 1,200*: McCaughey, *Stand, Columbia*, pp. 230–31.

31 *Cerf wrote "The Stroller"*: Cerf, a member of the Class of 1920, often listed himself as in the Class of 1919. He did graduate from Columbia College in October 1919 but attended the commencement in June 1920. *Columbia University Catalogue*, 1920–21, p. 280; Columbia University Archives; "Columbia to Honor Leaders in the War," *New York Times*, June 2, 1920, p. 11; Bennett Cerf, *At Random* (New York: Random House, 1977), pp. 12–57.

31 *majored in history and English*: Columbia has no record of the precise number of members of the Class of 1920 who completed this double major. However, 122 majored in English and 89 in history. The number of joint majors, therefore, would have been 89 or fewer.

31 *Joe Freeman*: Freeman entered Columbia in 1916 with the Class of 1920 but graduated in the spring of 1919. Joseph Freeman, *An American Testament: A Narrative of Rebels and Romantics* (New York: Farrar & Rinehart, 1936), pp. 81, 149; Bender, *New York Intellect*, p. 235.

31 *Class of 1920 is notable*: Like Oggins, Brown grew up in a New England mill town, but one founded by his great-grandfather. He left Columbia during Oggins's first term. In April 1917, like many students eager to get "over there" but not to abandon their pacifism, Brown went to France to join the Norton-Harjes Ambulance Corps. On the boat he met Edward Estlin Cummings, a young Harvard man also en route to the corps. E. E. Cummings and Brown became lifelong friends. Kenneth Burke, another member of Oggins's class, became a leading critic and philosopher of language. A close friend of Malcolm Cowley's, he also left Columbia early—not for the war but for Greenwich Village. Louis Bromfield (Oggins knew him as Brumfeld) was yet another classmate who left early for the ambulance corps. Not long after getting his B.A.—an honorary "war degree" given to those who had served—he turned to writing. In 1926, *Early Autumn*, his second novel, won the Pulitzer Prize. Not yet thirty, Bromfield was considered to be in the ranks of Dos Passos, Hemingway, and Wilder. Malcolm Cowley, *Exile's Return: A Literary Odyssey of the 1920s* (New York: Viking, 1951), p. 9.

32 *"what might be called"*: Ibid., p. 38.

33 *"So long as national policies"*: Butler, speech at Alumni Luncheon.

34 *"a part of the apparatus"*: *Columbia Spectator*, Sept. 26, 1919.

34 *"for any person"*: Butler, speech at Alumni Luncheon.

35 *"but a slip of a girl"*: "Columbia Students Face Federal Jury," *New York Times*, June 19, 1917, p. 2. See also "Anarchists Awed by Police Clubs," *New York Times*, June 5, 1917, p. 1; "3 Students Seized on Anti-Draft Charge," *The Call*, June 1, 1917; "Phillips Sticks to His Vow Not to Register," *The Call*, June 6, 1917; "Draft Slackers Must Face Trial," *New York Times*, June 7, 1917, p. 2; McCaughey, *Stand, Columbia*, p. 248; Dan La Botz, "American 'Slackers' in the Mexican Revolution," *The Americas* 62, 4 (2006): 563–90. The three students were Charles F. Phillips, Eleanor Parker, and Owen Cattell. Phillips and Parker, boyfriend and girlfriend, fled to Mexico in 1918. Phillips was reported to lead the national antidraft movement in the United States.

35 *more practitioners in the new field*: McCaughey, *Stand, Columbia*, pp. 198–99. In 1882–83, Cattell had been a fellow in philosophy with John Dewey at Johns Hopkins University, and Dewey and Cattell long remained close friends. Before Columbia, Cattell served as the first chairman of a psychology department in the United States.

35 *"association with the most irresponsible"*: N. M. Butler to H.W.L. Dana, Sept. 24, 1917, quoted in H.W.L. Dana to Allyn A. Young, Dec. 14, 1917; Central Files Record, Columbia University Archives.

36 *"The history of the world"*: Freeman, *American Testament*, p. 107. One of Oggins's professors, the historian Carlton Hayes, a convert to Catholicism who had come out against the war before April 1917, was shaken by Beard's resignation. Hayes's course on the war became a forum for the campus radicalism; two hundred students attended his lectures. On the morning Beard quit, according to Freeman, Hayes told his students, "Gentlemen, we have lost today in this university one of the most intelligent, honest and courageous men who ever lived. There is nothing I can say to you in my course today as important as Dr. Beard's resignation. The class is dismissed" (*American Testament*, p. 107).

36 *"War in the interests of democracy!"*: Randolph Bourne, *The Radical Will: Selected Writings, 1911–1918*, ed. Olaf Hansen (Berkeley: University of California Press, 1992), pp. 307–18, 336–47.

36 *"marked the literary voice"*: Frank, *Our America*, p. 199.

37 *"bulwark against democracy"*: John Recchiuti, "The Rand School of Social Science During the Progressive Era: Will to Power of a Stratum of the American Intellectual Class," *Journal of the History of the Behavioral Sciences*, 1995, 31 (2): 151.

37 *"To Hell with the flag!"*: McCaughey, *Stand, Columbia*, p. 251.

38 *Undergraduates wore uniforms*: Cerf, *At Random*, p. 14. Freeman includes a description of "bayonet practice" on campus; *American Testament*, pp. 126–27.

38 *"imperialism and militarism"*: Freeman, *American Testament*, pp. 122–23.

39 *"military service flags"*: Beardsley, "Willimantic in World War One," *Willimantic Chronicle*, May 18, 2005, p. 7.

39 *$150 a year*: McCaughey, *Stand, Columbia*, p. 300.

40 *BARBUSSE ON THE WAR*: Letter to the Editor, *New York Times*, Oct. 20, 1919, p. 14.

40 *"translated from the 100th"*: "Topics of the Times," *New York Times*, Oct. 17, 1919, p. 16.

41 *he was one of three men*: "To Draw Conscripts at War Department," *New York Times*, July 4, 1917, p. 10. On Sept. 14, 1918, at the age of thirty-two, David Oggins joined his brother in registering for the draft. David had been a naturalized U.S. citizen since he was a toddler—waived in when Simon Oggins took the oath.

41 *David had run for a delegate seat*: "Other 5—No title," *New York Times*, Mar. 28, 1915, p. 2.

41 *"David Oggins, (Rep.)"*: "Guide for Voters by Citizen's Union," *New York Times*, Oct. 28, 1917, p. E4.

41 *David got 2,093 votes*: "Hylan's Victory is a Tammany Record," *New York Times*, Nov. 8, 1917, p. 2. Edwin C. Brooks, the Socialist, received nearly as many votes as the Republican, 1,464.

41 *"The experience and training"*: "Nominees Analyzed by Citizens Union," *New York Times*, Oct. 27, 1918, p. 8. Election results: "City Vote for Senate," *New York Times*, Nov. 7, 1918, p. 3.

THE LUBYANKA: 1939

44 *In the 1930s*: Elizabeth Poretsky, *Our Own People: A Memoir of "Ignace Reiss" and His Friends* (London: Oxford University Press, 1969), p. 154.

44 *the real Egon Hein*: Born January 29, 1915, in Hranice, Hein moved to Prague as a medical student. The Prague address book for 1937–38 listed him: "Egon Hein st.—Podskalská 46, Praha II"; Czech National Archives.

45 *In the early 1930s*: Walter Krivitsky, *In Stalin's Secret Service* (New York: Enigma, 2000), p. 143.

47 *Twice a day*: Walter J. Ciszek, S.J., Collection, Special Collections, Georgetown University Library.

48 *"If you sit behind closed doors"*: Anna Larina, *This I Cannot Forget: The Memoirs of Nikolai Bukharin's Widow*, trans. Gary Kern (New York: Norton, 1993), p. 129.

48 *small red lights*: Ciszek Collection. See also Victor Sheymov, *Tower of Secrets: A Real-Life Thriller* (Annapolis, Md.: Naval Institute Press, 1993), pp. 160–61.

50 *It was a script*: Krivitsky, *In Stalin's Secret Service*, pp. 190–94.

50 *1.5 million people were arrested*: Marc Jansen and Nikita Petrov, *Stalin's Loyal Executioner: People's Commissar Nikolai Ezhov, 1895–1940* (Stanford, Calif.: Hoover Institution Press, 2002), pp. ix, 103.

CHAPTER 4. REVOLUTION

54 *Noyme Berman*: The microfilm was faded and the scrawl of the clerk hard to read, but there, halfway down the page, *Noima Bermann* was listed with her family. T. 715, Roll 1278, beginning June 1, 1909, NARA-DC.

55 *"Schipishke"*: Zarasai uezd, Kaunas gubernia, a province in what is today Lithuania. The shtetl was also known as Skopishki and Skopishok. Correspondence with Tim Baker, Apr. 11, 2002, coordinator of the Web site: www.shtetlinks.jewishgen.org/skopishok/skopishok.html.

55 *came with four children*: The *Zeeland* manifest appears to be an inaccurate record. Nerma is listed as eight years old, although every other known document lists her as born in 1898. Robin Oggins believed Chazan to be the brother later known as Moishe and had no knowledge of a sister named Feige. Another older brother, Abraham, was presumably already in the United States. Feige translates as "bird," Chazan as "Cantor," a rare name. Correspondence with David Roskies, Sept. 16, 2006, Jewish Theological Seminary, and David Brenner, Sept. 18, 2006, Kent State University.

58 *April 5, 1906*: Frederic Cornell, "A History of the Rand School of Social Science, 1906–1956," Ed.D. dissertation, Columbia University Teachers College, p. 29.

59 *a radical landmark*: The Rand School owed its name to Mrs. Carrie Rand, an Iowa widow of a gold rush titan, who endowed it with $200,000 in 1905. Mrs. Rand died the following year, but the name lived on. The gift had less to do with the widow's political leanings than with the charm of George D. Herron, her son-in-law. A Christian socialist, Herron is best remembered as the father of the Social Gospel but was also by turns a prairie preacher, professor, defrocked minister, published poet, would-be statesman, and agent of Woodrow Wilson at Versailles. Interview (New York, Dec. 2, 2005) and correspondence (Dec. 5, 2005) with Caroline Rand Herron; *A Socialist Wedding* (New York: Knickerbocker, date unknown), an account of the scandalous Rand-Herron wedding; Cornell, "History of the Rand School," pp. 17–20; "Prof. Herron Dies: Championed Allies," *New York Times*, Oct. 11, 1925, p. E5.

60 *"Women," cried Emma Goldman*: Matthew Josephson, *Life Among the Surrealists* (New York: Holt, Rinehart and Winston, 1962), p. 47.

60 *"He would go off"*: Ibid., p. 46. Joe Freeman also remembers the Rand School dances in *An American Testament*, p. 138.

62 *"eating its way"*: A. Mitchell Palmer, "The Case Against the Reds," *Forum* 63 (1920): 173.

62 *In July 1917*: Curt Gentry, *J. Edgar Hoover: The Man and the Secrets* (New York: Norton, 1991), p. 68.

63 *Ludwig Christian Alexander Karlovich Martens*: Benjamin Gitlow, *The Whole of Their Lives* (New York: Scribner's, 1948), pp. 58–60; Edward Jay Epstein,

Dossier: The Secret History of Armand Hammer (New York: Random House, 1996), pp. 39–61.

64 *On June 21, 1919*: "Raid Rand School, 'Left Wing,' and I.W.W. Offices," *New York Times*, June 22, 1919, p. 1. See also *Revolutionary Radicalism: Its History, Purpose and Tactics, Report of the Joint Legislative Committee Investigating Seditious Activities, filed April 24, 1920, in the Senate of the State of New York* (Albany: J. B. Lyons, 1920), four volumes that run to 4,428 pages (hereafter Lusk Committee Report). Of particular interest are the Lusk Committee's Investigation Files, 1918–20, which include numerous reports from informants to Ray W. Finch, the committee's chief investigator; Rand School Seized Files: 1913–19; Suspected Radical Organizations Seized Files, 1916–19; and Russian Soviet Bureau Seized Files, 1918–19. The committee's informants had access to a host of New York City left-wing organizations, including the Rand School.

66 *The state governor*: The governor was Joseph Grundy, a Republican. Scott Nearing, *A Scott Nearing Reader: The Good Life in Bad Times,* ed. Steve Sherman (Metuchen, N.J.: Scarecrow, 1989), p. 6.

66 *"The two per cent"*: "The Great Madness," in ibid., p. 78.

67 *"Some of those who believe"*: "Nearing Is Indicated on Sedition Charge," *New York Times*, Mar. 22, 1918, p. 4.

67 *"the greatest public question"*: Nearing, *A Scott Nearing Reader*, p. 90.

67 *"And you wanted to persuade"*: "Trail of Scott Nearing," in ibid., pp. 86–87.

68 *The police came before dawn*: Alexander Berkman, "The Log of the Transport Buford," *The Liberator* 3, 4 (Apr. 1920): 9–12.

71 *"One of Willimantic's"*: Obituary, *Willimantic Chronicle*, Dec. 13, 1918, n.p.

72 *"who when Belgium lay bleeding"*: "Columbia Honors Captains of War," *New York Times*, Jun. 3, 1920, p. 10.

73 *"If indeed"*: Ibid.

CHAPTER 5

INTO THE NIGHT

76 *"operatic baritone"*: Cowley, *Exile's Return*, pp. 222–23.

77 *breathed with the ideas*: Fellow residents included Clara Rieber, a schoolteacher and later a leader in the New York teachers' union. Two years later, Dushan Podgorshek, a Columbia classmate of Whittaker Chambers's—a Serb who helped him edit *The Morningside*, the campus literary magazine—moved in. Podgorshek was a Columbia undergraduate from 1922 to 1926. A mathematics major, he took out ads offering to tutor in math and engineering in the *New York Times* on Feb. 18 and 21, 1926, listing Watkins 00411 as his telephone number. This was the telephone number at 68 Perry Street. On Mar. 7, 1926, Podgorshek appeared on a *New York Times* list of newly licensed teachers in the public schools, living at 68 Perry. In the October 1922 issue of *The Morningside*, vol. 11, no. 1, he

is listed as one of eight associate editors. At the time, Chambers was editor in chief. The issue contains Chambers's scandalous "A Play for Pup-
pets" by "John Kelly." On the play, see Sam Tanenhaus, *Whittaker Chambers*
(New York: Random House, 1997), pp. 30–32.

77   *James C. Egbert*: Lusk Committee Report, p. 3307.

78   *the numbers attending extension classes*: *Columbia University 1923 Annual Report*, p. 7,
Columbia University Archives.

78   *He would teach*: New York City Bureau of Education application, 1922,
cited in FBI NY Field Report, NY 100-45923, Jan. 28, 1947, pp. 3–4. On
the application Oggins gave "his employment as a student in the day and
as a teacher in the evening, teaching English to foreigners from 1920 to
1922" (N.O. FBI Files). Oggins's NKVD file has "In 1921 as a student I
became a departmental assistant in History" (FSB).

80   *"Nerma Bermann"*: FBI Report, NY Field Report; NY 100-45923, Jan. 28,
1947, pp. 1–2, citing BOI informant report of May 13, 1922, N.O. FBI
Files.

81   *"in effect joining"*: Ibid.

81   *"recently organizing communist"*: Index Bureau telegram from [FNU] Harvey,
London, to Secretary of State, Washington, D.C., May 16, 1922. Relayed
May 17, 1922, to J. Edgar Hoover by telephone and "special messenger,"
811.10-Sc08, State Department Central File, RG 59, NARA-CP.

81   *"Unity Convention"*: Benjamin Gitlow, *The Whole of Their Lives* (New York:
Scribner's, 1948), pp. 89–96; correspondence with Tim Davenport
(Sept. 27, 2005, Nov. 20, 2006). The resort was called the Wulfskeel
Farm, owned by Karl Wulfskeel.

82   *"sylvan scene"*: Gitlow, *The Whole*, p. 90.

82   *K-97*: Theodore Draper, *The Roots of American Communism* (New York: Viking,
1957), pp. 366–72. Morrow may also have been a BOI source on Nerma
Berman's activities. In his memoirs, *Out of Step: An Unquiet Life in the 20th Century* (New York: Harper & Row, 1987), Sidney Hook remembers Nerma's
grudge against a BOI informer, "an Irishman recruited by Foster." Nerma,
according to Hook, hated it that he always demanded "the rest of [the
ticket proceeds from an event]" from her. "The suspicion that she'd kept
some of the take in her pockets made her apoplectic," he writes. "A few
months later (after this series of incidents) the man was exposed as a government agent, when he took action against his government contacts
because they failed to pay him his $5 a day, as promised" (pp. 94–95).

83   *Foster, too, was arrested*: "Foster Arrested in Chicago: 15 Radicals to Stand Trial
in Berrien; 2 To Be Deported," *St. Joseph Herald-Press*, Aug. 23, 1922, pp. 1, 4.

83   *enormous amount of money*: *Worker*, Oct. 14, 1922, p. 5. In the ad for the Opera
House event, Nerma Berman sought $90,000 for the cases in Michigan,
$15,000 for those in Pennsylvania, and $20,000 for those in New York.

83   *the Labor Defense Council*: "Workers Rally to Support of Victims of Michi-

gan Raids," *Worker*, Oct. 14, 1922, reported from a speaking tour by Ruthenberg and Foster in Toledo, Cleveland, Pittsburgh, and Youngstown. The tour raised funds for the defense of those arrested at Bridgman, advocated the idea of union amalgamation, and opened new local chapters of the LDC. The anonymous article was possibly the work of Nerma Berman.

83   *But Nerma Berman*: Richard Merrill Whitney, a Harvard graduate and conservative journalist for hire, published a volume with a remarkable title, *Reds in America: The Present Status of the Revolutionary Movement in the U.S., Based on Documents Seized by the Authorities in the Raid upon the Convention of the Communist Party at Bridgman, Mich., Aug. 22, 1922, Together with Descriptions of Numerous Connections and Associations of the Communists among the Radicals, Progressives, and Pinks* (New York: Beckwith, 1924). An extensive compilation of slurs and slanders, the book does at least merit historical interest as an early precursor of the McCarthy era. Among the documents (leaked from the BOI) reprinted in *Reds in America* is a letter dated April 6, 1923, from the "LABOR DEFENSE COUNCIL." By 1925, the LDC was subsumed by the International Labor Defense (ILD), which became the party's leading national organization. The same LDC letter found its way into the so-called Dies Index, also known as Appendix IX, entitled "Communist Front Organizations" and published by the Special Committee on Un-American Activities (Washington, D.C.: U.S. Government Printing Office, 1944), sec. 3, p. 961.

84   *"other similar cases"*: Whitney, *Reds in America*, p. 173. The FBI also found Nerma Berman in this circular; FBI New York Report, NY 100-45923, Jan. 28, 1947, p. 3, N.O. FBI files.

84   *Nerma had been appointed*: Whitney, *Reds in America*, p. 173; Elizabeth Kirkpatrick Dilling, *The Red Network: A "Who's Who" and Handbook of Radicalism for Patriots* (Kenilworth, Ill.: self-published, 1934), p. 182.

85   *"We must train": Lenin on Organization* (New York: Daily Worker, 1926), p. 44.

85   *"good Republicans and Democrats"*: Freeman, *An American Testament*, p. 120.

85   *3,434 dues-paying members*: Comintern Archive document f. 515, o. 1, d. 34,1. 22, RGASPI.

86   *308 East Eighteenth Street*: Meyer London, a Russian-born Jewish lawyer and Socialist politician, also lived at the address. In 1914, London, only the second Socialist to serve in Congress, had been elected from the Lower East Side. After waging three unsuccessful campaigns against Tammany Hall candidates, he triumphed in a landmark victory for the New York garment workers. By 1925 he was teaching a Saturday seminar on Soviet Russia at the Rand School. That fall he ran for a Supreme Court seat in New York, but in June 1926 he was killed in an automobile accident not far from Cy and Nerma's building. Nearly half a million people attended his funeral.

86 *keep up with his dues*: AHA Membership Lists, Box 880, Manuscript Reading Room, LOC.

88 *"According to Mr. RILEY"*: NY Field Report. NY 100-45923, Jan. 28, 1947, p. 4, N.O. FBI Files.

88 *Werner Rakov*: Rakov, who used the operational name Felix Wolf in the United States, recruited at least one prominent member of the New York underground, the Russian émigré dentist Philip Rosenbliett, in 1925. Recalled to Moscow, Rakov was executed in 1937. David Dallin interviewed Ray Murphy (Dec. 9, 1952) and Jay Lovestone (Dec. 12, 1952) regarding Wolf. Lovestone told Dallin that he had known Wolf in Germany during the Hamburg uprising and had seen him in Moscow during the American delegation's trip to the Sixth World Congress in 1928 (Dallin Papers, NYPL and Hoover). See also "Testimony to the United States Congress," in Walter C. Krivitsky, *MI5 Debriefing & Other Documents on Soviet Intelligence,* ed. and trans. Gary Kern (Riverside, Calif.: Xenos, 2004), p. 103; Lovestone testimony, *Investigation of Un-American Propaganda Activities in the United States: Hearings Before a Special Committee on Un-American Activities, 76th Congress, 1st Session, on H. Res. 282: Volume 11* (Washington, D.C.: Government Printing Office, 1939), pp. 7095–7188; William J. Chase, *Enemies Within the Gates?: The Comintern and the Stalinist Repression, 1934–1939* (New Haven, Conn.: Yale University Press, 2002), p. 492. In recent years Russian authors, with apparent access to the Soviet archives, have offered brief biographies of Rakov/Wolf: V. M. Lur'e and V. IA. Kochik, *GRU: dela i liudi* [GRU: Cases & People] (Sankt-Peterburg: Neva, 2002), p. 457; A. I. Kolpakidi and Dmitrii P. Prokhorov, *Imperia GRU: ocherki istorii rossiiskoi voennoi razvedki* [The Empire of the GRU: Essays in the History of Russian Military Intelligence] (Moskva: Olma, 2000), vol. 1, pp. 166–69, vol. 2, pp. 398–99; Vladimir V. Pozniakov, *Sovetskaia razvedka v Amerike, 1919–1941.* [Soviet Intelligence in America: 1919–1941] (Moskva: Mezhdunarodnye otnosheniia, 2005), pp. 117–23. On Rosenbliett: correspondence, Dec. 10, 2007, with John Earl Haynes, citing documents newly released from the KGB archives.

89 *more than 300 pages*: Markus Wehner, "Brat'ia Rakovy: nemetskie kommunisty v Rossii (1914–1918)" [The Brothers Rakov: German Communists in Russia, 1914–1918]. *Otechestvennaia istoriia* 4 (1996): 155–69.

90 *she petitioned for citizenship*: FBI NY Field Report, NY 100-45923, Aug. 31, 1943, p. 6, N.O. FBI Files. "Petition for Naturalization," dated June 13, 1924, and accompanying "Oath of Allegiance," dated Sept. 18, 1924. The petition was cosigned by Isaiah Oggins, "Research Worker", RG 21, NARA-NY.

91 *"travel to Germany"*: Washington, D.C., FBI Field Report, Feb. 27, 1947, 100–6367, p. 2, N.O. FBI Files. The 1926 return voyage to New York is recorded among the New York Passenger Lists, 1820–1957, RG 36, NARA-NY.

91 *By November 11*: Coincidence or not, Oggins returned to New York within days of Alfred Tilton, who arrived with his wife in New York on Nov. 2, 1926, to replace Rakov/Wolf; Kolpakidi and Prokhorov, *Imperia GRU*, vol. 1, p. 169. Kolpakidi and Prokhorov write that after their arrival in the United States in 1926, the Tiltons "immediately set to work strengthening and expanding the intelligence network. As a result, by year's end the network boasted 12 agents."

91 *severed all her party ties*: FBI Office Memorandum, SA [name redacted] to SAC, NEW YORK (65-14822) (#6-C), Subject: Jacob Albam, Espionage-R (MOCASE), Apr. 24, 1957, p. 2., N.O. FBI Files.

91 *"study and travel"*: Nerma Oggins Passport Application, Apr. 24, 1928, New York, R.O. Papers.

92 *born renegade*: Interview with John Hook, San Francisco, Aug. 13, 2003; interview with Arthur Kornberg, Stanford, Calif., Mar. 9, 2005. Kornberg was Katz's nephew; Katz and Hook were married at the Kornberg home in Brooklyn. On Katz and the Labor Defense Council: Sidney Hook to Carrie Katz, May 9, 1924; Hook Papers, Box 188, Folder 4, Hoover.

92 The Law of Social Revolution: Other chapters were by Carrie Katz's classmates, a number of whom appear in *Witness*, Chambers's 1952 book about his years in the underground.

94 *He never seemed comfortable*: Hook, *Out of Step*, p. 95.

95 *Cy rang Sidney*: Ibid. .

96 *the* Leviathan: Cy and Nerma were not alone. A headline in the *New York Times* (May 5, 1928), "Russia to Reopen Gold Import Issue," offered a clue. Moscow, the article reported, had undertaken "to reopen the question of imports of Soviet gold" into the United States. Facing a huge trade deficit, the Soviets were desperate to export gold to America—$30 million worth a year. The sum, and the headline, stemmed from the declarations of Saul G. Bron, chairman of Amtorg. The article noted the Russian's travel schedule. After a year in New York, Bron also boarded the *Leviathan*, bound "for a short stay in Russia" (p. 22).

CHAPTER 6. A CHANGE OF SKY

100 *deep roots in Berlin*: Evgeny Primakov, ed., *Ocherki istorii rossiiskoi vneshnei razvedki: v shesti tomakh* [Essays in the History of Russian Foreign Intelligence: in 6 Volumes] (Moskva: Mezhdunarodnye otnosheniia, 1996–2006), vol. 2, p. 15; Christopher Andrew and Vasili Mitrokhin, *The Sword and the Shield: The Mitrokhin Archive and the Secret History of the KGB* (New York: Basic, 1999), pp. 20–41; Ypsilon [pseud.], *Pattern for World Revolution* (Chicago: Ziff-Davis, 1947), pp. 1–34.

101 *"a host of typists"*: Jan Valtin, *Out of the Night* (New York: Alliance, 1941), p. 180.

101 *Embassies, consulates, official offices*: Frederick S. Litten, "The Noulens Affair," *China Quarterly* 138 (June 1994): 499.

103 *"was born in defeat"*: Peter Gay, *Weimar Culture: The Outsider as Insider* (New York: Harper & Row, 1968), p. 2. For a recent study of the Weimar culture, see Eric D. Weitz, *Weimar Germany: Promise and Tragedy* (Princeton, N.J.: Princeton University Press, 2007).

103 *Vera Nabokov*: Stacy Schiff, *Véra: Mrs. Vladimir Nabakov* (New York: Random House, 2004), p. 55.

104 *"the women of Berlin"*: Otto Friedrich, *Before the Deluge: A Portrait of Berlin in the 1920's* (New York: Harper & Row, 1972), p. 200.

105 *"plastered with slogans"*: Ruth Fischer, *Stalin and German Communism* (Cambridge, Mass.: Harvard University Press, 1948), p. 312.

106 RED FRONT FIGHTERS: Agnes Smedley, "Germany's Red Front," *The Nation* 127, 3291 (Aug. 1, 1928): 116–17.

108 *there were many machines*: Hook, *Out of Step*, p. 98.

109 *"parlor pink colony"*: Elizabeth Poretsky, *Our Own People: A Memoir of "Ignace Reiss" and His Friends* (London: Oxford University Press, 1969), p. 131.

110 *"Encounter with Espionage"*: Hook, *Out of Step*, pp. 94–101. Hook first published this as an article in *Midstream* (May 1985). Seven drafts of the manuscript of Hook's memoirs are preserved among his papers. By all appearances he considered this chapter essential to his early evolution—his turn away from communism. When his editor suggested cutting it, he stood firm; Hook Papers, Box 90, Folder 2, Hoover.

111 *"Politics," he wrote*: Sidney Hook to Herbert Hook, postcard, Oct. 13, 1928; Hook Papers, Box 3, Folder 12, Hoover.

114 *Lenin translation*: The book, Lenin's *Materialism and Empirio-Criticism* (1909), vol. 13 in his *Collected Works*, was published by Trachtenberg's International Publishers in New York in 1927.

115 *"Carrie's best friend"*: This sentence, not present in Hook's *Out of Step*, is found in the drafts of the manuscript; Hook Papers, Box 90, Folder 2, Hoover.

115 *His memory could have been faulty*: Hook almost certainly was wrong on one point. In *Out of Step* he writes that Cy and Nerma sailed from New York in 1926, not 1928. Hook went to Europe on his Guggenheim fellowship in the summer of 1928. The actual chronology calls into question his memory that "we were somewhat surprised that we received no word from them before we ourselves sailed for Europe in June 1928" (p. 96), as Cy and Nerma had left New York only in May 1928.

116 *"Soviet operatives in Berlin"*: A spy scandal did erupt in Berlin in the summer of 1928. On July 11, the *Berliner Tageblatt*, in an article entitled, "Luftfahrt Espionage in Adlershof: Sensationalle Verhaftungen bei der Deutschen Versuchsanstalt für Luftverkehr," broke the story how Dr. Eduard Ludwig, a twenty-seven-year-old aviation specialist, had been lured by the Soviets to steal secrets from the Aeronautical Research Institute in Berlin-Adlersdorf. Ludwig was convicted and received five years in jail.

Dallin Papers, Hoover. See also David J. Dallin, *Soviet Espionage* (New Haven, Conn.: Yale University Press, 1955), pp. 113–14.

117 *Stalin read Hitler's first speech*: The story of how Stalin received a copy of the speech awaits its full telling. The speech took place in the residence of General Kurt Equord von Hammerstein, head of the Wehrmacht. In recent years, German scholars have unearthed nearly stenographic copies of the speech in the Moscow archives and the East German archives. They also discovered the source: two of the general's daughters, Helga and Butsi, as Marie-Louise was called. As university students, Helga and Butsi not only mingled with Jews, they fell in love with Communists, among them Leo Roth (an early member of the Soviet underground in Germany), Werner Scholem (an early Communist Reichstag deputy and brother of the Israeli scholar Gershom Scholem), and Werner Hirsch (an aide to the KPD leader Thälmann and editor of *Die Rote Fahne*, the party paper). Helga and Butsi became Communists and spies. The Hammerstein sisters, Hirsch is said to have boasted, ranked "among the best agents of the Communist secret service in the German army" (Ypsilon, *Pattern for World Revolution*, p. 167). An independence of mind ran in the family; by 1939, General von Hammerstein had helped organize a failed attempt to kill Hitler, while his eldest sons, Kunrat and Ludwig, took part in the failed assassination of July 20, 1944, led by Claus von Stauffenberg (Interviews with Franz von Hammerstein [Berlin, Apr. 11, 2006] and Gottfried Paasche [telephone, Feb. 5, 2006, and Apr. 3, 2006]).

118 *$500,000 in fake bills*: "Physician Seized as Counterfeiter," *New York Times*, Jan. 5, 1933, p. 11. It is likely as well that a portion of the counterfeit bills was printed in Moscow.

118 *Nick Dozenberg*: On Dozenberg, telephone interview (Sept. 27, 2006) and correspondence (Oct. 10, 2006; Sept. 24, 2007; Sept. 25, 2007) with Alice Kramer. See also Dozenberg Statement and Affidavit, Hearings of Nov. 8, 1949, U.S. Congress, *House of Representatives*, Committee on Un-American Activities (HUAC), 81st Congress, 1st and 2d sess.; "Third Red Leader Is Seized By U.S. in Passport Case," *New York Times*, Dec. 10, 1939, p. 1; "Ship Plan Copied, Ex-Red Testifies," *New York Times*, Nov. 9, 1949, p. 34.

119 *Tilton visited Berlin*: Krivitsky, *In Stalin's Secret Service*, p. 129. Kolpakidi and Prokhorov, *Imperia GRU*, vol. 2, p. 421, also offers a biographical entry for Tilton.

119 *"A few million dollars' worth"*: Krivitsky, *In Stalin's Secret Service*, pp. 130–31.

119 *"the most genuine-appearing"*: "Flood of Fake Bills Is Traced to Russia," *New York Times*, Feb. 24, 1933, p. 1.

120 *"The national revolution"*: Friedrich, *Before the Deluge*, p. 140.

121 *More than thirty marchers*: For an examination of the violence and its victims, see Chris Bowlby, "Blutmai 1929: A Berlin Confrontation," *Historical Journal 29*, 1 (1986): 137–58.

121 *"Counterfeit $100 banknotes"*: "Fails to Show Soviet Counterfeited Notes," *New York Times*, Jan. 30, 1930, p. 11; Krivitsky, *In Stalin's Secret Service*, p. 119.

121 *General Berzin's men*: Krivitsky, *In Stalin's Secret Service*, pp. 116–38; Dallin, *Soviet Espionage*, pp. 393–96.

121 *Nerma went to get hers*: Nerma Oggins Passport Application, Apr. 7, 1930, Berlin; R.O. Papers.

122 *he had quit the party*: Rosenberg was a KPD member from 1920 to 1927 and a Reichstag deputy from 1924 to 1928. Telephone interview with Mario Kessler, Dec. 16, 2006. See also Kessler's recent biography, *Arthur Rosenberg: Ein Historiker im Zeitalter der Katastrophen (1889–1943)* [Arthur Rosenberg: A Historian In the Age of Catastrophe] (Köln: Böhlau Verlag, 2003).

122 *"splendiferous attire"*: Hook, *Out of Step*, p. 100.

123 *"Dear Sidney"*: John Dewey to Sidney Hook, 1928.07.25 (05717), in Larry A. Hickman, ed., *The Correspondence of John Dewey, 1871–1952*, 2d ed. (Charlottesville, Va.: InteLex Corp., 2005), vol. 2.

123 *"I wish Greenwich Village"*: Stephen J. Whitfield, *Scott Nearing: Apostle of American Radicalism* (New York: Columbia University Press, 1974), pp. 156–57.

123 *"GO TO SOVIET RUSSIA"*: Peter G. Filene, ed., *American Views of Soviet Russia, 1917–1965* (Homewood, Ill.: Dorsey, 1968), p. 141.

124 *"This is Moscow"*: Sidney Hook to Charlotte Hook, June 24, 1929; Hook Papers, Box 3, Folder 12, Hoover.

124 *The Comintern tried to install*: James R. Barrett, *William Z. Foster and the Tragedy of American Radicalism* (Urbana: University of Illinois Press, 1999), p. 157.

125 *"yellow eyes"*: Ella Wolfe, quoted in Ted Morgan, *A Covert Life: Jay Lovestone, Communist, Anti-Communist, and Spymaster* (New York: Random House, 1999), p. 91.

125 *"Who do you think you are?"*: Ibid., p. 99.

125 *"We not only responded"*: Hook, *Out of Step*, p. 99.

GULAG: 1940

129 *The NKVD tribunals*: Robert Conquest, *The Great Terror* (New York: Oxford University Press, 1990), p. 284.

130 *"You were arrested"*: Interrogation Report, May 9, 1939, FSB.

131 *"The accused has refused"*: Abakumov to Stalin and Molotov, May 21, 1947, TFR 18–20.

131 *a half-page document*: From Report No. 1, Special Tribunal of the People's Commissariat of Internal Affairs, Jan. 5, 1940, TFR 18–24.

131 *signed by the head*: Conquest, *The Great Terror*, p. 286, discusses the NKVD institution of "troikas," the three-man tribunals that Stalin introduced on July 30, 1937. The troikas streamlined the laborious process of sentencing. Oggins, however, was tried by an *Osoboe soveshchanie* (OSO) of the NKVD, an indication of the stature of his case.

132 *On January 16, 1940*: "Moscow-Ryazan-Oryol Convoy List," Jan. 16, 1940; Fond 18444, opis 2, delo 305, II. 36–7, RGVA.

132 *Almost always they departed*: There were, of course, exceptions. Four days after Oggins left the Lubyanka, an *etap* of thirteen Germans headed west to Brest-Litovsk, the border town en route to Berlin. The Germans, quite likely Communists stranded in Moscow after the Non-Aggression Pact of 1939, were handed over to the Nazis.

133 *476 camps*: Interview with Nikita Petrov, Memorial Society, Moscow, July 5, 2007. For a remarkable collection of statistics on the camps, guards, and prison contingent, see *GULAG: Glavnoe upravlenie lagerei: 1917 [sic]—1960, dokumenty* [The Gulag: The Main Directorate of Camps: Documents], compiled by Alexander Kokurin and Nikita Petrov (Moscow: Materik, 2000).

135 *the barge reached Dudinka*: Interviews with survivors of the Norilsk camps: Yulia Dorinskaya, Georgi Dorinsky, Josef Halski, Jadwiga Malewicz, Vera Pristupa, Vasily Romaskin, Igor Sobolyov, Olga Yaremchuk, and Olga Yaskina, Norilsk, Aug. 6–24, 2000; Bronius Zlatkus, Vilnius, Jan. 19, 2001; Jacques Rossi, Paris, Oct. 13, 2000, Apr. 18, 2001, Aug. 31, 2001. Interviews with Vasily Ksintaris, former head of the Dudinka port, Moscow, Sept. 6, 2000; Alexei Loginov, retired NKVD officer and former director of the Norilsk camps, Moscow, Aug. 28, 2000; Tatyana Lengyel, daughter of former Norilsk prisoner József Lengyel, telephone, Mar. 5, 2001. I have also relied on memoirs by the Norilsk survivors Valery Agranovsky, *Posledniy dolg* [The Last Duty] (Moskva: Akademia, 1994); A. A. Bayev, *The Paths of My Life*, *www.eimb.ru/English/history/bayev.htm*; Walter J. Cizsek, S.J., *With God in Russia* (New York: McGraw-Hill, 1964); Evfroseniia, Kersnovskaia, *Skol'ko stoit chelovek?* [How Much Is a Person Worth?] (Moskva: ROSSPEN, 2006); Unto Parvilahti, *Beria's Gardens: A Slave Laborer's Experiences in the Soviet Utopia* (New York: Dutton, 1960); Karlo Stajner, *Seven Thousand Days in Siberia* (New York: Farrar, Straus & Giroux, 1988).

138 *"The question of ferrous metals"*: May 1, 1925, *Izvestia*, p. 1.

CHAPTER 7. THE RED AND THE WHITE

146 *"A brilliant operation"*: Christopher Andrew and Oleg Gordievsky, *The KGB: The Inside Story of Its Foreign Operations from Lenin to Gorbachev* (New York: HarperCollins, 1990), p. 150.

147 *"Great movements"*: Ibid., p. 151.

147 *targeted three primary regions*: Christopher Andrew and Vasili Mitrokhin, *The Sword and the Shield: The Mitrokhin Archive and the Secret History of the KGB* (New York: Basic, 1999), p. 42.

150 *"for their integrity"*: Richard Sorge, quoted in Poretsky, *Our Own People*, p. 70.

150 *Dmitri Bystrolyotov*: Dmitri Alexandrovich Bystrolyotov went by the names Robert Grenville, Alexander Hallas, and at least a half-dozen other

aliases, but he was fondest of noble titles. Sent to the Norilsk camps in May 1939, he was released in 1954, after subsequent internment in other labor camps and prisons and at least one psychiatric hospital.

150 *"quickly became on close terms"*: Andrew and Mitrokhin, *The Sword and the Shield,* p. 44.

151 *Richard Sorge*: On Sorge (1895–1944), see Bryan T. Van Sweringen, ed., *The Case of Richard Sorge* (New York: Garland, 1989); Chalmers Johnson, *An Instance of Treason: Ozaki Hotsumi and the Sorge Spy Ring* (Stanford, Calif.: Stanford University Press, 1990); A. G. Fesiun, *Delo Rikharda Zorge: neizvestnye dokumenty* [The Case of Richard Sorge: The Unknown Documents] (Moskva: Letnii sad, 2000); Richard Whymant, *Stalin's Spy: Richard Sorge and the Tokyo Espionage Ring* (London: I.B. Tauris, 2006).

151 *He was one of six*: Two of the six were brothers, Mikhail and Berthold Umansky. Another was Fedia Fedin, alias Alfred Kraus. A fifth was Willy Stahl, alias "the Bear." Poretsky, *Our Own People*, pp. 5–26; Gary Kern, *A Death in Washington* (New York: Enigma, 2003), p. 12. Kolpakidi and Prokhorov, *Imperia GRU,* vol. 1, p. 102, lists the six "masters of Soviet espionage" from the town differently: "Alfred Glezner, Bertold Ilk [an alias for Bertold Umansky,], Mikahail Umansky, Wilhelm Stahl, Walter Krivitsky, and Ignatiy Reiss-Poretsky."

155 *"For Mother"*: Interview with Michel Romanoff, Paris, Apr. 6, 2006.

156 *Prince Fyodor Alexandrovich*: His sister Princess Irina of Russia was far better known. She married Prince Felix Yusupov, Rasputin's assassin, in 1914. Interview with Andrew Romanoff, Inverness, Calif., Apr. 3, 2007.

157 *"pronounced Semitic" types*: Princess Paley, *Memories of Russia, 1916-1919* (London: Herbert Jenkins, 1924), p. 88. Anti-Semitism runs deep in the memoirs, which first appeared as *Souvenirs de Russie* (Paris: Plon, 1923).

159 *The OGPU and GRU tried to infiltrate*: So effective was the *Comité* that Moscow created a front, the *Soyuz vozvrashcheniia* (Union for Repatriation), to lure White Russian émigrés; Kern, *Death in Washington*, p. 138. In an interview (Paris, Apr. 11, 2005), Dmitri Sezeman recalled how in 1936, when he was fourteen years old, his mother took him on a trip from Paris to the village of Hönefoss, Norway, where Trotsky was living at the time. Sezeman's mother and stepfather were NKVD operatives in Paris during the Ogginses' first residency in France; both worked in the Union for Repatriation with Sergei Efron, husband of the poet Marina Tsvetaeva. Sezeman and Tsvetaeva's son, Georgi (known as Mur), were best friends. In Hönefoss, Sezeman was sent to the door of a small house. "When I knocked," he recalled, "Lev Sedov opened the door—and there in the background, sitting by the fireplace, was Trotsky." His mother had used Sezeman as a decoy to confirm that Trotsky was living in the house. After the murder of Reiss in 1937, Sezeman's family fled to Moscow and lived with Efron, Tsvetaeva, and their children at a NKVD dacha outside

Moscow. In 1939 the NKVD arrested them all except for Sezeman, Tsvetaeva, and her son. Tsvetaeva committed suicide in 1942, Sezeman was
arrested in 1943, and his friend Mur was killed in the war in 1944.

161   *it had kept files*: At some point in the 1930s, Oggins had registered with the
      Paris police and been issued a *carte d'identité* valid until Nov. 9, 1940. The
      address on the card was 20 rue Cassette, a fashionable apartment build-
      ing near St. Sulpice.

161   *"The French said"*: Interview with Robert Conquest, Stanford, Calif., June
      15, 2004.

163   *To the horror*: The unraveling of the Switz ring was said to have led the
      French authorities to investigate 250 people. In the defendants' homes,
      police discovered a shortwave transmitter, photographic equipment and
      "moving picture machines" for filming documents, a darkroom, and even
      dressers and tables outfitted with secret compartments. Dallin, *Soviet Espi-
      onage*, pp. 60–67.

163   *"an exceptionally bookish"*: Janet Flanner [Genêt], *Paris Was Yesterday, 1925–1939*
      (New York: Harvest/HBJ, 1988), pp. 121–23. It is hard to imagine that
      Cy and Nerma did not know Stahl. In the late 1920s in New York, she
      had run a clandestine network of photographers and couriers. She had
      worked for Alfred Tilton, who arrived in New York in 1926 to replace
      Rakov/Wolf as the GRU *rezident*. She had received a master's degree at
      Columbia after Cy had left the university. During Cy and Nerma's time
      in Berlin, Stahl visited and renewed her passport at the U.S. consulate
      there in the fall of 1930.

164   *The Soviets were particularly keen*: Dallin, *Soviet Espionage*, p. 61.

164   *Izvestia noted*: *Izvestia* accused "rightest French circles, where many have
      refused up to now to reconcile themselves to the strengthening of
      French-Soviet relations, it appears tempting to inflate the case of the
      imaginary 'Soviet espionage' and thus distract attention from the Stavisky
      case and their part in it." Ibid., p. 66.

165   *"Two charming people"*: "Switzes Penitent, Says Paris Judge," *New York Times*,
      Apr. 1, 1934, p. 12.

165   *"I was tired"*: "Switz Terms Spies of Soviet Mercenary," *New York Times*, Apr.
      19, 1935, p. 12

165   *"I was hesitant"*: Ibid.

165   *The Aviator compromised*: Dallin, *Soviet Espionage*, p. 66; Nigel West, *MASK:
      MI5's Penetration of the Communist Party of Great Britain* (London: Routledge,
      2005), p. 230.

166   *boarded the SS Aquitania*: In his seventies, Robin remembered the boat's
      name. Nerma, however, had omitted the voyage on her passport applica-
      tions in 1934 and 1938. She claimed that the family had sailed from
      France on September 28, 1934, aboard the SS *Paris* to New York. Nerma
      may have had reason to lie. A Naum Eitingon, who claimed to be a Pol-

ish industrialist born in Orel, Russia, in 1899, was also onboard the *Aqui-tania.* This Eitingon was the namesake, and almost certainly a distant rel-ative, of the NKVD officer Naum Eitingon, who orchestrated Trotsky's assassination. The Eitingon family controlled the world's largest fur com-pany at the time, Eitingon-Schild. While accusations of complicity with the Soviet secret police have dogged the extended family for decades, they have been fiercely denied and never proven. The Naum Eitingon on the *Aquitania,* aged fifty-six at the time of the 1934 voyage, often sailed across the Atlantic—at least ten times between 1925 and 1939. That he and the Oggins family would take the same boat to New York in 1934 may have been coincidence. The fact, however, does little to quiet the debate about the relations between Soviet intelligence and the far-flung Eitingon family. The most contentious charges concern Max Eitingon (1881–1943), a psychoanalyst and one of Sigmund Freud's closest col-leagues, who served as a patron of Nadezhda Plevitskaya, the Russian émigré singer arrested in Paris after the kidnapping of General Miller. Plevitskaya and her husband, the double agent General Skoblin, had known Max Eitingon since their days in Berlin in the 1920s. After the singer's arrest, Max Eitingon tried to put forth his colleague Marie Bona-parte as a character witness at Plevitskaya's trial. He wrote several letters to Freud—published in *Sigmund Freud, Max Eitingon: Briefwechsel, 1906–1939* (Tuebingen: Edition Diskord, 2004)—arguing on the singer's behalf. Freud, for his part, was perplexed by the affair. In a letter to Freud dated Jan. 8, 1939, Eitingon condemned the French trial, comparing it to the Dreyfus case; *Briefwechsel,* pp. 915–18. On relations between the NKVD officer Naum Eitingon and his "prosperous relatives in Western Europe," see William Duff, *A Time for Spies* (Nashville: Vanderbilt University Press, 1999), p. 54. For a debate on the question of Max Eitingon's relationship to Plevitskaya and Skoblin, see Stephen Schwartz, "Intellectuals and Assassins—Annals of Stalin's Killerati," *New York Times,* Jan. 25, 1988; Theodore Draper, "The Mystery of Max Eitingon," *New York Review of Books,* Apr. 14, 1988; and their subsequent exchange, *New York Review of Books,* June 16 and Aug. 18, 1988. Robert Conquest weighed in with "Max Eitingon: Another View," *New York Times,* July 3, 1988, p. BR22.

BUTYRKA: 1942

169   *Llewellyn E. Thompson, Jr., and Francis Bowden Stevens:* Biographical and profes-sional information on Thompson and Stevens from interviews with vet-erans of the Moscow embassy in the 1930s and 1940s: James McCargar, Washington, D.C., Sept. 21, 2005; James W. Lewis, Washington, D.C., Nov. 11, 2002; Isaac Patch, telephone, June 22, 2005; and Thomas Whit-ney, telephone, May 4, 2002. Also interviews with Vladimir Toumanoff,

Washington, D.C., Feb. 23, 2004; Sherry Miller, telephone, Apr. 27, 2005; and Llewellyn E. Thompson, telephone, Mar. 4, 2003. Also correspondence with Sherry Miller, May 17, 2005; Nicholas Stevens, May 4, 2005, and June 7 and 13, 2005; U.S. Department of State, Office of the Historian, Apr. 18, 2003.

170   *The worst was the "kennel"*: Conquest, *The Great Terror*, pp. 277–78.

171   *"One fine morning"*: George F. Kennan, *Memoirs 1925–1950* (New York: Atlantic/Little, Brown, 1967), p. 84.

171   *Mr. Marjorie*: Interview with James W. Lewis, Washington, D.C., Nov. 11, 2002; David Mayers, *The Ambassadors and America's Soviet Policy* (New York: Oxford University Press, 1995), p. 40.

171   *"I never learned"*: Kennan, *Memoirs 1925–1950*, p. 84. Charles Bohlen, *Witness to History: 1929–1969* (New York: Norton, 1973), pp. 39–41, also notes the work of Kelley and the 1937 merger of the East European Division with the European Division in a White House–led purge that threatened to "dispose its valuable files and ship off for almost certain destruction the collection of newspapers, periodicals, and other literature that had been painstakingly assembled over the years."

172   *"very personal relationship"*: Arthur Hartman oral history, May 31, 1999, ADST, Foreign Affairs Oral History Project.

172   *"the best man"*: George F. Kennan, *At a Century's Ending* (New York: Norton, 1996), p. 23.

173   *the Roosevelt-Litvinov Agreement*: In a letter to Litvinov dated Nov. 16, 1933, FDR warned: "Let me add that American diplomatic and consular officers in the Soviet Union will be zealous in guarding the rights of American nationals, particularly the right to a fair, public and speedy trial and the right to be represented by counsel of their choice. We shall expect that the nearest American diplomatic or consular officer shall be notified immediately of any arrest or detention of an American national, and that he shall promptly be afforded the opportunity to communicate and converse with such national." The Soviets apparently never complied with the provision. As far as anyone at the State Department knew, Moscow had allowed U.S. diplomats to visit an American prisoner in a Soviet jail only twice before. *FRUS*, 1942, vol. 3 (Europe), pp. 768–70.

173   *"consular list"*: C. E. Dickerson, Jr., Kuibyshev, to Secretary of State, Washington, Jan. 9, 1943, "American Citizens Resident in the consular district of the Embassy as of January 1, 1943," 361.11 Citizens/12, p. 13, State Department Central File, RG 59, NARA-CP.

174   *"Black snow"*: Antony Beevor, *The Mystery of Olga Chekhova* (New York: Viking, 2004), p. 171, citing Vladimir Vladimirovich Knipper, *Pora galliutsinatsy* [A Time of Hallucinations] (Moscow: Spolokhi, 1995), p. 70.

174   *By late evening, as a blizzard*: Henry C. Cassidy, *Moscow Dateline: 1941–1943* (Boston: Houghton Mifflin, 1943), pp. 151–52.

174   *a mere twenty miles:* Charles W. Thayer, *Bears in the Caviar* (New York: Lippin-cott, 1950), pp. 219–31.

174   *"much in the way of food":* Clinton L. Olson oral history, Apr. 17, 1996, ADST, Foreign Affairs Oral History Project.

175   *an old three-story schoolhouse:* Ibid.; Interview with James L. Lewis, Washing-ton, D.C., Nov. 19, 2002.

175   *"where the Ritz Hotel":* Mayers, *The Ambassadors,* p. 133.

175   *"once the ornate":* William H. Standley and Arthur A. Ageton, *Admiral Ambas-sador to Russia* (Chicago: Regnery, 1955), p. 139.

176   *"There is always trouble":* Mayer, *The Ambassadors,* p. 142.

177   *"TELEGRAM RECEIVED":* Kuibyshev to Secretary of State, Telegram #130-11 a.m., Feb. 12, 1942, 361.1121/34, State Department Central File, RG 59, NARA-CP.

178   *"You are authorized":* Telegram, Sumner Welles to Kuibyshev, Apr. 15, 1942, 361.1121/34, p.2, State Department Central File, RG 59, NARA-CP.

178   *"Please take up this case":* Telegram, Cordell Hull to Kuibyshev, June 30, 1942, 361.1121/35, State Department Central File, RG 59, NARA-CP.

179   *"Oggins is now in Moscow":* Telegram, W. H. Standley to Secretary of State, Washington, Sept. 15, 1942, 361.1121/36, State Department Central File, RG 59, NARA-CP.

179   *"seek an appointment":* Telegram, #266-10 a.m., W. H. Standley to American Embassy Moscow, Sept. 15, 1942, 320-Oggins, Isaiah, RG 84, NARA-CP.

179   *"Foreign Office advises":* Telegram, #299-2 p.m., L.E. Thompson, Jr., to Kuibyshev, Sept. 18, 1942, 320-Oggins, Cy, RG 84, NARA-CP.

180   *For months they had prepped him:* During World War II, it could have taken months to travel by barge and train from Norilsk to Moscow. It is possi-ble, however, that Oggins was flown from the camps—an extraordinary flight from the Arctic at the height of the war. Whether brought by land or air, Oggins was kept out of sight for months in Moscow. One docu-ment seems to confirm that the Soviets kept him in prison for treatment before letting the U.S. diplomats meet with him. In 1998, the FSB reported to the Swedish-Russian Working Group investigating the case of Raoul Wallenberg, the Swedish diplomat abducted by the Soviets in Budapest in 1945, that in August 1942, Oggins was transported from the Norilsk camps to the Lubyanka, where he was imprisoned starting on Aug. 21; "FSB Answers to the Request Made by S. Mesinai on Nov. 30, 1998," correspondence with Susan Mesinai, Feb. 6, 2005.

181   *"allowed complete freedom":* Telegram, #409-4 p.m., L. E. Thompson, Jr., to American Embassy Kuibyshev, Dec. 9, 1942, 320-Oggins, Isaiah, p.1, RG 59, NARA-CP.

182   *"individuals residing in Soviet Russia":* Alan Cullison, "Stalin-Era Secret Police Documents Detail Arrest, Execution of Americans," *Los Angeles Times,* Nov. 9, 1997, p. 1.

183   *"Please endeavor":* Telegram, #409- 4 p.m., L. E. Thompson, Jr., to American

Embassy Kuibyshev, Dec. 9, 1942, 320-Oggins, Isaiah, p. 3, RG 84, NARA-CP.

184   *exchanging communiqués*: FRUS, Diplomatic Papers, 1942, vol. 3 (Europe), Dec. 8, 1942.

184   *"the Second Front"*: Walter Graebner to David Hulbard, July 25, 1942, *Time* Dispatches, First Series, Houghton Library, Harvard University.

184   *"Round Stalingrad"*: Joseph Stalin to Franklin Roosevelt, Dec. 6, 1942; reprinted in Susan Butler, ed., *My Dear Mr. Stalin: The Complete Correspondence of Franklin D. Roosevelt and Joseph V. Stalin* (New Haven, Conn.: Yale University Press, 2006), p. 102. FRUS, 1942, vol. 3 (Europe), has the same telegram in slightly different wording, owing to translation.

184   *Major General Patrick J. Hurley*: L. E. Thompson, Jr., sent the Hurley memorandum (nearly 10,000 words on the progress at Stalingrad) at 8 P.M., Dec. 8, 1942. FRUS, 1942, 668–73.

185   *Man of the Year*: "The trek of world dignitaries to Moscow in 1942 brought Stalin out of his inscrutable shell," *Time* wrote, and "revealed a pleasant host and an expert at playing his cards in international affairs. At banquets for such men as Winston Churchill, W. Averill Harriman and Wendell Willkie, Host Stalin drank his vodka straight, talked the same way." *Time*, Jan. 4, 1943, p. 23.

185   *"My impression"*: Telegram #409-4 p.m., L. E. Thompson, Jr., to American Embassy Kuibyshev, Dec. 9, 1942, 320-Oggins, Isaiah, p. 3, RG 84, NARA CP.

186   *"The impression gained"*: On the true nature of Oggins's visit to the USSR, neither Thompson nor Stevens was fooled. Stevens apprised Secretary of State Hull of his second interview with Oggins on Jan. 9, 1943: "From the applicant's statements it seems probable that he came to the Soviet Union with the assistance of agents of either the Soviet Union or another foreign power." "Opinion of Officer Taking Affidavit," found in "Form No. 213: Affidavit by Native American to Explain Protracted Foreign Residence" (Enclosure 2), sent, with "Passport Application of Isaiah Oggins" (Enclosure 1), in Despatch No. 37, L. E. Thompson, Jr. to Secretary of State, Jan. 11, 1943, "Subject: Transmitting passport application of Isaiah OGGINS," 130-Oggins, State Department Central File, RG 59, NARA-CP.

187   *"before the eventual release"*: Ibid., p. 2.

187   *"that a check-up be made"*: Untitled Memorandum [author's name redacted], State Department Political Division, Jan. 5, 1943, N.O. FBI Files.

CHAPTER 8. JOURNEY TO A WAR

189   *Hook, however, had left Carrie*: The couple separated in 1933 and soon divorced. Interview with John Hook, San Francisco, Aug. 13, 2003.

190   *"the black snake"*: Sidney Hook to Alan Wald, Feb. 4, 1985, p. 4, Hook Papers, Box 29, Folder 48, Hoover.

190   *"Radical unionism"*: *San Francisco Examiner*, Oct. 14, 1935, "Special Commemo-

rative Section," including a full-page, unsigned [unpaginated] advertisement extolling the importance of the shipping industry to the city.

191 *"fomenting strife"*: Ibid.

194 *The Japanese right wing*: On this point and others concerning Japan's imperial hunger in the 1930s, I am indebted to John Dower's "The Other Japanese Occupation," *The Nation*, July 7, 2003, pp. 11–14.

195 *"Foreigners came to Shanghai"*: Gerald Yorke, *China Changes* (New York: Scribner's, 1936), p. 26.

195 *"In no city"*: Aldous Huxley, *Jesting Pilate: An Intellectual Holiday* (New York: Doran, 1926), p. 271.

197 Histoire des arts anciens: Sirén's history was published by the Musée Guimet, home to the collection of Emile Guimet, one of the richest assemblies of Asian art in the West. It is likely that Cy also studied the Guimet's sculptures, paintings, and *objets*.

197 *a busy corner on the rue Wantz*: The corner was at one of the five crossing streets: rue Eugène Bard, rue Admiral Bayle, rue Brenier de Montmorand, rue Chapsal, or rue Dubail.

199 *a "listless depression"*: Yorke, *China Changes*, p. 59.

200 *"virginal naiveté"*: Jonathan D. Spence, *To Change China: Western Advisers in China 1620–1960* (New York: Penguin, 2002), p. 185.

201 *racial pyramid*: For an insightful history of the SMP, see Robert Bickers, *Empire Made Me: An Englishman Adrift in Shanghai* (London: Allen Lane, 2003), a biography of Maurice Tinkler, a British policeman who served in the British foreign police force in Shanghai in 1919.

201 *"suspected Soviet agents"*: SMP D 4718, Records of the Central Intelligence Agency, RG 263, SMP Files, NARA-CP. See also Bickers, *Empire Made Me*, p. 246.

201 *The SMP also caught*: On Noulens, see a work of deft historical sleuthing rare among studies of Soviet espionage in the 1920s and 1930s: Frederick S. Litten, "The Noulens Affair," *China Quarterly* 138 (June 1994): 492–512. I have also relied on Ruth Price, *The Lives of Agnes Smedley* (Oxford: Oxford University Press, 2005), pp. 217–24, which also details the case and Smedley's role in it.

201 *"A sub-agency"*: Robert F. Kelley to Mr. Secretary, July 12, 1932, 800.00B, Communist International/110, RG 59, cited in Price, *Agnes Smedley*, p. 218.

201 *"In general"*: Joseph Stalin to Vyacheslav Molotov, June 19, 1942, Letter 74 (author's translation); *Pisma I.V. Stalina V. M. Molotovu, 1925–1936 gg.: Sbornik dokumentov* [Letters of J. V. Stalin to V. M. Molotov, Collection of Documents] (Moskva: "Rossiia molodaia," 1995). The letter also appears in Lars T. Lih, Oleg V. Naumov, and Oleg Khlevniuk, eds., *Stalin's Letters to Molotov: 1925–1936* (New Haven, Conn.: Yale University Press, 1995), p. 229.

202 *"to assist Agnes Smedley"*: Harvey Klehr, John Earl Haynes, and Fridrikh Igorevich Firsov, *The Secret World of American Communism* (New Haven,

Conn.: Yale University Press, 1995), pp. 60–70, citing Earl Browder to Georgi Dimitrov, Sept. 2, 1935, 495-74-463, RGASPI. Original in English.

202   *"the Gorky of the Lower East Side"*: Michael Folsom, ed., *Mike Gold: A Literary Anthology* (New York: International, 1972), p. 10. Mike Gold's birth name was Itzok Granich.

202   *Eastern Publishing Company*: Also Far Eastern Publishing Company. D. S. Henchman to HBM Consulate-General, June 24, 1937, "Eastern Publishing Company and Max Granich," RG 263, SMP Files, NARA-CP.

203   *"radical to an extreme"*: SMP Report, June 24, 1937; p. 2, RG 263, SMP Files, NARA-CP.

203   *It is conceivable*: Oggins had at least one tie to the newspaper world in New York. In 1930, when he had just arrived in France, he enlisted the help of Ed Gottlieb, editor of the *Long Island Press*, to sponsor a letter of support from a member of Congress to Secretary of State Henry Stimson. The State Department special agents discovered the letter, dated Aug. 10, 1930, and questioned Nerma about it. She replied that Gottlieb had been "an old friend of her husband." Untitled Report, U.S. State Department, dated Jan. 5, 1943, p. 2, N.O. FBI Files.

203   *On November 30, 1936*: D. S. Henchman to HBM Consulate-General, "Eastern Publishing Company and Max Granich," June 24, 1937, RG 263, SMP Files, NARA-CP. The Graniches appeared before HUAC, Jan. 16–17, 1952.

203   *Often the journey posed risks*: One such voyage is described in a memoir by Frederick E. Landmann (1907–2003), *A Walk Through My Life*, privately published in 2004.

204   *The restoration*: "A New Act in a Weird Drama of Empire," *New York Times*, Feb. 25, 1934, p. SM3.

205   *"fat, defeated tribe"*: W. H. Auden and Christopher Isherwood, *Journey to a War* (London: Faber and Faber, 1939), p. 50.

206   *"the most modern city"*: "Will Rogers Reaches Dairen and Sees Relics of Other Wars," *New York Times*, Dec. 11, 1931, p. 29.

206   *"a sort of Japanese Hongkong"*: Peter Fleming, *One's Company: A Journey to China* (London: Jonathan Cape, 1934), p. 175.

207   *"The general atmosphere"*: Ibid.

207   *"the Manchukuo paradise"*: Wellington M. Ye, "Kings of Manchukuo," *Voice of China* I, 3 (Apr. 15, 1936): 17.

209   The Rote Kapelle: The CIA's historical study explained the origins of the name: " 'Rote Kapelle' ('Red Orchestra,' 'Red Band,' 'Red Choir,' or 'Red Chapel') was a cryptonym coined by the German central security office, the Reichsicherheitshauptamt (RSHA), to designate the Soviet networks of espionage and subversion discovered in Western Europe after the outbreak of the Russo-German war in 1941. The espionage reports

were transmitted primarily by radio. The 'music' on the air had its pianists (radio operators), a maestro in the field (the Grand Chef), and its conductor in Moscow (the Director)." U.S. Central Intelligence Agency, Counterintelligence Staff, *The Rote Kapelle: The CIA's History of Soviet Intelligence and Espionage Networks in Western Europe, 1936–1945* (Washington, D.C.: University Publications of America, 1979), p. xi.

209 *At first the CIA study*: Ibid., pp. 313–14. The CIA's book on the Rote Kapelle may have been authored by James M. Olson, a junior officer at the time. In "The Ten Commandments of Counterintelligence," a declassified article that appeared in *Studies in Intelligence*, unclassified edition, 11 (Fall-Winter 2001), n.p., published by the CIA's Center for the Study of Intelligence, Olson writes: "When I joined the CIA, one of my first interim assignments was with the old CI Staff. I found it fascinating. I was assigned to write a history of the *Rote Kapelle*, the Soviet espionage network in Nazi-occupied Western Europe during World War II." Available online at www.cia.gov.

212 *he had run Operation Korridor*: Max Steinberg left the USSR in 1923, moving to Belgium. From the late 1920s to the early 1930s he worked in France. For years he also worked in the Lubyanka, as a chief deputy to two of Stalin's secret police bosses. Steinberg makes several appearances in Russian memoirs. In 1931, Georgi Agabekov describes a scene in which Steinberg is called before a Lubyanka commission purging cadres in 1929. "They called in this Steinberg. A young fellow, a Jew from Bessarabia. He had only just started in the Foreign Department and ran the intelligence network in Rumania"; *Ch. K. za rabotoi* [The Cheka at Work] (Berlin: Izdatel'stvo "Strela," 1931), pp. 290–91. Steinberg, in Agabekov's account, had also by then worked in Belgium and France as a secret agent. Pavel Sudoplatov, in *Raznie dni tainoi voini i diplomatii* [Various Days of the Secret War and Diplomacy] (Moskva: OLMA, 2003), pp. 52–53, states that "Maks Steinberg worked for Vyacheslav Menzhinsky, on operation 'Corridor' in the late 1920s, exploiting émigré circles to infiltrate Western countries," adding that Steinberg took over the operation from A. Fyodorov, hero of the operation "Sindikat."

212 *Dr. Eugenio Carutti*: Carutti may have been a legitimate business partner who was used *v tyomnuiu* ("in the dark"), that is, kept unaware of the clandestine nature of Charles Martin & Co. Alternately, he could have been a knowing participant in the scheme. In the latter case, as seems probable, Carutti would have also been an NKVD operative.

213 *In the summer of 1935*: Charles Martin told the Swiss that they flew from Kaliningrad to Berlin, then on to Paris. In Paris, Carutti gave him 80,000 Swiss francs, his "first commission." From France the Martins went to Zurich, where Max deposited 50,000 francs into a Swiss bank account. They next traveled to Lausanne, where he registered with the

police and the army, paying a fine in lieu of military service. Then on to Lake Geneva and Italy, to conclude negotiations with the firms he would represent, before leaving for China. Swiss Dossier.

213   *The case of Mr. Roth*: Isaac Patch, *Closing the Circle: A Buckolino Journey Around Our Time* (Wellesley, Mass.: Wellesley Printing Services, 1996), p. 172.

214   *Freda Utley*: Freda Utley, *The Dream We Lost: Soviet Russia, Then and Now* (New York: John Day, 1940), p. 22.

214   *"Every Saturday Evening"*: Advertisement in *Manchuria* (fortnightly publication of *The Manchuria Daily News,* Dairen, Manchuria), July 15, 1936, p. 95.

215   *Three weeks earlier*: See Jonathon Spence, *The Search for Modern China* (New York: Norton, 1990), pp. 444–45. For a reevaluation of the conventional historical wisdom using Japanese military sources, see James B. Crowley, "A Reconsideration of the Marco Polo Bridge Incident," *Journal of Asian Studies* 22, 3 (May 1963): 277.

216   *"The only course"*: Spence, *Modern China*, pp. 445–46.

216   *"Dairen Scene"*: "Japan Faces Peril of War on 2 Fronts," *New York Times*, Aug. 14, 1937, p. 3.

218   *Several Caruttis did appear*: Telephone interview with Carlo Alberto Carutti, Mar. 4, 2007. In 1951, Dr. Eugenio Carutti's wife, Tatyana Yakoleff (Yakovleva), and their son, Marcello, left Italy and moved to Argentina. Marcello Carutti died in 2006; Tatyana died earlier. Marcello did, however, have a son, also named Eugenio Carutti, an astrologer living in Buenos Aries. The grandson, Eugenio Carutti, explained that he knew little of his grandfather's life and work. What he did know, however, was revealing. "My father and my grandmother," wrote Eugenio Carutti, "were terribly anti-Communist—and I never knew why." Correspondence, Mar. 28, 2007.

218   *"about one hundred in all"*: Telephone interview with Carlo Alberto Carutti, Mar. 4, 2007.

218   *"Charles Martin & Co."*: J. A. Cimperman, Legal Attaché (U.S. Embassy, London), to Bundespolizei, Bern, July 9, 1952, stamped "GEHEIM," translation from English, Swiss Dossier.

219   *"Mussolini was openly courting"*: "Italian Economic Mission in Manchuria," *Manchuria*, June 15, 1938, pp. 421–29.

219   *"1 FIAT file"*: "Inventaire, des pieces deposes par M. Charles Martin," dated Jan. 15, 1953, Lausanne, signed Insp. [Robert] Pache (Ministère Public Fédéral), Swiss Dossier.

219   *"The enterprise was involved"*: Cimperman to Bundespolizei, Swiss Dossier.

219   *"1,500 foreigners"*: "Current Events: Population," *Manchuria*, June 15, 1937, p. 355. Further statistics on nationalities: "What Races Inhabit Manchoukuo," *Manchuria*, Feb. 15, 1937, pp. 102–3; *The Japan–Manchoukuo Yearbook* (Tokyo: Japan–Manchoukuo Year Book, 1934–1941). The 1936 edition lists the figure as 134 American men and 92 American women.

Under Japanese visas issued to American visitors to Manchukuo, it lists 8 journalists, 268 businessmen, 49 missionaries, 49 diplomats; p. 656 (statistics as of June 30, 1935).

220 *General Khanzhin*: Mikhail Vasilievich Khanzhin (1871–1961) was a leader of the White army in Siberia who lived in Harbin from 1928 to 1930 and headed the Far Eastern branch of the White Russian Officers' Union (ROVS). From October 1933, Khanzhin worked for the South Manchurian Railroad as a cartographer. After the Soviets occupied Manchuria in World War II, he was arrested by SMERSH in Dairen on September 15, 1945, and spent a decade in the gulag.

220 *The force, however*: Correspondence with Akira Takizawa, May 12, 2006. Takizawa pointed me to the official history of the Manchukuoan Defense Forces, edited by veterans of the army: Ranseikai, ed., *Manshūkokugunshi* [History of the Manchukuoan Army] (Tokyo: Manshukokugun kankōkai, 1970).

220 *Cy and Max's operation*: The question of Italian aircraft manufacturers working with the Japanese regime in Manchukuo has not been closely studied by military historians of the period. Rana Mitter, a specialist at Oxford and author of *The Manchurian Myth: Nationalism, Resistance, and Collaboration in Modern China* (Berkeley: University of California Press, 2000), said in a telephone interview (Mar. 27, 2005), "Such a deal would seem an anomaly, but it's not impossible. The Japanese were eager to procure aircraft and loath to deal with the Americans, or Soviets." Mark Peattie, an expert on the Sino-Japanese war at the Hoover Institution, said in a telephone interview (May 11, 2006), "It seems an odd initiative, but one not inherently unimaginable." John W. M. Chapman, honorary senior research fellow of the University of Glasgow and author of "A Dance on Eggs: Intelligence and the 'Anti-Comintern,' " *Journal of Contemporary History* 22, 2 (Apr. 1987): 333–72, knew of the Japanese purchases. "The IJA bought aircraft models from Germany and Italy at this period," Chapman wrote, "partly because the IJAAF [Army Air Force] was technically inferior to IJNAF [Navy Air Force] and up to 1936 all its modern aircraft were imported or produced under foreign licence"; Correspondence, Nov. 20, 2006.

220 *After 1937, the Texan*: For a summary of Chennault's corps, see Spence, *To Change China*, pp. 228–41.

221 *"The aircraft now purchased"*: "Equipment Purchased by Italy," National Institute for Defense Studies, Defense Agency, Army, Dainikki, Ministry of War, Mitsu Dainikki, vol. 6, 1938, Reference Code: C01004464200. Available at www.jacar.go.jp; Japan Center for Asian Historical Records (JACAR), National Archives of Japan.

221 *"provided good insurance"*: Bericht, Schweizerische Bundesanwaltschaft, Polizeidienst, In Sachen: "RADO, FOOTE et consorts, espionage et emissions en faveur de Moscou", Insp. [Robert] Pache; Feb. 24, 1953, p. 8, Swiss Dossier.

CHAPTER 9. THE STAMP MARKET

226   *Only one or two of the agents*: Early defectors were Boris Bazhanov, Grigory Bessodovsky, and George Agabekov. All wrote memoirs. For a general overview, see Gordon Brook-Shepherd, *The Storm Petrels: The First Soviet Defectors 1928–1938* (London: Collins, 1977). The word "defector" was first used in Hanson W. Baldwin, "What We Know—and Do Not Know— About Russia," *New York Times*, Aug. 22, 1948, p. E3.

226   *Alexander Barmine*: See his memoir, *One Who Survived: The Life Story of a Russian under the Soviets* (New York: Putnam, 1945).

227   *"Up until this moment"*: Reiss's letter of July 17, 1937, is cited in Poretsky, *Our Own People*, pp. 1–3.

228   *"The Assistant Producer"*: The Kutepov and Miller cases have been extensively documented. Among the more detailed sources on the Kutepov kidnapping is one of the earliest, Boris Bazhanov, *L'Enlevement du General Koutepov* (Paris: Spes, 1930). For a scholarly treatment of the Miller case as the source for the Nabokov story (published in January 1943), see Gennady Barabtarlo, "Life's Sequel," *Nabokov Studies* 8 (2004): 1–21. The case also informed an Erich Rohmer Film, *The Third Agent*.

228   *Café les Deux Magots*: Krivitsky, *In Stalin's Secret Service*, p. 240.

228   *"For eighteen years"*: The full text of the quoted letter is found in the MI5 dossier on Krivitsky, PRO, KV/2/805, National Archives, UK. Within weeks the letter was published in Russian in Paris: *Begstvo ot Stalina*, "Flight from Stalin," in *Sotsialisticheskii vestnik*, Paris, No 23–24, (403–4), Dec. 24, 1937.

229   *Léon Sedov*: Sedov—Sedoff in the French spelling—was Trotsky's legal name. He had been born Bronstein. He took the name Sedov when he married Natalya Sedova. They had two children, Lev (Léon), born 1906, and Sergei, born 1908. In "Thermidor and anti-Semitism," an article dated Feb. 22, 1937, Trotsky explained the reason for the name change: "In order not to oblige my sons to change their name, I, for 'citizenship' requirements, took on the name of my wife (which, according to the Soviet law, is fully permissible)." See Irving Howe, ed., *The Basic Writings of Trotsky* (New York: Random House, 1963), pp. 206–15.

229   *Trotsky by then had left*: Of the dozens of books on Stalin's hounding of Trotsky, one of the most detailed is *With Trotsky in Exile, From Prinkipo to Coyoacan* (Cambridge, Mass.: Harvard University Press, 1978), by Jean van Heijenoort, a young French secretary and bodyguard.

229   *"The Robinson-Rubens affair"*: The *New York Times* reported extensively on the case, from "American Couple Vanish Mysteriously in Moscow," Dec. 10, 1937, p. 1, to "Passports of Reds Being Investigated," Oct. 22, 1939, p. 1.

229   *The Ikals had been recalled*: The Ikals left New York aboard the *Rex* on Oct. 16, 1937, and entered the USSR on Nov. 5. Part of Ikal's NKVD interrogation records, dated Jan. 8, 1939, are held in the Tanenhaus Papers, Box 46, Folder "Ikal, Arnold," Hoover.

230 *"100 to 150 passports"*: Krivitsky interview with Ruth Shipley of the State Department, June 28, 1939, cited in J. A. Cimperman to Freda M. Small, May 10, 1948; PRO, KV/2/805, Image Reference: 50, p. 5. Tanenhaus, *Whittaker Chambers*, p. 99, citing Chambers's "Faking," puts the figure at "at least 100 passports" produced each month.

231 *Poyntz had not been seen*: "Woman Communist Missing 7 Months; Disappearance of Miss Poyntz Made Known as Robinson Clue Is Sought Here," *New York Times*, Dec. 18, 1937, p. 10. See also Herbert Solow Papers, Box 10, Folder "Poyntz, Juliet Stuart, 1935–1940," Hoover; Herbert Solow, "Missing a Year!," *New Leader,* July 2, 1938; Dorothy Gallagher, "Disappeared," *Grand Street* 9, 2 (Winter 1990): 142–56.

231 *"an agent in New York for the receipt"*: Krivitsky interview with Ruth Shipley, cited in Cimperman to Small.

237 *dispatched two loyal agents*: One was Panteleimon Takhchianov, an intelligence officer known for his ruthlessness, and the other was Mikhail Alakhverdov, a loyal and high-ranking Armenian officer.

237 *Naum Eitingon*: Pavel Sudoplatov and Anatoli Sudoplatov, with Jerrold L. and Leona P. Schecter, *Special Tasks: The Memoirs of an Unwanted Witness—A Soviet Spymaster* (New York: Little, Brown, 1994), pp. 72–73; Pavel Sudoplatov, *Razvedka i Kreml': zapiski nezhelatel'nogo svidetelia* [Intelligence and the Kremlin: Notes of an Unwanted Witness] (Moskva: Geia, 1996), pp. 84–85. At least one source, A. I. Kolpakidi and Dmitrii P. Prokhorov, *KGB-prikazano likvidirovat': spetsoperatsii sovetskikh spetssluzhb 1918–1941* [The KGB Is Ordered to Liquidate: Special Operations of the Soviet Special Services] (Moskva: IAuza/EKSMO, 2004), p. 404, claims that Eitingon entered the United States on an Iraqi passport. Sudoplatov's account seems to indicate that Eitingon left France on a French passport.

238 *traveling as Frank Jacson*: Ship manifest, *Ile de France*.

238 *"in a terrible state"*: Joseph P. Kennedy to Cordell Hull, Sept. 8, 1939, Franklin D. Roosevelt Library (Hyde Park, New York), cited in Barbara Leaming, *John Kennedy: The Education of a Statesman* (New York: Norton, 2006), p. 92. In all, more than 100 people died in the incident, including 28 American citizens. More than 200 American citizens were rescued. See also Robert Dallek, *An Unfinished Life, John F. Kennedy, 1917–1963* (New York: Little, Brown, 2003); pp. 58–59.

239 *"amid the throng"*: Thomas Mann to Heinrich Mann, Nov. 26, 1939, in Hans Wysling, ed., *Letters of Heinrich and Thomas Mann, 1900–1949* (Berkeley: University of California Press, 1998), p. 229.

239 *"ordered home"*: "British Liner Athenia Torpedoed, Sunk; 1,400 Passengers Aboard, 292 Americans; All Except a Few Are Reported Saved," *New York Times,* Sept. 4, 1939, p.1.

CHAPTER 10. TRUTH WILL WIN

242 *"I have been patching them"*: Mrs. Merle Martin to N. Oggins, n.d.; R. O. Papers.

242 *8 Barrow Street*: New York City "Tax Photographs," Municipal Archives, New York, N.Y.

245 *"My dear Mrs. Oggins"*: Franklin C. Gowen, Asst. Chief, Special Division, Dept. of State, Mar. 4, 1943, to Mrs. Isaiah Oggins, R.O. Papers.

246 *"FUNDS REQUIRED"*: Western Union Telegram, Sumner Welles, Acting Secy of State, to Mrs. Isaiah Oggins, Mar. 9, 1943, R.O. Papers.

246 *"competent Soviet authorities"*: Franklin C. Gowen, Asst. Chief, Special Division, Dept. of State, June 22, 1943, to Mrs. Isaiah Oggins, R.O. Papers. The Soviets' decision not to reconsider the Oggins case is found in Diplomatic Note from the People's Commissariat for Foreign Affairs to U.S. Embassy, Moscow, June 9, 1943; transmitted June 10, 1943, W. H. Standley, Moscow Embassy, to Secretary of State, Washington, 320-Oggins, RG 84, NARA-CP.

247 *Ben Mandel was known*: Richard Merrill Whitney, *Reds in America* (New York: Beckwith, 1924), p. 173, reprinted the LDC letter listing Mandel and Berman on the letterhead. The letter also appeared in the Dies Committee's Appendix IX and was cited by the FBI; FBI New York Field Report, NY 100-45923, Jan. 28, 1947, p. 3, N.O. FBI files.

248 *He worked first*: At the Dies Committee, Mandel helped his boss, J. B. Matthews, the committee's lead investigator, compile witness lists. With Mandel by his side, Matthews built the country's longest list of alleged Communists and party front organizations. See Robert M. Lichtman, "J. B. Matthews and the 'Counter-subversives': Names as a Political and Financial Resource in the McCarthy Era," *American Communist History* 5, 1 (June 2006): 1–36.

248 *when his name first emerged*: "7 Teachers Face Contempt Action in School Inquiry," *New York Times,* June 6, 1941, p. 1; "Teacher Is Tried in Absentia As Red," *New York Times,* Sept. 18, 1941, p. 1.

248 *singing to the FBI*: Robert Gordon Switz testified before HUAC on Sept. 27 and 28, 1948, and Feb. 27 and Mar. 1, 1950, Transcripts of Executive Session Testimony, 1945-1974, RG 233, NARA-DC.

249 *"Note: When Loy Henderson interviewed"*: Tanenhaus, *Whittaker Chambers,* p. 162. Berle's notes became a government exhibit at Alger Hiss's second trial; see vol. 7 of the trial transcript, attachment to p. 3325.

250 *"ever employed by MI5"*: Kim Philby, *My Silent War* (New York: Grove, 1968), p. 105. The full quote is: "After Guy Liddell, Jane was perhaps the ablest professional intelligence officer ever employed by MI5 . . . Jane would have made a very bad enemy."

250 *It was a shock*: The Krivitsky case has inspired more than one book, and still the debate concerning his death endures. In addition to his 1939 mem-

oirs and *Saturday Evening Post* articles, two important works have recently appeared: Gary Kern, *A Death in Washington: Walter G. Krivitsky and the Stalin Terror* (New York: Enigma, 2003), a biography, and Gary Kern, ed., *MI5 Debriefing and Other Documents on Soviet Intelligence* (Riverside, Calif.: Xenos, 2004), a collection of documents relating to the case, including the transcript of his debriefing by British intelligence in January 1940.

250 *"Any fool can commit a murder"*: Whittaker Chambers, *Witness* (New York: Random House, 1952), p. 485. Louis Waldman devotes a chapter of his memoirs, *Labor Lawyer* (New York: Dutton, 1944), to the "suicide."

251 *"OGGINS"*: Handwritten telegram, N. Oggins to I. Oggins, enclosure to letter to J. D. Hickerson, Div. of European Affairs, State Department, Oct. 17, 1942, 361.1121/38, State Department Central File, RG 59, NARA-CP.

252 *"Oggins wants to go home"*: Telegram 409, L. E. Thompson, Moscow, to Kuibyshev, Dec. 9, 1942; Telegram 1080, L. Henderson, Kuibyshev, to Secretary of State, Dec. 11, 1942, 130—Oggins, Isaia "Desire of," State Department Central File, RG 59, NARA-CP.

252 *"I recieved your message"*: F. C. Gowen, Asst. Chief, Special Division, State Department, to Mrs. Isaiah Oggins, Jan. 1, 1943, R.O. Papers.

252 *"I send my deepest love"*: F. C. Gowen, Asst. Chief, Special Division, State Department, to Mrs. Isaiah Oggins, Jan. 22, 1943, R.O. Papers.

252 *"searched this name"*: Handwritten "Memo for P.D." [Political Division] by [FNU] Siegel, Feb. 17, 1942, Division of Communication and Records, State Department, 361.1121 Oggins-I, State Department Central File, RG 59, NARA-CP.

253 *T. F. Fitch and Daniel H. Clare*: On Fitch's biographical and professional details, correspondence with Doris (Fitch) Scott, June 25, 2005, and Sept. 10, 2005; "Thomas Freeman Fitch Retirement," U.S. Department of State, press release, May 19, 1950. On Clare, telephone interview (Aug. 15, 2005) and correspondence (July 27, 2005) with Richard Clare.

253 *"IT IS POSSIBLE"*: Telegram 173, Sumner Welles to American Embassy, Kuibyshev, Apr. 15, 1942, 361.1121/34, State Department Central File, RG 59, NARA-CP.

254 *"It is believed"*: Untitled memorandum [author's name redacted], State Department Political Division, Jan. 5, 1943, N.O. FBI Files. The State Dept. memorandum led the FBI to initiate its investigation; J. Edgar Hoover to SAC NYC; "SUBJECT: MRS. NERMA OGGINS, INTERNAL SECU-RITY-R," Mar. 8, 1943, N.O. FBI Files. Nerma Oggins was interviewed by Daniel H. Clare, State Department special agent, on Mar. 23, 1943.

255 *"With obvious relish"*: Bohlen, *Witness to History*, p. 41.

255 *"HAVE COURAGE"*: Paraphrase of telegram, N. Oggins to I. Oggins, Telegram 269, Cordell Hull, Washington, to American Embassy, Moscow, Apr. 30, 1943, 130-Oggins, State Department Central File, RG 59, NARA-CP.

256 *"second mission to Moscow"*: William H. Standley and Arthur A. Ageton, *Admi-*

ral Ambassador to Russia (Chicago: Regnery, 1955), p. 365. Standley offers a blistering account of Davies's visit and its "oil of publicity" for his book and film. See also *New York Times*: "Stalin Gets Letter from Roosevelt; Davies Talks with Soviet Leader", May 21, 1943, p. 1; "Russians Not to See 'Mission To Moscow,' " July 21, 1943, p. 12; "J. E. Davies Objects to Story on 'Mission,' " July 24, 1943, p. 7. For an account of the film as a U.S. government effort to overcome domestic distrust of the USSR and to curry favor with Stalin, see Todd Bennett, "Culture, Power, and Mission to Moscow Film and Soviet-American Relations during World War II," *Journal of American History* 88, 2. (Sept. 2001): 489–518.

256   *"no leaders of a nation"*: Ronald Radosh and Allis Radosh, *Red Star Over Hollywood: The Film Colony's Long Romance with the Left* (San Francisco: Encounter, 2005), p. 100; David Culbert, ed., *Mission to Moscow*, Wisconsin/Warner Bros. Screenplay Series (Madison: University of Wisconsin Press, 1980).

256   *"competent Soviet authorities"*: Telegram 639, W. H. Standley to Secretary of State, June 10, 1943, 361.1121/41, State Department Central File, RG 59, NARA-CP. "Competent" was the official State Department translation. The Russian, *sootvetstvuyushchie organy*, should be translated as "corresponding organs." A Soviet bureaucratic term, it usually refers to the intelligence or law enforcement services.

257   *"those funny little men"*: "It's the Gremlins That Delay the 'El' Now; Thousands Affected Mutter Just the . . . ," *New York Times*, Jan. 9, 1943, p. 15.

258   *"a long lanky lean"*: Irwin Shapiro, *The Gremlins of Lieut. Oggins* (New York: Julian Messner, 1943), n.p.

259   *A former colleague*: Telephone interview with Ann McGovern, Mar. 10, 2005.

259   90 Percent of the People: Shapiro's play was undated and marked "194-?," but its political references, in particular to the "O'Connell Peace Act" pending before Congress, makes it clear that it was written in 1938. The sketch was intended as anti-isolationist propaganda.

259   *"First thing you should know"*: Telephone interview with Jonathan S. Shapiro, Mar. 14, 2007.

260   *"to try and oil"*: Bill MacDonald, *The True Intrepid: Sir William Stephenson and the Unknown Agents* (Vancouver: Raincoast, 2001), p. 239.

260   *"BIRTHDAY GREETINGS"*: N. Oggins to Cordell Hull, July 17, 1944, 361.1121/7-1744; State Department Central File, RG 59, NARA-CP.

262   *"Dear Mr. Marshall"*: Robin Oggins to George Marshall, Enclosure to N. Oggins to G. Marshall, Mar. 3, 1947, 361.1121/3-347; State Department Central File, RG 59, NARA-CP.

263   *Hoover's men believed*: FBI NY Field Report, 100-191369, June 28, 1946, pp. 1–2; citing FBI NY Field Report, 100-187340, Aug. 6, 1945, "in the case entitled 'Ruth Domino Jerusalem, WAS; Internal Security-R.' It is shown that upon her arrival in the United States in 1941, she took up residence with Mrs. NERMA OGGINS at 8 Barrow Street, New York

City. RUTH JERUSALEM is now residing with ANGELA IDA MAR-JORIE JUDITH CARMEL HAYDEN GUEST, a member of the Communist Party of Great Britain and formerly a nurse with the International Brigade in the Spanish Civil War." N.O. FBI Files.

263   *"reported wife of Gerhard Eisler"*: FBI NY Field Report, NY 100-45923, Jan. 28, 1947, p. 2: "Testifying before a Visa Committee on June 21, 1944, RUTH DOMINO JERUSALEM, alleged propaganda agent of the USSR and reported wife of GERHARD EISLER, stated that she resided with one NERMA OGGINS at 8 Barrow Street, New York City." Ruth was either not telling the truth or misinformed; by June 1944, Nerma had moved to Fifteenth Street. On FBI interview of Ruth Jerusalem: FBI Field Report, NY 100-45923; Apr. 26, 1948, p. 8: "RUTH D. JERUSALEM, who formerly lived with NERMA OGGINS, was recently interviewed by agents of the Philadelphia Office regarding her knowledge of NERMA OGGINS with whom she lived in February of 1942, but she claimed that she knew nothing of Mrs. OGGINS other than that she was a woman of good moral and social character." N.O. FBI Files.

264   *"Angela Ida Marjorie"*: FBI Field Report, NY 100-45923, Nov. 5, 1947, p. 3, N.O. FBI Files.

264   *"A theosophist"*: Bertrand Russell, *Autobiography of Bertrand Russell* (London: Allen & Unwin, 1968), vol. 2, p. 102, cited in Stephen White, "British Labour in Soviet Russia, 1920," *English Historical Review* 109, 432 (June 1994): 627.

264   *"Everyone is afraid to speak"*: Haden Guest, *Fabian News*, Aug. 1920, pp. 33–34, cited in White, "British Labour," p. 629.

265   *"over five-sixths"*: M. Y. Lang, in Carmel Haden Guest, ed., *David Guest: A Scientist Fights for Freedom (1911–1938)*, (London: Lawrence & Wishart, 1939), p. 85.

265   *"with a hammer and sickle"*: Maurice Cornforth, in ibid., p. 97.

265   *the first Communist cell*: Ibid., p. 98.

265   *"pierced by the bullet"*: Ibid., p. 195.

265   *She was also reported*: NY Field Report, NY 100-45923, Nov. 5, 1947, pp. 3–4: "It is pointed out that ANGELA GUEST also was receiving mail at 8 Barrow Street, New York City as of August 8, 1942, and it is probable that NERMA OGGINS is acquainted with her inasmuch as OGGINS did not move from 8 Barrow Street until the expiration of her lease on October 1 1942." The same report (p. 4): "As of September 2, 1947 [name redacted] reported that GUEST had been attending monthly meetings of the Sacco-Vanzetti Club of the Communist Party at 273 Bleecker Street, New York City, since April, 1947." N.O. FBI Files.

266   *On June 26, a call was placed*: Ibid., p. 3.

266   *"Page 3 of referenced report"*: Boston FBI Field Report, 100-22161, Dec. 6, 1947, p. 2, N.O. FBI Files.

EXECUTION

269   *the summer of 1947*: Although there is no known date of death for Isaiah
      Oggins, it may have been July 5, 1947. The available evidence remains
      inconclusive and the official Soviet accounts differ. The Soviet Foreign
      Ministry in March 1948 provided a death certificate to the U.S. embassy.
      Certificate No. 008576, issued on Jan. 20, 1948, purportedly by the reg-
      istration bureau of the town of Penza, claims that Oggins had died nearly
      a year earlier, on Jan. 13, 1947, and that his death was recorded on Jan. 30,
      1947. A copy of this certificate was among the documents given to the
      U.S. government by the Russian government in September 1992 (TFR
      18-28). At the National Archives in College Park, Maryland, I found a
      second copy of this certificate (Despatch 298, Mar. 25, 1948; Moscow
      Embassy to Washington). The dates and certificate numbers on the two
      documents were identical. In 2006, however, the FSB provided a photo-
      copy of a different death certificate to Robin Oggins. According to Cer-
      tificate No. 008548, Isaiah Oggins died on Jan. 14, 1947, the death was
      registered on Jan. 15, 1947, and the certificate was issued—also by the
      Penza registration bureau—on Jan. 17, 1948. Both certificates were falsi-
      fied. No. 008548, however, appears to be a recent falsification. The paper
      contains no watermarks, even though it bears the imprint "Goznak," the
      state printing house, which only produced paper with watermarks (inter-
      views with Vadim Birstein, New York, Oct. 29, 2007, and Nikita Petrov,
      Moscow, July 5, 2007).
         Although neither death certificate gives the true date of Oggins's
      death, General Volkogonov may have inadvertently revealed it to the
      American side of the Joint POW/MIA Commission. In a session on
      Sept. 21, 1992, he spoke of an American citizen killed by the Soviets,
      "FNU [first name unknown] Anderson," and gave his death date as July
      5, 1947. Volkogonov referred to Anderson as "entirely without guilt"—a
      phrase that frequently accompanied official Soviet descriptions of
      Oggins. Moreover, in September 1992, the KGB archivist Vladimir
      Vinogradov stated that Oggins was killed "in July 1947"; Ken Fireman,
      "Russia Details Americans' Deaths," *Newsday*, Sept. 25, 1992, p. 15. He is
      the only known official to give a date of execution.
         A further clue may found in an internal report unearthed in the Soviet
      Foreign Ministry archives: Memorandum "No. 131/USA," dated January
      31, 1947, from V. I. Bazykin in the USA Department to V. G. Dekanozov,
      then the department head, entitled "Questions That May Be Raised by
      the U.S. Ambassador [Walter Bedell] Smith in His Meeting with Com-
      rade Molotov, 10 July 1947." The memorandum reveals the fear at the
      highest levels of the Soviet government that Washington, at an upcoming
      summit of foreign ministers, would again raise the question of Oggins's
      whereabouts after the expiration of his prison sentence. The prisoner's

"liquidation," then, would have occurred on the eve of the Molotov-Smith meeting. The memorandum is cited in Vladimir Pozniakov, "Taynaia voyna Iosifa Stalina: Sovetskie razvedyvatel'nye sluzhby v SSHA nakanune i v nachale kholodnoi voiny, 1943–1953" ["The Secret War of Joseph Stalin: Soviet Intelligence Services in the U.S. on the Eve and Start of the Cold War, 1943–1953"], in *Stalinskoe desiatiletie kholodnoi voiny* [*The Stalinist Decade of the Cold War*] (Moskva: Nauka, 1999), fn. 6, p. 201.

269 *his journey through the prisons*: The precise record of Oggins's internment in the USSR from 1943 to his death remains to be discovered. In 1992, Russian government sources claimed that he had last been in a prison in the town of Penza and hence had been buried in a cemetery there. That scenario, while possible, seems unlikely. There is a far greater likelihood that he was returned, at least after World War II, to the Butyrka Prison. In 1998, the FSB, in written responses to questions from the Swedish-Russian Working Group investigating the Wallenberg case, stated that Oggins was imprisoned after January 1943 "in the Butyrka Prison until December 1946 when he returned to the Internal [Lubyanka] Prison"; "FSB Answers to the Request Made by S. Mesinai on Nov. 30, 1998," correspondence with Susan Mesinai, Feb. 6, 2005.

270 *"toxicological laboratory"*: Vadim Birstein, *The Perversion of Knowledge: The True Story of Soviet Science* (Cambridge, Mass.: Westview, 2002), p. 97. Of the historical works on Soviet intelligence that describe the laboratory, Birstein's study offers the most detailed history of the laboratory and Mairanovsky.

271 ptichki: Interview with Vladimir Bobrenov, Moscow, Sept. 3, 2003.

271 *"loss of voice"*: Mairanovsky testimony quoted in V. Bobrenov, *Doktor Smert', ili Varsonof'evskie prizraki* [Doctor Death, or The Ghosts of Varsonofyevsky Lane] (Moscow: Olimp, 1997), pp. 256–57, cited in Birstein, *Perversion of Knowledge,* p. 116. On curare, see Will H. Blackwell, *Poisonous and Medicinal Plants* (Englewood Cliffs, N.J.: Prentice Hall, 1990).

CHAPTER 11. THE NOTE TO STALIN

273 *Yeltsin had summoned Toon*: Ambassador Straus took notes of the meeting in the Kremlin. His report went not only to the State Department but to the White House. Straus reported Yeltsin's revelations concerning the Oggins case, and in closing wrote, "After disclosing details like that, Yeltsin wondered whether some people still have doubt about Russia's desire to find out the fate of each and every American." Straus Notes, Toon Papers, Container 2, LOC. On the Kremlin and White House meetings and the work of the POW/MIA Commission: telephone interview with Malcolm Toon, Mar. 18, 2004.

275 *"Our archives have shown"*: Jim Wolf, "Yeltsin Hits Raw Nerve in U.S. with Vietnam Prisoner Report," Reuters, June 16, 1992.

275 *"the highest priority"*: Gene Gibbons, "Bush Confident Russians Will Clear Up POW Mystery," Reuters, June 16, 1992.

276 *"cynicism"*: Straus Notes, Toon Papers, Container 2, LOC.

276 *"not averse to taking"*: Alexander Solzhenitsyn, *The Gulag Archipelago 1918–1956*, trans. Thomas P. Whitney and Harry Willets (New York: HarperCollins Perennial, 2002), p. 60.

277 *Translated into English*: TFR 18–20 to TFR 18–22; available at lcweb2.loc .gov/frd/tfrussia/tfrhtml/tfr018–1.html. The U.S. government translation differs slightly from mine. The text as quoted retains the original State Department translation for *sootvetstvuyushchie sovetskie organy*— "*competent* Soviet authorities"—for the sake of consistency.

280 *"Isaiah H. Oggins"*: Celestine Bohlen, "Advice of Stalin: Hold Korean War P.O.W.'s", *New York Times*, Sept. 25, 1992, p. A10. The name Oggins had appeared in the Russian press earlier. Throughout the summer of 1992, news of Volkogonov's search in the archives leaked into the Russian press. On July 23 and 25, *Trud* published two articles under the headline "Murders Were Ordered in the Kremlin," about Pavel Sudoplatov. On July 23, *Trud* revealed Sudoplatov's letter of appeal to the 23rd Party Congress in 1966, which had been found in the archives of the Central Committee. On July 25, *Trud* named the American prisoner executed by Sudoplatov as "Oggin." On July 30, *Izvestia* printed a story, promising "Possible Sensations" regarding Americans in the USSR during the cold war. On July 31, *Rossiiskaya gazeta*, the new state newspaper, published Volkogonov's list of twenty-five U.S. citizens who may have still been residing in the former USSR. On Aug. 2, *Moskovskie novosti* published the Sudoplatov exposé, naming Oggins. On Aug. 9, the English-language version of the article ran in the *Moscow News*. On Aug. 13, *Izvestia* published a column by Volkogonov, "The Search Continues for American Citizens on the Territory of the ex-USSR," mentioning Abakumov's 1947 note to Stalin.

The news soon went overseas. On Aug. 13, Reuters ran an article by Jonathan Lyons, citing the *Izvestia* story and the *Moscow News* story to name Oggins. On Aug. 14, the *Chicago Sun-Times* and the *Baltimore Sun* published the Lyons report: "Stalin OK'd Postwar Killing of American" (*Sun-Times*, p. 15; *Baltimore Sun*, p. 3A). Throughout the fall of 1992, a number of U.S. news accounts of Volkogonov's revelations mentioned the Oggins case. The reports often misspelled the surname Oggins—rendering it as Ogens, Oggens, or Oginz, among other variations—largely because of inaccurate transliterations in the Russian. Isaiah, similarly, became Isaak, Isaac, Ysai, or even, as in the first POW/MIA Commission translations, Esau. See "Russia Says It Holds No Living U.S. Missing," Associated Press, Sept. 22, 1992; TASS, Sept. 23, 1992 (Toon Papers, Container 2, Tab 28, LOC); "U.S.-Russian POW Team Reveals Deaths of Two Americans," Reuters, Sept. 23, 1992; ABC News report by David Ensor, Sept. 24, 1992; Michael Dobbs, "U.S. POW Prober 'Not Satisfied,' He Tells

Yeltsin,' Kremlin Meeting Fails to Resolve Fate of Korean War Prisoners," *Washington Post,* Sept. 24, 1992, p. A20; "Russian Tells of Americans' Fate," *New York Times,* Sept. 24, 1992, p. A3; Ken Fireman, "Russia Details Americans' Deaths," *Newsday,* Sept. 25, 1992, p. 15; Vasilii Kononenko, "*Bez Vesti Propavshie Amerikantsy Pogibli v Stalinskikh Lageryakh*" [Americans Disappeared Without Trace, Died in Stalin's Camps], *Izvestia,* Sept. 24, 1992; Vladimir Strakhov, "*Slishkom Mnogo Znali*" [They Knew Too Much], *Kuranty,* Sept. 24, 1992; Elizabeth Shogren, "No Evidence of American POWs in Russia," *Los Angeles Times,* Sept. 25, 1992, p. A7; Fred Hiatt, "Stalin, Mao Plotted to Hold U.S. POWs; Joint Probers Say They Lack Proof 1950s Plan Was Carried Out," *Washington Post,* Sept. 25, 1992, p. A22; Jon Auerbach, "Mass. Native Was Executed in Soviet Gulag, Panel Says," *Boston Globe,* Sept. 25, 1992, p. 2.

On Nov. 7, 1992, *Trud* published Abakumov's 1947 note to Stalin under the headline, "*On Slishkom Mnogo Znal*" ["He Knew Too Much"]. On Nov. 11, Reuters followed with "Yeltsin Adviser Says Six Americans Held During Korean War," by Jim Adams, which reported, "Volkogonov's interpreter quoted him as saying . . . a man named Oggins was supposed to be released but Stalin ordered him executed on the grounds that he knew too much." On Nov. 12, the *New York Times* listed Oggins in a report on Volkogonov's Senate testimony: Steven A. Holmes, "Moscow Says Some G.I.'s Held in Camps Are Alive," Nov. 12, 1992, p. A5.

In 1994, when the Sudoplatov memoirs were published in English, one reporter picked up his allegations on the Oggins case: Paul Quinn-Judge, "Ex-Soviet Spy Stirs Debate," *Boston Globe,* May 8, 1994, p. 25. In addition, Arkady Vaksberg published three articles on Sudoplatov's revelations in *Literaturnaia gazeta:* "*Nemoi zagovoril*" [The Mute One Has Spoken], No. 23 (5503), June 8, 1994, p. 12; "*Spetsgruppa tovarishchei*" [A "Special Group" of Comrades], No. 30 (5510), July 27, 1994, p. 12; "*Svidetel' po delu o sebe*" [Witness in the Case About Himself], No. 38 (5620), Sept. 18, 1996. Vaksberg, citing Soviet documents—"Archival-Investigative *delo* OS 101257" and "V. 2, Criminal Case OS 101257"—reported that Sudoplatov and Eitingon not only organized the Oggins murder but witnessed it.

280 *"because he had seen too much":* Volkogonov testimony, *Hearings on Cold War, Korea, WWII POWS: Hearings Before the Select Committee on POW/MIA Affairs,* U.S. Senate, 102d Congress, 2d session, Nov. 10 and 11, 1992 (Washington, D.C.: Government Printing Office, 1993), pp. 322–47.

281 *"You're doing the Lord's work":* Meeting notes, Jan. 14, 1993, Toon Papers, Container 4, Tab 20, LOC. The notes also concern another of Volkogonov's purported discoveries: the absence of incriminating documents in the Soviet archives relating to Alger Hiss. In the fall of 1992, Volkogonov created a furor when he declared in a videotaped interview with John Lowenthal that Hiss was innocent. Volkogonov based his conclusion on

his examination of the archives, where "not a single document—and a great amount of materials has been studied—substantiates the allegation that Mr. Hiss collaborated with the intelligence service of the Soviet Union"; Sam Tanenhaus, "The Hiss Case Isn't Over Yet," *New York Times,* Oct. 31, 1992, p. 1.21. The Toon Papers (Container 2, Tab 31, LOC) record an exchange at a Sept. 21, 1992, reception in Moscow in which Volkogonov tells Toon, "An old man by the name [of] Alger Hiss Noble [*sic*] wrote to me that [he] was accused of being a spy in the US and spent 5 years in prison and wondered if in my research I could find proof to exonerate him from the spy charges. I will answer him in a half official way, by saying that as a historian I cannot find any documents stating he was a Soviet spy. Let the old man pass away in peace."

Materials from Toon's debriefing in Washington, D.C., Oct. 27–28, 1992, during which he met with Robert Gates, CIA director, among others, include notes by Major General Bernand Loeffke, Pentagon representative on the POW/MIA Commission, which record Volkogonov as saying, "The American press keeps asking me about Alger Hiss. I did not look at all the files. There may be something somewhere else. I only looked at some of the archives"; Container 3, Tab 18, Toon Papers, LOC.

281 *"Likvidatsia, of course"*: Interview with Anatoli Sudoplatov, Moscow, Sept. 7, 2003.

282 *"on balance, Stalin"*: Poll taken on the 50th anniversary of Stalin's death by the All-Russian Public Opinion Center (VTsIOM), Mar. 4, 2003.

282 *"in the pay of foreign intelligence"*: *Pravda,* cited in Amy Knight, *Beria: Stalin's First Lieutenant* (Princeton N.J.: Princeton University Press, 1993), p. 218.

283 *"strong-acting chemicals"*: Birstein, *The Perversion of Knowledge,* p. 447. The second charge was "abuse of office." Mairanovsky was arrested on Dec. 13, 1951, sentenced on Feb. 14, 1953; Mairanovsky Vladimir Prison Cards, cited in ibid., pp. 446–49.

284 *"which hung on him"*: Anatol Marchenko, *Moi pokazaniia* [My Testimony] (Paris: Presse Libre, 1969), p. 147; cited in B. G. Menshagin, *Vospominaniia: Smolensk-Katyn-Vladimirskaia tiurma* [Memoirs: Smolensk–Katyn–The Vladimir Prison] (Paris: YMCA, 1988), pp. 209–10.

284 *handler and hangman even shared*: Sudoplatov and Steinberg were cellmates in Corpus 2, Cell 32; telephone interview (Mar. 2, 2006) and correspondence (Mar. 5, 2007) with Marvin W. Makinen. See also Marvin W. Makinen and Ari D. Kaplan, *Cell Occupancy Analysis of Korpus 2 of the Vladimir Prison,* Report Submitted to the Swedish-Russian Working Group on the Fate of Raoul Wallenberg (Chicago, Ill.), Dec. 15, 2000, available at www.raoulwallenberg.net.

Anatoli Marchenko, Boris Menshagin, and Revolt Pimenov also recorded their memories of Steinberg in prison. See Marchenko, *My Testimony* (New York: Dutton, 1969); Menshagin, *Vospominaniia*; Pimenov,

Vospominaniia, 2 vols.; "Dokumenty po istorii dvizheniia inakomys-liashchikh" [Memoirs; "Documents from the History of the Dissident Movement"] (Moskva: Informatsionno-ekspertnaia gruppa "Panorama," 1996). Pimenov published an earlier version of the memoirs under a pseudonym, "O. Volin": "S Berievtsami vo Vladimirskoi tyur'me" ["With the Beria Men in the Vladimir Prison"], in *Minuvshee. Istoricheskii al'manakh* (Paris: Atheneum, 1989), pp. 357–72. The Menshagin and Pimenov memoirs, in Russian, are available at www.sakharovcenter.ru.

284   "*betraying the Motherland*": Pavel Sudoplatov, *Razvedka*, p. 467.

284   *Max was shuffled*: In fewer than eight years in the Vladimir Prison, Stein-berg was moved eighteen times.

284   "*luxury apartment*": Marchenko, *My Testimony*, p. 157.

285   "*Things were not easy*": Interview with Anatoli Sudoplatov, Moscow, Sept. 7, 2003.

285   "*eliminating the enemy*": Sudoplatov, *Razvedka*, pp. 331–32.

286   Special Tasks: The book, cowritten with his son Anatoli, appeared in 1994 and stirred a worldwide sensation. It was written and published with the aid of an American couple, Leona and Jerrold Schecter, the for-mer a literary agent, the latter a journalist and author who served as *Time* magazine's Moscow bureau chief (1968–1970), National Security Council spokesman under President Carter, and coeditor of the third volume of Nikita Khrushchev's memoirs in English. *Special Tasks* became a lightning rod in the debate over the Soviets' reach into the Manhattan Project. Above all, Sudoplatov alleged that J. Robert Oppenheimer, Niels Bohr, Enrico Fermi, and Leo Szilard had knowingly aided Soviet intelligence. The criticism was robust. David Holloway, a military histo-rian and expert on the Soviet atomic program, wrote, "Almost nothing in these charges stands up to scrutiny"; "Charges of Espionage," *Science*, n.s. 264, 5163 (May 27, 1994): 1346–47. In an interview with *Nezavisimaya gazeta* days before his death, Sudoplatov himself seemed to backtrack. Oppenheimer and Bohr, he said, were "sources of information, but never Soviet spies"; "Soviet Spymaster Pavel Sudoplatov Dies at 89," Associated Press, Sept. 26, 1996. Sudoplatov is an often contradictory—and inaccurate—witness. In 1992, when he began to record his oral his-tory, he was eighty-five years old and in poor health. The Russian and English editions of his memoirs, moreover, often diverge. Nonetheless, his voice remains essential to any attempt to reconstruct and understand the machinery of Stalin's terror.

286   "*The West by then*: Sudoplatov, *Razvedka*, pp. 331–32.

286   "*Today, recalling this man*": Ibid., p. 332; The English-language edition of Sudoplatov's memoirs is not as revealing: "Looking back at this episode, I feel sorry for him; but in those Cold War years we did not concern our-selves with what methods were used to eliminate people who knew too

much"; Pavel Sudoplatov and Anatoli Sudoplatov, with Jerrold L. and Leona P. Schecter, *Special Tasks: The Memoirs of an Unwanted Witness—A Soviet Spymaster* (New York: Little, Brown, 1994), p. 282.

287   *"the people who were in charge"*: Sudoplatov, *Razvedka*, p. 163.

288   *"A second-category"*: F. Orekhov, Ministry of Foreign Affairs, USSR, to E. Durbrow, Moscow Embassy, Jan. 7, 1948, trans. G. F. Reinhardt, PC 320-1948, RG 84, NARA-CP.

CHAPTER 12. AFTERLIFE

290   *"It's just the price"*: Matt Chayes, "Retiring Harpur Scholar Has No Regrets," *Binghamton University Pipe Dream*, Apr. 8, 2003, pp. 3, 6.

292   *"We have been unable to locate"*: William Daniels to Robin Oggins, Dec. 31, 1992, R.O. Papers.

294   *"Mr. Oggins was captured"*: M. Naito to N. Oggins, Feb. 15, 1957, R.O. Papers.

295   *"Oggins had come to the Soviet Union"*: Ken Fireman, "Russia Details Americans' Deaths," *Newsday*, Sept. 25, 1992, p. 15.

295   *"You can never escape"*: Ruth Werner, *Sonya's Report*, trans. Renate Simpson (London: Chatto and Windus, 1991), pp. 297–98.

295   *On February 10, 1949*: Report of FBI interview with Esther Chambers, Feb. 10 and 11, 1949; FBI File NY 65–14920 (Serial 3230, Doc. #84, May 17, 1949), p. 205; Tanenhaus Papers, Box 38, Folder "Esther Chambers," Hoover.

296   *In case after case*: From 1942 to 1957, Nerma Oggins's name appeared in FBI investigations, including the 1957 arrests that resulted from the cooperation of Boris Morros, a Hollywood producer who served as a Soviet agent before becoming a double agent for the FBI in 1947. The investigations often relied on previous reports, sometimes even BOI reports dating from as far back as the early 1920s.

297   *Nerma proved surprisingly "cooperative"*: FBI Office Memorandum, SA [name redacted] to SAC, NEW YORK (65-14822) (#6-C), Subject: Jacob Albam, Espionage-R (MOCASE), Apr. 24, 1957, p. 2, N.O. FBI Files.

298   *"We were looking"*: Telephone interview with David Othmer, Aug. 18, 2006.

BIBLIOGRAPHY

NOTE: All materials collected during the research of this book will be made available for public use at the Hoover Archives in Stanford, California.

PRIVATE COLLECTIONS AND PUBLIC LIBRARIES (UNITED STATES)

Association for Diplomatic Studies and Training, Arlington, Va.: Frontline Diplomacy: The U.S. Foreign Affairs Oral History Collection

Columbia University Archives: Columbia student and faculty registries, course bulletins, yearbooks, 1916–1923; *The Jester, The Spectator,* and *The Morningside;* Papers of Randolph Bourne; Papers of Bennett Cerf; Papers of Joseph Freeman

Cornell University, Kheel Center for Labor: International Ladies' Garment Workers' Union Archives

Georgetown University Library, Special Collections: Walter Ciszek, S.J., Collection.

Harvard University, Houghton Library Archives: Papers of Randolph Bourne; Papers of Ruth Fischer; Papers of Alger Hiss (Langdell Law Library); Papers of John Reed; Papers of Boris Souvarine; Papers of Leon Trotsky

Hoover Institution Archives: Papers of Paul Crouch; Papers of David Dallin; Papers of Ralph de Toledano; Papers of George H. Herron; Papers of Sidney Hook; Papers of Maxim Lieber; Papers of Jay Lovestone; Papers of Herbert Solow; Papers of Sam Tanenhaus; Papers of Karl Wittvogel

Library of Congress, Manuscripts Reading Room: FBI file on the House Committee on Un-American Activities; Papers of Charles E. Bohlen; Papers of W. Averell Harriman; Papers of Loy Henderson; Papers of Owen Lattimore; Papers of William H. Standley; Papers of Malcolm Toon; Records of the Communist Party of the USA, 1914–1920

New York Public Library, Manuscripts and Archives: New Theatre League Records, 1932–42 (Performing Arts/Theatre Special Collections); "The Pageant of America" Photograph Archive (Photography Collection); Papers of David Dallin; Papers of Babette Deutsch; Papers of Norman Thomas; Papers of Louis Waldman

New York University, Robert F. Wagner Labor Archives, Tamiment Institute Library: Archives of the Rand School; Papers of Simon Gerson; Papers of Mike Gold; Papers of Grace and Max Granich; Papers of Algernon Lee; Papers of Norman Thomas; Socialist and Radical Pamphlet Collection

Swarthmore College, Swarthmore College Peace Collection: Papers of H.W.L. Dana; Papers of Scott Nearing

Teacher's College, New York: NYC Board of Education Records

Truman Library: Oral history of G. Frederick Reinhardt; Papers of Charles W. Thayer

University of Connecticut, Storrs: Papers of Walter Snow

University of Oregon, Special Collections and University Archives: Papers of Grace Hutchins; Papers of Anna Rochester

University of North Carolina, Chapel Hill: Papers of Katherine Du Pre Lumpkin

University of South Carolina: Papers of Grace Lumpkin

GOVERNMENT ARCHIVES (UNITED STATES)

FBI Reading Room: Central Files; "Cointelpro," CPUSA; Whittaker and Esther Chambers Documents; Maxim Lieber Documents; Field Office Files (FOIA)

National Archives, Washington, D.C., College Park, Md., and New York, N.Y.: U.S. State Department Records: Central Files, Moscow Embassy Files, Records of Dairen Consulate, Shanghai Company Registration Files, Shanghai Correspondence; CIA Records, Shanghai Municipal Police Records, Raymond E. Murphy Collection on International Communism, 1917–1958, Passenger Lists (New York, New York), 1922–1939; Records of the House Un-American Activities Committee, 1945–75; Records of the Special Subcommittee to Investigate the Administration of the Internal Security Act and Other Internal Security Laws, 1951–77, more commonly known as the Senate Internal Security Subcommittee (SISS); Naturalization Certificates

National Security Agency, National Cryptological Museum Library: MASK Archive, transcripts of coded Comintern messages between Moscow and Europe, 1934–1937, captured by the British Government Communications Headquarters

New York State Archives: Archives of the Lusk Commission; Rand School Seized Files; Soviet Bureau in New York Seized Files

New York City Municipal Archives: Marriage, Birth, and Death Certificates; Collection of "Tax Photographs"; Civil Service Lists

ARCHIVES IN OTHER COUNTRIES

China: Beijing: Archives of the Chinese Communist Party; Shanghai: Archives of the French Concession and International Settlement

England: National Archives (Public Record Office)

France: Archives of the Sûreté Generale; *Poslledniye novosti* (émigré newspaper)

Germany: Archives of the German Communist Party (SAPMO); Berlin Landesarchiv; Bundesarchiv; Archive of Charlottenburg and Wilmersdorf; Humboldt University Archive

Holland: International Institute of Social History; Papers of Boris Souvarine

Japan: Japan Center for Asian Historical Records (JACAR), National Archives of Japan

Russia: Moscow: APRF, Archive of the President of the Russian Federation; FSB and SVR, Archives of the Russian Security and Foreign Intelligence Services; GARF, State Archives of the Russian Federation; MEMORIAL, Archive of the Memorial Society; RGASPI, Russian Archive of Social and Political History; RGVA, Russian State Military Archive

Norilsk: Norilsk Museum and Memorial Society Collections

Krasnoyarsk: Ministry of the Interior, Noril'lag Prisoner Index (Gulag *Kartoteka*)

Switzerland: Schweizerisches Bundesarchiv; Archives of Contemporary History, Institute of History, Federal Institute of Technology; Archives of the Swiss Federal Foreign Police (E 4301), Federal Persecutor (E 4320 B), and Foreign Department (E 2001 C); Cantonal Archives (Archives cantonales vaudoises)

BOOKS AND ARTICLES

Agabekov, George. *OGPU: The Russian Secret Terror.* Translated by Henry W. Bunn. New York: Brentano's, 1931. Reprint: Westport, Conn.: Hyperion, 1975.

Akhmedov, Ismail. *In and Out of Stalin's GRU: A Tatar's Escape from Red Army Intelligence.* Frederick, Md.: University Publications of America, 1984.

American Trade Union Delegation to the Soviet Union. *Soviet Russia in the Second Decade: a Joint Survey by the Technical Staff of the First American Trade Union Delegation.* New York: John Day, 1928.

Andrew, Christopher. *Secret Service: The Making of the British Intelligence Community.* London: Heinemann, 1985.

——, and Oleg Gordievsky. *The KGB: The Inside Story of Its Foreign Operations from Lenin to Gorbachev.* New York: HarperCollins, 1990.

——, and Vasili Mitrokhin. *The Sword and the Shield: The Mitrokhin Archive and the Secret History of the KGB.* New York: Basic, 1999.

Anglo-Russian Parliamentary Committee (Great Britain). *Raid on Arcos Ltd. and the Trade Delegation of the U.S.S.R. Facts and Documents.* London: 1927. 50 p. Microfilm. New York: Columbia University Libraries, 1997.

Auden, W. H., and Christopher Isherwood. *Journey to a War.* London: Faber & Faber, 1939.

Bailey, Geoffrey [pseud.]. *The Conspirators.* New York: Harper, 1960.

Baldwin, Roger N. *Liberty Under the Soviets.* New York: Vanguard, 1928.

Barmine, Alexandre. *Memoirs of a Soviet Diplomat: Twenty Years in the Service of the U.S.S.R.* Westport, Conn.: Hyperion, 1973.

————. *One Who Survived: The Life Story of a Russian Under the Soviets.* New York: Putnam, 1945.

Barron, John. *Operation Solo: The FBI's Man in the Kremlin.* Washington, D.C.: Regnery, 1996.

Barrett, James R. *William Z. Foster and the Tragedy of American Radicalism.* Urbana: University of Illinois Press, 1999.

Baum, Vicki. *Shanghai '37.* Translated by Basil Creighton. New York: Doubleday, Doran, 1939.

Bayerlein, Bernhard. *Les Partis communistes et l'Internationale communiste dans les années 1928–1932.* Boston: Kluwer, 1988.

————. *Les Partis communistes et l'Internationale communiste dans les années 1923–27.* Boston: Kluwer, 1981.

Bazhanov, Boris. *Bazhanov and the Damnation of Stalin.* Translated by David W. Doyle. Athens: Ohio University Press, 1990. Published in French as *Avec Stalin dans le Kremlin,* Paris: Les Editions de France, 1930; in German as *Der rote Diktator, von seinen ehemaligen Privatsekretaer,* Berlin: Editions P. Aretz, 1931.

————. *L'Enlèvement du Général Koutepov.* Paris: Spes, 1930.

Beal, Fred C. *Proletarian Journey.* New York: DaCapo, 1971 [c. 1937].

————. *The Red Fraud, an Expose of Stalinism.* New York: Tempo, 1949.

————. *Word from Nowhere: The Story of a Fugitive from Two Worlds.* London: R. Hale, 1937.

Beardsley, Thomas R. "Willimantic: Textile City." *Connecticut History* 42, 2 (Fall 2003): 97–104.

————. *Willimantic Industry and Community: The Rise and Decline of Connecticut Textile City.* Willimantic, Conn.: Windham Textile & History Museum, 1993.

————. *Willimantic Women: Their Lives and Labors.* Willimantic, Conn.: Windham Textile & History Museum, 1990.

Beck, F., and W. Godin [pseud.]. *Russian Purge and the Extraction of Confession.* Translated by Eric Mosbacher and David Porter. New York: Viking, 1951.

Bender, Thomas. *New York Intellect: A History of Intellectual Life in New York City, from 1750 to the Beginnings of Our Own Time.* New York: Knopf, 1987.

Bentley, Elizabeth. *Out of Bondage.* London: R. Hart-Davis, 1952. Reprinted as *Out of Bondage: The Story of Elizabeth Bentley,* New York: Ivy, 1988.

Beria, Sergo Lavrentevich. *Beria, My Father: Inside Stalin's Kremlin.* Edited by Francoise Thom. Translated by Brian Pearce. London: Duckworth, 2001.

Bern, Gregory G. *Behind the Red Mask.* Los Angeles: Bern, 1947.

Bessedovsky, Grigorij. *Im Dienste der Sowjets. Erinnerungen.* Leipzig: Grethlein, 1930.

Bey, Essad [Lev Nussibaum]. *OGPU: The Plot Against the World.* New York: Viking, 1933.

————. *Stalin: The Career of a Fanatic.* New York: Viking, 1932.

Bickers, Robert. *Empire Made Me: An Englishman Adrift in Shanghai.* London: Allen Lane, 2003.

Birstein, Vadim. "Eksperimenty na lyudiakh v stenakh NKVD" [Experiments on Humans Behind the Walls of the NKVD]. *Chelovek* (May 1997): 114–32.

———. *The Perversion of Knowledge: The True Story of Soviet Science.* Cambridge, Mass.: Westview, 2002.

Blackstock, Paul. *The Secret Road to World War II: Soviet versus Western Intelligence 1921–1939.* Chicago: Quadrangle, 1969.

Bloor, Ella Reeve. *We Are Many: An Autobiography by Ella Reeve Bloor.* New York: International, 1940.

Blunden, Godfrey. *A Room on the Route.* New York: Lippincott, 1947.

Bobrenev, Vladimir. *Doktor Smert', ili Varsonof'evskie prizraki* [Doctor Death, or The Ghosts of Varsonofyevsky Lane]. Moskva: Olimp, 1997.

Bobrenev, Vladimir, and Valerii Riazantsev. "Varsonof'evskie prizraki" [The Ghosts of Varsonofyevsky Lane]. *Rodina* (Fall 1995): 52–57.

———. *Palachi i zhertvy* [Executioners and Victims]. Moskva: Voennoe izd–vo, 1993.

Bohlen, Charles. *Witness to History: 1929–1969.* New York: Norton, 1973.

Boltunov, Mikhail. *Agenturoi GRU ustanovleno* [The GRU Network Has Established]. Moskva: Russkaia razvedka, 2003.

Bourne, Randolph. *The Radical Will: Selected Writings, 1911–1918.* Edited by Olaf Hansen. Berkeley: University of California Press, 1992.

———. *War and the Intellectuals: Collected Essays, 1915–1919.* Edited by Carl Resek. Indianapolis: Hackett, 1999.

Boyle, John Hunter. *China and Japan at War, 1937–1945: The Politics of Collaboration.* Stanford, Calif.: Stanford University Press, 1972.

Braun, Otto. *A Comintern Agent in China, 1932–1939.* Translated by Jeanne Moore. Stanford, Calif.: Stanford University Press, 1962.

Brook-Shepherd, Gordon. *The Storm Birds: Soviet Postwar Defectors, The Dramatic True Stories, 1945–1985.* New York: Henry Holt, 1989.

———. *The Storm Petrels: The First Soviet Defectors, 1928–1938.* London: Collins, 1977.

Broué, Pierre. *Léon Sedov, fils de Trotsky, victime de Staline.* Collection "La Part des hommes." Paris: Editions Ouvrières, 1993.

Browder, Earl. "The American Communist Party in the Thirties." In *As We Saw the Thirties: Essays on Social and Political Movements of a Decade,* pp. 216–53. Edited by Rita J. Simon. Urbana: University of Illinois Press, 1967.

———. *Communism in the United States.* New York: International Publishers, 1935.

Brown, Anthony Cave, and Charles B. MacDonald. *On a Field of Red: The Communist International and the Coming of World War II.* New York: Putnam, 1981.

Buckmiller, Michael, Dietrich Heimann, and Joachim Perels. *Judentum und Politische Existenz: Siebzehn Portraets Deutsch-Juedischer Intellektueller.* Hannover: Offizin, 2000.

Budenz, Louis. *The Bolshevik Invasion of the West: Account of the Great Political War for a Soviet America.* Linden, N.J.: Bookmailer, 1966.

———. *Men Without Faces: The Communist Conspiracy in the U.S.A.* New York: Harper, 1950.

Bullitt, William C. "How We Won the War and Lost the Peace." *Life*, August 30, 1948, p. 94.

———. *It's Not Done.* New York: Harcourt, Brace, 1926.

Burmeister, Alfred. *Dissolution and Aftermath of the Comintern.* New York: Research Program on the U.S.S.R., 1955.

Butler, Nicholas Murray. *Butler's Commencement Addresses.* Edited by David Andrew Weaver. Alton, Ill.: Shurtleff College, 1951.

———. "The Russian Revolution." Address at a Meeting at the Hudson Theatre, New York, April 23, 1917, under the auspices of the National Institute of Arts and Letters. Washington, D.C.: Carnegie Endowment for International Peace, 1917. Reprinted in *A World in Ferment: Interpretations of the War for a New World*, pp. 206–18. Edited by Nicholas Murray Butler. New York: Scribner's, 1917.

Cannon, James Patrick. *American Stalinism and Anti-Stalinism.* New York: Pioneer, 1947.

———. *Notebook of an Agitator.* New York: Pioneer, 1958.

Carr, E. H. *Twilight of the Comintern, 1930–1935.* New York: Pantheon, 1982.

Carter, Miranda. *Anthony Blunt: His Lives.* New York: Farrar, Straus, and Giroux, 2001.

Cassidy, Henry C. *Moscow Dateline: 1941–1943.* Boston: Houghton Mifflin, 1943.

Cerf, Bennett. *At Random: The Reminiscences of Bennett Cerf.* New York: Random House, 1977.

Chambers, Whittaker. "The Faking of Americans." Unpublished manuscript. Papers of Herbert Solow, Hoover Archives.

———. "Welcome, Soviet Spies!" Unpublished manuscript. Papers of Herbert Solow, Hoover Archives.

———. *Witness.* New York: Random House, 1952.

Chase, William J. *Enemies Within the Gates?: The Comintern and the Stalinist Repression, 1934–1939.* New Haven, Conn.: Yale University Press, 2002.

Chikov, Vladimir. *Razvedchiki-nelegaly* [Intelligence Agents and Illegals]. Moskva: Eksmo: Algoritm-kniga, 2003.

———. *Russkie nelegaly v SSHA* [Russian Illegals in the U.S.A.]. Moskva: Eksmo: Algoritm-kniga, 2003.

Ciszek, Walter J. *With God in Russia.* New York: McGraw-Hill, 1964.

Clark, Evans. *Facts and Fabrications about Soviet Russia.* New York: Rand School of Social Science, 1920.

Conquest, Robert. *The Great Terror.* New York: Oxford University Press, 1990.

———. *Inside Stalin's Secret Police: NKVD Politics 1936–39.* Stanford, Calif.: Hoover Institution Press, 1985.

Coox, Alvin. *Nomonhan: Japan Against Russia, 1939.* Stanford, Calif.: Stanford University Press, 1985.

Cornell, Frederic. "A History of the Rand School of Social Science, 1906–1956." Ed.D. dissertation, Columbia University Teachers College, 1976.

Costello, John, and Oleg Tsarev. *Deadly Illusions: The KGB Orlov Dossier Reveals Stalin's Master Spy.* New York: Crown, 1993.

Counts, George S. *A Ford Crosses Soviet Russia.* Boston: Stratford, 1930.

———. *The Soviet Challenge to America.* New York: John Day, 1931.

Cowley, Malcolm. *Exile's Return: A Literary Odyssey of the 1920s.* New York: Viking, 1951.

Cullison, Alan. "How Stalin Repaid the Support of Americans." Associated Press, November 9, 1997.

Cutler Schwartz, Rachel. "The Rand School of Social Science, 1906–1924: A Study of Worker Education in the Socialist Era." Ed.D. dissertation, State University of New York at Buffalo, 1984.

Dallin, David J. *Soviet Espionage.* New Haven, Conn.: Yale University Press, 1955.

Damaskin, Igor, with Geoffrey Elliott. *Kitty Harris: The Spy with Seventeen Names.* London: St. Ermin's, 2001.

Davies, Joseph E. *Mission to Moscow.* New York: Pocket Books, 1943.

Deakin, F. W., and G. R. Storry. *The Case of Richard Sorge.* London: Chatto & Windus, 1966.

Dement'eva, Irina. *Tovarishch Zorge: dokumenty, vospominaniia, interv'ie o podvige sovekskogo razvedchika* [Comrade Sorge: Documents, Memoirs, and Interviews Concerning the Triumph of a Soviet Agent]. Moskva: Sovetskaia Rossiia, 1965.

Dennis, Peggy. *Autobiography of an American Communist: A Personal View of a Political Life, 1925–1975.* Westport, Conn.: L. Hill, 1977.

Deriabin, Peter, and Joseph C. Evans. *Inside Stalin's Kremlin.* Washington, D.C.: Brassey's, 1998.

———, and Frank Gibney. *The Secret World.* New York: Doubleday, 1959.

De Toledano, Ralph. *Spies, Dupes and Diplomat.* New Rochelle, N.Y.: Arlington House, 1967.

Dewey, John. *Impressions of Soviet Russia and the Revolutionary World.* New York: New Republic, 1929.

Dies, Martin. *The Trojan Horse in America.* New York: Dodd, Mead, 1940.

Dilling, Elizabeth Kirkpatrick. *The Red Network: A "Who's Who" and Handbook of Radicalism for Patriots.* Chicago: self-published, 1934.

Dimitrov, Georgi. *The Diary of Georgi Dimitrov, 1933–1949.* Edited by Ivo Banic. New Haven, Conn.: Yale University Press, 2003.

Dodd, Martha. *My Years in Germany.* London: Gollancz, 1941.

———. *Through Embassy Eyes.* New York: Harcourt, Brace, 1939.

Dodd, William E. *Ambassador Dodd's Diary: 1933–1938.* New York: Harcourt, Brace, 1941.

Dolgun, Alexander, and Patrick Watson. *Alexander Dolgun's Story: An American in the Gulag.* New York: Knopf, 1975.

Dong, Stella. *Shanghai: The Rise and Fall of a Decadent City.* New York: Morrow, 2000.

Draper, Theodore. *American Communism and Soviet Russia.* New Brunswick, N.J.: Transaction, 2003.

————. *A Present of Things Past.* New Brunswick, N.J.: Transaction, 2002.

————. *The Roots of American Communism.* New York: Viking, 1957.

————. "Sidney Hook's Revolution." *New York Review of Books*, April 9, 1998.

Duff, William. *A Time for Spies.* Nashville, Tenn.: Vanderbilt University Press, 1999.

Dumbadze, Evgenii. *Na sluzhbe Cheka i Kominterna: lichnyia vospominaniia* [In the Service of the Cheka and Comintern: Personal Remembrances]. Orange, Conn.: Antiquary, 1986.

Enstad, Nan. *Ladies of Labor, Girls of Adventure: Working Women, Popular Culture, and Labor Politics at the Turn of the Twentieth Century.* New York: Columbia University Press, 1999.

Epstein, Edward Jay. *Dossier: The Secret History of Armand Hammer.* New York: Random House, 1996.

Farrell, James T. *Sam Holman.* Buffalo, N.Y.: Prometheus, 1983.

Feklistov, Alexander, and Sergei Kostin. *Man Behind the Rosenbergs.* New York: Enigma, 2001.

Fesiun, A. G. *Delo Rikharda Zorge: neizvestnye dokumenty* [The Case of Richard Sorge: The Unknown Documents]. Moskva: Letnii sad, 2000.

First, Wesley, ed. *Columbia Remembered.* New York: Columbia University Press, 1967.

————. *University on the Heights,* New York: Doubleday, 1969.

Fischer, Ben C. *Okhrana: The Paris Operations of the Russian Imperial Police.* History Staff, Center for the Study of Intelligence, Central Intelligence Agency, 1997.

Fischer, Benjamin B. "Farewell to Sonia, the Spy Who Haunted Britain." *International Journal of Intelligence and Counterintelligence* 15, 1 (January 2002): 61–76.

Fischer, Ruth. *Stalin and German Communism.* Cambridge, Mass.: Harvard University Press, 1948.

Fleming, Peter. *One's Company: A Journey to China.* London: Jonathan Cape, 1934.

Flicke, Wilhelm F. *Die Rote Kapelle.* Hilden/Rhein: Vier-Bruecken Verlag, 1949.

————. *War Secrets in the Ether.* Translated by Ray W. Pettengill. 2 vols. (microform). Fort Meade, Md.: Office of Training Services, National Security Agency, June 1959. Reissued by Aegean Park Press, Laguna Hills, Calif. 1994.

Foote, Alexander. *A Handbook for Spies.* London: Museum Press, 1949.

Fox, Dylan Ryan. *The Decline of Aristocracy in the Politics of New York.* New York: Columbia University Press, 1918.

————. *Herbert Levi Osgood: An American Scholar.* New York: Columbia University Press, 1924.

Freeman, Joseph. *An American Testament: A Narrative of Rebels and Romantics.* New York: Farrar & Rinehart, 1936.

————. *The Soviet Worker: An Account of the Economic, Social and Cultural Status of Labor in the USSR.* New York: Liveright, 1932.

Freud, Sigmund, and Max Eitingon. *Briefwechsel 1906–1939.* 2 vols. Tübingen: Edition Diskord, 2004.

Friedrich, Otto. *Before the Deluge: A Portrait of Berlin in the 1920s.* New York: Harper & Row, 1972.

Gay, Peter. *Weimar Culture: The Outsider as Insider.* New York: Harper & Row, 1968.

Gentry, Curt. *J. Edgar Hoover: The Man and the Secrets.* New York: Norton, 1991.

Gide, André. *Back from the U.S.S.R.* London: Secker and Warburg, 1937.

Gitlow, Benjamin. *I Confess: The Truth About American Communism.* New York: Dutton, 1939.

———. *The Whole of Their Lives.* New York: Scribner's, 1948.

Gold, Michael. *Jews Without Money.* New York: Avon, 1965.

———. *Mike Gold: A Literary Anthology.* Edited by Michael Folsom. New York: International, 1972.

Gorman, George. *Manchoukuo, the World's Newest Nation: Facing Facts in Manchuria.* Moukden: Manchuria Daily News, 1932.

Gouzenko, Igor. *The Iron Curtain.* New York: Dutton, 1948.

———. *This Was My Choice.* 2d ed. Montreal: Palm, 1968.

Grant, Natalie, with John Dziak. *Murder in the Tiergarten: The Political Life of Vladimir Orlov, Intelligence Agent and Disinformer.* Washington, D.C.: Nathan Hale Institute, 1997.

Green, William. *Reports [sic] on Communist Propaganda in America as Submitted to the State Department, United States Government.* Washington, D.C.: American Federation of Labor, 1935.

Gregory, Paul, and Valery Lazarev, eds. *The Economics of Forced Labor: The Soviet Gulag.* Stanford, Calif.: Hoover Institution Press, 2003.

Gross, Babette. *Willi Münzenberg: A Political Biography.* Translated by Marian Jackson. East Lansing: Michigan State University Press, 1974.

Hayes, C.J.H. *Political and Social History of Modern Europe.* Vol. 1. New York: Macmillan, 1916.

Haynes, John Earl, and K. M. Anderson. *The Soviet World of American Communism.* New Haven, Conn.: Yale University Press, 1998.

———, and Fridrikh Igorevich Firsov. *The Secret World of American Communism.* New Haven, Conn.: Yale University Press, 1995.

———, and Harvey Klehr. *Venona: Decoding Soviet Espionage in America.* New Haven, Conn.: Yale University Press, 1999.

Heijenoort, Jean van. *With Trotsky in Exile: From Prinkopo to Coyoacan.* Cambridge, Mass.: Harvard University Press, 1978.

Henderson, Loy W. *A Question of Trust: The Origins of U.S.-Soviet Diplomatic Relations. The Memoirs of Loy W. Henderson.* Edited by George W. Baer. Stanford, Calif.: Hoover Institution Press, 1986.

Herman, Victor. *Coming Out of the Ice: An Unexpected Life.* New York: Harcourt Brace Jovanovich, 1979.

Hillquit, Morris. *Loose Leaves from a Busy Life.* New York: Macmillan, 1934.

Hochschild, Adam. "Never Coming Home: An Exclusive Look at the KGB's Secret Files on Americans in Stalin's Prisons." *Mother Jones,* October 1992, pp. 50–56.

Höhne, Heinz. *Der Krieg im Dunkeln: Macht und Einfluss der Deutschen und Russischen Geheimdienste.* Frankfurt:Ullstein, 1988.

Holubnychy, Lydia. *Michael Borodin and the Chinese Revolution, 1923–1925.* Ann Arbor, Mich.: University Microfilms International, 1979.

Hook, Sidney. "Communism and the Intellectuals." *American Mercury,* February 1949, pp. 133–44.

——. "The Faiths of Whittaker Chambers." *New York Times Book Review,* May 25, 1952.

——. *John Dewey: An Intellectual Portrait.* Amherst, N.Y.: Prometheus, 1995.

——. *Letters of Sidney Hook.* Edited by Edward S. Shapiro. Armonk, N.Y.: M. E. Sharpe, 1995.

——. *The Metaphysics of Pragmatism.* Chicago: Open Court, 1927.

——. *Out of Step: An Unquiet Life in the 20th Century.* New York: Harper & Row, 1987.

——. *Towards the Understanding of Karl Marx: A Revolutionary Intrepretation.* New York: John Day, 1933.

Hoover, J. Edgar. *Menace of Communism: Statement of J. Edgar Hoover . . . before the Committee on Un-American Activities,* House of Representatives, March 26, 1947. Washington, D.C.: Government Printing Office, 1947.

Hornstein, David P. *Arthur Ewert: A Life for the Comintern.* Lanham, Md.: University Press of America, 1993.

Huber, Peter. *Stalins Schatten in die Schweiz. Schweizer Kommunisten in Moskau: Verteidiger und Gefangene der Komintern.* Zürich: Chronos Verlag 1994.

Isaacs, Harold. *The Tragedy of the Chinese Revolution.* London: Secker & Warburg, 1938.

Isserman, Maurice. *Which Side Were You On? The American Communist Party During the Second World War.* Middletown, Conn.: Wesleyan University Press, 1982.

Jaffe, Philip J. "China's Communists Told Me." *New Masses,* October 12, 1937, pp. 3–10.

——. *The Rise and Fall of American Communism.* New York: Horizon, 1975.

Jansen, Marc, and Nikita Petrov. *Stalin's Loyal Executioner: People's Commissar Nikolai Ezhov, 1895–1940.* Stanford, Calif.: Hoover Institution Press, 2002.

Japan-Manchoukuo Yearbook. Tokyo: Japan-Manchoukuo Year Book, Co., 1934–1941.

Jeffery, Inez Cope. *Inside Russia: The Life and Times of Zoya Zarubina.* Austin, Tex.: Eakin, 1999.

Johanningsmeier, Edward. *Forging American Communism: The Life of William Z. Foster.* Princeton, N.J.: Princeton University Press, 1994.

Johnston, Robert H. *New Mecca, New Babylon: Paris and the Russian Exiles, 1920–1945.* Kingston, Ont.: McGill-Queen's University Press, 1988.

Josephson, Matthew. *Infidel in the Temple: A Memoir of the Nineteen-Thirties.* New York: Knopf, 1967.

——. *Life Among the Surrealists.* New York: Holt, Rinehart and Winston, 1962.

Kaufmann, Bernd. *Der Nachrichtendienst der KPD 1919–1937.* Berlin: Dietz, 1993.

Kempton, Murray. *Part of Our Time: Some Monuments and Ruins of the Thirties.* New York: Dell, 1967.

Kennan, George F. *At a Century's Ending: Reflections, 1982–1995.* New York: Norton, 1996.

———. *Memoirs: 1925–1950.* Boston: Atlantic/Little & Brown, 1967.

———. *Sketches from a Life.* New York: Pantheon, 1989.

Kern, Gary. *Death in Washington.* New York: Enigma, 2003.

———. "How 'Uncle Joe' Bugged FDR." *Studies in Intelligence* 47, 1 (2003).

Kessler, Mario. *Arthur Rosenberg ein Historiker im Zeitalter der Katastrophen (1889–1943).* Zeithistorische Studien, Bd. 24. Köln: Böhlau, 2003.

KGB: vchera, segodnya, zavtra: mezhdunarodnye konferentsii i kruglye stoly [The KGB Yesterday, Today, and Tomorrow: International Conferences and Roundtables]. Moskva: Obshchestvenniy fond Glasnost', 1996.

Kinel, Lola. *This Is My Affair.* Boston: Little, Brown, 1937.

Klehr, Harvey. *The Heyday of American Communism: The Depression Decade.* New York: Basic, 1984.

———, with Ronald Radosh. *The Amerasia Spy Case: Prelude to McCarthyism.* Chapel Hill: University of North Carolina Press, 1996.

Koestler, Arthur. *The Invisible Writing.* London: Macmillan, 1954.

———. *The Yogi and the Commissar.* London: Macmillan, 1945.

Kolpakidi, A. I. *Entsiklopediia sekretnykh sluzhb Rossii* [An Encyclopedia of the Russian Secret Services]. Moskva: Izd-vo AST: Izd-vo Astrel: Tranzitkniga, 2003.

———. *Entsiklopediia voennoi razvedki Rossii* [Encyclopedia of Russian Military Intelligence]. Moskva: Izd-vo AST: Izd-vo Astrel, OAO VZOI, 2004.

———. *Likvidatory KGB: spetsoperatsii sovetskikh spetssluzhb* [The Liquidators of the KGB: Special Operations of the Soviet Special Services]. Moskva: IAuza: Eksmo, 2004.

———. *Shchit i mech: rukovoditeli organov gosudarstvennoi bezopasnosti Moskovskoi Rusi, Rossiiskoi Imperii, Sovetskogo Soiuza i Rossiiskoi Federatsii: entsiklopedicheskii spravochnik* [The Sword and Shield: Leaders of the State Security Organs from the Age of Muscovy to the Russian Federation]. Moskva: Olma, 2002.

Kolpakidi, A. I., and Dmitrii P. Prokhorov. *Imperia GRU: ocherki istorii rossiiskoi voennoi razvedki* [The Empire of the GRU: Essays in the History of Russian Military Intelligence]. 2 vols. Moskva: Olma, 2000.

———. *KGB-prikazano likvidirovat': spetsoperatsii sovetskikh spetssluzhb 1918–1941* [The KGB Is Ordered to Liquidate: Special Operations of the Soviet Special Services, 1918–1941]. Moskva: IAuza: Eksmo, 2004.

———. *KGB: spetsoperatsii sovetskoi razvedkoi* [KGB: Special Operations of Soviet Intelligence]. Moskva: Olimp, 2000.

———. *Vneshniaia razvedka Rossii* [The Foreign Intelligence Service of Russia]. Moskva: Olma, Seriya dos'e', 2001.

——. *Vse o vneshnei razvedke* [All About Foreign Intelligence]. Moskva: AST: Olimp, 2002.

Krammer, Arnold. "Russian Counterfeit Dollars: A Case of Early Soviet Espionage." *Slavic Review* 30, 4 (December 1971): 762–73.

Krasilnikov, R. *Prizraki s ulitsy Chaikovskogo: Shpionskie aktsii TsRU SShA v Sovetskom Soiuze i Rossiiskoi Federatsii v 1979–1992 godakh* [Ghosts of Tchaikovsky Street: CIA Espionage in the USSR and Russian Federation, 1979–1992]. Moskva: Geia, 1999.

Kravchenko, Victor. *I Chose Freedom: The Personal and Political Life of a Soviet Official.* New York: Scribner's, 1946.

——. *I Chose Justice.* New York: Scribner's, 1950.

Krivitsky, Walter G. *In Stalin's Secret Service.* New York: Enigma, 2000.

——. *In Stalin's Secret Service: An Exposé of Russia's Secret Policies by the Former Chief of the Soviet Intelligence in Western Europe.* Frederick, Md.: University Publications of America, 1985. First published by Harper & Brothers, 1939.

——. *MI5 Debriefing and Other Documents on Soviet Intelligence.* Edited and translated by Gary Kern. Riverside, Calif.: Xenos, 2004.

Kuznetsov, Ilia. "KGB General Naum Isakovich Eitingon." *Journal of Slavic Military Studies* 14, 1 (March 2001): 37–52.

——. "Stalin's Minister V. S. Abakumov, 1908–1954." *Journal of Slavic Military Studies* 12, 1 (1999): 149–65.

Kvitko, David. *Ocherki sovremennoi anglo-amerikanskoi filosofii* [Essays in Contemporary Anglo-American Philosophy]. Moskva: Gos. Sotsial'no-ekonomicheskoe izd-vo, 1936.

——. "A Philosophic Study of Tolstoy." Master's thesis, Columbia University, 1927.

Labor Research Study Group. *The Law of Social Revolution: A Co-operative Study by the Labor Research Study Group, Scott Nearing, Leader.* New York: Social Science, 1926.

Lamphere, Robert J., and Tom Schactman. *The FBI-KGB War: A Special Agent's Story.* New York: Random House, 1986.

Larina, Anna. *This I Cannot Forget: The Memoirs of Nikolai Bukharin's Widow.* Translated by Gary Kern. New York: Norton, 1993.

Lasch, Christopher. *The New Radicalism in America, 1889–1963: The Intellectual as a Social Type.* New York: Knopf, 1965.

Lee, Janet. *Comrades and Partners: The Shared Lives of Grace Hutchins and Anna Rochester.* Lanham, Md.: Rowman & Littlefield, 2000.

Lenin, V. I. *Materialism and Empirio-Criticism.* Translated by David Kvitko and Sidney Hook. Vol. 13, *Collected Works of V. I. Lenin.* New York: International Publishers, 1927.

Leonard, Raymond W. *Secret Soldiers of the Revolution: Soviet Military Intelligence, 1918–1933.* Westport, Conn.: Greenwood, 1999.

Levine, Isaac Don. *The Mind of an Assassin.* New York: Farrar, Straus, and Cudahy, 1959.

Lewis, Flora. *Red Pawn: The Story of Noel Field.* New York: Doubleday, 1965.

Li, Lincoln. *The Japanese Army in North China, 1937–1941: Problems of Political and Economic Control.* New York: Oxford University Press, 1975.

Lichtman, Robert M. "J.B. Matthews and the 'Counter-subversives': Names as a Political and Financial Resource in the McCarthy Era." *American Communist History* 5, 1 (June 2006): 1–36.

Litten, Frederick S. "Die Goldštajn/Goldenstein-Verwechslung: Eine biographische Notiz zur Komintern-Aktivität auf dem Balkan." *Forschungen* 50 (1991): 245–50.

———. "The Myth of the 'Turning-Point': Towards a New Understanding of the Long March." *Bochumer Jahrbuch zur Ostasienforschung* 25 (December 2001): 3–44.

———. "The Noulens Affair." *China Quarterly* 138 (June 1994): 492–512.

———. "Otto Braun's Curriculum Vitae: Translation and Commentary." *Twentieth-Century China* 23, 1 (1997): 31–61.

Lockhart, R.H.B. *British Agent.* New York: Putnam, 1933.

Luk, Michael. *The Origins of the Communist Bolshevism: An Ideology in the Making, 1920–28.* New York: Oxford University Press, 1990.

Lumpkin, Grace, and Esther Shemitz. "The Artist in a Hostile Environment." *World Tomorrow* 9, 4 (April 1926).

Lur'e, V. M., and V. IA. Kochik. *GRU dela i liudi* [GRU: Cases and People]. Rossiia v litsiakh. Sankt-Peterburg: Neva, 2002.

Lyons, Eugene. *The Red Decade: The Stalinist Penetration of America.* Indianapolis. Bobbs-Merrill, 1941.

MacLean, Elizabeth Kimball. *Joseph E. Davies: Envoy to the Soviets.* Westport, Conn.: Praeger, 1992.

Manchuria: Bifortnightly Supplement of the Manchuria Daily News. Dairen. Vol. 1, July 1936–January 1940.

Massie, Robert. *The Romanovs: The Final Chapter.* New York: Random House, 1995.

Massing, Hede. *This Deception.* New York: Duell, Sloan, and Pearce, 1951.

Mayers, David. *The Ambassadors and America's Soviet Policy.* New York: Oxford University Press, 1995.

McCaughey, Robert. *Stand, Columbia: A History of Columbia University in the City of New York, 1757–2004.* New York: Columbia University Press, 2003.

McCormick, Charles H. *Seeing Reds: Federal Surveillance of Radicals in the Pittsburgh Mill District, 1917–1921.* Pittsburgh, Pa.: University of Pittsburgh Press, 1997.

McKnight, David. *Espionage and the Roots of the Cold War: The Conspiratorial Heritage.* Portland, Ore.: Frank Cass, 2002.

McMeekin, Sean. *The Red Millionaire: A Political Biography of Willy Münzenberg, Moscow's Secret Propaganda Tsar in the West, 1917–1940.* New Haven, Conn.: Yale University Press, 2004.

Meissner, Hans Otto. *The Man with Three Faces.* New York: Rinehart, 1956.

Menshagin, Boris Georgievich. *Vospominaniia: Smolensk-Katyn-Vladimirskaia tiurma* [Memoirs: Smolensk–Katyn–The Vladimir Prison]. Paris: YMCA, 1988.

Michels, Tony. *A Fire in Their Hearts: Yiddish Socialists in New York.* Cambridge, Mass.: Harvard University Press, 2005.

Mickenberg, Julia. "Communist in a Coonskin Cap? Meridel Le Sueur's Books for Children and Reformulation of America's Cold War Frontier Epic." *The Lion and the Unicorn* 21, 1 (January 1997): 59–85.

Mieder, Sabine. "*Deckname Sonja—das geheime Leben der Agentin Ruth Werner*". Documentary film broadcast on ARD, German television, February 7, 2001.

Mishler, Paul. *Raising Reds: The Young Pioneers, Radical Summer Camps, and Communist Political Culture in the United States.* New York: Columbia University Press, 1999.

Mitter, Rana. *The Manchurian Myth: Nationalism, Resistance, and Collaboration in Modern China.* Berkeley: University of California Press, 2000.

Morgan, Ted. *A Covert Life: Jay Lovestone, Communist, Anti-Communist, and Spymaster.* New York: Random House, 1999.

———. *Reds: McCarthyism in Twentieth-Century America.* New York: Random House, 2003.

Morros, Boris. *My Ten Years as a Counterspy.* New York: Viking, 1959.

Moss, Norman. " 'Sonya' Explains." *Bulletin of the Atomic Scientists* 49, 6 (July 1993): 9–12.

Müller, Reinhard. *Herbert Wehner: Moskau 1937.* Hamburg: Hamburger Edition, 2004.

———. "Hitlers Rede vor der Reichswehr und Reichsmarineführung am 3. Februar 1933: Eine neue Moskauer Überlieferung." *Mittelweg 36*, 1, 10 (Jahrgang, Februar/März 2001): 79–90.

———. *Menschenfalle Moskau: Exil and stalinistische Verfolgung.* Hamburg: Hamburger Edition, 2001.

Müller-Enbergs, Helmut, with Jan Wielgohs and Dieter Hoffmann. *Wer War Wer in Der DDR?: Ein Biographisches Lexikon.* Berlin: Ch. Links Verlag, 2000.

Murphy, Raymond E., Francis Bowden Stevens, Howard Trivers, and Joseph Morgan Roland. *National Socialism: Basic Principles, Their Application by the Nazi Party's Foreign Organization, and the Use of Germans Abroad for Nazi Aims.* Washington, D.C.: Government Printing Office, 1943.

Nearing, Scott. *Poverty and Riches: A Study of the Industrial Regime.* Philadelphia: John C. Winston Co., 1916.

———. *A Scott Nearing Reader: The Good Life in Bad Times.* Edited by Steve Sherman. Metuchen, N.J.: Scarecrow, 1989.

———. *Where Is Civilization Going?.* New York: Vanguard, 1917.

———, and Joseph Freeman. *Dollar Diplomacy.* New York: B. W. Huebsch/Viking, 1926.

Olin, John Myers. *Review of the Mooney Case: Its Relations to the Conduct in this Country of Anarchists, I.W.W. and Bolsheviki. Facts That Every True American Should Know.* [Madison, Wisc.], 1919.

Olmsted, Kathryn S. *Red Spy Queen: A Biography of Elizabeth Bentley.* Chapel Hill: University of North Carolina Press, 2002.

Orlov, Alexander. *Handbook of Intelligence and Guerrilla Warfare.* Ann Arbor: University of Michigan Press, 1963.

———. *The Secret History of Stalin's Crimes.* New York: Random House, 1953.

Oshinsky, David. *A Conspiracy So Immense: The World of Joe McCarthy.* New York: Free Press, 1983.

Packer, Herbert L. *Ex-Communist Witnesses: Four Studies in Fact Finding.* Stanford, Calif.: Stanford University Press, 1962.

Palei, Kniaginia. *Memories of Russia, 1916–1919, by Princess Paley.* London: H. Jenkins, 1924.

———. *Souvenirs de Russie, 1916–1919.* Paris: Plon-Nourrit, 1923.

Patch, Isaac. *Closing the Circle: A Buckolino Journey Around Our Time.* Wellesley, Mass.: Wellesley Printing Services, 1996.

———. *They Made a Difference: Friends Remembered.* Self-published, 2002.

Pavlov, Vitaly. *Operatsiia "Sneg": polveka vo vneshnei razvedke KGB* [Operation "Snow": Half a Century in the Foreign Intelligence Service of the KGB]. Moskva: Geia, 1996.

Peattie, Mark. *Ishiwara Kanji and Japan's Confrontation with the West.* Princeton, N.J.: Princeton University Press, 1975.

Pepper, John [Joseph Pogany]. *"Underground Radicalism": An Open Letter to Eugene V. Debs and to All Honest Workers Within the Socialist Party.* New York: Workers Party of America, 1923.

Perrett, Geoffrey. *America in the Twenties: A History.* New York: Simon & Shuster, 1982.

Pfannestiel, Todd. *Rethinking the Red Scare: The Lusk Committee and New York's Crusade Against Radicalism, 1919–1923.* New York: Routledge, 2003.

Phelps, Christopher. *Young Sidney Hook.* Cornell, N.Y.: Cornell University Press, 1997.

Philby, Kim. *My Silent War.* New York: Grove, 1968.

Pilat, Oliver. *The Atom Spies.* New York: Putnam, 1952.

Poretsky, Elizabeth. *Our Own People: A Memoir of "Ignace Reiss" and His Friends.* London: Oxford University Press, 1969.

Pozniakov, V. V. *Sovetskaia razvedka v Amerike, 1919–1941* [Soviet Intelligence in America: 1919–1941]. Moskva: Mezhdunarodnye otnosheniia, 2005.

———. "Tainaia voina Iosifa Stalina: Sovetskie razvedyvatel'nye sluzhby v SShA nakanune i v nachale kholodnoi voiny 1943–1953" [Joseph Stalin's Secret War: Soviet Intelligence Services in the U.S.A. on the Eve of the Cold War]. In I. V. Gaiduk, N. I. Yegorova, and A. O. Chubar'ian, eds., *Stalinskoe desiatiletie kholodnoi voiny: Fakty I gipotezy* [The Stalinist Decade of the Cold War: Facts and Hypotheses], pp. 115–17. Moskva: Nauka, 1999.

Price, Ruth. *The Lives of Agnes Smedley.* Oxford: Oxford University Press, 2005.

Primakov, Evgeny, ed. *Ocherki istorii rossiiskoi vneshnei razvedki: v shesti tomakh* [Essays in the History of Russian Foreign Intelligence: in 6 Volumes]. Moskva: Mezhdunarodnye otnosheniia, 1996–2006.

Ranseikai, ed., *Manshūkokugunshi* [History of the Manchukuoan Army]. Tokyo: Manshukokugun kankōkai, 1970.

Recchiuti, John. "The Rand School of Social Science During the Progressive Era: Will to Power of a Stratum of the American Intellectual Class." *Journal of the History of the Behavioral Sciences* 31, 2 (1995): 149–61.

Reinhardt, Guenther. *Crime Without Punishment: The Secret Soviet Terror Against America.* New York: Hermitage House, 1952.

Reisner, Larisa. *Hamburg at the Barricades, and Other Writings on Weimar Germany.* Translated and edited by Richard Chappell. London: Pluto, 1977.

Reynold, Quentin. *The Curtain Rises.* New York: Random House, 1944.

Ristaino, Marcia. *Port of Last Resort: The Diaspora of Communities of Shanghai.* Stanford, Calif.: Stanford University Press, 2001.

Ritter, Ernst. *Lageberichte (1920–1929) und Meldungen (1929–1933) Bestand R 134 des Bundesarchivs, Koblenz veröffentlicht als Microfiche–Ausgab: Einleitung und Indices.* München: K. G. Saur, 1979.

Roehr, Edward van der. *The Shadow Network.* New York: Scribner's, 1983.

Rommerstein, Herbert, and Eric Breindel. *The Venona Secrets: Exposing Soviet Espionage and America's Traitors.* Washington, D.C.: Regnery, 2000.

——, with Stanislav Levchenko. *The KGB Against the "Main Enemy": How the Soviet Intelligence Service Operates Against the United States.* Lexington, Mass.: Lexington Books, 1989.

Rosenberg, Arthur. *Einleitung und Quellenkunde zur Roemischen Geshichte.* Berlin: Weimann, 1921.

Rossi, Jacques, with Sophie Benech. *Fragments de vies.* Paris: Elikia, 1995.

——, and Michèle Sarde. *Jacques, Le Français, pour mémoire du Goulag.* Paris: Le Cherche Midi, 2002.

Roth, Joseph. *What I Saw: Reports from Berlin, 1920–1933.* New York: Norton, 2005.

Rowan, Richard W. *Secret Agents Against America.* New York: Doubleday, Doran, 1939.

——. *Spy and Counterspy: The Development of Modern Espionage.* New York: Viking, 1928.

Ryan, Alan. *John Dewey and the High Tide of American Liberalism.* New York: Norton, 1995.

Ryan, James G. *Earl Browder. The Failure of American Communism.* Tuscaloosa: University of Alabama Press, 1997.

Saich, Anthony. "The Comintern and China: An Overview and Sources." In Jürgen Rojahn, ed., *Comintern and National Communist Parties Project.* Amsterdam: International Institute of Social History, forthcoming.

Schecter, Jerrold L., and Leona P. Schecter. *Sacred Secrets: How Soviet Intelligence Operations Changed American History.* Washington, D.C.: Brassey's, 2002.

Schlögel, Karl. *Berlin-Ostbahnhof Europas. Russen und Deutsche in ihrem Jahrhundert.* Berlin: Siedler Verlag, 1998.

Scholem, Gershom. *From Berlin to Jerusalem.* Translated by Harry Zohn. New York: Schocken, 1980.

Sgovio, Thomas. *Dear America! Why I Turned Against Communism.* Kenmore, N.Y.: Partners, 1979.

Shapiro, Irwin. *The Gremlins of Lieut. Oggins.* New York: Julian Messner, 1943.

———. "90 Percent of the People." Unpublished play. New York Public Library for the Performing Arts, Theatre Division.

Shi, David E. *Matthew Josephson: Bourgeois Bohemian.* New Haven, Conn.: Yale University Press, 1981.

Sibille, Claire. "Les Archives du ministère de la Guerre recuperées de Russie." *Gazette des Archives* 176 (1997): 64–77.

Singer, Kurt D. *Communist Agents in America: A Who's Who of American Communists, 1947.* New York: News Background, 1947.

Slesinger, Tess. *The Unpossessed.* New York: Simon and Schuster, 1934.

Smith, Bradley F. *The Shadow Warriors, O.S.S. and the Origins of the C.I.A.* New York: Basic, 1983.

Smith, Walter Bedell. *My Three Years in Moscow.* Philadelphia: Lippincott, 1950.

Snow, Edgar. *Red Star Over China.* New York: Random House, 1938.

Solow, Herbert. "Stalin's American Passport Mill." *American Mercury,* July 1939, pp. 302–9.

Spence, Jonathan. *To Change China: Western Advisers in China, 1620–1960.* New York: Penguin, 1980.

———. *The Search for Modern China.* New York: Norton, 1990.

Spolansky, Jacob. *The Communist Trail in America.* New York: Macmillan, 1951.

Stajner, Karlo. *Seven Thousand Days in Siberia.* New York: Farrar, Straus and Giroux, 1988.

Stalin, Joseph. *Pisma I.V. Stalina V. M. Molotovu, 1925–1936 gg: sbornik dokumentov.* [Letters of J. V. Stalin to V. M. Molotov, 1925–1936]. Edited by L. Kosheleva et al. Moskva: Rossiia molodaia, 1995.

———. *Stalin's Letters to Molotov, 1925–1936.* Edited by Lars T. Lih, Oleg V. Naumov, and Oleg V. Khlevniuk. Translated by Catherine A. Fitzpatrick. New Haven, Conn.: Yale University Press, 1995.

Standley, William H., and Arthur A. Ageton. *Admiral Ambassador to Russia.* Chicago: Regnery, 1955.

Stansell, Christine. *American Moderns: Bohemian New York and the Creation of a New Century.* New York: Metropolitan, 2000.

Stavinsky, Ervin. *Zarubiny: semeinaia rezidentura* [The Zarubins: A Family Spy Station]. Moskva: Olma, 2003.

Stepakov, Viktor N. *Pavel Sudoplatov: genii terrora* [Pavel Sudoplatov: A Genius of Terror]. Moskva: Olma, 2003.

Stewart, John Robert. *Manchuria Since 1931. Prepared for the Sixth Conference of the Institute of Pacific Relations, held at Yosemite Park, California, from August 15th to 29th, 1936.* New York: Institute of Pacific Relations, 1936.

Stone, Geoffrey R. *Perilous Times: Free Speech in Wartime.* New York: Norton, 2004.

Stranahan, Patricia. *Underground: The Shanghai Communist Party and the Politics of Survival, 1927–1937.* Lanham, Md.: Rowman & Littlefield, 1998.

Stripling, Robert E. *The Red Plot Against America.* Edited by Bob Considine. Drexel Hill, Pa.: Bell, 1949.

Strong, Anna Louise. *I Change Worlds: The Remaking of an American.* Seattle: Seal, 1979. First published by Holt, Rinehart and Winston, 1935.

Sudoplatov, Anatolii. *Tainaia zhizn' Generala Sudoplatova: Pravda i vymysly o moem ottse* [The Secret Life of General Sudoplatov: The Truth and Myths About My Father]. 2 vols. Moskva: Olma, 1998.

Sudoplatov, Pavel. *Raznye dni tainoi voini i diplomatii. 1941 goda* [Various Days from the Secret War and Diplomacy, 1941]. Moskva: Olma, 2001.

———. *Razvedka i Kreml', zapiski nezhelatel'nogo svidetalia* [Intelligence and the Kremlin: Notes of an Unwanted Witness]. Moskva: Geia, 1996.

———. *Spetsoperatsii: Lubianka i Kreml', 1930–1950 gody* [Special Operations: The Lubyanka and Kremlin, 1930–1950]. Moskva: Olma, 1997.

———, and Anatoli Sudoplatov, with Jerrold L. and Leona P. Schecter. *Special Tasks: The Memoirs of an Unwanted Witness—A Soviet Spymaster.* New York: Little, Brown, 1994.

Tanenhaus, Sam. *Whittaker Chambers.* New York: Random House, 1997.

Thayer, Charles W. *Bears in the Caviar.* New York: Lippincott, 1950.

Thompson, Dorothy. *The New Russia.* New York: Henry Holt, 1928.

Titarenko, Mikhail L. *VKP(b), Komintern i Kitai: dokumenty.* v. 1–4 [The Comintern and China: Documents, vols. 1–4]. Moskva: ROSSPEN (Rossiiskaia politicheskaia entsiklopediia), 1996–2007.

Tripp, Wendell. "Dylan Ryan Fox, 1887–1944." *American National Biography,* vol. 8, pp. 336–37.

Ulianovskaia, Maia, and Nadezhda Ulianovskaia. *Istoriia odnoi semyi* [History of One Family]. Benson, Vt.: Chalidze, 1982.

U.S. Central Intelligence Agency. Counterintelligence Staff. *The Rote Kapelle: The CIA's History of Soviet Intelligence and Espionage Networks in Western Europe, 1936–1945.* Washington, D.C.: University Publications of America, 1979.

U.S. Congress. House of Representatives, Committee on Un-American Activities. *The Shameful Years: Thirty Years of Soviet Espionage in the United States.* December 30, 1951.

Usov, Viktor. *Sovietskaia razvedka v Kitaye 20-e godyi XX veka* [Soviet Intelligence in China in the 1920s]. Moskva: Olma, 2002.

Utley, Freda. *The Dream We Lost: Soviet Russia, Then and Now.* New York: John Day, 1940.

———. *Lost Illusion.* Philadelphia: Fireside 1948.

———. *Odyssey of a Liberal: Memoirs.* Washington, D.C.: Washington National Press, 1970.

Valtin, Jan [Richard Julius Herman Krebs]. *Bend in the River.* New York: Alliance, 1942.

———. "Communist Agent." *American Mercury,* November 1939.

———. *Out of the Night.* New York: Alliance, 1941.

Van Sweringen, Bryan T., editor. *The Case of Richard Sorge.* New York: Garland, 1989.

The Voice of China, vols. 1–2, nos. 18–21, March 15, 1936–November 1, 1937, Shanghai.

Volin, O. [Revolt Ivanovich Pimenov]. "S Berievtsami vo Vladimirskoi tiur'me" [With the Beria Men in the Vladimir Prison]. In *Minuvshee. Istoricheskii al'manakh,* pp. 357–72. Paris: Atheneum, 1989.

Von Waldenfels, Ernst. *Der Spion, der aus Deutschland kam: Das geheime Leben des Seemanns Richard Krebs.* Berlin: Aufbau Verlag, 2002.

Wadleigh, Julian. "Why I Spied for the Communists." *New York Post,* July 11–24, 1949.

Wakeman, Frederic, Jr., *Policing Shanghai, 1927–1937.* Berkeley: University of California Press, 1995.

Wald, Alan. *The New York Intellectuals.* Chapel Hill: University of North Carolina Press, 1987.

Waldman, Louis. *Labor Lawyer.* New York: Dutton, 1944.

Watson, Bruce. *Bread and Roses: Mills, Migrants, and the Struggle for the American Dream.* New York: Viking, 2005.

Webb, G. Gregg. "Intelligence Liaison Between the FBI and State, 1940–1944." *Studies in Intelligence* 49, 3 (2005).

Wechsler, James. *The Age of Suspicion.* New York: Primus, 1953.

Weinstein, Alan. *Perjury: The Hiss-Chambers Case.* New York: Random House, 1997.

———, and Alexander Vasiliev. *The Haunted Wood.* New York: Random House, 1999.

Weissman, Susan. *Victor Serge: The Course Is Set on Hope.* London: Verso, 2001.

Werner, Ruth. *Sonya's Report.* Translated by Renate Simpson. London: Chatto & Windus, 1991. First published as *Sonjas Rapport,* Berlin: Verlag Neues Leben, 1977.

West, Nigel. *MASK: MI5's Penetration of the Communist Party of Great Britain.* London: Routledge, 2005.

———, and Oleg Tsarev. *The Crown Jewels: The British Secrets at the Heart of the KGB Archives.* London: HarperCollins, 1998.

Wetzsteon, Ross. *Republic of Dreams: Greenwich Village, the American Bohemia, 1910–1960.* New York: Simon & Schuster, 2002.

White, Steven. "British Labour in Soviet Russia, 1920." *English Historical Review* 109, 432 (June 1994): 621–40.

Whitney, Richard Merrill. *Reds in America: The Present Status of the Revolutionary Movement in the U. S. Based on Documents Seized by the Authorities in the Raid upon the Convention of the Communist Party at Bridgman, Mich., Aug. 22, 1922, Together with Descriptions of Numerous Connections and Associations of the Communists among the Radicals, Progressives, and Pinks.* New York: Beckwith, 1924.

Wilbur, C. Martin, and Julie Lien-ying How. *Missionaries of Revolution: Soviet Advisers and Nationalist China, 1920–1927.* Cambridge, Mass.: Harvard University Press, 1989.

——, eds. *Documents on Communism, Nationalism, and Soviet Advisors in China, 1918–1927. Papers Seized in the 1927 Peking Raid.* New York: Columbia University Press, 1956.

Williams, David. "The Bureau of Investigation and Its Critics, 1919–1921: The Origins of Federal Political Surveillance." *Journal of American History* 68 (1981): 560–79.

Willoughby Charles. *Shanghai Conspiracy: The Sorge Spy Ring, Moscow, Shanghai, Tokyo, San Francisco, New York.* New York: Dutton, 1952.

Wirschung, Andreas. "Hitlers Rede vor den Spitzen der Reichswehr am 3. Februar 1933." *Vierteljahrshefte fuer Zeitgeschichte* 49 (2001): 517–50.

Wohl, Paul. "Walter G. Krivitsky." *Commonweal*, February 28, 1941.

Wolfe, Bertram. *Strange Communists I Have Known.* Briarcliff Manor, N.Y.: Stein and Day, 1982.

Wolff, David. *To the Harbin Station: The Liberal Alternative in Russian Manchuria, 1898–1914.* Stanford, Calif.: Stanford University Press, 1999.

Wolton, Thierry. *Le KGB en France.* Paris: B. Grasset, 1986.

Wright, Peter. *Spycatcher: The Candid Autobiography of a Senior Intelligence Officer.* New York: Viking, 1987.

Yardley, Herbert O. *The American Black Chamber.* London: Faber & Faber, 1931.

Yorke, Gerald. *China Changes.* New York: Scribner's, 1936.

Ypsilon [pseud.]. *Pattern for World Revolution.* Chicago: Ziff-Davis, 1947.

Zeutschel, W. *Im Dienst der Kommunistische Terrororganisation.* Berlin: J.H.W. Dietz, 1931.

INDEX

Page numbers in *italics* refer to illustrations.
Page numbers beginning with 321 refer to endnotes.

Standley, William, 175–76, 178–79, 185, 256
Stanislavsky, Constantin, 259
State Department, U.S., 7, 170, 179, 182–84, 186–87, 201, 249, 266, 288, 292, *309*, 354
    EUR/X unit of, 186
    Nerma questioned by, 263, 297, 343
    Nerma's correspondence with, 245–47, 250–52, 256, 260, 262, 293
    Oggins investigated by, 252–54
    Passport Division of, 251
    Political Department of, 252, 254
    Robin's letter to, 262
    Russian Division of, 171
    Special Division of, 252
Stauffenberg, Claus von, 333
Stavisky, Alexandre, 163, 164
Steinberg, Max (Matus), 208–13, 233–34, 236–37, 266, 284–85, 287, 295, 344–45, 357–58
Steinhardt, Lawrence, 175
Stevens, Francis Bowden "Franny," 169–70, 172–73, 180–83, 185–87, 251–52, 254, 341
Stimson, Henry, 201, 204, 343
stock market crash of 1929, 123, 189, 190, 265
Stony Point, 90
Straus, Robert, 273, 280, 354
strikes, 242
    in Willimantic, 23–25
Strong, Anna Louise, 123
Student Army Training Corps, 38
Stuyvesant High School, 261–62
Sudoplatov, Anatoli, 281–82, 285, 358
Sudoplatov, Pavel, 281–86, 355, 356, 357
Sulzberger, Cyrus, 174
Sun Yat-sen, 199–200
Sun Yat-sen, Madame, 201
Sûreté Générale, 153, 161, 166

SVR (Foreign Intelligence Service), 150
    archives of, 150
Swiss Federal Archives, 210
Switz, Marjorie Tilley, 162–66, 203, 248, 337
Switz, Robert Gordon "the Aviator," 162–66, 203, 248, 337
Switzerland, 210–11, 212–13, 218, 233–34, 235, 236–37, 284, 295
Szilard, Leo, 358

Taft, William Howard, 28
Takhchianov, Panteleimon, 348
Tangku, 216
Teachers' Union, 84, 247
Thälmann, Ernst, 105, 106, 108, 200, 333
Third International, *see* Comintern
Thomas, Norman, 68, 84, 296
Thompson, Llewellyn E. "Tommy," Jr., 169–73, 179–87, 251–52, 341
Threepenny Opera, The, 104
Tiger Moths, 257
Tilden, Bill, 239
Tilton, Alfred, 118–19, 164, 230, 258, 331, 337
Tilton, Maria, 119, 331
Tokyo, 151, 194, 196, 213
Tolstoy, Leo, 150
Toon, Malcolm, 273–75, 280–81, 357
Trachtenberg, Alexander, 65, 94, 114, 332
trade unions, 77, 83, 120, 190–91
Trans-Siberian Railway, 204, 221–23
Treasury Department, U.S., 117–18, 119
Trilling, Lionel, 93
Trotsky, Leon, 110, 190 229, 231, 264, 276, 336, 347
    assassination of, 232, 236–38, 281, 282, 338
    in France, 161
    Stalin's expulsion of, 93, 113, 123, 144, 145–46, 190, 215

In 2000, while on a reporting trip to Russia's northernmost city, Andrew Meier first heard rumors of an American lost to Stalin's gulag. *The Lost Spy* is the result of seven years of sleuthing on three continents. Meier is the author of the award-winning *Black Earth: A Journey Through Russia After the Fall*, named a Book of the Year by *The Economist*. A graduate of Wesleyan and Oxford Universities, he was a Moscow correspondent for *Time* from 1996 to 2001. The recipient of fellowships from the National Endowment for Humanities, Alicia Patterson Foundation, and Woodrow Wilson International Center for Scholars, Meier was most recently a Whiting Foundation Fellow at the Dorothy and Lewis B. Cullman Center for Scholars & Writers at the New York Public Library.

One of America's leading authorities on Russia, Meier has published widely on foreign affairs, contributing to *Harper's*, *National Geographic*, the *New Republic*, the *New York Times Magazine*, and the *Washington Post*, among many other publications. A frequent commentator on the BBC, CNN, and NPR, he has also reported for PBS television documentaries. Meier lives in New York City with his wife and two daughters, where he is a writer-in-residence at the New School University.